EVIDENCE PRINCIPLES & PRACTICES

150 Things You Were Never Taught, Forgot, or Never Understood

PROFESSOR PAUL R. RICE

American University
Washington College of Law
Washington, D. C. 20016-8181

Library of Congress Cataloging-in-Publication Data

Rice, Paul R.

Evidence principles & practices : 150 things you were never taught, forgot, or never understood /
Paul R. Rice.

p. cm.

Includes index.

ISBN 0-8205-7058-3 (softbound)

1. Evidence (Law) — United States. I. Title. II. Title: Evidence principles and practices.

KF8935.R487 2006

347.73'6 — dc22   2006019822

Editorial Offices
744 Broad Street, Newark, NJ 07102 (973) 820-2000
201 Mission St., San Francisco, CA 94105-1831 (415) 908-3200
701 East Water Street, Charlottesville, VA 22902-7587 (434) 972-7600
www.lexis.com

(Pub.3224)

NOTE TO THE PRACTITIONER

In forty years of teaching, practicing and consulting with regard to the common law and the Federal Rules of Evidence, I have seen recurring misunderstandings of certain evidentiary principles. Although these often have been in some of the more complex areas of the subject, many have concerned fundamental issues that every lawyer should understand. Some principles were never learned correctly. Some were not taught correctly. Most simply have been forgotten. All of these principles, however, will eventually be important in most practices.

This book presents and discusses 150 of these principles. Some principles are comparatively unnoticed recent additions to the Federal Rules of Evidence. Some are illogical rules or practices that have become so deeply ingrained in our jurisprudence that they are entrenched doctrine. These are identified because eventually they will be successfully attacked and changed. Finally, some of the issues are so inherently complex and difficult, they are quickly forgotten when not regularly reviewed and used.

More than two dozen **Diagrams** have been used throughout the text to assist the practitioner in understanding some of the more complex concepts, including multiple level hearsay, the application of the state of mind exception to the hearsay rule, and the application of the attorney-client privilege to pre-existing documents and responsive communications of attorneys. In addition, numerous **Applications** are given to illustrate principles.

Equally important to the practitioner, however, is understanding the relationships between the rules within the evidence code. Therefore, at the end of many topic areas a **Relationship to Other Rules** section can be found where these relationships are examined. In addition, at the beginning of the text an **Index of Rules** is supplied to indicate their interrelationship and where relevant discussions can be found.

Although this book reviews basic concepts relevant to the 150 practices, it is not an Evidence primer. It is designed as a focused refresher for practitioners and a supplement to basic casebooks and manuals (including EVIDENCE: COMMON LAW AND FEDERAL RULES OF EVIDENCE (LEXIS 5th ed. 2005). For the convenience of the reader, all evidence rules relevant to each discussion have been reproduced within the text.

BIOGRAPHICAL SKETCH
Paul R. Rice

Paul Rice is a professor of law at the American University Washington College of Law where he has taught Evidence, Civil Procedure and Criminal Procedure for thirty-five years.

He is the author of two treatises on the attorney-client privilege, ATTORNEY-CLIENT PRIVILEGE IN THE UNITED STATES (West Group 2d ed. 1999) (with annual supplements) and ATTORNEY-CLIENT PRIVILEGE: STATE LAW (Rice Publishing 2006). On the topic of electronic evidence he is the author of ELECTRONIC EVIDENCE: Law and Practice (ABA 2005) that explores issues from discovery through trial. He also has published a popular law school textbook, PAUL R. RICE & ROY A. CATRIEL: EVIDENCE: COMMON LAW AND FEDERAL RULES OF EVIDENCE (LEXIS Publishing 5th ed. 2005), from which significant material in this book was taken. His other books include: Rice, COMPARATIVE EVIDENCE RULES PAMPHLET (1987) and Brazil, Hazard & Rice, MANAGING COMPLEX LITIGATION: A PRACTICAL GUIDE TO THE USE OF SPECIAL MASTERS (Am. Bar Foundation 1983).

Professor Rice is the Director of the Evidence Project at the Washington College of Law that has published comprehensive proposals for the revision of the Federal Rules of Evidence, 171 F.R.D. 330 (1997), see www.wcl.american.edu/pub/journals/evidence, and a report on the Project's experience in working with the Federal Rules of Evidence Advisory Committee, 191 F.R.D. 678 (2000). He has published over one hundred articles in law reviews and specialized journals on topics of evidence and procedure and has been a contributor to the Legal Times and National Law Journal.

Professor Rice has served as a special master or special counsel in the *Consolidated Microsoft Cases* (both consumer and competitor cases from both federal courts and the state of California), *United States v. American Telephone & Telegraph* (the government's divestiture action); *Southern Communication Corporation v. American Telephone & Telegraph* (a private antitrust action); and *In re Amoxicillin* (a multi-district antitrust and patent infringement action). He has lectured to law firms, corporate legal departments, judges and professional associations on an array of evidence topics, served as a litigation consultant to the firm of Finnegan, Henderson, Farabow, Garrett & Dunner in Washington, D.C. and is regularly consulted by a number of firms on attorney-client privilege and other evidentiary issues.

DEDICATION

To my partner and best
friend Jane Bird Rice.

ACKNOWLEDGMENTS

To borrow a phrase from the Beatles, all of my scholarly accomplishments have been made possible "with a little help from my friends." The laborious task of editing and supplementing footnote materials in this text was accomplished by Ben Marcoux. For that I am deeply grateful.

As with all of my scholarship, this project was made possible by the financial support of the Washington College of Law and its Dean, Claudio Grossman.

Most importantly, without the consistent support, encouragement, tolerance and sound advice from my partner Jane Bird Rice, I would never accomplish anything.

INTRODUCTION

This book attempts to resolve for practitioners, in a manual format, many common problems and misunderstandings which have existed since evidence rules evolved under the common law. Unfortunately, many of those problems were perpetuated when the common law rules were codified in 1974 in the Federal Rules of Evidence. Though the evidence code provided some solutions to existing problems and created consistency among the federal courts, it also created new problems that have not been addressed in the last quarter of the 20th century.

Codification has radically changed the dynamic of the evolution of evidence rules. Unlike common law rules, which judges are expected to modify based on principles of equity and fairness in light of the facts before them, codified rules are intended to minimize judges' discretion in interpreting and applying them. Consequently, judges have had to ignore the language of codified rules, or resort to strained interpretations of their language in order to achieve a level of fairness in their application.

Rule changes are now quasi-legislative. They must be adopted by the Federal Rules of Evidence Advisory Committee after public hearings, and become law only after being accepted by (1) the Committee on the Rules of Practice & Procedure of the Federal Judicial Conference, (2) the full Judicial Conference, (3) the Supreme Court and (4) Congress. If Congress does not act to reject proposed changes, they automatically become law the following December 1. Because this process is detached from individual cases, the evolution of codified rules is now more influenced by special interest groups than the equities of situations in which they must be applied. This, coupled with the lethargy of the committee process, has left many problems unaddressed. This book identifies some of these problems and traces their development through the common law, codification in the Federal Rules of Evidence and evolution through judicial decisions.

The 150 principles identified in this book are organized under a specific sequence of topical areas as they are addressed in my basic evidence course and textbook, PAUL R. RICE & ROY A. KATRIEL, EVIDENCE: COMMON LAW AND FEDERAL RULES OF EVIDENCE (LEXIS 5th ed. 2005). The diagrams illustrating the logic of hearsay and the sections entitled **Relationship To Other Rules** have been taken, in substantial part, from that textbook.[1]

Chapter One discusses principles relating to the making of the record and the most fundamental of all issues, logical relevance, the universal hurdle all evidence must clear. Identifying witnesses and authenticating tangible items about which testimony is being offered are essential to logical relevance. This chapter discusses and predicts the practical failure of a new provision in the Federal

---

[1] These excerpts have been reprinted by permission of LEXIS Publishing.

Rules of Evidence that dispenses with the requirement of contemporaneous objections at trial when *in limine* rulings have been declared "dispositive."

Chapter Two deals with issues of authentication. The is a fundamental issue logical relevance. Nothing is admissible unless it has been authenticated. This chapter explores various doctrines of authentication, the concept of self-authentication, and the application of these common law doctrines in the new world of electronic evidence.

Chapter Three examines the concept of relevance, as well as specific exclusionary rules — similar occurrence evidence, remedial measures, offers of compromise, and the least understood of these historically, character evidence.

Chapter Four, which constitutes the largest portion of these materials, analyzes hearsay, the most frequently raised evidentiary objection. It is a difficult concept further complicated with numerous exceptions. Under the Federal Rules of Evidence its complexity is compounded by (1) the assertive/nonassertive distinction in the definition of hearsay, (2) the exclusion of a class of statements from the definition of hearsay that is equivalent to the creation of a third category of hearsay exceptions, (3) the inconsistent incorporation of constitutional principles in a fashion that has misinterpreted and misapplied the right, and (4) the inadequate and occasionally inconsistent ways comparable policies and exceptions are codified.

Chapter Five reviews writings, specifically the topics of authentication and best evidence. Authentication is a difficult and growing problem with the advent of electronic communications and the Internet. The old wine can easily be poured into these new bottles if basic principles and the context in which they are being employed are understood. Changes to the common law best evidence rule incorporated into the Federal Rules of Evidence, are one of the most striking successes within the evidence code. Article X has virtually eliminated frivolous best evidence objections through its recognition of "duplicates" in lieu of originals (unless genuine questions of authenticity and accuracy are raised by the parties). The most serious problem in Article X has been created by judges who minimize the importance of the summary rule, Rule 1006, by treating summaries like pedagogical devices, rather than an exception to the original writing requirement. Another problem identified in this chapter has existed since the common law — the effect of self-authentication. It continues to be unresolved under the Federal Rules of Evidence, in significant part because of the continuing debate over the appropriate effect of presumptions, which lies at the foundation of self-authentication.

Chapter Six discusses the significant problems that continue to plague expert opinion rules. Practices codified in Rules 702 and 703 are illogical, inadequate and inappropriate. While mimicking a limited practice under the common law with medical doctors, Rule 703 stretches the practice beyond its breaking point, and in doing so, changes the nature of our adjudicatory system and the role of the players within it. The poor work of the Advisory Committee in drafting and maintaining Rules 702 and 703 is trumped only by the Supreme Court's unhelpful, perhaps even naive, interpretation of those rules. Judges have been assigned a role previously relegated to scientific and technological experts under the *Frye* "general acceptance" test, and have been forced to do indirectly what they previously did directly.

The common law problems with opinion testimony from lay witnesses were resolved by the elimination of the common law rule of exclusion in Rule 701 of the Federal Rules of Evidence. While only minor problems continue, a recent revision in Rule 701, preventing lay witnesses from offering opinions "based on scientific, technological, or other specialized knowledge," may create significant problems.

Chapter Seven addresses the problems within the various methods of impeachment — bias, prior convictions, character evidence, psychiatric condition and inconsistent statements. These rules have perpetuated many of the problems that existed under the common law, created new problems through codified language, and expanded the scope of admissibility where severe restrictions were previously imposed. The most significant problems under this topic exist with regard to proving bias. The Federal Rules of Evidence ignore this topic, compelling courts to fashion rules from conflicting common law principles.

Chapter Eight examines the attorney-client privilege — the most complicated and litigated of all privileges. Although it is premised on a requirement of secrecy, most judges have indicated, through their decisions on a variety of issues, that they do not believe secrecy is a necessary condition for the privilege. As the fundamental purpose of the privilege is being forgotten, basic principles are evolving through misinterpretation and misapplication. In addition, the application of the privilege to the corporate entity has *never* been critically evaluated and justified in a published judicial opinion. Case law has developed on little more than *ipse dixit*.

Chapter 9 deals with presumptions. In general, the profession is probably least familiar with this evidentiary principle. When this unfamiliarity is coupled with judicial interpretations and uses that are inconsistent with the theory of presumptions adopted in Article III of the Federal Rules of Evidence, it is little wonder there is such wide-spread confusion. Presumptions should prove to be particularly relevant to the authentication of electronic communications.

SUMMARY OF CONTENTS

TABLE OF CONTENTS

CHAPTER 1
MAKING THE RECORD

CHAPTER 2
AUTHENTICATION

CHAPTER 3
RELEVANCE — RULES BALANCING PROBATIVE
VALUE AGAINST POTENTIAL PREJUDICE

CHAPTER 6
OPINION TESTIMONY

CHAPTER 7
IMPEACHMENT AND CROSS-EXAMINATION

CHAPTER 9
SHORTCUTS TO PROOF

TABLE OF RULES

[References are to page numbers]

Chapter 1

MAKING THE RECORD

I. THE STRUCTURE OF THE TRIAL AND THE PRESENTATION OF EVIDENCE

Understanding the evidentiary rules that regulate the presentation of evidence in judicial proceedings requires an understanding of the structure within which those rules apply, because their application frequently varies with the circumstances in which the court applies them. This first chapter, therefore, explains the structure, process and general rules that apply to the presentation of evidence.

In litigation in common law courts (both civil and criminal), one can visualize the trial as a rectangle divided into four parts.

TRIAL

1 Plaintiff's Case-in-Chief	3 Plaintiff's Rebuttal
2 Defendant's Case-in-Chief or Case-in-Defense	4 Defendant's Rejoinder

As illustrated in the above diagram, the first stage of the trial is the plaintiff's case-in-chief. In this part of the trial, the plaintiff must present sufficient evidence from which a reasonable jury could find that the plaintiff has proven all of the elements of the claim upon which his cause of action is based. After the plaintiff completes his presentation by resting his case, the defendant can test whether the plaintiff has satisfied this burden through a motion to the court for a directed verdict. If, at this point, the presiding judge concludes that the plaintiff has not presented sufficient evidence upon which a jury could find that the plaintiff has established all the elements of his cause of action — a *prima facie* standard — the judge will grant the defendant's motion for a directed verdict. Granting the motion for a directed verdict ends the action and the judge will

1

enter a judgment for the defendant before the defendant has even presented any evidence; the trial never advances to the second stage.

Assuming the judge denies the motion for a directed verdict, and the defendant wishes to present evidence in response to the plaintiff's case, the defendant may do so in the second stage of the trial, the defendant's case-in-chief or case-in-defense. If the defendant does not wish to present such evidence, the trial will end after the first stage and the judge will submit the action to the trier of fact for determination.

The defendant's case may take several different forms: (1) the defendant may offer evidence to disprove directly the facts the plaintiff's witnesses have attempted to establish; (2) the defendant may offer evidence attacking the credibility of the witnesses upon whom the plaintiff has relied, and thus the validity of their testimony; or (3) the defendant may present evidence to establish an affirmative defense precluding judgment for the plaintiff even if the jury concluded that the plaintiff had proved his case.

After the defendant has concluded the presentation of his defense, the plaintiff has the opportunity to respond to any affirmative defense which the defendant might have presented, and to "shore-up" or reinforce his case relative to those issues and facts contested in the defendant's presentation. This third stage of trial is called "rebuttal."

The fourth and last stage of the trial is the rejoinder. In this stage, the defendant has an opportunity to respond to the additional issues raised and the evidence presented in the plaintiff's rebuttal.

Courts at common law and federal courts generally follow this same trial structure. Rule 611(a) of the Federal Rules of Evidence, however, has codified only the courts' common law power and responsibility to regulate the order of presenting evidence. It has not codified the structure itself.

RULE 611 FRE
Mode and Order of Interrogation and Presentation

(a) **Control by court.** The court shall exercise reasonable control over the mode and order of interrogating witnesses and presenting evidence so as to (1) make the interrogation and presentation effective for the ascertainment of the truth, (2) avoid needless consumption of time, and (3) protect witnesses from harassment or undue embarrassment.

II. THE PRESENTATION OF TESTIMONY

Within each phase of the trial, the parties will present evidence through the testimony of witnesses. One can visualize the presentation of this testimony, like the structure of the trial itself, as a rectangle that is divided into four parts.

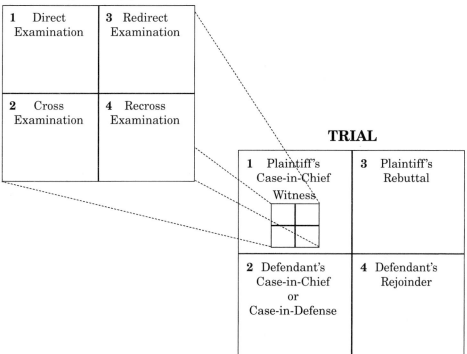

The initial presentation of testimony by the party who called the witness — the proponent of the testimony — is denoted "direct examination." During direct examination, to the extent permitted by evidentiary rules, the proponent may elicit first-hand information that the witness possesses concerning facts related to the claims or defenses raised in the cause of action, as well as facts relating to the credibility of any witness who has testified.

Following direct examination, the opposing party has an opportunity to test the witness' credibility and the reliability of the facts elicited from the witness on direct examination. This second stage of the presentation of testimony — the testing stage — is denoted "cross-examination."

Most jurisdictions limit the scope of cross-examination to those issues the proponent raised directly or by implication during the direct examination, even though the witness might have more relevant information on other issues involved in the cause of action. Courts have adopted this limitation on the belief that it contributes to the orderly presentation of evidence.[1] An additional

---

[1] *E.g.*, United States v. White, No. 99-3470, 2000 WL 1022326, at *5 (7th Cir. July 25, 2000) (finding that the district court had discretion to prohibit the defendant's cross-examination of an FBI rebuttal witness because the potential to confuse the jury and waste the court's time outweighed its probative value under Fed. R. Evid. 403 and because it exceeded the scope of direct examination).

reason for this limitation in criminal cases is the defendant's Fifth Amendment privilege against compelled self-incrimination. A defendant who takes the witness stand can fairly be held to have voluntarily waived the privilege only with regard to the issues addressed in the defendant's direct testimony.[2]

A number of state jurisdictions impose no such limitation on cross-examination; they permit wide-open cross-examination. In those jurisdictions, the party conducting the cross-examination can elicit all the relevant information that the witness possesses, regardless of whether, during direct examination, the proponent touched on the issues to which this information relates. This broad approach has been said to facilitate the search for truth by allowing all that a witness knows to be brought to light at one time, thereby preventing adversaries from making their cases and misleading the jury through the controlled disclosure of facts. Even in these jurisdictions, however, the Fifth Amendment privilege against compelled self-incrimination limits the breadth of the defendant's cross-examination in criminal cases.

Under the Federal Rules of Evidence, Rule 611(b) limits the scope of cross-examination. It provides as follows:

RULE 611 FRE
Mode and Order of Interrogation and Presentation

(b) Scope of cross-examination. Cross-examination should be limited to the subject matter of the direct examination and matters affecting the credibility of the witness. The court may, in the exercise of discretion, permit inquiry into additional matters as if on direct examination.

Of course, both at common law and under the Federal Rules, the exploration of facts relevant to the witness' credibility is always appropriate on cross-examination because courts consider the proponent's presentation of the witness to put the witness' credibility at issue automatically.[3] Because each witness must take an oath before testifying, the silent preface to each answer given is "You can believe me when I say . . . ." Therefore, on cross-examination that unstated assertion can be tested.

If the opposing party is successful in raising questions as to credibility and reliability, and the witness was not given an opportunity to explain during cross-examination, the proponent may elicit those explanations in the third phase of the witness' examination, which has been denoted "redirect examination." The final phase of examination is recross-examination. In this phase the opposing party is given another opportunity to test any new information that the proponent may have brought out during redirect examination.

---

[2] Brown v. United States, 356 U.S. 148, 154-56 (1958).

[3] *See* United States v. Wallace, 722 F.2d 415, 416 (8th Cir. 1983).

At any time during the parties' examination of a witness, the presiding judge may propound questions to clarify preceding testimony or to elicit new information. This power exists under both the common law and Rule 614 of the Federal Rules of Evidence. The judge must be careful, however, not to assume the role of an advocate and thereby influence the jury's decision.[4] Of course, if there is no jury because the case is being tried to the court, this concern does not exist; in these circumstances, there are virtually no restrictions on the judge's power to conduct examinations that will assist in rendering a fair decision.

A. Leading Questions

PRINCIPLES

A leading question suggests its own answer. Because it is a way of coaxing a witness to testify to things that the lawyer wants to hear, rather to what the witness is inclined to say without prompting, the rule precludes an attorney from asking such questions of witnesses who are *aligned in interest* with the examining attorney's client (for example, a relative or friend).

Because parties usually call witnesses who favor their side of the case (and therefore are aligned with them), and the opposing side (the party with whom the witnesses are not aligned) must cross-examine them, leading questions are usually forbidden on direct examination and permitted on cross examination. Of course, if the adverse party, a witness obviously aligned with himself, or a hostile witness is called to testify, the reverse is true — leading questions may be used in direct examination and may not be used in cross-examination.[5]

RULE 611 FRE
Mode and Order of Interrogation and Presentation

(c) **Leading questions**. Leading questions should not be used on the direct examination of a witness except as may be necessary to develop the witness' testimony. Ordinarily leading questions should be permitted on cross-examination. When a party calls a hostile witness an adverse party, or a witness identified with an adverse party, interrogation may be by leading questions.

---

[4] United States v. Albers, 93 F.3d 1469, 1486 (10th Cir. 1996).

[5] Alpha Display Paging, Inc. v. Motorola Communications & Elecs. Inc., 867 F.2d 1168, 1171 (8th Cir. 1989).

1 PRACTICES

Questions calling for yes or no answers — not necessarily leading. It is a common practice for judges to characterize all questions calling for a yes or no answer as leading. This definition is over-inclusive because many questions calling for such abbreviated answers do not suggest the answer that the questioner desires.

Example 1

If you asked the next person you meet whether she intends to travel overseas this year, her answer may be yes or no, but neither answer is suggested by the question or the context in which it was being asked.

Example 2

If the witness who observed the accident is asked "Did you hear anything being said while the accident was happening?" this would be a leading question because it suggests that someone said something. However, depending on the context in which the question was asked, it may be of little consequence.

2 PRACTICES

Leading is often loaded. Loaded questions are questions that assume facts not in evidence.

Example: In a product liability action for a fire caused by faultily wired machinery, the employer's lawyer asks an employee/witness, "When you went to the back of the machine, did you take the back off of it?" After the employee responds, "Yes" the next question is "And when the inside of the machine was exposed, did you find a loose red wire?" Both of these question are leading and loaded. They are leading because they suggest that the lawyer wants the employee to say that he took the back off the smoking machinery and found a loose red wire. The leading nature of questions is exaggerated by the fact that they assume the unproven facts that (1) the employee examined the back of the machine, (2) took the back off the smoking machine, (3) this action exposed the inner working of the machine, (4) a loose wire was found, and (5) that the wire was red in color.

If the witness had independently testified to those five facts without leading questions ("What did you see?" "What did you do in response?"), it would have been appropriate to use them in a follow-up question: "After you took the back off the machine and found the loose red wire, did you see anything else that immediately caught your attention?"

B. Offers of Proof

PRINCIPLES

When a witness is asked a question at trial and the adverse party objects, the witness will not be permitted to answer if the objection is sustained. Assuming that this ruling was erroneous, and the proponent later finds it necessary to appeal the judgment, this error cannot result in the reversal of the judgment unless the proponent can demonstrate that the error was *harmful*.[6]

Error alone is not a sufficient basis for reversing a judgment. Few trials are error free. An error justifies overturning a judgment only if it can be demonstrated that the error adversely affected the proponent.

Often this demonstration requires an offer of proof because the nature of the excluded evidence is not apparent from the context within which the question was asked. Conversely, "[f]ailure to make an offer of proof . . . is excused . . . when the substance of the excluded evidence is apparent from the context within which the questions were asked."[7]

Such offers of proof can be made in a variety of ways:

1. ***Question and answer format.*** The most complete way this can be done is by eliciting from the witness (immediately after the objection is upheld) the same testimony that was excluded from the hearing of the finder of facts. Courts disfavor this because it is time-consuming and inconvenient because the jury has to be excluded.

2. ***Proffer.*** The attorney can proffer — orally represent — to the presiding judge what the witness would have said if permitted to answer. If the successful objecting party disputes this representation, the first method can be pursued. Oral proffers are the most efficient, and therefore the most common, means of making the offer of proof.

3. ***Transcript or affidavit.*** A middle ground between live testimony and proffer could be a transcript of earlier testimony (from a trial or deposition) or an affidavit from the witness.

---

[6] *E.g.,* K-B Trucking Co. v. Riss Int'l Corp., 763 F.2d 1148, 1156 (10th Cir. 1986) ("[E]rror in the admission or exclusion of evidence is harmless if it does not affect the substantial rights of the parties, and the burden of demonstrating that substantial rights were affected rests with the party asserting the error.").

[7] Waltzer v. Transidyne Gen. Corp., 697 F.2d 130, 134 (6th Cir. 1983).

RULE 103 FRE
Rulings on Evidence

(a) Effect of erroneous ruling. Error may not be predicated upon a ruling which admits or excludes evidence unless a substantial right of the party is affected, and

(1) Objection. In case the ruling is one admitting evidence, a timely objection or motion to strike appears of record, stating the specific ground of objection, if the specific ground was not apparent from the context, or

(2) Offer of proof. In case the ruling is one excluding evidence, the substance of the evidence was made known to the court by offer or was apparent from the context within which questions were asked. Once the court makes a definitive ruling on the record admitting or excluding evidence, either at or before trial, a party need not renew an objection or offer of proof to preserve a claim of error for appeal.

(b) Record of offer and ruling. The court may add any other or further statement which shows the character of the evidence, the form in which it was offered, the objection made, and the ruling thereon. It may direct the making of an offer in question and answer form.

(c) Hearing of jury. In jury cases, proceedings shall be conducted, to the extent practicable, so as to prevent inadmissible evidence from being suggested to the jury by any means, such as making statements or offers of proof or asking questions in the hearing of the jury.

(d) Plain error. Nothing in this rule precludes taking notice of plain errors affecting substantial rights although they were not brought to the attention of the court.

When testimony is being offered, it is preferable to make the offer of proof through the question and answer format when the testimony is complex, and particularly when the evidentiary theory for admitting the evidence could be clarified for the presiding judge by hearing it in its entirety. The judge can change her mind, and winning below is far better than winning on appeal. Judges, however, will favor proffers because they are more efficient.

3 PRACTICES

Is the pretrial ruling definitive? Rule 103(a) FRE excuses a contemporaneous objection at trial when evidence is offered, if (1) a motion to exclude it was made *in limine*, (2) that motion was denied, and (3) the ruling was "definitive."[8]

Parties should request a decision from the ruling judge on the status of the pretrial ruling — whether "definitive" or not. For the losing party, this will preserve an option at trial: (1) objecting, if there is a different presiding judge and a reasonable possibility that the issue may be heard again and resolved differently, or (2) standing mute when evidence is offered by the opposing party because objecting will only elevate the level of attention that jurors will give to it.

This revision of the contemporaneous objection rule will not change the result in *Luce v. United States*.[9] In *Luce,* the Supreme Court held that a criminal defendant who lost an *in limine* motion to suppress evidence of his prior convictions on cross-examination if he testified at trial, could not raise the issue on appeal unless he actually took the witness stand at trial — making an offer of proof of what he would have testified to at trial, had the convictions been excluded, was held to be inadequate.

Luce was premised on a number of factors that continue to compel the same result:

1. The defendant might never have intended to take the witness stand in his own defense, but might have raised the issue of prior conviction only for the purpose of creating potentially reversible error.

2. Even though the government was permitted to raise the prior convictions during its cross-examination of the defendant, it might have chosen not to do so.

3. Under the pressures of trial — oath, cross-examination, public hearing and the immediate potential of a loss of freedom — there is no assurance that what the witness testified to before trial (at the pretrial hearing, for example), or what the lawyer proffers (orally represents) that his client will say, is precisely what the client would have said at trial.*

---

[8] *See* Wilson v. Williams, 182 F.3d 562, 565 (7th Cir. 1999) (en banc) (adopting the logic of the new rule). *See also* Unit Drilling Co. v. Enron Oil & Gas Co., 108 F.3d 1186, 1193 n.10 (10th Cir. 1997) (noting, before the revision, that "an issue may be preserved for appeal by a motion *in limine*, even when a party fails to object at trial, if '(1) the matter was adequately presented to the district court; (2) the issue was of a type that can be finally decided prior to trial; and (3) the court's ruling was definitive.'").

[9] 469 U.S. 38 (1984).

* *See* PRACTICE 119, *infra.*

As a matter of practice, judges should be hesitant to label pretrial evidentiary rulings "definitive" when there is a distinct possibility that a different judge may be presiding at the trial.[10] This determination can deprive that trial judge of an opportunity to rule independently on the issue, and thereby avoid potentially reversible error — the very purpose of the contemporaneous objection rule.

C. Evidentiary Foundations

PRINCIPLES

In a jury trial, the judge is usually a finder of fact on far more issues than will be submitted to the jury. The judge must find the facts upon which all evidentiary objections are resolved. For example, if evidence is objected to because it is hearsay, that objection will turn on why the evidence is relevant. If relevant because of the truth of the matter asserted in the writing, it is excluded as hearsay unless made admissible under one of the many exceptions to the hearsay rule. If, for example, the proponent relies upon the business record exception in Rule 803(6) the following factual foundation must be established by the proponent:

> The statement in question was made by someone with (1) *personal knowledge and* (2) *a business duty*; (3) *at or near the time* of the event recorded; in the (4) course of a *regularly conducted activity*; and the record must have been (5) *relied upon*. In addition all of this has to be established by a (6) *custodian of the records* or someone with equivalent knowledge of the record keeping activities.

All of these requirements are factual in nature and resolved by the judge by a preponderance of the evidence standard, even in the context of a criminal case.[11] Of course, the presence or absence of these factors in varying degrees can be argued to the jury in closing arguments on the question of weight that should be assigned to the evidence during deliberations.

RULE 104 FRE
Preliminary Questions

(a) **Questions of admissibility generally.** Preliminary questions concerning the qualification of a person to be a witness, the existence of a privilege, or the admissibility of evidence shall be determined by the court, subject to the provision of subdivision (b). In making its deter-

---

[10] Clausen v. Sea-3, Inc., 21 F.3d 1181, 1190 (1st Cir. 1994) (stating the "renewal gives the trial judge a chance to reconsider the ruling with the concrete evidence presented in the actual context of the trial.").

[11] *See* Lego v. Twomey, 404 U.S. 477, 486 (1972).

mination it is not bound by the rules of evidence except those with respect to privileges.

4 PRACTICES

Not bound by the rules being enforced. In resolving these factual issues, the judge will often hear evidence from witnesses, but more often than not will base her decision on proffers from the attorneys. The evidence that the judge considers does not have to be evidence that could be heard and considered by the jury at trial. Under Fed. R. Evid. 104(a) the judge is not bound by the rules of evidence when ruling on the admissibility of evidence. Therefore, the judge can hear and consider hearsay in ruling on the admissibility of hearsay.[12] The only evidence rules that the judge may not disregard in analyzing admissibility issues are those relating to privilege.

Example 1

If a judge is determining the admissibility of a dead man's dying declaration, it must be established that the deceased was *contemplating imminent death* when the statement was made. In making this determination, the court can consider hearsay testimony from individuals who repeat what others have said about the deceased's conduct. Although this testimony could not be heard by the jury, because it is hearsay for which there is no exception, it can nevertheless be considered by the judge in this context.

5 PRACTICES

Burden of persuasion on factual questions of admissibility. Regardless of the nature of the proceedings (civil or criminal) and the ultimate burden of persuasion that must be satisfied (preponderance of evidence, clear and convincing evidence or beyond a reasonable doubt), the proponent of evidence need only convince the presiding judge by a preponderance of the evidence that all foundation facts are true. This is true even when the question is the voluntariness of a confession in a criminal action or the admissibility of co-conspirator admissions when the defendant has been charged with criminal conspiracy, and even though the accumulation of evidence at the end of the trial (including the admission) must prove guilt beyond a reasonable doubt.[13]

This burden varies when the question of admissibility overlaps with the issue to be decided by the jury. In that instance, the presiding judge decides

---

[12] *See* United State v. Franco, 872 F.2d 1136, 1139 (7th Cir. 1989) (allowing the use of hearsay evidence to determine whether the trial court could admit certain business records under Fed. R. Evid. 803(6).).

[13] *See* Bourjaily v. United States, 483 U.S. 171, 175-78 (1987).

[14] *See* Lentz v. Mason, 32 F. Supp. 2d 733, 744 (D.N.J. 1999).

the preliminary factual question by a *prima facie* standard — sufficient evidence upon which a reasonable jury could find that the foundation facts are true.[14]

RULE 104 FRE
Preliminary Questions

(b) Relevancy conditioned on fact. When the relevancy of evidence depends upon the fulfillment of a condition of fact, the court shall admit it upon, or subject to, the introduction of evidence sufficient to support a finding of the fulfillment of the condition.

Example 1

If the authenticity of a will is the subject of the cause of action, the proponent cannot admit the will into evidence so the jury can examine it until the judge first determines that it is authentic. Because the judge is being asked to decide, for admissibility purposes, the same thing the jury will ultimately be asked to decide, the judge makes the preliminary determination by a *prima facie* standard, rather than the preponderance standard that is usually employed.

Example 2

When a criminal defendant's out-of-court confessions are offered into evidence, the court must first determine that (1) it was voluntarily made (2) by the defendant. The court will make this determination by a preponderance of the evidence standard. Once it is admitted, the jury must be convinced of the same facts before it credits the confession and factors it into its determination of whether the defendant committed the crime beyond a reasonable doubt.

6 PRACTICES

Prima facie is the how, not the what. The *prima facie* standard is not a characterization of the level of the burden. It is only a characterization of how the decision is made — on the face of the evidence without considerations of credibility. With the *prima facie* standard the court must apply a burden of persuasion. As with all other admissibility decisions, this burden of persuasion is by a preponderance of the evidence. The judge must be convinced, by a preponderance of the evidence, that a reasonable juror *could* find, not that the judge *would* find if she considered credibility factors, that the facts being proven are true. Many lawyers and judges misinterpret the *prima facie* con-

---

[15] *See* United States v. Reilly, 33 F.3d 1396, 1405 (3d Cir. 1994) ("[O]nce the court finds that evidence has been introduced sufficient to permit a reasonable juror to find that the matter in question is what its proponent claims [the preponderance of the evidence standard], a sufficient foundation for introduction in evidence has been laid [the *prima facie* standard].").

cept as a burden of persuasion that is something less than a preponderance of the evidence.[15]

D. Rule of Completeness

PRINCIPLES

When part of a writing is offered as evidence, the opposing party has the right, at the time of that offering, to introduce whatever remainder is necessary to give context and meaning to the initial offering.[16]

RULE 106 FRE
Remainder of or Related Writings or Recorded Statements

When a writing or recorded statement or part thereof is introduced by a party, an adverse party may require the introduction at that time of any other part or any other writing or recorded statement which ought in fairness to be considered contemporaneously with it.

7 PRACTICES

A rule of timing, applying only to writings. The rule of completeness is nothing more than a rule of timing. To avoid the misleading presentation of evidence, it permits the opposing party to offer evidence in the middle of the opposing party's case. This is permitted because the offering of the additional materials will not unfairly interfere with the initial party's adversarial presentation.

While the same distortion of evidence can result from limited *testimony* being presented, the *rule of completeness does not apply* to this form of evidence.[17] In fairness to the party presenting his case, the opposing party may not ask cross-examination questions until direct-examination has been completed, and certainly cannot insist that other testimony he is prepared to present be heard contemporaneously.

The rule of completeness also is not an independent basis for admitting otherwise inadmissible evidence.[18] If the initially omitted portion of the writing

---

[16] *See* United States v. Haddad, 10 F.3d 1252, 1258 (7th Cir. 1993) ("To determine whether a disputed portion is necessary, the district court considers whether (1) it explains the admitted evidence, (2) places the admitted evidence in context, (3) avoids misleading the jury, and (4) insures fair and impartial understanding of the evidence.").

[17] *See United States Ortego*, 203 F.3d 675, 682 (9th Cir. 2000) (reiterating that the rule of completeness does not apply to oral testimony).

[18] *See id.* ("[R]ule 106 does not compel the admission of otherwise inadmissible evidence.").

is essential to understanding the portion that was offered, the entire writing must be seen as one piece of evidence. Consequently, if the omitted portions are inadmissible, by definition, the initial portion that was offered should be inadmissible for the same reason.

E. Applications — Remainder of or Related Writings

At the defendant's trial, inconsistencies between the officer's trial testimony, grand jury testimony, testimony at the suppression hearing, and police report were highlighted. In response, the trial court permitted the government to offer the entire transcript of the officer's prior testimony before the grand jury and suppression hearing, as well as the entire police report claiming it was permitted under the rule of completeness. The appellate court concluded that this was erroneous because all of this evidence was not necessary in the interest of fairness and completeness to give context and meaning to the portions that had been brought out to impeach. Without offering just the portions that were relevant to the issues raised on cross-examination, the government's evidence amounted to little more than prior consistent statements of a witness on matters that had not been impeached. *United States v. Ramos-Caraballo*, 2004 WL 1647383 (8th Cir. 2004).

Chapter 2

AUTHENTICATION

I. AUTHENTICATION

PRINCIPLES

Authentication is an issue of logical relevance. Every tangible piece of evidence that is offered at trial must be authenticated; that is, a witness must identify it and show its relevance to issues being tried. This can be accomplished in a variety of ways — directly, through personal knowledge of the item, or indirectly (circumstantially), through surrounding circumstances (e.g., the sound of a voice, the content of a written instrument, or a series of events that give assurance that a writing is a reply to a prior communication — the reply doctrine).[19]

RULE 401 FRE
Definition of "Relevant Evidence"

"Relevant evidence" means evidence having any tendency to make the existence of any fact that is of consequence to the determination of the action more probable or less probable than it would be without the evidence.

8 PRACTICES

Authentication is an issue of conditional relevance. The question of authenticity, whether it is of the principal document in issue or of an exemplar from which the authenticity of another document is determined, is one of conditional relevance that the jury must ultimately resolve pursuant to Rule 104(b). *See* **PRACTICES NO. 5**, *supra.* After the presiding judge determines that the proponent has established a *prima facie* case of a document's authenticity — that is, the proponent has introduced sufficient evidence upon which a reasonable jury could find that the document is authentic — the judge must allow the jury to resolve the matter.

---

[19] *See* United States v. Espinoza, 641 F.2d 153 (4th Cir. 1981) (illustrating these various methods of authentication).

As the court explained in *United States v. Goichman*[20]:

> [T]he showing of authenticity is not on a par with more technical evidentiary rules, such as hearsay exceptions, governing admissibility. Rather, there need be only a *prima facie* showing, to the court, of authenticity, not a full argument on admissibility. Once a *prima facie* case is made, the evidence goes to the jury and it is the jury who will ultimately determine the authenticity of the evidence, not the court. The only requirement is that there has been substantial evidence from which they could infer that the document was authentic.[21]

A proponent need not establish authenticity to any degree remotely resembling a certainty. In *Mauldin v. The Upjohn Co.*,[22] for example, a pathologist had prepared photographs displaying slides of certain tissue from the plaintiff. When the doctor, on cross-examination, could not attest "with absolute certainty" that the paraffin blocks contained tissue from the plaintiff, the defendant objected that the photographs were insufficiently authenticated to be admissible. Concluding that the trial court's admission of the photographs was appropriate, the appellate court pointed out that the doctor did testify that the numbers on the pathology reports identified as Mauldin's were identical to the numbers on the paraffin blocks identified as Mauldin's, and that he had observed nothing to indicate a mix-up. In addition, the doctor had expressed no doubt as to the match itself. The court then commented: "The Federal Rules of Evidence do not require absolute certainty in authentication, but rather 'evidence sufficient to support a finding that the matter in question is what its proponent claims.'"[23]

To identify a document sufficiently to warrant its admission into evidence, a witness need not be able to attest familiarity with every page; an identification of the signature on the signature page is sufficient. This only gets the document into evidence and before the trier of facts for its consideration. It does not ensure that the trier of facts will give any credibility and probative force to the document.[24] Once the document is admitted, the jury must make the ultimate determination of the genuineness of the evidence.

9 PRACTICES

Chain of custody not an imperative. If a piece of real evidence (*e.g.*, the item that was purchased, the gun that was found at the scene of a crime, the

---

[20] 547 F.2d 778 (3d Cir. 1976).

[21] *Id.* at 784.

[22] 697 F.2d 644, 648 (5th Cir.), *cert. denied*, 464 U.S. 848 (1983).

[23] *Id.* at 648.

[24] *See* United States v. Whittington, 783 F.2d 1210, 1215 (5th Cir.), *cert. denied*, 479 U.S. 882 (1986).

blood-stained clothing of the victim, the consumer good that caused the plaintiff's injuries) has been handled by several people before having been brought to a hearing, that chain of custody does *not* have to be accounted for if a single individual can identify the item. Identification by a person with personal knowledge is all that is required.

A *chain of custody* is *necessary* only when:

1. The item cannot be identified by a single individual, and the chain is necessary to link the evidence back to the scene of the accident or crime; or

2. The item is being used as a source of latent evidence (results of blood, fingerprints, or ballistic tests) that needs to be linked to a specific unaltered item and no single witness can do that because those factors are not detectable by the naked eye.[25]

Demonstrating a chain of custody may be desirable, even though not required, to reinforce the testimony of the identifying witness.

A *chain of custody may prove to be invaluable* when authenticating electronic and digital evidence because it may be the only realistic way of give adequate assurances that the documents or photographs have not been altered. *See* **PRINCIPLE NO. 14**, *infra*.

Flaws in the chain of custody that do not preclude admission may influence the weight the jury will give to the evidence.[26]

II. SELF-AUTHENTICATION

A. PRINCIPLES

The identity of some items is so self-apparent that courts have made them self-authenticating. These items, therefore, are admissible without the presentation of any additional foundational evidence. Under the common law such items included certified copies of public records and acknowledged (notarized) private documents. Rule 902 of the Federal Rules of Evidence expanded the list of self-authenticating documents.[27]

---

[25] *See, e.g.*, United States v. Cardenas, 864 F.2d 1528, 1531 (10th Cir.), *cert. denied*, 491 U.S. 909 (1989) ("The condition precedent to the admission of real evidence is met by providing the proper foundation. If the proffered evidence is unique, readily identifiable and relatively resistant to change, the foundation need only consist of testimony that the evidence is what the proponent claims. . . . However, when the evidence, as here, is not readily identifiable and is susceptible to alteration by tampering or contamination, the trial court requires a more stringent foundation entailing a chain of custody of the item with sufficient completeness to render it improbable that the original item has either been exchanged with another or been contaminated or tampered with.")

[26] *See* United States v. Washington, 11 F.3d 1510, 1514 (10th Cir. 1993).

[27] For examples of the different methods of authentication, *see generally*, United States v. McGlory, 968 F.2d 309, 328-31 (3d Cir. 1992), *cert. denied*, 507 U.S. 962 (1993); United States v.

RULE 902 FRE
Self-Authentication

Extrinsic evidence of authenticity as a condition precedent to admissibility is not required with respect to the following:

(1) Domestic public documents under seal. A document bearing a seal purporting to be that of the United States, or of any State, district, Commonwealth, territory, or insular possession thereof, or the Panama Canal Zone, or the Trust Territory of the Pacific Islands, or of a political subdivision, department officer, or agency thereof, and a signature purporting to be an attestation or execution.

(2) Domestic public documents not under seal. A document purporting to bear the signature in the official capacity of an officer or employee of any entity included in paragraph (1) hereof, having no seal, if a public officer having a seal and having official duties in the district or political subdivision of the officer or employee certifies under seal that the signer has the official capacity and that signature is genuine.

(3) Foreign public documents. A document purporting to be executed or attested in an official capacity by a person authorized by the laws of a foreign country to make the execution or attestation, and accompanied by a final certification as to the genuineness of the signature and official position (A) of the execution or attesting person, or (B) of any foreign official whose certificate of genuineness of signature and official position relates to the execution or attestation or is in a chain of certificates of genuineness of signature and official position relating to the execution or attestation. A final certification may be made by a secretary of embassy or legation, consul general, consul, vice consul, or consular agent of the United States, or a diplomatic or consular official of the foreign country assigned or accredited to the United States. If reasonable opportunity has been given to all parties to investigate the authenticity and accuracy of official documents, the court may, for good cause shown, order that they be treated as presumptively authentic without final certification or permit them to be evidenced by an attested summary with or without final certification.

(4) Certified copies of public records. A copy of an official record or report or entry therein, or of a document authorized by law to be recorded or filed and actually recorded or filed in a public office, including data compilations in any form, certified as correct by the custodian or other person authorized to make the certification, by certificate com-

---

Stone, 604 F.2d 922, 925-26 (5th Cir. 1979); United States v. Wilson, 532 F.2d 641, 644-45 (8th Cir.), *cert. denied*, 429 U.S. 846 (1976).

plying with paragraph (1), (2), or (3) of this rule or complying with any Act of Congress or rule prescribed by the Supreme Court pursuant to statutory authority.

(5) Official publications. Books, pamphlets, or other publications purporting to be issued by public authority.

(6) Newspapers and periodicals. Printed materials purporting to be newspapers or periodicals.

(7) Trade inscriptions and the like. Inscriptions, signs, tags, or labels purporting to have been affixed in the course of business and indicating ownership, control, or origin.

(8) Acknowledged documents. Documents accompanied by a certificate of acknowledgment executed in the manner provided by law by a notary public or other officer authorized by law to take acknowledgments.

(9) Commercial paper and related documents. Commercial paper, signatures thereon, and documents relating thereto to the extent provided by general commercial law.

(10) Presumptions under Acts of Congress. Any signature, document, or other matter by Act of Congress to be presumptively or *prima facie* genuine or authentic.

(11) Certified domestic records of regularly conducted activity. The original or a duplicate of a domestic record of regularly conducted activity, that would be admissible under Rule 803(6), if accompanied by a written declaration of its custodian or another qualified person, in a manner complying with any Act of Congress or rule prescribed by the Supreme Court pursuant to statutory authority, certifying that the record —

(A) was made at or near the time of the occurrence of the matters set forth, by or from information transmitted by, a person with knowledge of those matters;

(B) was kept in the course of the regularly conducted activity; and

(C) was made by the regularly conducted activity as a regular practice.

A party intending to offer a record in evidence under this paragraph must provide written notice of that intention to all adverse parties, and must make the record and declaration available for inspection sufficiently in advance of their offer into evidence to provide an adverse party with a fair opportunity to challenge them.

(12) Certified foreign records of regularly conducted activity. In a civil case, the original or a duplicate of a foreign record of regularly conducted activity, which would be admissible under Rule 803(6), if accompanied by a written declaration by the custodian or another qualified person that the record —

(A) was made at or near the time of the occurrence of the matters set forth, by or from information transmitted by, a person with knowledge or those matters;

(B) was kept in the course of the regularly conducted activity; and

(C) was made by the regularly conducted activity as a regular practice.

The declaration must be signed in a manner that, if falsely made, would subject the maker to criminal penalty under the laws of the country where the declaration is signed. A party intending to offer a record into evidence under this paragraph must provide written notice of that intention to all adverse parties, and must make the record and declaration available for inspection sufficiently in advance of their offer into evidence to provide an adverse party with a fair opportunity to challenge them.

10 PRACTICES

Effect of self-authentication. For as long as the concept of self-authentication has existed its effect has been debated. Three approaches have emerged:

(1) One view is that the concept of self-authentication permits a jury to find, without additional evidence being presented, that the document is what the proponent claims. The concept, however, does not automatically satisfy the proponent's burden of going forward with evidence of authenticity. It only permits an instruction to the jury that it *may* find that the document is authentic.

(2) A second view treats the concept of self-authentication as satisfying the proponent's burden of coming forward with evidence of authenticity. Accordingly, even though the proponent still has the burden of persuasion on the question of authenticity, the jury is instructed that it *must find* the document authentic *absent compelling evidence to the contrary*. If such evidence is forthcoming, the jury must resolve the issue based on the evidence before it, with appropriate consideration being giving to the factors that prompted the law to recognize its self-authenticating status.

(3) The third view is much like the second, except that the concept of self-authentication *shifts* to the adversary the *burden of persuading the jury* that it is not what is presumed — proving lack of authenticity. Accordingly, the jury is instructed that authenticity is pre-

sumed — the jury must accept the fact, unless the adversary convinces them otherwise.[28]

The continuing disagreement about the effect of self-authentication appears to be related to the continuing debate over the effect of presumptions. Article III of the Federal Rules of Evidence explicitly adopted the "bursting bubble" view of presumptions, which serves only to shift the burden of going forward with evidence to the adversary. Once *any evidence* of the *non-existence* of the *presumed fact* is presented, the *presumption bubble bursts* and is no longer mentioned to the jury.

Though professing to follow this "bursting bubble" approach, judges have taken many inconsistent positions relative to how the jury is instructed about the destroyed presumption. Most of these practices have, in effect, been subtle efforts to change the "bursting bubble" theory to one more akin to the second approach — one that shifts to the adversary the burden of disproving what has been presumed. Until this debate is resolved, it is unlikely that the debate of the effect of self-authentication will be resolved. *See* **PRACTICES NOS. 148-150,** *infra.*

11 PRACTICES

Electronic Evidence — Old wine in new bottles. Authentication is the most challenging evidentiary problem facing litigators in the Internet/Information age. The mutability of electronic data has prompted some to question the continued validity of traditional authentication methods. It shouldn't. While digital technology has expanded the ways in which documents can be corrupted or forged, it has also expanded the ways in which they can be authenticated. At the same time, existing circumstantial methods of authentication remain available, and those methods can be modified to accommodate the unique difficulties posed by e-evidence. The following are a few examples of how "appearance, contents, substance, internal patterns, or other distinctive characteristics, taken in conjunction with circumstances" under Fed. R. Evid. 901(b)(4) have been successfully employed.

Example 1

E-mail was found to be sufficiently authenticated because (1) it bore the appellant's e-mail address, (2) the reply automatically dialed the appellant's e-mail address as the sender, (3) the factual details of the message were known to the appellant, (4) the message bore his nickname, and (5) it was followed by a phone conversations involving the same subject matter. *United*

---

[28] *See also* 5 CHRISTOPHER B. MUELLER & LAIRD C. KIRKPATRICK, FEDERAL EVIDENCE, § 538, at 150-51 (Lawyers Cooperative 2d Ed. 1994) and PAUL R. RICE & ROY A. KATRIEL, EVIDENCE: COMMON LAW AND FEDERAL RULES OF EVIDENCE § 7.02 [B][2][b] (LEXIS Publishing 2005).

States v. Siddiqui, 235 F.3d 1318 (11th Cir. 2000), *cert. denied*, 533 U.S. 940 (2001).

Example 2

Chat room log printouts authenticated by (1) appellant's admission that he used the screen name "Cessna" when participating in such conversation, (2) several co-conspirators confirmed through their testimony that appellant used the name "Cessna", and (3) when a meeting was arranged with the person who used the screen name "Cessna," the appellant showed up. *United States v. Tank*, 200 F.3d 627 (9th Cir. 2000)

Example 3

E-mails were authenticated when (1) the victim recognized the appellant's e-mail address, (2) the e-mails discussed things only the victim, the appellant, and a few other people knew about, (3) the messages were written in the way in which the appellant would communicate, and (4) a third party had witnessed the appellant sending a similar threatening e-mail to the victim previously. *Massimo v. State*, 144 S.W.3d 210 (Tex. Ct. App. 2004).

12 PRACTICES

Cumulative doctrines. No method of authentication is exclusive or preclusive. The use of one does not preclude the use of as many others as are relevant. The more that different methods of authentication point to a conclusion of authenticity, the more likely the court and the jury are to find the evidence authentic. In the above examples you see personal knowledge, content, circumstances, and context all being used to provide the most convincing demonstration from which the most convincing argument can be made.

13 PRACTICES

Old, but still kicking. Most of the circumstantial methods of authentication were designed for the era of "snail mail," but they are still as viable in the electronic communication age as they were when they were first recognized. Two important methods are the reply doctrine and the ancient document rule.

The *ancient document rule* serves to authenticate a document and to make it admissible under an exception to the hearsay rule by the same name. Under Fed. R. Evid. 803 (16) a document need only be 20 years old to be ancient. Under the common law it had to be 30 years old. In addition, the hearsay exception requires that the document's authenticity be otherwise established. This indirectly incorporates Fed. R. Evid. 902(b)(8), which declares that a 20 year old document is sufficiently authentic to be admitted into evidence if it is "in such condition as to create no suspicion concerning its authenticity," and "was in a place where it, if authentic, would likely be." If these conditions cannot be met, that does not mean the ancient document is not admissible. It only means that you will have to resort to another rule to establish authenticity.

The hard drive of a computer could easily meet the requirement of these rules. To increase the capacity of computers, hard drives are often replaced and discarded. This practice has occurred for more than 20 years. Therefore the ancient document rule could be used to authenticate documents retrieved from the discarded hard drives and ensure their admissibility for truth as well.

The documents retrieved would be originals for best evidence purposes, and all printouts made of those images would also be originals. *See* Fed. R. Evid. 1001(3) which states that "if data are stored in a computer or similar device, any printout or other output readable by sight, shown to reflect the data accurately, is an 'original.' "

The *reply doctrine* could have similar utility. Under the common law, if one establishes that he properly addressed, stamped, and posted a letter, a presumption arose that the addressee received it. If, in the due course of mail, without undue delay, a reply was received that purported to be from the original addressee and refers to the original letter, this authenticated the response as being from the addressee. That doctrine still exists under the Federal Rules of Evidence, although no rule specifically incorporates the doctrine by title. Fed. R. Evid. 902 (b)(4), however, delineates the concept on which the common law doctrine was premised — "appearance, contents, substance, internal patterns, or other distinctive characteristics, taken in conjunction with circumstances." While no courts appear to have relied on the doctrine, it could be applicable to e-mail communications. There is little reason for not presuming that a responsive e-mail is from the original addressee if evidence establishes that the original message was properly addressed and sent, and a prompt response is received claiming to be in reply, with the original addressee's name listed on the header as the sender, and the original message attached to the reply.

14 PRACTICES

In the digital age, a chain of custody provides the critical link. Digital photography poses significant problems of authentication because technology has advanced to the point where photographs can be significantly manipulated with little possibility of detection. This problem materializes primarily in situations where there are no eyewitnesses to assure accuracy. One answer to authentication is a chain of custody of the digital card that was used in the digital camera and the computer onto which the images on the digital card were downloaded.

If a digital card that was used in a camera has been in the exclusive custody of a single person, that person's testimony that he had not tampered with the image on the card should be sufficient authentication of the card. The digital photograph on that card can either be printed or displayed on a monitor on a portable computer in the courtroom.

If the digital print is made outside the courtroom, and that print is offered into evidence, a chain of custody of the computer on which it was stored and from which it was printed would also have to be established, with testimony by each person having access that he did not tamper with it. If there were changes, such as enhancements that increased the quality of the image, rather than manipulations of what was recorded, this also would have to be acknowledged and explained.

III. RELATIONSHIP OF AUTHENTICATION RULES TO OTHER RULES[29]

Rule 406. Habit; Routine Practice. A party can use an individual's habits or an organization's routine practices to authenticate documents. For example, in *In re James E. Long Constr. Co.*,[30] the issue before the bankruptcy court involved the validity of certain lien waivers. To establish the genuineness of the signatures that appeared on these waivers, the plaintiff presented the testimony of the attorney who had prepared the lien waiver form for signatures.

He stated that his office had prepared the form and that the signatures were apparently obtained by Long, which returned it to his office after signatures. Crawford, the vice-president of Long, testified that Moran, superintendent of Long, was dead and had apparently obtained the signatures on the reverse side of the document; that he did not specifically recall the document but possibly took it to the attorney's office after completion; that the waiver in question was customarily executed by Long and the subcontractor in the regular course of business on other projects; and that there must have been outstanding liabilities on the project for the signatures to have been required. Nothing in the record suggests that the lien waiver was obtained other than in the ordinary course of business.[31]

The court then concluded that this was sufficient to make out a *prima facie* case of authenticity.

---

[29] PAUL R. RICE & ROY A. KATRIEL, EVIDENCE: COMMON LAW AND FEDERAL RULES OF EVIDENCE § 7.02 [C] (LEXIS Publishing 2000)

[30] 557 F.2d 1039 (4th Cir. 1977).

[31] *Id.* at 1040-41.

Rule 701. Opinion Testimony by Lay Witnesses. All witness identifications, whether they are of persons, documents, voices, or photographs, are nothing more than opinions. Although there was a basic rule at common law excluding opinion testimony, courts always admitted such identifications because they were helpful and because requiring the witness to describe the facts upon which he based his identification (for example, describing the handwriting style of another) so that the jury could make the identification without the witness' opinion would have been virtually impossible.

Under the Federal Rules of Evidence there is no longer a rule excluding opinion testimony. Rule 701 makes lay opinion admissible so long as it is "(a) rationally based on the perception of the witness and (b) helpful to a clear understanding of the witness' testimony or the determination of a fact in issue." Consequently, opinions about the authorship of documents are admissible so long as the proponent demonstrates that the witness based his opinion on his familiarity with such things as the author's handwriting style, choice of words or grammatical styles.

IV. APPLICATIONS — AUTHENTICATION

ONE

The defendant was captured selling drugs to a paid informant on a hidden video camera. At his trial for possession and distribution of crack cocaine the government put the videotapes of the transactions into evidence through the agents who had monitored the transactions. To introduce the drugs that were purchased the prosecution built a "chain of custody" to establish they were the same unaltered substances seen on the tapes. This chain was established in the following way: (1) the videotape showed the defendant giving the drugs to the informant; (2) the DEA agents testimony describing the government's surveillance of the informant before, during, and after the transaction; (3) the DEA agent's testimony about field-testing and storage of the drugs; and (4) the testimony of the forensic chemist who tested the purchased substance. The defendant objected to the chain of custody because (1) the informant's absence from the video camera's field of view was not accounted for and (2) the informant delivered four rocks to the DEA agents, whereas the video showed the defendant counting and giving five rocks to the informant. The court rejected the argument that this broke the chain of custody. The court noted that the government need not rule out all possibilities inconsistent with authenticity, or prove beyond any doubt that the evidence is what it purports to be. The identified problems in the chain of custody go to the weight of the evidence, not its admissibility. *United States v. Jackson*, 345 F.3d 59 (2d Cir. 2003).

TWO

In a breach of contract action, notes written by one of the parties were admitted into evidence as an admission. These notes were objected to as having been inadequately authenticated. On a page of the notes acknowledged to have been written by the party, appeared an eighteen-word sentence written in a different hand stating: "the more you say, the more you will get hurt on cross unless it is our party line." The theory of the party offering the sentence was that someone (possibly a lawyer) had written the note before or during the party's deposition. Because authentication requires only enough evidence to enable a reasonable juror to find genuineness, the court need not be convinced of genuineness to admit it. Because (1) the party owned the notebook, (2) took it to his deposition, (3) it contained the party's handwritten notes from the year of his deposition, and (4) he wrote the five lines that immediately preceded the "party line" notation, the court did not abuse its discretion in admitting the evidence. *SCS Communications, Inc. v. Herrick Co., Inc.,* 360 F.3d 329 (2d Cir. 2004).

THREE

Defendants are on trial for conspiracy to defraud the city through a partnership. The partnership paid the mayor of the town funds that had been funneled from the Town to defendants, SRC, and then to the conspirators' Plaza partners; the mayor reported these sums on her income tax returns. If her signatures on the checks were genuine, the inference arose that she knew that the partnership was an instrument of fraud. The mayor claims that her husband forged all of her signatures. The government presented uncontested handwriting exemplars to the jury so that the jurors could compare them to the checks and decide authorship. No handwriting expert testified. This was an acceptable means of authentication under Rule 901(b)(3) which permits "comparison by the trier of fact . . . with specimens which have been authenticated." *United States v. Spano,* 2005 421 F.3d 599 (7th Cir. 2005).

Chapter 3

RELEVANCE

I. BALANCING PREJUDICE AGAINST PROBATIVE VALUE

PRINCIPLES

Evidence probative of a provable proposition is logically relevant. Logically relevant evidence is admissible unless excluded by other rules of evidence.

RULE 401 FRE
Definition of "Relevant Evidence"

"Relevant evidence" means evidence having any tendency to make the existence of any fact that is of consequence to the determination of the action more probable or less probable than it would be without the evidence.

RULE 402 FRE
Relevant Evidence Generally Admissible;
Irrelevant Evidence Inadmissible

All relevant evidence is admissible, except as otherwise provided by the Constitution of the United States, by Act of Congress, by these rules, or by other rules prescribed by the Supreme Court pursuant to statutory authority. Evidence which is not relevant is not admissible.

RULE 403 FRE
Exclusion of Relevant Evidence on Grounds
of Prejudice, Confusion, or Waste of Time

Although relevant, evidence may be excluded if its probative value is substantially outweighed by the danger of unfair prejudice, confusion of the issues, or misleading the jury, or by considerations of undue delay, waste of time, or needless presentation of cumulative evidence.

15 PRACTICES

A promise is just as good. When the relevance of evidence is dependent upon proof of other facts (for example, evidence that the plaintiff could both hear and understand English is not relevant in a tort action until there is evidence that a verbal warning was given in English before the accident occurred), Rule 104 requires the court to admit it into evidence subject to the conditioning facts being proven at a later time. In the old Perry Mason TV series, Perry would embark on a line of questioning that the prosecutor would vehemently object to on the ground of relevance. In response, Perry would always say, "Your honor, the relevance of this line of questioning will become apparent in a moment." In response, the judge would say, "OK, Mr. Mason, I'll give you a little rope here." What was discretionary in the Perry Mason trials is mandatory now. Of course, the judge could ask for an offer of proof in the form of a proffer.

16 PRACTICES

Simply prejudicial is not enough. Even if there is no specific rule (e.g., hearsay, remedial measures, privileges) that otherwise excludes relevant evidence, this evidence can still be excluded by the presiding judge under Fed. R. Evid. Rule 403, but only if its probative value is shown to be *substantially outweighed* by the danger of "unfair prejudice, confusion of the issues, or misleading the jury, or by considerations of undue delay, waste of time, or needless presentation of cumulative evidence." There is a strong bias in favor of admitting relevant evidence.

In our adversarial system each party is expected to present evidence that is prejudicial to the opposing side. That is how the party with the burden of persuasion wins the law suit. The only prejudice that will warrant the exclusion of probative evidence is prejudice that *unfairly biases the jury* against the opposing side by appealing to their emotions rather than their minds (creating more heat than light), or that needlessly encumbers the trial by the introduction of cumulative or repetitive material.[32]

---

[32] As the court in United States v. Mills, 704 F.2d 1553, 1559 (11th Cir. 1983), *cert. denied*, 467 U.S. 1243 (1984), stated when admitting evidence of Aryan Brotherhood gang activities,

> Relevant evidence is inherently prejudicial; but it is only unfair prejudice, substantially outweighing probative value, which permits exclusion of relevant matter under Rule 403. Unless trials are to be conducted as scenarios, or unreal facts tailored and sanitized for the occasion, the application of Rule 403 must be cautious and sparing. Its major function is limited to excluding matter of scant or cumulative probative force, dragged in by the heels for the sake of its prejudicial effect.

II. CHARACTER EVIDENCE — TO ESTABLISH THE PROPENSITY OF A PARTY OR WITNESS

A. PRINCIPLES

1. Character an element of claim or defense

When character is an element of a claim, for example, in a prosecution for statutory rape of a child of previous chaste character, the chaste character of the victim must be proven. When the defense of truth is raised in a defamation action, character evidence is not only admissible, it *must* be proven for the defense to prevail.[33]

The evidence, of course, must be directed toward a relevant character trait. That trait will be defined by the nature of the claim or defense. If chastity were the issue, morality would be the relevant trait. If self-defense were claimed, the victim's traits of violence or peacefulness would be relevant.

2. Character to establish <u>past</u> propensity of party

When character evidence is used to establish the propensity of a party, and therefore his conduct *in the past*, the evidence is generally excluded. *See* F.R. Evid. 404(a). The only exception to this general rule of exclusion is *criminal cases*. Even then, the topic of propensity evidence must be *initiated by the criminal defendant,* except in criminal homicide cases where the defendant claims self-defense (in which case the government can initiate the character evidence favorable to the alleged victim.). The criminal defendant can initiate positive character evidence about himself and negative character evidence about the alleged victim of the crime. Such evidence is excluded in virtually all civil cases.

3. Character to establish <u>current</u> propensity of a witness

Propensity evidence has probative worth beyond the *past conduct* of a party or alleged victim. It is also relevant to the *current conduct of witnesses* who are testifying. If a witness has a bad character trait for truth and veracity, this could indicate that he is not worthy of belief while testifying under oath. In this context, character/propensity evidence is admitted more often than it is excluded. *See* Fed. R. Evid. 608, discussed below.

4. Methods of proof

Theoretically, there are three types of proof: (1) reputation — the collective opinion of people in the community; (2) opinion — the personal belief of the witness; and (3) specific act evidence — things that the individual has done in the past that reflect on the type of person he is.

---

[33] *See* Schafer v. Time, Inc., 142 F.3d 1361, 1372-73, *en banc denied*, 162 F.3d 1179 (11th Cir. 1998) (discussing the admissibility of certain forms of character evidence under Rule 404(a) when a specific trait comprises an essential element of the claim).

a. Elements of claim or defense

When character is an element of the claim or defense, all three types of proof are admissible.

b. Past general propensity of a party in a criminal case

When the propensity of a party or victim has been placed in issue by the criminal defendant, Fed. R. Evid. 405 allows it to be proven with two types of evidence: (1) reputation testimony (the sole means of proof under the common law) and (2) opinion testimony. Specific act evidence is the only form of character evidence that is not explicitly sanctioned.

c. Current, general propensity of all witnesses

When witnesses take the witness stand, they place their own character trait for truth and veracity in issue. Silently they preface each answer with "You can believe me when I say. . . ." Proof of any witness' propensity to not tell the truth may take the following forms:

(1) On cross-examination. Rule 608(b) permits propensity to be explored on cross-examination by asking the witness about specific instances of his prior conduct that are inconsistent with that character trait. For example, the witness can be asked whether it is true that he was fired from his past job for filing false travel vouchers. The limitation on this examination, however, is that if the witness denies the conduct, the cross-examiner must take the answer — she is not permitted to prove the denied conduct through independent evidence.[34] This is a bit perverse since the issue being explored is the credibility of the witness who has just lied, under oath, in front of the jury making the credibility assessment, and that cannot be proven to the jury. Misplaced fears of distraction and delay have driven this limitation.

(2) Character witnesses about previous witnesses. In the next stage of the case, the opposing party, pursuant to Rule 608(a), can call a character witness against a previous witness. As with character witnesses called under Fed. R. Evid. 404(a), these character witnesses may only testify (1) to their personal opinions about the prior witness' character trait for truth and veracity, or (2) to the prior witness' reputation for truth and veracity in a relevant business or residential community.

As with any other witness, *see* discussion above, a character witness can be cross-examined about her prior specific conduct that reflects on her credibility. For example, perhaps she too was discharged from her job for filing false travel vouchers.

---

[34] *See* Carter v. Hewitt, 617 F.2d 961, 969 (3d Cir. 1980).

TRIAL

Plaintiff will elicit from the witness facts about the incident that give rise to the causes of action.

On cross-examination the defendant will likely explore the factual account given during the direct examination relative to the accuracy of the witness' perception and memory and the sincerity with which he is testifying, and will clarify any ambiguities that may exist in the witness' testimony.

In addition, the defendant may probe the credibility of the witness by asking him questions about his prior conduct that reflects negatively on his credibility. Example: "Is it not true that you have filed false travel vouchers with your employer?" If the witness denies these acts, the defendant will not be allowed to prove that the witness actually committed them by calling additional witnesses, such as Witness 1's employer, during his case-in-defense.

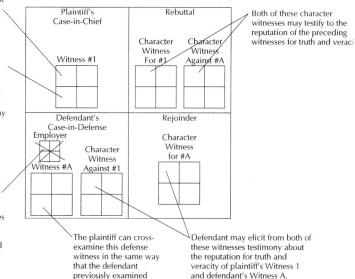

Both of these character witnesses may testify to the reputation of the preceding witnesses for truth and veraci

The plaintiff can cross-examine this defense witness in the same way that the defendant previously examined Witness 1.

Defendant may elicit from both of these witnesses testimony about the reputation for truth and veracity of plaintiff's Witness 1 and defendant's Witness A.

CRIMINAL TRIAL

The government may not introduce evidence in its case-in-chief for the purpose of establishing the defendant's propensity.

If the propensity of either the defendant or victim is to become an issue in the trial, the defendant must initiate the use of character evidence in his case-in-defense.

These character witnesses may give only reputation or opinion testimony about the relevant character trait of the victim or the defendant.

The government may cross-examine to determine how credible their testimony is. This is done by asking "Have you heard . . .?" (for reputation witnesses) or "Do you know . . . ?" (for opinion witnesses) question addressed to prior conduct of the person about whom he has testified that is inconsistent with the character trait that has been opened for examination.

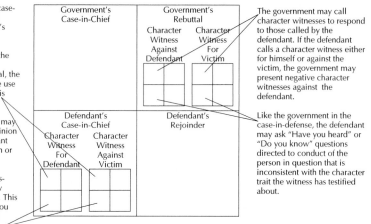

The government may call character witnesses to respond to those called by the defendant. If the defendant calls a character witness either for himself or against the victim, the government may present negative character witnesses against the defendant.

Like the government in the case-in-defense, the defendant may ask "Have you heard" or "Do you know" questions directed to conduct of the person in question that is inconsistent with the character trait the witness has testified about.

The government might ask the pro-defendant witness if he had heard or knew that the defendant had been charged with murder five years ago (even if the charge resulted in an acquittal).

The government might also ask the anti-victim witness if he had heard or knew that the victim was the organizer of the Social Change Through Non-Violence lobbying group.

Character Rules for the Propensity of a Party

RULE 404 FRE
Character Evidence Not Admissible to Prove Conduct; Exceptions; Other Crimes

(a) **Character evidence generally.** Evidence of a person's character or a trait of character is not admissible for the purpose of proving action in conformity therewith on a particular occasion, except:

(1) **Character of accused.** Evidence of a pertinent trait of character offered by an accused, or by the prosecution to rebut the same, or if evidence of a trait of character of the alleged victim of the crime is offered by an accused and admitted under Rule 404 (a)(2), evidence of the same trait of character of the accused offered by the prosecution.

(2) **Character of alleged victim.** Evidence of a pertinent trait of character of the alleged victim of the crime offered by an accused, or by the prosecution to rebut the same, or evidence of a character trait of peacefulness of the alleged victim offered by the prosecution in a homicide case to rebut evidence that the victim was the first aggressor;

(3) **Character of witness.** Evidence of the character of a witness, as provided in rules 607, 608, and 609.

(b) **Other crimes, wrongs, or acts.** Evidence of other crimes, wrongs, or acts is not admissible to prove the character of a person in order to show action in conformity therewith. It may, however, be admissible for other purposes, such as proof of motive, opportunity, intent, preparation, plan, knowledge, identity, or absence of mistake or accident, provided that upon request by the accused, the prosecution in a criminal case shall provide reasonable notice in advance of trial, or during trial if the court excuses pretrial notice on good cause shown, of the general nature of any such evidence it intends to introduce at trial.

RULE 405 FRE
Methods of Proving Character

(a) **Reputation or opinion.** In all cases in which evidence of character or a trait of character of a person is admissible, proof may be made by testimony as to reputation or by testimony in the form of an opinion. On cross-examination, inquiry is allowable into relevant specific instances of conduct.

(b) **Specific instances of conduct.** In cases in which character or a trait of character of a person is an essential element of a charge, claim or defense, proof may also be made of specific instances of that person's conduct.

Character Rules for the Propensity of Witnesses

RULE 608 FRE
Evidence of Character and Conduct of Witnesses

(a) Opinion and reputation evidence of character. The credibility of a witness may be attacked or supported by evidence in the form of opinion or reputation, but subject to these limitations: (1) the evidence may refer only to character for truthfulness or untruthfulness, and (2) evidence of truthfulness character is admissible only after the character of the witness for truthfulness has been attacked by opinion or reputation evidence or otherwise.

(b) Specific instances of conduct. Specific instances of the conduct of a witness, for the purpose of attacking or supporting the witness' character for truthfulness, other than conviction of crime as provided in rule 609, may not be proved by extrinsic evidence. They may, however, in the discretion of the court, if probative of truthfulness or untruthfulness, be inquired into on cross-examination of the witness (1) concerning the witness' character for truthfulness or untruthfulness, or (2) concerning the character for truthfulness or untruthfulness of another witness as to which character the witness being cross-examined has testified.

RULE 609 FRE
Impeachment by Evidence of Conviction of Crime

(a) General rule. For the purpose of attacking the credibility of a witness,

(1) evidence that a witness other than an accused has been convicted of a crime shall be admitted, subject to Rule 403, if the crime was punishable by death or imprisonment in excess of one year under the law under which the witness was convicted, and evidence that an accused has been convicted of such a crime shall be admitted if the court determines that the probative value of admitting this evidence outweighs its prejudicial effect to the accused; and

(2) evidence that any witness has been convicted of a crime shall be admitted if it involved dishonesty or false statement, regardless of the punishment.

17 PRACTICES

A criminal defendant no longer gets a risk-free shot at the victim. As previously noted, under the common law, if a criminal defendant offered negative character evidence of the relevant character trait of the victim of a crime (the form of which was limited under the common law to reputation testimony), the prosecution could respond in kind — with positive character evidence (in the form of reputation testimony) for the victim.

Rule 404(a) has changed the common law practice in two ways:

(1) When the criminal defendant opens this line of inquiry, by attacking the victim, under the 2000 revision to Rule 404(a), he opens *both* the victim's and his own relevant character traits to a full inquiry. The criminal defendant no longer gets a risk-free shot at the victim.[35]

(2) After the inquiry has been opened by the criminal defendant, both the criminal defendant and the prosecutor may prove the relevant character trait through opinion as well as reputation evidence.

18 PRACTICES

Cross-examining with the specific acts that cannot be used on direct. After the character evidence has been introduced through the opinion or reputation witnesses, the opposing party is entitled in its cross-examination to explore the credibility of each witness. To do this, the opposing party can ask each witness if he "has heard" (if a reputation witness) or "knows" (if an opinion witness) of certain prior acts of the criminal defendant that are inconsistent with the character trait placed in issue.

This practice *appears* to be *disproving* the character trait with specific act evidence, when the proponent was not permitted to prove the same character trait with specific act evidence. While this may be the practical effect of the line of questioning (because that is the way the jury will probably see and use it), the theoretical purpose is to show that the reputation witness, for example, is not credible because he has not heard about things that a credible reputation witness should have heard. Similarly, if an opinion witness does not "know" about relevant conduct, his opinion should be questioned.[36]

---

[35] See Fed. R. Evid. 404(a) Advisory Committee's notes (proposed amendment 2000) (stating "[t]he amendment makes clear that the accused cannot attack the alleged victim's character and yet remain shielded from the disclosure of equally relevant evidence concerning the same character trait of the accused").

[36] *See* United States v. Bruguier, 161 F.3d 1145, 1150 (8th Cir. 1998) (discussing the extent of the government's need for a good-faith basis when questioning witness' opinion).

Another reason this subtle distinction is probably lost on the jury (even though a limiting instruction is given under Fed. R. Evid. 105) is the fact that the only types of acts that can be inquired about on cross-examination are those that are inconsistent with the character trait placed in issue. Jurors find it difficult to understand how this is not disproving on cross what the proponent sought to prove on direct.

Logically, when the basis of a reputation witness' testimony is questioned, the cross-examiner should be permitted to ask the witness about *all* of the conduct rumored to be true (regardless of the rumor's accuracy) which a credible reputation witness should have heard. To the extent that he hasn't heard, his credibility is proportionately diminished. Logic, however, has not prevailed in practice because of the fear that cross-examination will become a general character assassination. There must be a factual basis for believing he committed the acts, and the substance of the acts must relate to the character trait under inquiry. These limitations are an institutionalized Rule 403 balance.

The potential for misuse by the jury of specific act cross-examination questions is particularly acute with opinion witnesses. When opinion witnesses are asked on cross-examination about their knowledge of specific conduct of the defendant, the implicit assumption is that the conduct actually occurred, and therefore, should have been factored into the opinion. How the jurors are supposed to use this evidence to assess the diminished credibility of another person's opinion, without factoring the same conduct into their own opinions and conclusions — thereby using specific act evidence to prove or disprove a character trait — is unclear.

19 PRACTICES

Methods of proof — expanding one to two may indirectly have expanded to three. Because of this unique problem with opinion testimony and the way it is impeached on cross-examination, the expansion of the permissible method of proof from reputation to reputation *and opinion* may result in the *indirect* expansion of the permissible methods of proof to specific act evidence as well because:

1. Opinions are only as valuable as their bases (unlike reputation, the quality of the witness' opinion can be explored);

2. Many opinions will have been based on specific acts that the witness observed or was told;

3. The only way the jury can serve as an independent finder of facts is by being given the relevant information from which it can assess the reliability of each proposed conclusion.

4. While it will be argued that introducing the opinion's basis will violate Rule 405's exclusion of specific act evidence, this argument should not prevail for the same reason the cross-examiner is permitted to ask the opinion witness the "Have you heard?" questions — the jury is merely being given an opportunity, as the sole finder of facts, to assess the value that it should assign to the opinion evidence.

5. Potential unfair prejudice from the juror's possible misuse of the information should be adequately addressed by a limiting instruction under Rule 105 — the "What is good for the goose is good for the gander" argument.

If the judge does not accept the previous argument when the character witness' opinion is initially being elicited, the merits of the argument increase after opposing counsel has asked "Have you heard . . ." questions on the pretext of challenging the witness' credibility. The fact that the opposing side has been permitted to destroy the opinion with specific act questions should open the door for the proponent to demonstrate a basis for the seemingly unjustified opinion.

20 PRACTICES

No "Perry Mason" defense with general propensity evidence. Rule 404(a) permits a criminal defendant to place in issue the relevant character traits of either himself or the alleged victim. When this is done, Rule 405 excludes evidence of prior specific instances of conduct to establish those relevant character traits.

If a criminal defendant wants to put forward a "Perry Mason" defense — suggesting that a third party committed the crime — he cannot do this through general predisposition evidence. He may, however, employ the form of character evidence that usually is forbidden — evidence of specific instances of conduct — to establish more specific facts that would tend to establish an individual's culpability.[37] Under Rule 404(b), for example, such evidence may be admitted to establish such things as motive, intent, common scheme, design, opportunity, and modus operandi.[38]

---

[37] *See* United States v. Willington, 754 F.2d 1457, 1465 (9th Cir.) (unpublished), *cert. denied*, 474 U.S. 1032 (1985) (finding the admission of evidence not barred by Rule 403 because, as the evidence only detailed a third party's bad acts, its risk of improper prejudice to the defendant was remote).

[38] The reasons for offering the evidence of conduct delineated in Rule 404(b) are only illustrative. Other reasons more focused than "general predisposition" have also been recognized. *See generally*, E. Imwinkelreid, UNCHARGED MISCONDUCT EVIDENCE (Thomson/West 2005).

B. Relationship of Character Rules to Other Rules[39]

Rule 105. Limited Admissibility. If evidence is admissible for one purpose, but not for another, the trial judge should instruct the jury on the restricted purpose for which he admitted the evidence. Rule 105 requires the judge to give this instruction if a party requests it. The following is a typical instruction that a judge might give if a court admits evidence of a prior act for a limited purpose under Rule 404(b).

You are about to hear testimony that the defendant previously committed other [crimes] [wrongs] [acts] not charged here. I instruct you that the testimony is being admitted only for the limited purpose of being considered by you on the question of defendant's [intent] [motive] [opportunity] [preparation] [plan] [knowledge] [identity] [absence of mistake] [absence of accident] and for no other purpose.

Manual of Model Criminal Jury Instructions for the Ninth Circuit § 2.10 (2003).

Rule 410. Inadmissibility of Pleas, Plea Discussions, and Related Statements. The plea of *nolo contendere* is a plea through which a criminal defendant can admit, for the purposes of the criminal action, all the facts alleged in support of a charge without that plea being construed as an admission of those facts in subsequent actions. Rule 410 explicitly makes these pleas inadmissible against the defendants who entered them. This protection, however, does not preclude future adversaries from using other evidence to prove that the defendant committed the prior offense if evidence of that prior offense were admissible, for example, under Rule 404(b) to prove such things as motive, intent, knowledge, common scheme, or design.[40]

Rule 412. Sex Offenses; Relevance of Victim's Past Behavior. Consistent with the exception for character evidence of the victim in criminal homicide cases, the common law allowed the defendant in a prosecution for forcible rape, in which he claimed consent as a defense, to present evidence of the alleged victim's unchaste character in support of his defense.

Under the Federal Rules of Evidence, Rule 412 precludes this use of character evidence to establish the sexual propensities of the prosecutrix in cases — establishing a protective shield for victims of all sex offenses, not just victims in prosecutions for the technical crime of rape.

---

[39] PAUL R. RICE & ROY A. KATRIEL, EVIDENCE: COMMON LAW AND FEDERAL RULES OF EVIDENCE § 3.02 [F] (LEXIS Publishing 2000)

[40] *See* United States v. Wyatt, 762 F.2d 908, 911 (11th Cir. 1985).

Rule 412
Sex Offense Cases; Relevance of Alleged Victim's Past Sexual Behavior or Alleged Sexual Predisposition

(a) Evidence generally inadmissible. The following evidence is not admissible in any civil or criminal proceeding involving alleged sexual misconduct except as provided in subdivisions (b) and (c):

(1) Evidence offered to prove that any alleged victim engaged in other sexual behavior.

(2) Evidence offered to prove any alleged victim's sexual predisposition.

(b) Exceptions.

(1) In a criminal case, the following evidence is admissible, if otherwise admissible under these rules:

(A) evidence of specific instances of sexual behavior by the alleged victim offered to prove that a person other than the accused was the source of semen, injury or other physical evidence;

(B) evidence of specific instances of sexual behavior by the alleged victim with respect to the person accused of the sexual misconduct offered by the accused to prove consent or by the prosecution; and

(C) evidence the exclusion of which would violate the constitutional rights of the defendant.

(2) In a civil case, evidence offered to prove the sexual behavior or sexual predisposition of any alleged victim is admissible if it is otherwise admissible under these rules and its probative value substantially outweighs the danger of harm to any victim and of unfair prejudice to any party. Evidence of an alleged victim's reputation is admissible only if it has been placed in controversy by the alleged victim.

(c) Procedure to determine admissibility.

(1) A party intending to offer evidence under subdivision (b) must —

(A) file a written motion at least 14 days before trial specifically describing the evidence and stating the purpose for which it is offered unless the court, for good cause requires a different time for filing or permits filing during trial; and

(B) serve the motion on all parties and notify the alleged victim or, when appropriate, the alleged victim's guardian or representative.

(2) Before admitting evidence under this rule the court must conduct a hearing in camera and afford the victim and parties a right to attend and be heard. The motion, related papers, and the record of the hearing must be sealed unless the court orders otherwise.

Rule 609(a). Impeachment by Evidence of Conviction of Crime. A defendant's prior conviction which may be inadmissible under Rule 609(a) because it was not a felony or one involving dishonest or false statement or because its prejudicial effect outweighed its probative value, may still be admissible under Rule 404(b) for other purposes, such as proof of intent, opportunity, and knowledge. *See Huddleston v. United States,*[41] where evidence of a defendant's previous receipt of stolen goods was introduced to show that his later possession of stolen goods likely took place with knowledge that they were stolen.

Rule 609(b). Time Limit on the Use of Prior Convictions. The prior acts that one may offer under Rule 404(b) may have resulted in the actor's conviction. Evidence of these convictions is usually admissible for impeachment purposes under Rule 609(a). Rule 609 will generally render these convictions inadmissible, however, if they are over 10 years old. Despite this time limitation on the use of convictions for impeachment purposes, no comparable limitation is placed on the use of the evidence of the acts that gave rise to those convictions if such evidence is also admissible under Rule 404(b). Under Rule 404(b), the prior remoteness in time is only a factor that weakens the probative value of the evidence. Although this factor may ultimately affect the "prejudice versus probative value" analysis that a court must make concerning the admissibility of the prior act evidence, the time factor is not by itself dispositive under Rule 403.[42]

Rule 702. Testimony by Experts. Rule 405(a) provides that character may now be proven by opinion testimony as well as reputation testimony — this includes both expert and lay opinions. Under Rule 702, opinions by acknowledged experts are admissible if based on an adequate factual foundation. Accordingly, the Third Circuit has found error when the trial court excluded an opinion by a clinical psychologist about the defendant's character trait of susceptibility to inducement in an action in which the defendant had raised entrapment as a defense. *See United States v. Hill.*[43] Similarly, in *United States v. Staggs,*[44] the Seventh Circuit held that it was error to exclude testimony of a psychologist who would have testified that a particular personality trait of the defendant was inconsistent with the specific intent that was required for him to be guilty of the crime charged.

Rule 803(21). Reputation as to Character. If character is the proper subject of proof through reputation evidence under Rules 404(a) and 405, it is unclear whether that evidence constitutes hearsay. The character witness who testifies to reputation must have personal knowledge of what the people in the community are saying about the individual in question. That witness, in effect,

---

[41] 108 S. Ct. 1496 (1988).

[42] *See* United States v. Rubio-Gonzalez, 674 F.2d 1067, 1075 (5th Cir. 1982).

[43] 655 F.2d 512, 517 (3d Cir. 1981).

[44] 553 F.2d 1073, 1075-76 (7th Cir. 1977).

is allowed to summarize that information and offer it in the form of a conclusion about the general reputation of the individual. The purpose for which reputation testimony is offered determines whether it is hearsay. For example, if offered in a defamation action for the purpose of establishing what the plaintiff's reputation was prior to the publication of the libelous article, it would not constitute hearsay because its relevance would stem from its mere existence, not its truth. On the other hand, if such testimony were offered in a criminal action to prove the good or bad character of the defendant or victim, in order to prove, in turn, that one or the other was or was not the first aggressor, it would constitute hearsay because it would be relevant only if accepted as true.

If reputation evidence is otherwise admissible, its hearsay character will not preclude its admission because of an exception to the hearsay rule Congress recognized in Rule 803(21). This rule provides as follows:

Rule 803
HEARSAY EXCEPTIONS

AVAILABILITY OF DECLARANT IMMATERIAL. The following are not excluded by the hearsay rule, even though the declarant is available as a witness:

(21) Reputation as to character. Reputation of a person's character among associates or in the community.

C. Applications — Character Evidence

ONE

The defendant was charged with a robbery during which a person was murdered. At his trial the government offered evidence of sixteen prior robberies in which the defendant had been involved. The court admitted the evidence because the government was prosecuting a racketeering offense and the uncharged crimes established the criminal enterprise. The court noted that case law favors admissibility where the prior acts arose out of the same transaction or series of transactions. When the evidence is inextricably intertwined with the crime charged it is often necessary to complete the story being told at the trial. *United States v. Baez*, 2003 WL 22682305 (2d Cir. 2003).

TWO

An officer was fired for making false statements to a superior. In an action for wrongful discharge the plaintiff offered seven documents that allegedly demonstrated his propensity for truthfulness. These included performance reviews containing positive evaluations, and letters from the Chief of Police and Mayor lauding his dedication, courage and hard work. The defendant opposed these pieces of evidence contending that they were little more than general character evidence in a civil action where character is not an element of the claim or defense. The court agreed. Just because character may be relevant to issues in the case does not make it an essential element of a claim or defense and therefore provable under Rule 405(b). It is only essential if it alters the rights and liabilities of the parties under the substantive law; if a party loses when it is not proven. *Gibson v. Mayor & Council of the City of Wilmington*, 2004 WL 36059 (3d Cir. 2004).

III. SIMILAR OCCURRENCE EVIDENCE

A. PRINCIPLES

Evidence of occurrences similar to the occurrence in dispute may be relevant to establishing such things as (1) that the event occurred; (2) that the event occurred in the way the proponent alleges; (3) the nature and condition of an instrumentality; (4) the value of property; or (5) notice.[45] These occurrences can be both spontaneous or created (demonstrations). With the exception of notice (which logically could not be given in the past by a future event), both prior and subsequent occurrences can be used to establish these factors.

What must be similar? The level of similarity required and the other factors relating to the occurrences that must be considered are determined by the standard of logical relevance. For example, in a demonstration of the value of condemned property from some previous sales, the conditions of the sales (voluntary or coerced), as well as the location, size, use, condition, time-frame, and surrounding properties would have to be similar. To demonstrate something about an instrumentality (such as an automobile) involved in a tort claim, the instrumentality, its condition, and the circumstances of use would have to be similar.

How similar must it be? The level of similarity required depends on what is being proven. For example, in offering similar occurrences to establish notice of a defective condition, only marginal similarity may be required.[46] On the other hand, if the prior occurrences are being offered to establish the nature or condition of something, a substantial level of similarity would be necessary.[47]

As a rule of thumb, courts generally employ a "substantial similarity" requirement. This is the same "substantial similarity" requirement that is used in

---

[45] *See, e.g.*, Burke v. Deere & Co., 6 F.3d 497, 506 (8th Cir. 1993), *cert. denied*, 510 U.S. 1115 (1994) ("Under [Rule 401], evidence of similar occurrences may be relevant to the defendant's notice of a defect, the magnitude of the danger involved, the defendant's ability to correct a known defect, the lack of safety for intended uses, the standard of care, or causation.").

[46] *See* Jackson v. Firestone Tire & Rubber Co., 788 F.2d 1070, 1083 (5th Cir. 1986).

[47] *See* Nachtsheim v. Beech AirCraft Corp., 847 F.2d 1261, 1268-69 (7th Cir. 1988).

Rule 404(b), when prior bad acts are being offered to demonstrate such factors as motive, intent, common scheme, design and modus operandi.[48]

When demonstrations are being prepared for courtroom use, too much similarity to the factual circumstances of the cause of action can be misleading, prompting the jury to misconstrue its purpose. In such circumstances, the court may be justified in excluding the evidence. For example, if a party were attempting to demonstrate the absorption qualities of a particular type of wood, the only factors that would need to be duplicated for the experiment from the scene of the accident would be the wood and the combustible fluid that was poured on it. While the amount of fluid could be important, larger variations from the time of the injury would be tolerable if precise measurements were being taken.

Properly structured, a filmed, or in-court, demonstration should consist of a sample of wood, being held above a collecting container, a measured amount of the same combustible fluid being poured over it, and subsequently measured and compared to the original amount. In contrast, setting the demonstration in the context of a tent where the injury occurred, with a young woman who looks like the plaintiff, sloppily pouring the fluid over a piece of wood being held by her, with the residue dropping to the floor, would be inappropriate because it gives the impression that the scene of the accident is being recreated.[49] The same problem arises when animated computer-generated recreations are employed.

21 PRACTICES

Non-occurrence evidence to prove a negative. Non-occurrence evidence can be probative of some of the same factors that occurrences may prove.[50] Use of such evidence, however, involves exaggerated problems of ambiguity in two ways:

(1) How do you know it didn't happen? If a condition is not formally or informally monitored (like all passengers stepping onto a bus beside the driver), how is the fact of nonconcurrence established? The answer stems from the absence of complaints, but this method of proof remains problematic because nothing assures that injured persons would have complained (particularly if the injury was slight), and if complaints occurred, that they were made to the person testifying. Therefore, the probative value of nonoccurrence evidence is less than prior occurrences. It also takes many more nonoccurrences to be as probative as

---

[48] *See* United States v. Beechum, 582 F.2d 898, 912 n. 15 (5th Cir. 1978) (en banc). *See also United States v. Richards*, 204 F.3d 177, 200-01 (5th Cir. 2000) (relying on the *Beechum* test to permit the admissibility of extrinsic evidence showing the defendant's intent to commit mail and wire fraud).

[49] *See* Randall v. Warnaco, Inc., 677 F.2d 1226, 1233-34 (8th Cir. 1982).

[50] *See, e.g.*, Espeaignnette v. Gene Tierney Co., 43 F.3d 1, 9-10 (1st Cir. 1994).

occurrences. For example, if two people fell down a flight of stairs to their death in the past month, that would be more probative of the condition of the stairs than the fact that 20 other people used the stairs and were not injured. This is true because there are so many unknown variables with nonoccurrences.

(2) How do you know conditions were sufficiently similar? How can it be determined that the conditions surrounding a prior nonoccurrence were sufficiently similar if they never happened? While this poses a difficult problem, it is surmountable. Three interdependent factors typically have to be considered:

(a) *contemporaneity* — closeness in time of the period of nonoccurrences to the event that gave rise to the cause of action. If conditions relevant to use are permanently changing, contemporaneity is crucial.

(b) *status or nature of instrumentality* - was it static or changing.

(c) *circumstances of its use* — was it used in the same manner and under the same conditions. If conditions of use are cyclical (like the weather), a longer time-frame ensures that conditions have periodically been the same or substantially similar.

(d) *frequency of the use* — was there enough usage during the period of alleged nonoccurrences to make nonoccurrence evidence relevant. The higher the usage the more probative the evidence.

Example

To establish that a sidewalk was not defectively constructed, the defendant offers evidence that during the past two years adjacent store owners have not received any complaints of people stumbling or falling. While the sidewalk is a static condition, the conditions surrounding the use of the walk vary considerably with the seasons (snow and ice in winter, wet and slippery throughout the year, hot pavement on bare feet in summer), people's dress (boots in winter, bare feet in summer, women with high heeled shoes during business hours) and social activities at that location (skateboarding, children spilling ice cream, holiday shoppers walking with cumbersome packages). Nevertheless, because all these conditions are cyclical, a number of times throughout the year all of the conditions will be substantially the same as they were at the time the cause of action arose. Therefore, if no complaints were made, and the frequency of use was consistently high, this fact could be probative to show the area was not defective.[51]

---

[51] *See* Simon v. Town of Kennebunkport, 417 A.2d 982, 984-86 (Me. 1980).

B. Relationship of Similar Occurrence Rule to Other Rules[52]

Rule 404. Character Evidence Not Admissible to Prove Conduct; Exception; Other Crimes

Rule 405. Methods of Proving Character. Similar occurrence evidence is not the same as prior act evidence of an individual offered to prove the past conduct of that individual because of his general propensities. When offered for such *general purposes*, this type of evidence is excluded by Rule 405. When similar occurrences involve the conduct of individuals, (as with the sale of property) the level of similarity needed in the details of the occurrence make the evidence more akin to specific act evidence under Rule 404(b) when limited issues are being proven, like motive, intent, common scheme, design, and modus operandi. The more focused the purpose and the details, the more probative the evidence. The more probative the evidence, the greater the likelihood of its admissibility.

C. Applications — Similar Occurrence Evidence

ONE

In 1983, the plaintiff in a personal injury action was injured when her car collided with another car at an intersection. She sued the city for negligent maintenance of the overhead traffic signal at the intersection. It was undisputed that the cause of the accident was a defective overhead traffic signal that turned green in two directions at one time. Consequently, a primary issue in the case was whether the city had notice that the traffic signal in question was defective and therefore was negligent in failing to repair it. To establish that the city did have notice of the defect, the plaintiff sought to introduce evidence of thirty-five other motor vehicle accidents occurring at the intersection in question from 1965-1983. The plaintiff did not introduce evidence as to the cause of these prior accidents. The trial court should not admit this evidence of similar occurrences to prove the defendant's knowledge of a dangerous defective condition. The evidence at best establishes that due to a number of accidents over a protracted period of time, the city was aware of the intersection's generally dangerous nature. The plaintiff's theory of negligence, however, was that the city failed to repair a defective overhead traffic signal. Absent some indication that the previous accidents were also caused by a defective traffic signal, evidence of the other accidents, particularly those remote in time, would not meet the similarity requirement that courts impose for the introduction of such evidence. *Whitman v. Riddell*, 324 Pa. Super. 185, 471 A.2d 521 (1984).

---

[52] PAUL R. RICE & ROY A. KATRIEL, EVIDENCE: COMMON LAW AND FEDERAL RULES OF EVIDENCE § 3.03 [D](LEXIS Publishing 2000)

TWO

A train derailed and ran into a warehouse, causing extensive damage. The derailment was caused by three teenagers who tampered with the track's switching and signaling systems and caused the train to be shunted without warning from a main track into a short spur track. The plaintiff, the owner of the warehouse, sued the train company, claiming it had acted negligently by maintaining switching and signaling systems it knew were vulnerable to the type of vandalism which led to this accident. There have been a number of other incidents of train derailment due to switch tampering.

The principal factor in determining the admissibility of these other incidents will be whether they involved the same type of switching device, or at least ones sufficiently close to the one in question so that the tampering with them would reasonably have led the company to the conclusion that the others could also be vandalized in the same manner. Other important considerations will be whether and when the other event occurred and whether the same type of tampering was involved. The fact that notice and foreseeability is being demonstrated should result in a more relaxed standard of similarity being imposed. *See, e.g., Ponder v. Warren Tool Corp.*, 834 F.2d 1553, 1560 (10th Cir. 1987); *Exum v. General Elec. Co.*, 819 F.2d 1158, 1162-63 (D.C. Cir. 1987); *Jackson v. Firestone Tire & Rubber Co.*, 788 F.2d 1070, 1083 (5th Cir. 1986); *Borden, Inc. v. Fla. East Coast Rwy. Co.*, 772 F.2d 750 (11th Cir. 1985).

IV. SUBSEQUENT REMEDIAL MEASURES

A. PRINCIPLES

Theoretically, remedial measures might be construed as an admission by the person who made the repairs that the changed instrumentality was defective or dangerous before the repairs, or that he acted negligently in not taking those actions to remedy the problem before injuries were caused by it. To encourage such remedial measures, and thereby enhance the general safety of the public, the law excludes evidence of remedial measures when they have been offered as an admission of negligence. When, however, the manufacturer performs the remedial measure *before* the accident takes place, exclusion under Rule 407 does not apply. In such cases, many courts will employ Rule 403 to determine that the possibility of unfair prejudice from the admission of evidence of a remedial measure substantially outweighs its probative value.[53]

Because product liability does not depend upon proof of negligence — only upon the placing of a defective product in commerce — there was a lengthy debate over whether the "subsequent repairs" or "subsequent remedial measures" rule was applicable to strict liability cases.[54] After virtually all courts

---

[53] *See* Bogosian v. Mercedes-Benz of North America, 104 F.3d 472, 481 (1st Cir. 1997).

[54] *See* Werner v. Upjohn Co., 628 F.2d 848, 857-58 (4th Cir. 1980).

had agreed on its resolution, Rule 407 was revised to explicitly preclude remedial measures from being used as an admission that the changed product was defective without the change.

RULE 407 FRE
Subsequent Remedial Measures

When, after an injury or harm allegedly caused by an event, measures are taken that, if taken previously, would have made the injury or harm less likely to occur, evidence of the subsequent measures is not admissible to prove negligence, culpable conduct, a defect in a product, a defect in a product's design, or a need for a warning or instruction. This rule does not require the exclusion of evidence of subsequent measures when offered for another purpose, such as proving ownership, control, or feasibility of precautionary measures, if controverted, or impeachment.

22 PRACTICES

Product liability cases — a perverse result. In an effort to clarify the application of the remedial measures rule to product liability claims, where negligence or culpable conduct is not at issue, Rule 407 was revised to include "a defect in a product, a defect in a product's design, or a need for a warning or instruction" within the list of things that remedial measures evidence may not be used to prove.

Unfortunately, the application of this rule is limited to measures taken "after an injury or harm allegedly caused by an event." While such an event usually gave notice to the defendant in a negligence action, and allowed his conduct to be interpreted as an admission, there is little justification for the limitation in product liability cases. Because general safety of the public is the policy behind the rule, it is difficult to understand why there is any limitation on the rule's applicability in either negligence or product liability actions.

As the rule is currently written, a manufacturer cannot change the design of its product or repair a faulty part, or replace damaged components before someone is injured, without the change being used against the manufacturer when someone is subsequently injured by a product designed in the previous manner. The evidence code creates a perverse situation in which a rule designed to make the environment safer gives a manufacturer incentive to wait until someone is injured before it can act without evidentiary repercussions!

23 PRACTICES

The impeachment ploy won't work. A party cannot get around the remedial measures rule by calling the opposing party as a witness and asking him if he believes his product was safe (to which he must respond in the affirmative) and then offer his remedial measures against him, not as an admission, but for its impeachment value because his prior conduct was inconsistent with his trial testimony.[55] Such an exception would eliminate the remedial measures prohibition.

The only time this evidence may be used for impeachment purposes is when the opposing party *volunteers testimony* inconsistent with the remedial measure taken, and thereby attempts to gain an unfair advantage. For example, in *Muzyka v. Remington Arms Co., Inc.*,[56] the defendant, in its opening statement, claimed it would show that its rifle was one of the "safest rifles" on the market. Through subsequent testimony, the defendant asserted that its two-position, bolt-lock safety was the best available and that its rifle was the best and safest on the market. The Court held that the plaintiff should have been permitted to present evidence of design changes in the gun's safety for the purpose of impeaching the witness who made the extreme claims. *See also* **PRACTICES NO. 23**, *infra*.

B. Relationship of Subsequent Remedial Measures Rule to Other Rules[57]

Rule 105. Limited Admissibility. If the proponent of evidence avoids the exclusion of testimony on the ground it is not being offered for a purpose other than an admission of negligence of culpable conduct, the opposing party is entitled to a jury instruction limiting the jury's use of the information. This decision always involves a tactical consideration because the admonition may suggest something that the jurors had not yet considered, as they are being told not to do that.

C. Applications — Subsequent Remedial Measures Rule

Prior to cardiac surgery the patient had been placed on an anti-coagulant, Heparin, to reduce chest pains and shortness of breath. Hours before surgery, consistent with existing practice, the anesthesiologist discontinued the drug

---

[55] *See* Probus v. K-Mart, Inc., 794 F.2d 1207 (7th Cir. 1986).

[56] 774 F.2d 1309 (5th Cir. 1985).

[57] PAUL R. RICE & ROY A. KATRIEL, EVIDENCE: COMMON LAW AND FEDERAL RULES OF EVIDENCE § 3.04 [C] (LEXIS Publishing 2005)

so that the patient's system could metabolize the drug by the time of the operation. Because the operation was delayed three to four hours, the attending physician considered putting the patient back on the drug but decided against it in light of his stable condition and the complications it may create during surgery. The patient went into cardiac arrest and died. From this experience the hospital changed its protocol to maintain the anti-coagulant drug until the patient is ready for surgery. The trial judge would not permit the plaintiff to use this change of protocol as evidence of the hospital's admission of negligence in not reintroducing the drug after the delay. It was a subsequent remedial measure that Rule 407 excluded on the question of negligence. "The fact that the protocol was changed following Mr. Tuer's death in no way suggests that Dr. McDonald did not honestly believe that his judgment call was appropriate at the time. The only reasonable inference from his testimony coupled with counsel's proffer as to why the protocol was changed, was that Dr. McDonald and his colleagues reevaluated the relative risks in light of what happened to Mr. Tuer and decided that the safer course was to continue the Heparin. That kind of reevaluation is precisely what the exclusionary provision of the Rule was designed to encourage." *Tuer v. McDonald*, 347 Md. 507, 701 A.2d 1101 (1997).

V. OFFERS OF COMPROMISE

A. PRINCIPLES

To encourage litigants to settle their disputes, the law has made offers of compromise — offers to pay or take less on claims — privileged. The offers cannot be used by the opposing party as an implied admission of the validity, invalidity or amount of a claim. While the claim still has to be *disputed* for the privilege to apply — disputed as to either validity or amount — unlike the common law, no distinction is made between the offer and statements made during negotiations about the offer. The rule excludes all statements made in compromise negotiations, including documents prepared for those negotiations.

RULE 408 FRE
Compromise and Offers to Compromise

Evidence of (1) furnishing or offering or promising to furnish, or (2) accepting or offering or promising to accept, a valuable consideration in compromising or attempting to compromise a claim which was disputed as to either validity or amount, is not admissible to prove liability for or invalidity of the claim of its amount. Evidence of conduct or statements made in compromise negotiations is likewise not admissible. This rule does not require the exclusion of any evidence otherwise discoverable merely because it is presented in the course of compromise negotiations. This rule also does not require exclusion when the evidence if offered for another purpose, such as proving bias or prejudice of a witness, negating a contention of undue delay, or proving an effort to obstruct a criminal investigation or prosecution.

The completed compromise is privileged along with statements made in the compromise negotiations. The rule precludes either from being used as admissions in future proceedings. Since the rule addresses offers of compromise only in a civil context, it has been held that civil compromises may be used as admissions in future criminal proceedings.

An amended pleading is not privileged. While it no longer constitutes a judicial admission of its contents, thereby precluding any evidence controverting the facts admitted, it is converted to an evidentiary admission that can be used against the party.

All statements made in the process of attempting to negotiate a compromise to a civil dispute are protected by Rule 408.

Judgments in civil cases are not admissible under Rule 803(22) in future proceedings to prove facts essential to those judgments. Nothing is Rule 408 is inconsistent with this hearsay exception.

The Federal Rules of Evidence have specifically addressed the issue of compromises in criminal cases in Rule 410. Under rules of statutory construction, the specific prevails over the general. Therefore, in criminal matters Rule 410 controls.

RULE 410 FRE
Inadmissibility of Pleas, Plea
Discussions, and Related Statements

Except as otherwise provided in this rule, evidence of the following is not, in any civil or criminal proceeding, admissible against the defendant who made the plea or was a participant in the plea discussions:

(1) a plea of guilty which was later withdrawn;

(2) a plea of nolo contendere;

(3) any statement made in the course of any proceedings under Rule 11 of the Federal Rules of Criminal Procedure or comparable state procedure regarding either of the foregoing pleas; or

(4) any statement made in the course of plea discussions with an attorney for the prosecuting authority which do not result in a plea of guilty or which result in a plea of guilty later withdrawn.

However, such a statement is admissible (i) in any proceeding wherein another statement made in the course of the same plea or plea discussions has been introduced and the statement ought in fairness be considered contemporaneously with it, or (ii) in a criminal proceeding for perjury or false statement if the statement was made by the defendant under oath, on the record and in the presence of counsel.

When the protections in Rules 408 and 410 are applicable, they apply to both the offer of compromise and communications in furtherance of those compromise efforts. The two Rules, however, protect strikingly different things:

A successful plea bargain results in a guilty plea that sticks. In contrast to civil compromises, these pleas are is admissible in all future civil and criminal proceedings, even though they were the product of a plea bargain. If the criminal defendant wants protection from future use as an admission, he must seek permission to enter a *nolo contendere* plea. The only compromise offers that are protected by Rule 410 are those that were not successful — did not result in a guilty plea. They are not admissible in "any civil or criminal proceeding."

A withdrawn guilty plea is not admissible against the defendant after he enters a not guilty plea and goes to trial. It is feared that if the withdrawn plea were admissible as an admission, the trial would become a slow guilty plea.

Only statements made to "an *attorney* for the prosecuting authority" are protected under Rule 410. This limitation is to preclude defendants from successfully claiming that they were engaged in plea negotiations when they confessed to the police. Some courts are extending the coverage of this rule to statements made to "agents" of the prosecuting authority, which leaves open the possibility of this claim.

Judgments in criminal cases are admissible under Rule 803(22) to prove facts essential to sustain those judgments, only if they are felony convictions. Guilty pleas to misdemeanor charges, however, are admissible in subsequent proceedings even though the judgment entered on those pleas are not.

24 PRACTICES

Confidentiality irrelevant. The evidence rule that excludes offers of compromise is not dependent upon the presence of confidentiality.[58] Even though the parties may place a premium on confidentiality, or it may be a precondition for settlement negotiations, the public disclosure does not waive the protection of Rule 408.

---

[58] Alpex Computer Corp. v. Nintendo Co., Ltd., 770 F. Supp. 161, 166 (S.D.N.Y. 1991), *vacated in part*, No. 86-Civ.-1499, 1999 WL 381659 (S.D.N.Y. July 21, 1999).

Indeed, the lack of importance of confidentiality is reflected in the fact that compromise information may be discoverable, even though it is not admissible. Although discovery is not automatic, it will be required if the demanding party can show that it will likely lead to the discovery of other admissible evidence.[59]

25 PRACTICES

Compelled waiver of protection for statements made in plea bargaining negotiations. Plea bargaining in criminal cases is a seller's market, and the prosecutor holds all the goods. As a consequence, many have required a waiver by the defendant of the protection under Rule 410 before they will discuss a plea agreement. To date this waiver has been limited to using the defendant's statements to impeach him if the plea discussions are unsuccessful, the defendant pleas not guilty, and testifies at his trial inconsistently with the plea bargaining statements. This has been upheld by the Supreme Court in *United States v. Mezzanatto*[60] where the court noted "[r]ather than deeming waiver presumptively unavailable absent some sort of express enabling clause, we instead have adhered to the opposite presumption."

It is not clear from the Court's decision in *Mezzanatto* whether it would sanction an effort by prosecutors to have defendants waive the protection of Rule 410 so the government could use the statements for their substantive truth, rather than just impeachment. The reality is that jurors are probably using the prior statement for truth now even though they are given a limiting instruction by the court. The single factor that suggests that the Court might see this as prosecutorial overreaching is that fact that unlike use for impeachment, the defendant would not be "in control." The Court referred to this as "the most compelling fact." With impeachment, the defendant "is the one who will be truthful or not, and having been untruthful, will be the one to decide whether he will testify inconsistently at trial." None of this would necessarily be true if the prosecution were permitted to use the statements to prove the defendant's guilt regardless of the actions he may take at his trial.

---

[59] *Bottaro v. Hatton*, 96 F.R.D. 158, 160 (E.D.N.Y. 1982). *See also* Fidelity Federal Sav. & Loan Assoc. v. Felicetti, 148 F.R.D. 532, 534 (E.D. Penn. 1993) and Morse/Diesel, Inc. v. Trinity Indus. Inc., 142 F.R.D. 80 (S.D.N.Y. 1992).

[60] 513 U.S. 196, 130 L. Ed. 2d 697, 115 S. Ct. 797 (1995).

B. Relationship of Offers of Compromise Rule to Other Rules[61]

Rule 409. Payment of Medical and Similar Expenses. For offers of compromise to be privileged, there must have been a dispute as to either the validity of a claim or its amount. Rule 408 is designed to encourage the settlement of disputes. Rule 409, on the other hand is designed to encourage "good Samaritan" acts. Therefore, unlike Rule 408, a dispute is not necessary. However, the privilege created is quite limited. First, it only applies to offers to pay "medical, hospital, or similar expenses." Second, unlike Rule 408, it does not protect any statement that the party may make that accompanies his offer.

Rule 410. Inadmissibility of Pleas, Plea Discussions, and Related Statements

Rule 803(22). Judgment of previous conviction. Unlike the successful compromise of a civil claim, a successful compromise of a criminal charge — a guilty plea resulting from a plea bargain — is admissible. The guilty plea that is entered for the bargained disposition is admissible in subsequent judicial proceedings as an admission by the criminal defendant. Curiously, however, the judgment entered on that admissible plea is not equally admissible. *See* Rule 803(22). Such judgments are admissible only from felony prosecutions. *See* **PRACTICES NO. 88**, *infra*.

C. Applications — Offers of Compromise

ONE

Hajek ran a stop sign and seriously injured Athey. Hajek had only limited coverage. Hajek had underinsured motorist coverage with Farmers Insurance Exchange. When Farmers refused to make additional payments under the policy, Hajek brought an action for breach of contract and bad faith in failing to investigate the plaintiff's claims and by putting off his settlement. After settling with the Hajek's insurance carrier a settlement conference was held between Hajek and Farmers before a Magistrate. Farmers, however, refused to make a settlement offer unless plaintiff agreed to abandon his bad faith claim. The plaintiff declined and the action went to trial. Hajek's counsel in the settlement negotiations withdrew so he could testify about the settlement negotiations and did so at the trial. While this was objected to under Rule 408, the court held that generally such discussions are privileged, but under South Dakota law, an insurer's attempt to condition the settlement of a breach of contract claim on the release of a bad faith claim may be used as evidence of bad faith. Therefore, the trial judge did not abuse his discretion by admitting the evidence. *Athey v. Farmers Ins. Exchange,* 234 F.3d 357 (8th Cir. 2000).

---

[61] PAUL R. RICE & ROY A. KATRIEL, EVIDENCE: COMMON LAW AND FEDERAL RULES OF EVIDENCE § 3.05 [C] (LEXIS 5th ed. 2005)

TWO

The parties were in litigation in both California and Illinois. In an effort to settle the California action an offer of compromise was made to the plaintiff. This offer was used as evidence in the Illinois action for the purpose of determining whether there was an arbitrable dispute under the deductible agreements. It was not used to prove liability for or invalidity of the claim or its amount. On appeal the defendant protested that had it been known "that settlement efforts would be used by the court as proof of the need for an arbitration, [it] would not have engaged in settlement efforts," the appellate court saw the admission of such evidence as within the discretion of the trial judge, and that discretion is often exercised in favor of admission "when the settlement communication arises out of a dispute distinct from the one for which the evidence is being offered." Notwithstanding the defendant's protestations, the court concluded that it "did not believe that the policy behind Rule 408 is thwarted by admission of this evidence in the instant case." *Zurich American Ins. Co. v. Watts Indus., Inc.*, 2005 WL 1804771 (7th Cir. 2005).

THREE

Patricia McInnis was injured when the motorcycle she was riding was involved in a collision with a car. As a result of this collision, the clutch housing on her motorcycle shattered, causing severe injuries to McInnis' leg. As a result of these injuries, McInnis' leg was amputated. McInnis initiated separate actions against both the automobile driver and the manufacturer of her motorcycle. McInnis settled her claim against the automobile driver for $60,000 but was unable to settle with the motorcycle manufacturer. In the subsequent trial of McInnis' strict liability claim against the manufacturer for defective design, the manufacturer called McInnis to the stand to elicit testimony concerning her settlement with the automobile driver. McInnis' counsel objected to the elicitation of this testimony, and the manufacturer countered by arguing that it was eliciting the information for the purpose of attacking McInnis' credibility rather than proving it was the collision and not a defective clutch housing that caused McInnis' injuries. The manufacturer claims that the testimony it was seeking concerning the settlement agreement tends to show that McInnis brought the suit against the manufacturer knowing all the while it was the driver of the car and not the manufacturer who caused the injury to her leg.

Rule 408 precludes admission of settlement agreements to prove the validity or invalidity of a claim or its amount. It is clear that the rule precludes the admission of such agreements against defendants. A number of federal courts have also construed the rule as prohibiting evidence of a settlement agreement between a plaintiff and a third party. *See Quad/Graphics v. Fass*, 724 F.2d 1230, 1235 (7th Cir. 1983); *McHann v. Firestone Tire & Rubber Co.*, 713 F.2d 161, 165-66 (5th Cir. 1983); *United States v. Contra Costa Co. Water Dist.*, 678 F.2d 90, 92 (9th Cir. 1982). Thus, Rule 408 applies to the settlement agreement described in this problem between McInnis, the plaintiff, and the third party automobile driver.

Although Rule 408 precludes the introduction of evidence of a settlement agreement to prove liability or the validity of a claim, the rule expressly allows parties to introduce such evidence for other purposes. The defendants in this problem suggested that the settlement agreement is admissible to attack the plaintiff's credibility. Although the argument is superficially appealing, it is ultimately unpersuasive because the alleged attack on the plaintiff's credibility is actually a poorly-masked attempt to establish causation in fact. Causation in fact is an integral element of a determination of a claim's validity, and as such is not provable under Rule 408. *See McInnis v. A.M.F., Inc.*, 765 F.2d 240, 248-49 (1st Cir. 1985). Consequently, evidence of the settlement agreement should be excluded.

Chapter 4
HEARSAY RULE

[handwritten: ten/written]

I. THE DEFINITION

[handwritten: OUT-OF-COURT STATEMENT TO PROVE THE TRUTH OF THE MATTER ASSERTED]

PRINCIPLES

Hearsay is a statement originally made outside of the proceedings in which the statement is now being repeated for the purpose of proving the truth of the matter asserted in the statement. Testimony about a hearsay statement involves *two truths*:

The first truth is the fact that certain words were uttered. *[handwritten: 1st ORIGINAL SPEAKER'S]*

The second truth is the substance of what those uttered words describe.

The concerns giving rise to the hearsay rule are the original speaker's untested (1) perception, (2) memory, (3) sincerity and (4) ambiguity. These concerns exist only when the statement is being offered to prove the second truth — that the words accurately describe something. The first truth — that the statement was actually spoken — can be tested by cross-examining the individual who claims to have heard it. That person is before the jury and under oath.

RULE 801 FRE
Definition

The following definitions apply under this article:

(a) Statement. A "statement" is (1) an oral or written assertion or (2) nonverbal conduct of a person, if it is intended by the person as an assertion.

(b) Declarant. A "declarant" is a person who makes a statement.

(c) Hearsay. "Hearsay" is a statement, other than one made by the declarant while testifying at the trial or hearing, offered in evidence to prove the truth of the matter asserted.

Example

D shoots X. Witness #1 observes this act and subsequently states: "D shot X!" Witness #2 hears this statement and is later called as a witness at D's criminal trial for murder and asked to repeat Witness #1's statement. It is being repeated for the purpose of proving that D actually did shoot X. This testimony by Witness #2, therefore, is hearsay. This is illustrated in the following diagram:

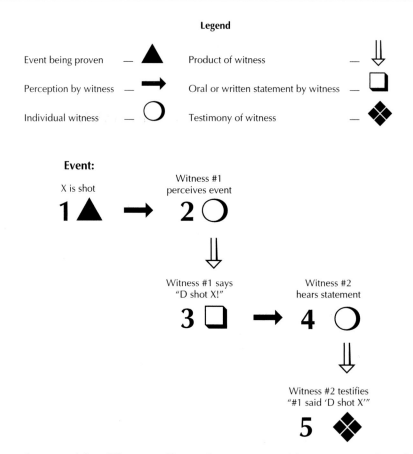

To go from position Witness #2's testimony, at position 5, to proving that D shot X, at position 1, requires the listener to rely on the untested perception of Witness #1 who is not under oath and testifying subject to cross-examination.

26 PRACTICES

Direct and indirect hearsay. The testimony about the truth of what another said can be *direct*, *e.g.*, "He said . . . .", or *indirect*, by proposing a factual conclusion that is based on information from third parties that is not explicitly stated.[62] Both forms are equally inadmissible, absent an applicable hearsay exception.

Always insist that the proponent of testimony first establish the basis of the witness' testimony. If the witness does not have personal knowledge, her testimony is either hearsay or inadmissible speculation.

---

[62] *See* United States v. Brown, 548 F.2d 1194 (5th Cir. 1977) (it was hearsay for an IRS supervisor to testify that the taxpayer overstated his deductions by a certain percentage, since that information had been reported to her by subordinates).

27 PRACTICES

Why is it relevant? Fundamental to assessing whether testimony involves hearsay is answering the question, "Why is the evidence relevant?" If its relevance requires the fact finder to rely on the mind of someone who is not testifying — the out-of-court declarant — the statement is hearsay.

Example 1

Customer A tells a woman walking down the aisle of a store, "Watch out! The floor is wet and slippery." Ignoring the warning, the woman proceeds down the aisle and falls. In the resulting negligence action for the injuries suffered in the fall, Customer B, who heard the warning, is asked to repeat it in the courtroom.

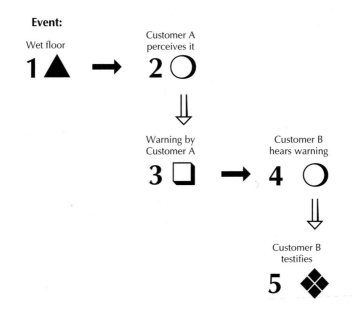

Event:

Wet floor

Customer A perceives it

1 ▲ ➡ **2** ◯

Warning by Customer A

Customer B hears warning

3 ▢ ➡ **4** ◯

Customer B testifies

5 ◆

Q — Why is this statement relevant?

A — It is relevant for two reasons: (1) to prove that the plaintiff was given notice of the danger, and therefore was contributorily negligent, and (2) to prove that the floor was wet.

(1) If the defendant offered the statement to prove contributory negligence, the testimony would not be hearsay. The statement's relevance is in the fact that it was said, audible and with a particular sound of urgency. Customer B has personal knowledge of those facts. In the diagram, the testimony at position 5 is offered only to establish the fact of utterance in position 3. Therefore only the credibility of Customer B is in issue, and he is in court, under oath, and subject to cross-examination.

(2) If, on the other hand, the plaintiff offers the statement to prove that the floor was wet, it would be hearsay because its relevance turns on the truth of what Customer A perceived, position 1. In the diagram, testimony from Customer B at position 5 is offered to establish what Customer A perceived at position 1. Therefore, the jury must rely on the untested perception, memory and sincerity of Customer A, at position 2.

If words or conduct are relevant for more than one reason, and one of those reasons is the truth of what was uttered, the hearsay nature of the words or conduct will turn on the reason the proponent gives for offering the communication.

Example 2

Sheriff Vinson was accused of taking bribes. Undercover agents set up a payoff through one of the complainants and made payment to an intermediary for the sheriff in an envelope marked "Sheriff Charles Vinson." This envelope was later found in the Sheriff's possession and offered at his trial to establish his receipt of the payment.

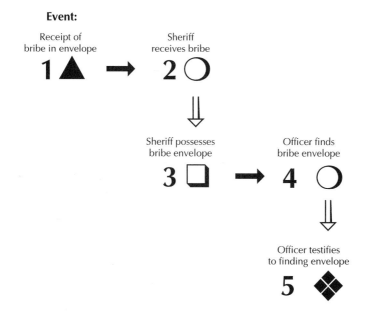

Q — Why is this statement relevant?

A — The evidence is relevant because the envelope in which the bribe was paid was found in the Sheriff's possession. No message must be read into the fact of possession (from either the officer who wrote the name, or the Sheriff) for it to be relevant to prove the Sheriff's culpability. His mere possession of the envelope does that and the officer who found it has personal knowledge of that fact. The testimony at position 5 is being offered to prove that the envelope was possessed, position 3, and the officer has personal knowledge of that fact. The fact that the envelope had his name on it is relevant because that mark — his name — is being used *only as a means of identifying the envelope* in which the bribe was paid. Had the undercover agent drawn a picture of a duck on the envelope and colored it pink it would have served the same purpose and neither would have constituted hearsay. The name on the envelope is not being used to prove Sheriff Vinson took a bribe because the author of the mark believed it to be so. The name on the envelope is not being used as an admission by the Sheriff that he received what previously had been placed in it — the bribe. In the diagram we are not offering the possession at position 3 to prove the receipt at position 1. The circumstance of possession immediately after the payment of the bribe circumstantially proves this. Therefore, the fact-finder is not relying on the mind of any person who is not testifying under oath.

Example 3

The defendant is charged with keeping a house for the purpose of taking bets. The prosecution offers the testimony of police officers who, while in the house, received telephone calls from individuals attempting to place bets.

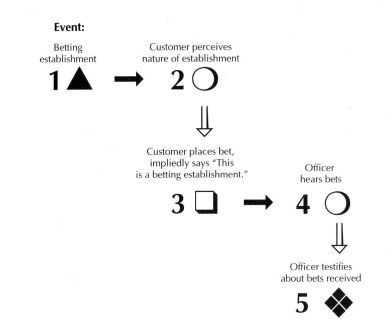

Event:

Betting establishment

1 ▲ ➡ 2 ◯

Customer perceives nature of establishment

Customer places bet, impliedly says "This is a betting establishment."

3 ◻ ➡ 4 ◯

Officer hears bets

Officer testifies about bets received

5 ◆

Q — Why are the telephone calls relevant?

A — They are relevant as circumstantial evidence that the house was a betting establishment because bets were placed there. That, however, does not make them non-hearsay. Through each bet the callers are *impliedly saying* that they believe that this is a betting establishment and the prosecution is offering those implied statements for their truth. In the diagram, the testimony at position 5 is being offered to prove the nature of the establishment at position 1. This requires the jurors to rely on the untested perception, memory, and sincerity of each caller. Consequently, each call is hearsay. While the *number* of calls may reinforce the probative value of each, and therefore its ultimate admissibility under an exception to the hearsay rule, it does not change the hearsay character of each. *See* **PRACTICE NO. 55**, *infra*.[63]

Example 4

The defendant was seen running from the scene of the crime. Witness #1 will testify to that fact.

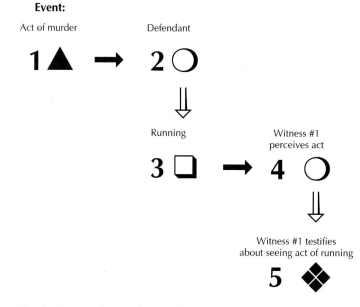

Event:

Act of murder   Defendant

1 ▲ → 2 ○

Running   Witness #1
                       perceives act

3 □ → 4 ○

Witness #1 testifies
about seeing act of running

5 ◆

Q — Why is the conduct relevant?

A — It is relevant for two reasons: (1) flight from the scene of a crime can be construed as an implied admission of guilt; and (2) the flight shows the defendant's presence at the scene of the crime, and therefore, that she had opportunity to have committed the crime.

(1) Under the common law when offered as an implied admission by conduct it was considered hearsay, but admissible under the admissions exception. Into the diagram the testimony about flight, at position five, is being offered to *prove* the defendant's guilt, at position one. In the act of running we are reading the unintended assertion "I'm guilty." This is being offered for its

---

[63] *See, e.g.,* People v. Barnhart, 60 Cal. App. 2d 714, 723-24, 153 P.2d 214, 219 (Dist. Ct. App. 1944) (Doran J., concurring) (noting the evidence of implied statements that the house was a betting establishment constituted hearsay).

truth. This use requires the finder of facts to rely on the untested perception, memory, sincerity and ambiguity of the defendant (the out-of-court declarant).

Under the Federal Rules of Evidence admissions have been excluded from the definition of hearsay. This is a difference with no substantive consequences. Proving the fact of flight, position 3 — the first truth, is not hearsay because Witness #1 has personal knowledge and is testifying under oath at position 5.

Under the Federal Rules of Evidence the act of running could also be considered non-hearsay because the declarant did not intend to make a statement through his flight. *See* **PRACTICES NO. 36**, *infra* (relating to the distinction between assertive and non-assertive conduct).

(2) When the evidence of the defendant's running from the scene of the crime is offered to establish only an *opportunity* on the defendant's part, the only truth we are concerned about is the first truth in the previous scenario — the fact of running — because it establishes presence. Since Witness #2 has personal knowledge of this fact, his testimony is not hearsay.

28 PRACTICES

The dogs and nuns rule. Under the common law there was disagreement over whether animals and machines, like watches, produced hearsay. For example, if you followed a blood hound who trailed the defendant from the scene of a crime and barked at his feet, offering testimony about that dog's conduct would be using the dog's "statement" as a declaration that the defendant was the one who left his scent at the scene of the crime, and therefore, is probably the assailant. Also, if I asked you for the time, and you looked at your watch and said it was 1:00 PM, when your statement is repeated in court by a third party who heard what you said, that third party's testimony would be hearsay. But what about the statement being made by the watch? Are you not offering what the watch was "saying" for the truth of the matter it was asserting? Does this create a double level hearsay problem — your statement and the watch's statement? Because neither the dog's "statement" nor the watch's "statements" involve mendacity or insincerity problems, most common law courts said that neither animal nor machine produced hearsay if they were properly authenticated.

By contrast, if a carload of nuns witnessed an accident and each were interviewed separately and told virtually the same story, even though it is unlikely that the nuns would give insincere statements, and their consistency reinforced the accuracy of each account, common law courts called their statements hearsay because they could be insincere or mistaken, and unlike machines, they are not wholly explicable, or unlike dogs, acting out of instinct. Therefore, the line was drawn between human utterances and animals, ergo the dogs and nuns rule.

This issue has been resolved in Fed. R. Evid. 801(b) which defines a "declarant," as a "person" and Fed. R. Evid. 801(a) that defines a "statement" as either an oral or written assertion or nonverbal conduct of a "person."

29 PRACTICES

Writings as hearsay — think of them as paper people. Writings, no less than oral statements, are hearsay when offered to prove the truth of the matter asserted by the author. In both instances, the author is not in the courtroom, under oath, and subject to cross-examination. The writing is the equivalent of another individual to whom the author has "spoken."

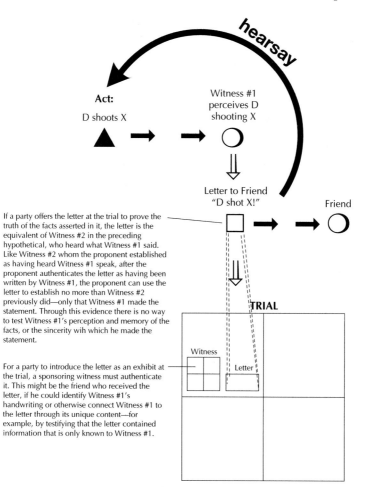

If a party offers the letter at the trial to prove the truth of the facts asserted in it, the letter is the equivalent of Witness #2 in the preceding hypothetical, who heard what Witness #1 said. Like Witness #2 whom the proponent established as having heard Witness #1 speak, after the proponent authenticates the letter as having been written by Witness #1, the proponent can use the letter to establish no more than Witness #2 previously did—only that Witness #1 made the statement. Through this evidence there is no way to test Witness #1's perception and memory of the facts, or the sincerity wih which he made the statement.

For a party to introduce the letter as an exhibit at the trial, a sponsoring witness must authenticate it. This might be the friend who received the letter, if he could identify Witness #1's handwriting or otherwise connect Witness #1 to the letter through its unique content—for example, by testifying that the letter contained information that is only known to Witness #1.

The writing is the equivalent of a paper "person" repeating what was heard. While the writing is not under oath and subject to cross-examination, this circumstance is inconsequential because the writing has perfect perception and memory and no possibility of insincerity, assuming authorship has been proven. Unlike an individual to whom an oral statement could have been made, when the writing repeats the written statement made by the author, the writing's memory is absolute.

Through the writing the proponent attempts to establish the first truth of hearsay — that the declarant actually uttered certain words. After proper authentication, the writing, having been written by the declarant, has "personal knowledge" of what the declarant said — similar to a witness repeating what the declarant might have said orally. Unlike another individual testifying from recollection, however, there is no need to administer an oath and cross-examine the letter because it presents none of the hearsay dangers. Therefore, it establishes the first truth — that the statement was made by the author — without creating another level of hearsay. The second truth — the substance of the message conveyed by the declarant — requires the finder of facts to rely on the fallible and untested perception, memory and sincerity of the declarant — the person who authored the letter.

30 PRACTICES

Multiple-level hearsay. When a declarant does not have personal knowledge of the event he is relating, because he acquired the information from someone else, the offering of the declarant's out-of-court statement may involve two levels of hearsay — the first level being the individual who is the source of the information (Witness #1), and second level being the declarant (Witness #2) who related that information to the testifying witness, Witness #3. Two levels of hearsay exist if the declarant's statement is being offered to prove the truth of what was described by the first witness. When multiple levels of hearsay exist, the testimony is admissible only if hearsay exceptions are found for every hearsay link. The following diagram illustrates the multiple levels of hearsay. Exceptions for each level of hearsay will be discussed and diagramed later.

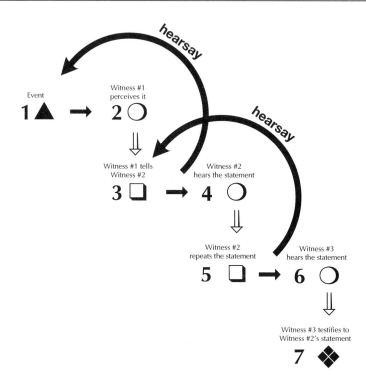

If Witness #3 at position 7 is being asked to repeat what Witness #2 at position 5 uttered, that link in the chain of communication would not involve hearsay because Witness #3 has personal knowledge of what Witness #2 said and is testifying under oath.

The fact alone that Witness #2 uttered certain words, however, does not establish anything that is relevant to the case without believing the truth of what was said — namely what Witness #1 had previously described something. Since Witness #3 does not have personal knowledge of what Witness #1 described, the link from position 5 to position 3 involves the first level of hearsay. Witness #2's reiteration of what Witness #1 previously said is being offered not just for the truth that it was uttered, but also for the truth of what it described — what Witness #1 initially said.

What Witness #1 said does not prove how the event occurred without believing the truth of his utterance. As Witness #3 before him, Witness #2 only has personal knowledge of what he heard. He does not have personal knowledge of how the event occurred. Therefore, there is a second level of hearsay through Witness #1, from position 3 to position 1. It is relevant only if it accurately describes what Witness #1 perceived. That requires the finder of facts to rely on the untested perception, memory, sincerity and ambiguity of Witness #1, and therefore, is a second level of hearsay.

There is only one level of hearsay if the declarant's statement is relevant simply because the first witness uttered particular words on a prior occasion, not because his previous statement reflected the truth. This result usually occurs when Witness #1 testifies at trial and the declarant's statement is being offered to impeach Witness 1 by showing that he told a different story on a previous occasion. In his instance, Witness #1's statement is not being offered because what he described was true — only because he uttered certain words and told a different story from what he is saying now. In this instance, a hearsay exception is only needed to establish that the statement was uttered (position 3).

Example

A witness to a hit and run accident described the driver of the car as a heavyset Asian male with a bald head. The police take this statement and put it in a police report. At trial, the witness describes the driver of the car as a thin Caucasian male with long stringy, blond hair.

Q — Why is this statement relevant?

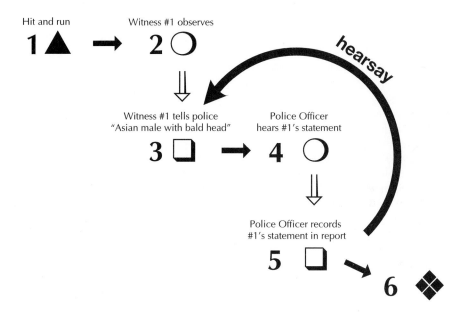

A — To impeach Witness #1 who told inconsistent stories.

If the police officer testified to the truth that the prior statement was made there would be no hearsay problem. The officer has personal knowledge of what the witness said and would be testifying under oath. The officer, however, is not present. In his stead, we are using the report that he wrote. This report is testifying like an independent person who is saying that the officer told it that the witness made certain statements, and we are being asked to believe the truth of what the officer said: that the witness said the culprit was a heavyset Asian man with a bald head. This need gives rise to the only level of hearsay because, for the purpose of relevance, the report only needs to establish the fact that there was an utterance with a particular content. Because the officer had personal knowledge of the utterance of what Witness #1 said, and a duty to report it, the report would probably be admitted under either the public records exception in Rule 803(8)(B), as matters observed pursuant to a duty imposed by law, or the business records exception in Rule 803(6).

The same analysis applies when a witness testifies one way at one trial and another way at another trial. When the transcript of the first trial is offered into evidence just to prove the witness' previous testimony, there is one level of hearsay — the transcript. Like the police officer in the above example, the court reporter is the declarant in this situation. His prior testimony is not being offered to prove the truth of what he previously testified to — only to prove that he testified differently. The court reporter has personal knowledge of this fact and records the statement simultaneously pursuant to a duty. The transcript could be admitted under the exceptions mentioned above, and, since the declarant made the transcript simultaneously with hearing the words, the present sense impression exception in Rule 803(1) might be applicable, as well as the exception for past recollection recorded, Rule 803(5), if the reporter is available to authenticate the transcript he made and to verify its accuracy.

If the prosecution intends to use the report to establish the truth of what Witness #1 asserted — that a heavy-set Asian male with a bald head was driving the vehicle — then a second level of hearsay appears. As discussed above, the first level of hearsay is the truth that Witness #1 uttered the statement. The business records exception in rule 803(6) will satisfy only this first level of hearsay. The second level, however, cannot be satisfied through the same business records exception because the officer who wrote the report took the statement from the hearsay statement of Witness #1.[64] Thus, to admit the report, the prosecution must employ an additional hearsay exception — perhaps excited utterance under Rule 803(2) — together with Rule 803(6) to overcome the multiple levels of hearsay.

31 PRACTICES

Offered for truth. For an out-of-court statement to be hearsay it must be relevant for the truth of what was said, and it must be offered for that purpose. If a statement is relevant simply because the declarant was conversing

---

[64] *See* Johnson v. Lutz, 253 N.Y. 124, 127, 170 N.E. 517, 518 (1930) (finding a police report inadmissible under the business record exception because it "was made from hearsay statements of a third person who happened to present at the scene of the accident" rather than the personal knowledge of officer who was making the report pursuant to a business duty.)

(to demonstrate that there was a relationship with another person or that he could speak in English), his utterances are not hearsay, even if their content is the same as the fact being proven.

Example

If after a serious automobile accident, in which the declarant was injured, he awakens in the ambulance and mutters, "I'm actually alive! I survived that horrible experience!" If he died before he reached the hospital and, in a subsequent wrongful death action, damages are sought for the pain and suffering he experienced from the scene of the accident to the hospital, his statement would establish that he survived the accident and was alive and could have suffered for a period of time. We know this, in part, because he said it. But we also know it because he was able to utter anything. Had he said "I forgot to lock my car" instead of the statement he uttered, it would still prove the proposition that he was alive and could have experienced pain. The fact being proven and the fact stated in the utterance were the same, but that is simply a coincidence. This statement should be admitted as non-hearsay. The following diagram illustrates.

Event:

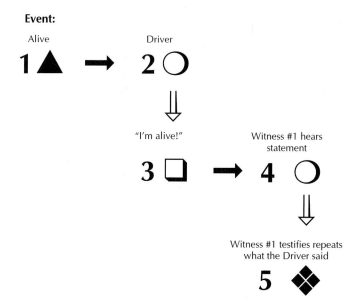

For the Witness #1's testimony to prove that Driver was alive in the ambulance, all that he needs to do it prove that there was a statement uttered at position 3. What was uttered is not particularly important.

32 PRACTICES

Silence as hearsay. When communications are being read into silence, and those communications are being introduced for their truth, silence is no less hearsay than an explicit assertion through either words or conduct. In every instance the value of the assertion depends on the perception, memory, and sincerity of the silent declarants, as well as the ambiguity of their silence — none of which can be tested and explored through an examination of the declarants while under oath.[65]

Example 1

A manufacturer maintains a record of all complaints that customers have filed with the company regarding its product. Their records reflect no complaints about a particular product.

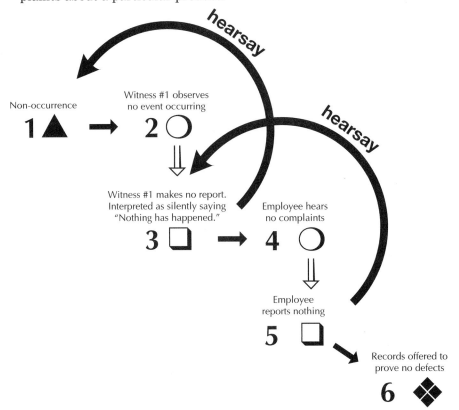

This absence of complaints is offered as evidence that the product was not defective. The silence in the business records and from the customers is interpreted as an assertion by customers that there is not anything to complain about, and that implied assertion is being offered for its truth. All hearsay concerns are present at two levels — the business record at positions 5 & 6 to prove that no complaints were made at position 3, and the silence of

---

[65] For further discussion of the implications of silence as hearsay, *see* Falknor, *Silence as Hearsay*, 89 U. PA. L. REV. 192, 209 (1940).

the customers at position 3 to prove that there was nothing to complain about at position 1.

Example 2

Unauthorized actions were taken by an executive of a corporation. In an action against that executive, a member of the board will testify that he attended all board meetings and the conduct complained of has never been discussed and certainly has not been sanctioned.

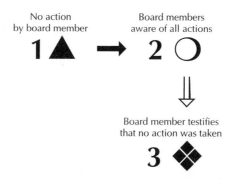

This testimony is *not hearsay* because only the fact of silence is relevant and the board member has personal knowledge of that silence. No messages need to be read into the silence and accepted for their truth.[66]

33 PRACTICES

Made in the presence of the opponent fallacy. Judges occasionally have refused to recognize a statement as hearsay if it was made in the presence of the party against whom it is offered. This fact is *totally irrelevant* to the hearsay nature of the statement, which is determined by the purpose for which it is being offered at trial, not the context in which it was made.

These judges appear to have confused the definition of hearsay with the concept of adoptive admissions by silence. The theory of this type of admission is that if an accusation is made to an individual which calls for a response if not true, and the evidence shows that that individual heard and understood the statement, but without any impediment to responding remained silent, his silence can be construed as an acknowledgment of the

---

[66] *See* Murray v. American Builders Supply, Inc., 472 P.2d 738, 740 (Colo. Ct. App. 1970).

[67] *See, e.g.,* United States v. Aponte, 31 F.3d 81, 87 (2d Cir. 1994); United States v. Flecha, 539 F.2d 874, 877 (2d Cir. 1976).

statement's truth.[67] The sole fact that a statement was made in the presence of the opposing party is hardly a foundation for such an admission.

34 PRACTICES

The literal assertion mistake. The literal words spoken do not have to be offered for their truth for a statement to be hearsay. This approach to hearsay puts form over substance. The problems with hearsay arise because the source of information is not in court, under oath and being tested through cross-examination. If a message is being read into a statement that is different from the words uttered, the problems of perception, memory, sincerity and ambiguity are still the same. All of the problems stemming from having relied on the untested mind of an out-of-court declarant are still present.

Example 1

If a witness to a hit and run stated that the fleeing car "looked like a canary" when that statement is repeated in court by someone who heard it, for the purpose of proving that the car was bright yellow, it would be hearsay. It is irrelevant that the statement was indirect rather than a direct assertion about the color. All that the indirect nature of the communication does is add additional ambiguity problems — canaries come in a lot of different colors.

Example 2

When the doctor writes a prescription for a particular drug, the pharmacist may "know" the disease being treated because the drug has been used for that limited purpose. If the druggist testified that the patient had Acquired Immune Deficiency Syndrome, or AIDS, this would be hearsay. The pharmacist has no personal knowledge of that fact. He has drawn the conclusion from the message he read into the prescription. Even though that message in the prescription was both indirect and unintended, it would still be hearsay under the common law. For the jurors to credit the pharmacist's testimony, they would have to rely on the untested perception, memory and sincerity of the doctor who is not testifying. Under the Federal Rules of Evidence, even though the indirect message was unintended, the statement should still be classified as hearsay despite the assertive/non-assertive distinction in Rule 801(a), but the courts are in conflict. *See also* **PRACTICES, NO. 36**, *infra.*

Example 3

A survey is taken to discover whether people believe that a certain product is orange juice. After tasting the product, half of those surveyed stated, "I *believe* this is orange juice." The other half stated, "This *is* orange juice." Both statements are hearsay even though the latter statement is not being offered to prove the truth of the literal words spoken — that the product *is* orange juice. It is hearsay because the latter statement is relevant only because of the implied assertion that is being read into it, the assertion that was explicitly stated by the other half — what they "believed."

35 PRACTICES

Circumstantial evidence trap. Occasionally, courts will try to avoid the hearsay exclusion by noting that the testimony or conduct in question is only "circumstantial evidence" of whatever it is being offered to prove. This fact is irrelevant to the hearsay assessment. Hearsay can be both direct and circumstantial. The label "circumstantial" refers only to the indirect manner in which the evidence tends to establish the fact or proposition it was offered to prove. It is totally unrelated to the evidence's reliability with respect to the dangers of perception, memory and sincerity. Judges often misinterpret this notion, finding that circumstantial evidence is not hearsay, despite the fact it is an out-of-court statement used to prove the truth of the matter asserted, because the evidence is merely used to prove the circumstantial relationship between the parties.[68]

The circumstantial evidence label is frequently used with regard to conduct as hearsay. For example, when an individual stops his car at a street light, if one reads into that conduct the statement that the light is red in the direction he is driving, the conduct is hearsay when offered to prove the color of the light, even though it is only circumstantial evidence of the color of the light. The reliability of the conduct as evidence of the color of the light requires the jury to depend on the untested perception, memory, and sincerity of the driver, as well as the unexplored ambiguity of the conduct — people stop in many places, for many reasons.

Another example of circumstantial hearsay through the use of words is the previous hypothetical about a physician's writing a prescription for a particular drug that has been used only to treat one specific disease. When the pharmacist testifies that the patient has a particular medical condition he is actually testifying that the doctor indirectly "said" the patient has a particular medical condition through the circumstances of his treatment — the prescription. As a basis for this message, however, the prescription is laden with ambiguity. The physician may be trying a new drug regimen for a completely different medical condition. And, of course, as previously noted, even if the physician were treating the usual medical condition, the reliability of the indirect statement depends on the untested quality of the doctor's perception, memory and sincerity.

---

[68] *See, e.g.,* United States v. David, 96 F.3d 1477, 1481 (D.C. Cir. 1996); United States v. Marino, 658 F.2d 1120, 1124 (6th Cir. 1981).

II. THE ASSERTIVE/NON-ASSERTIVE DISTINCTION

PRINCIPLES

The hearsay rule is premised on four concerns: (1) perception, (2) memory, (3) sincerity, and (4) ambiguity. Rule 801(a) FRE has excluded *unintentionally implied* statements from the definition of hearsay, on the ground that the lack of an intention to communicate the implied message eliminates the problem of insincerity. From the conclusion that these implied statements are sincere, it is assumed, without more, that they also are reliable.

RULE 801 FRE
Definition

The following definitions apply under this article:

(a) Statement. A "statement" is (1) an oral or written assertion or (2) nonverbal conduct of a person, if it is intended by the person as an assertion.

. . . .

(c) Hearsay. "Hearsay" is a statement, other than one made by the declarant while testifying at the trial or hearing, offered in evidence to prove the truth of the matter asserted.

36 PRACTICES

Conduct, not oral or written assertions. If the premise upon which the assertive/non-assertive distinction is based were true — that sincerity guarantees accuracy — many of us would not be losing so many wagers with friends over past events that have been remembered differently. Nevertheless, given this irrational distinction, it should be applied in a fashion that is consistent with its own unique logic.

The definition of hearsay in Rule 801(c) involves the use of the term "statement." Hearsay is defined as an out of court "statement" offered in evidence to prove the truth of the matter asserted. This is the common law definition except for the fact that the term "statement" is previously defined in Rule 801(a) as "(1) an oral or written assertion or (2) nonverbal conduct of a person, if it is intended by the person as an assertion." There are two ways to view the definition of "statement."

1) The grammatical construction of the rule — two alternatives followed by a modifying clause set off with a comma — would compel the conclusion that unintended implications of both oral and

written assertions, as well as nonverbal conduct are not "statements" under Rule 801(a), and therefore, not hearsay under Rule 801(c).[69]

2) Since the logic of the distinction between intentionally assertive and unintentionally assertive statements flows from the assured absence of insincerity with unintended assertions, implied statements from spoken words should not be subject to the distinction because spoken words invariably involve an intention to communicate something to someone. Because of that intention, the declarant's direct message may be insincere. If the direct message is the basis for finding other implied messages, those implied messages can be no more reliable than their source.[70]

Example 1

A doctor writes a prescription for a particular drug. When the patient takes the prescription to the drugstore to be filled, the pharmacist interprets it as a statement that the individual has the particular medical condition treated with that drug. Because the doctor did not intend to communicate the nature of the patient's medical condition through the prescription, courts *may* hold that the use of the prescription to prove the nature of the disease is not hearsay.

The logic used is that since the doctor didn't intend the indirect message, it must be sincere. In the context of a prescription, few would quarrel with that conclusion. The problem, of course, is that we are still left with percep-

---

[69] *See, e.g.,* United States v. Zenni, 492 F. Supp. 464, 465-69 (E.D. Ky. 1980) (finding all unintended, non-assertive actions — whether verbal conduct (spoken or written) or nonverbal conduct — do not fall within the definition).

[70] Stoddard v. State, 389 Md. 681, 887 A.2d 564 (Md. Ct. App. 2005) ("The notion that evidence 'untested with respect to the perception, memory, and narration (or their equivalents) of the actor' poses minimal dangers 'in the absence of an intent to assert' has been labeled a *non sequitur* on the grounds that the inferences of perception, memory, and narration are wholly independent from any intention to assert. The fact that a declarant may not have intended to communicate a particular factual proposition reveals nothing about the circumstances under which the declarant came to believe that proposition, nor about the clarity with which the declarant remembers the underlying events."); Mosley v. State, 141 S.W.3d 816, 829 (Tex. Ct. App. 2004) ("'Matter asserted' includes any matter explicitly asserted, and any matter implied by a statement, if the probative value of the statement as offered flows from the declarant's belief as to the matter."); Iowa v. Dullard, 668 N.W.2d 585 (2003) ("[E]ven the danger of insincerity may continue to be present in those instances where the reliability of the direct assertion may be questioned. If the expressed assertion is insincere, such as a fabricated story, the implied assertion derived from the expressed assertion will similarly be unreliable. Implied assertions can be no more reliable than the predicate expressed assertion). *See,* United States v. Palma-Ruedas, 121 F.3d 841 (3d Cir. 1997); United States v. Reynolds, 715 F.2d 99, 103 (3d Cir. 1983) and Lyle v. Koehler, 720 F.2d 426 432-33 (6th Cir. 1983)(implicitly adopting the view that only non-assertive, non-verbal conduct does not qualify as hearsay). *See generally,* Paul R. Rice, *Should Unintended Implications of Speech be Considered Nonhearsay? The Assertive/Nonassertive Distinction Under Rule 801(a) of the Federal Rules of Evidence,* 65 TEMP. L. REV. 529 (1992). *See also* Paul R. Rice, *Back to the Future with Privileges: Abandon Codification, Not the Common Law,* 38 LOY. L.A. L. REV. 739, 764-65 (2004).

tion, memory and ambiguity problems. How can we know that the doctor is not trying a new drug regimen for another medical condition — creating ambiguity problems? How do we know that the doctor accurately assessed the nature of the patient's medical condition — creating perception problems? The answer is that we cannot know, but that those are the dangers of hearsay that the assertive/non-assertive distinction has chosen to ignore.

A more difficult theoretical issue is presented by this problem. Even though the doctor did not intend to communicate the implied message taken by the pharmacist, did he not intend to communicate some message by writing the prescription? The answer, of course, is yes. Therefore, the act of communicating what drug to dispense injects the possibility of insincerity. While this possibility is slight in the context of a doctor writing a prescription, in other contexts of less serious potential consequences, it is more likely. As a consequence, this prescription should be seen as hearsay. Whenever the declarant intends to communicate anything to anyone, a theoretical insincerity problem exists and the basis for the assertive/non-assertive distinction disappears.

Example 2

"Yes, John is a very 'special' member of the family. I have a particular fondness for him." By making this satirical statement, the uncle clearly did not intend to say that John was his favorite nephew. Nevertheless, by the assertive/non-assertive distinction some would argue that the implied statement is not hearsay. This is nonsense. Since the declarant is intending to convey *a message* through his use of words, potential insincerity is injected into the equation. As a consequence, any indirect message, intended or not, is as unreliable as the direct message.

III. RELATIONSHIP OF HEARSAY RULE TO OTHER RULES[71]

Rule 103 (a). Rulings on Evidence. If a timely objection is not made to the admission of hearsay, it may be used by the opposing side for any purpose for which it may be relevant. The use of such hearsay, however, does not open the door for the opposing party to use a selected piece of hearsay at his discretion. The theory of "opening the door" applies only to *subjects*, not to types of evidence.

For example, if the door to character evidence was inappropriately opened in a civil case by the introduction of evidence without objection, the proponent of that evidence could not later prevent the opposing side from responding with a similar type of evidence. The responsive evidence, of course, must be an admissible form of character evidence — reputation and opinion, rather than specific

---

[71] PAUL R. RICE & ROY A. KATRIEL, EVIDENCE: COMMON LAW AND FEDERAL RULES OF EVIDENCE § 4.02 [D] (LEXIS 5th ed. 2005).

instances of conduct. Therefore, in theory, if a timely and proper objection is raised by the party who initiated this inquiry, the responding party may not use specific act evidence, even if the objecting party used that impermissible form of evidence when the matter originally was broached. In practice, however, this would be permitting the objecting party to have his cake and eat it too— an unfairness to the responding party. Consequently, when the form of evidence and the subject matter of the evidence coalesce (as with character and specific acts) courts are likely to overrule the objection and permit the party to respond in kind to the subject of the evidence, with the same type of evidence.

Rule 104(a). Preliminary Questions. When the judge decides whether evidence that has been objected to is hearsay (because it is being offered for the truth of the matter asserted) and, if hearsay, whether it nevertheless is admissible under an established exception (like the business records exception in Rule 803(6), because it was regularly made, at or near the time of the event, from personal knowledge and business duty), the judge may hear and consider evidence in making that determination that she would not permit the jury to hear. She is not bound by the rules she is enforcing.

Rule 106. Remainder of or Related Writings or Recorded Statements. When hearsay is in written form, the opponent has the right to offer with it whatever additional portions of the same writing, or any other writings, which in fairness should be considered contemporaneously in order to establish the proper context and give the full and intended meaning.

Rule 806. Attacking and Supporting Credibility of Declarant. When hearsay evidence is proven through the testimony of a third party who heard it, the credibility of both the witness who is testifying and the out-of-court hearsay declarant (whose statement is being repeated) may be attacked though character evidence, prior convictions, bias evidence, inconsistent statements and evidence of psychiatric disorders.

Rule 901. Requirement of Authentication or Identification. All evidence must be proven to be what the proponent claims it is. Documents and other objects must be authenticated and individuals must be identified in order to establish their relevance to the cause of action. All direct (*e.g.*, witnesses with personal knowledge of the sound of a voice, or style of handwriting) and circumstantial (comparison of voices or handwriting exemplars, distinctive characteristics) means of authentication may be employed.

Rule 1002. Requirement of Original. When written hearsay is offered as evidence, it also will involve a best evidence problem because the proponent will be proving the content of that writing, in order to be proving the truth of that content. If the writing is material to the litigation, the best evidence rule requires that the original of the writing be used unless it is shown to be unavailable due to no serious fault of the proponent. In lieu of the original, if a genuine question has not been raised as to the authenticity of the original, the proponent can also offer a mechanically produced copy — a duplicate — without accounting for the unavailability of the original.

IV. HEARSAY THAT IS NOT HEARSAY — RULE 801(D)(1) — PRIOR STATEMENTS OF WITNESSES

A. PRINCIPLES

Under the common law, exceptions to the hearsay rule were of two types: (1) those that required the out-of-court declarant to be unavailable before they could be used (e.g., former testimony, declarations against interest, dying declarations) and (2) those that did not require unavailability but instead allowed statements to be admitted regardless of whether the out-of-court declarant was in court and even when he repeated his own prior statement (e.g., excited utterances, present physical condition, present state of mind, business records).

The federal rules have perpetuated these two categories of exceptions under Rules 803 and 804, respectively, but have complicated the equation by allowing additional types of statements to be used for the truth of the matter asserted in them, without classifying them as "hearsay." These statements, are denoted as "exclusions" from the definition and are classified by Rule 801(d)(1)(A)-(C) as prior inconsistent statements, prior consistent statements, and prior identifications.

RULE 801 FRE
Definition

The following definitions apply under this article:

. . . .

(d) Statements which are not hearsay. A statement is not hearsay if —

(1) Prior statement by witness. The declarant testifies at the trial or hearing and is subject to cross-examination concerning the statement, and the statement is (A) inconsistent with the declarant's testimony, and was given under oath subject to the penalty of perjury at a trial, hearing, or other proceeding, or in a deposition, or (B) consistent with the declarant's testimony and is offered to rebut an express or implied charge against the declarant of recent fabrication or improper influence or motive, or (C) one of identification of a person made after perceiving the person; . . . .

37 PRACTICES

Ducks that are not ducks — indirect recognition of a third class of hearsay exceptions. If the out of court declarant is present and testifying, Rule

801(d)(1) permits certain prior statements of that witness (prior inconsistent statement made under oath, prior consistent statement offered in response to an express or implied charge of recent fabrication, and prior identifications) to be offered for their truth without being classified as hearsay. These are statements that are classified as non-hearsay are like birds that look like ducks and quack like ducks, but, for no compelling reason, are not called ducks. They are statements, which because of their use, are within the definition of hearsay under both the common law and Rule 801(c) of the Federal Rules of Evidence, except for the fact that they have been explicitly excluded from the definition by Rule 801(d)(1).

In substance, Rule 801(d) creates a third class of hearsay exceptions — exceptions that *require the out of court declarant to be present* before they can be used. This would have been an appropriate place to codify the past recollection recorded exception (presently in rule 803(5)) that requires the maker of the recorded recollection to be present to identify the writing, but unavailable in the sense that he has an inadequate memory to testify fully and accurately.

B. Prior Inconsistent Statements

PRINCIPLES

Prior inconsistent statements of a witness used only for impeachment purposes do not create a hearsay problem. The theory of impeachment is that by making inconsistent statements, the witness is not credible. The inconsistent statement is not being offered for the truth of what the witness previously said, but only for the fact that the inconsistent statement was uttered (the first truth that is not hearsay because the witness has personal knowledge of that fact).[72]

There is a possibility, however, that jurors may misunderstand the theory of the offer and use the prior statement for the truth of what was said. Therefore, the opposing party can ask for a limiting instruction from the presiding judge under Rule 105, in which the limited purpose is spelled out for the jury.[73]

---

[72] *See* United States v. Boa, 189 F.3d 860, 866 (9th Cir. 1999) ("a prior inconsistent statement is admissible to raise the suggestion that if a witness makes inconsistent statements, then his entire testimony may not be credible; such an inference does not depend on whether either the prior statement or the subsequent in-court statement is true.").

[73] *See, e.g.,* United States v. Tafollo-Cardenas, 860, 866 (9th Cir. 1999) (finding, based upon the strength of the hearsay evidence, the failure to give a limiting instruction constituted reversible error).

RULE 801 FRE
Definition

The following definitions apply under this article:

. . . .

(d) Statements which are not hearsay. A statement is not hearsay if —

(1) Prior statement by witness. The declarant testifies at the trial or hearing and is subject to cross-examination concerning the statement, and the statement is (A) inconsistent with the declarant's testimony, and was given under oath subject to the penalty of perjury at a trial, hearing, or other proceeding, or in a deposition . . . .

RULE 607 FRE
Who May Impeach

The credibility of a witness may be impeached by any party, including the party calling the witness.

RULE 105 FRE
Limited Admissibility

When evidence which is admissible as to one party or for one purpose but not admissible as to another party or for another purpose is admitted, the court, upon request, shall restrict the evidence to its proper scope and instruct the jury accordingly.

38 PRACTICES

Surprise and damage / "good faith." Under the common law a party could not impeach his own witness. The party vouched for the credibility of the witnesses he called. The only exceptions to the prohibition were: (1) when that party was *surprised* by the witness' testimony and *affirmatively damaged* by what he said (as opposed to being just disappointed); and (2) when the witness was the adverse party or was declared an adverse or hostile witness by the presiding judge.

Under Rule 607, a party may now impeach his own witness. This raises the possibility of a party calling a witness knowing that he will give unfavorable testimony, solely for the purpose of impeaching him with his prior inconsistent statement, hoping that the jury, having heard the prior statement, will use it as substantive evidence of what the witness previously said. Because the Federal Rules of Evidence did not codify the common law "surprise and damage" limitation, courts have addressed this problem by creating a "good faith" requirement. If the party calling the witness cannot demonstrate that he has a good faith basis for believing that the witness will give favorable testimony (thereby appearing to have called the witness solely for the purpose of "impeaching"), the court will not permit the inconsistent statement to be explored. This practice was announced in 1984 in *United States v. Webster*,[74] and has been followed by most other circuits.[75] What apparently has not been perpetuated is the "damage" requirement, but the judicially created rule may still be evolving.

39 PRACTICES

Other basis for admitting inconsistent statement. Rule 801(d)(1) changes the common law. Now, prior inconsistent statements cannot only be used to impeach the witness, they also can be used to prove the truth of what witnesses previously said without creating hearsay problem because they have been defined out of the hearsay rule. If the prior inconsistent statement was (1) made under oath (2) in a prior trial, hearing or other proceedings, Rule 801(d)(1) makes them admissible to prove the truth of what was previously said. Even though they look like ducks, walk like ducks, and quack like ducks, they are no longer called ducks.

Because such statements are independently admissible for truth, they are not subject to the "good faith" requirement announced in *United States v. Webster*, see **PRACTICES NO. 38**, *supra*. The proponent of the inconsistent statements is no longer offering them under the guise of impeachment, when, in fact, he is seeking an inappropriate gain through jurors' misuse. The gain is now sanctioned.

40 PRACTICES

From foundation to roof. Under the common law, when a prior inconsistent statement was used for impeachment purposes, a foundation had to be laid

---

[74] 734 F.2d 1191, 1192 (7th Cir. 1984).

[75] *See* United States v. Ince, 21 F.3d 576, 581 (4th Cir. 1994); United States v. Kane, 944 F.2d 1406, 1411 (7th Cir. 1991); United States v. Gomez-Gallardo, 915 F.2d 553 (9th Cir. 1990); United States v. Peterman, 841 F.2d 1474 (10th Cir. 1988); United States v. Johnson, 802 F.2d 1459 (D.C. Cir. 1986); United States v. Miller, 664 F.2d 94, 97 (5th Cir. 1981), *cert. denied*, 459 U.S. 854 (1982); United States v. DeLillo, 620 F.2d 939, 946 (2d Cir.), *cert. denied*, 449 U.S. 835 (1980); United States v. Morlang, 531 F.2d 183, 190 (4th Cir. 1975). Some courts note, however, that when the Government calls "a witness whose corroborating testimony is instrumental to constructing the Government's case, the Government has the right to question the witness, and to attempt to impeach him about those aspects of his testimony that conflict with the government's account of the same events," despite the good-faith exception. United States v. Eisen, 974 F.2d 246, 262-63 (2d Cir. 1994).

before the inconsistent statement could be proven through the testimony of other witnesses — extrinsic evidence. This foundation required the examiner to confront the witness with the inconsistency, so that other witnesses might not have to be called if the inconsistency was admitted.[76]

The foundation requirement appears to have been abolished in Rule 613. In subsection (a), the rule states that when examining a witness concerning his prior statement, he need not be shown the statement (if it is in writing) or otherwise informed of its content. This eliminates the common law foundation requirement. However, subsection (b) creates a problem. It permits extrinsic evidence of prior inconsistent statements (testimony of third parties), but it makes that testimony inadmissible if the witness being impeached is not "afforded an opportunity to explain or deny the same and the opposite party is afforded an opportunity to interrogate the witness thereon, or the interests of justice otherwise require." How can the witness have been afforded an opportunity to confront and explain if a foundation has not been laid? The answer may lie in a process equivalent to conditional relevance where the court must admit the evidence subject to the later admission of the conditioning fact. The proponent will have to ensure that the witness can be confronted at a later time by asking the court not to excuse him. Therefore, in the metaphor of building from a foundation, the proponent of extrinsic evidence needs only to put a "roof" on it after it has been developed. Courts have split on the question of whether a foundation is required.[77]

41 PRACTICES

Always lay a foundation even if it isn't required. While Rule 613 may have eliminated the foundation *requirement*, a foundation is still advisable for two reasons:

(1) If the witness becomes unavailable before being recalled and given a chance to confront, admit, and explain the alleged inconsistent statement, that inconsistent statement will be stricken from the record and the jury will be instructed to ignore it during its deliberations.

(2) By laying a foundation when the witness initially testifies, the proponent creates additional possibilities for impeachment. First, the witness may *volunteer other inconsistent statements* when the examination begins to generally focus on the time, place, manner, and individuals to whom inconsistent statements may have been made. Second, if he

---

[76] *See* McCormick on Evidence, § 37 (West Group 5th ed. 1999); Ladd, *Some Observations on Credibility; Impeachment of Witnesses*, 52 Cornell L.Q. 239 (1967).

[77] *See* Wammock v. Celotex Corp., 793 F.2d 1518, 20 Fed. R. Evid. Serv. 1281. *See also* United States v. Elliott, 771 F.2d 1046; United States v. Young, 248 F.3d 260; United States v. Hudson, 970 F.2d 948, 36 Fed. R. Evid. Serv. 297.

denies the inconsistency, he can be impeached with both the fact of his inconsistency and his false testimony about it while under oath. While the witness *may admit the inconsistency* and offer a plausible explanation, that same possibility exists during a later confrontation after the statement has been independently proven. While this will preclude further testimony about the inconsistency from a third party, there is no substantive loss, and in balance, one has much more to potentially gain through laying the foundation.

C. Prior Consistent Statements of a Witness

PRINCIPLES

Prior consistent statements are relevant for rehabilitation of a witness who has been impeached, and they do not constitute hearsay when offered for this limited purpose. Their relevance is in the fact that the witness has told consistent stories, and not necessarily in the truth of the prior consistent story.[78]

Although courts disagreed under the common law, to be admissible under the Federal Rules of Evidence solely for rehabilitative purposes, the prior consistent statement must have been made *before the motive to fabricate arose. Tome v. United States.*[79] Although this is not necessarily a logical imperative, in *Tome* the Court struck a balance and excluded post motive statements because the potential for misuse and waste of court time is too great relative to its probative value. States, of course, are free to construe their own evidence rule differently since *Tome* was only interpreting Federal Rules of Evidence 804(b)(3).

Like inconsistent statements in Rule 801(d)(A), Rule 801(d)(1)(B) makes consistent statements admissible for their truth.

RULE 801 FRE
Definition

The following definitions apply under this article:

. . . .

(d) Statements which are not hearsay. A statement is not hearsay if —

(1) Prior statement by witness. The declarant testifies at the trial or hearing and is subject to cross-examination concerning the

---

[78] *See, e.g.,* United States v. Barrett, 39 F.2d 244 (1st Cir. 1976). For an extensive discussion of the use of prior consistent statements to rehabilitate a witness, *see* Thomas, *Rehabilitating the Impeached Witness with Consistent Statements*, 32 MO. L. REV. 472 (1967).

[79] 513 U.S. 150, 156 (1995).

statement, and the statement is . . . (B) consistent with the declarant's testimony and is offered to rebut an express or implied charge against the declarant of recent fabrication or improper influence or motive. . . .

42 PRACTICES

Consistent statements admissible for truth — an inconsequential change. Rule 801(d) (1)(B) makes prior consistent statements admissible for truth, as well as for rehabilitative purposes. This change is meaningless, however, because the witness has already testified to the substance of the statement, and it, therefore, is already in the record. Therefore, the only value in the consistent statements is in their impact on the juror's perception of the witness' credibility. If a consistent statement convinces the jury to believe the witness, the jurors will believe what the witness said under oath in front of them. If the prior consistent statement fails to rehabilitate the witness, they will not believe either statement. Consequently, the expanded substantive use recognized by Rule 801(d)(1)(B) is of no consequence.

D. Relationship of Prior Consistent and Inconsistent Statements to Other Rules[80]

Rule 104. Preliminary Questions. Whether testimony is hearsay under Rule 801(a) or is excluded from the definition of hearsay under Rule 801(d) involves a question of admissibility that will be decided exclusively by the presiding judge pursuant to Rule 104 (a). For example, the determination of whether statements are hearsay only because the truth of their content is relevant, or because they were the product of nonverbal conduct intended by the actor as an assertion, is reserved exclusively for the presiding judge. Similarly, whether a statement is non-hearsay because it is inconsistent with the witness' testimony or because there has been an implied charge of recent fabrication that the statement rebuts is also a determination reserved for the judge.

Rule 106. Remainder of or Related Writings or Recorded Statements. Rule 106 is a rule of completeness. It provides that when part or all of a writing is introduced, the opponent may introduce the remainder of that writing or any other writing if, in fairness, it ought to be considered contemporaneously with the first document. The second dimension of the Rule — the placing of the statement in context — has long been an accepted basis for admitting such statements. Such was the basis upon which the Second Circuit in *United States v. Rubin*[81] held prior consistent statements to be admissible.

---

[80] PAUL R. RICE & ROY A. KATRIEL, EVIDENCE: COMMON LAW AND FEDERAL RULES OF EVIDENCE § 4.02 [D] (LEXIS 5th ed. 2005).

[81] 609 F.2d 51 (2d Cir. 1979), *aff'd on grant of cert. limited to other issues*, 449 U.S. 424 (1981).

Subsequently explaining its decision in *Rubin*, the Court of Appeals suggested that the doctrine of completeness should limit offers of evidence under Rule 106 to the same purpose for which the original offering is being made. If the first document were not introduced as substantive evidence, but only to impeach credibility, "the document offered for completeness would seem to be appropriately introduced also not as substantive evidence, but only to rehabilitate credibility."[82]

E. Applications — Prior Consistent and Inconsistent Statements

ONE

Mark Carpenter was arrested in Mexico on drug charges. While in Mexican custody, Carpenter made statements to U.S. law enforcement officials that implicated both himself and Barry and Brad Hogan in a conspiracy to import large quantities of cocaine into the United States. The Hogans were subsequently arrested and indicted in the United States.

Following Carpenter's release by the Mexican authorities and return to the United States, he was called to testify before the grand jury in a related case pending in the same court in which the Hogans were later to be tried. Carpenter initially refused to testify. Upon a grant of immunity, he then denied that he or the Hogans had any involvement in a drug conspiracy and testified that his confessions while imprisoned in Mexico were wholly fabricated and resulted from torture. The prosecutor in the Hogans' case was informed of Carpenter's reversal of position. During a pretrial suppression hearing, Carpenter reiterated his grand jury testimony.

At the Hogans' trial, the prosecutor announced during his opening argument that he would call Carpenter, but that he expected the witness to exculpate the Hogans. The prosecutor then stated, "If Mr. Carpenter testifies as I anticipate, we will show you that his testimony is untruthful by bringing you his prior statements regarding the culpability of himself and his co-conspirator." When Carpenter was called to the stand, he denied involvement in any drug-smuggling operation and reaffirmed his grand jury testimony of torture and fabrication. Following Carpenter's testimony, the Government seeks to call the U.S. law enforcement officials who took Carpenter's confession in Mexico to impeach Carpenter's testimony. Defense counsel objects. As trial judge, how should you rule?

Rule 607 of the Federal Rules of Evidence provides that a party has the right to impeach the credibility of its own witnesses. A party may not, however, introduce such a statement under the guise of impeachment for the *primary*

---

[82] United States v. Pierre, 781 F.2d 329, 332 n.2 (2d Cir. 1986).

purpose of placing before the jury substantive evidence that is not otherwise admissible. *United States v. Hogan*, 763 F.2d 697, 703 (5th Cir. 1985). In the problem, the Government announced to the jury that Carpenter would be hostile and that it would impeach him. Carpenter adhered to his grand jury testimony under oath during the pretrial suppression hearing. Knowing that Carpenter would testify as he did, it is clear that the Government's primary purpose in calling him to the stand was to place before the jury Carpenter's prior inconsistent statements, and thus a trial court would probably not allow the Government to cross-examine Carpenter as to these statements.

TWO

In a civil rights action against police officers for allegedly using excessive force in arresting the plaintiff, the officers told a very different story from the plaintiff's. The plaintiff seeks to introduce a description of the events in question that had been telephoned into police headquarters and recorded by the police. You conclude as the presiding judge that the statement is not admissible under an exception to the hearsay rule, like the excited utterance or present sense impression, because the declarant is not shown to have had personal knowledge of the events that he was describing or sufficiently close to the time of the event described. In response to this ruling, the plaintiff offers the statement solely for impeachment value as an inconsistent statement.

Since the police did not make the report, but instead only recorded it, the different description of the event by witnesses is not an inconsistent statement of the police. Recording what another says is not an adoption of that statement. Therefore, the statement is relevant only if the substance of what was said is accepted as true. This makes it hearsay and inadmissible because an applicable exception cannot be found.

THREE

The defendant is prosecuted for sexually molesting his daughter while she was in his custody. After the daughter testified, cross-examination extended over two days. During that cross-examination it was suggested that she fabricated her accusations because she wanted to live with her mother. To rehabilitate the witness, the prosecution offers the testimony of several witness who can testify to the witnesses prior accounts to them of the father's sexual assaults on her. The Court concluded that the statements were not admissible to rebut a charge of recent fabrication because they were not shown to have been made before the witness' alleged motive to fabricate arose. *Tome v. United States*, 513 U.S. 150, 130 L. Ed. 2d 574, 115 S. Ct. 696 (1995). Characterizing such an absolute rule as one of convenience in application rather than logic, the dissent argued that the post-motive statements could be relevant to rehabilitate if the circumstances of their utterance suggested a more powerful motive to tell the truth.

FOUR

Co-conspirators were arrested and charged with robbing computer gear from a UPS truck. After the arrests, Palacios, a co-conspirator, pled guilty and became a government witness giving details of the crime at trial. After suggestions on cross-examination that the witness was fabricating his testimony to get a deal from the prosecution, the government offered prior consistent statements that had been made relating the same details. The question presented was whether the prior statements were made before the witness' motive to fabricate had arisen. The government argued that since the statements were made before the cooperation agreement was entered into, they preceded the motive to fabricate. While acknowledging that there are many motives that may drive a person's decision to disgorge details of a crime both before and after a cooperation agreement has been signed (such as conscience or a desire to curry favor), this is a question of fact that must be resolved based on the specific evidence presented in each case. Ordinarily appellate courts will defer to the trial court's findings. *United States v. Prieto*, 232 F.3d 816 (11th Cir. 2000).

FIVE

The defendant was charged with assault. He offered an alibi defense and claimed that another individual, Hayes, had confessed committing the crime to his cell mates. In his defense he called Hayes as a witness, but Hayes denied any involvement. The defendant then attempted to call the two cell mates to impeach Hayes. The trial court excluded this testimony because it was perceived as a ruse. The judge saw the defendant as trying to get around the inadmissibility of the third-party confessions for substantive truth (they were not declarations against interest because the declarant was available) by offering them as inconsistent statements for impeachment purposes. In truth, the judge accused the defendant of offering them in anticipation that the jury would ignore a limiting instruction for impeachment use only and accept the statements for the truth of what they asserted (namely, Hayes' responsibility). The appellate court reversed, holding that it is a different balancing determination when the prosecution attempts to offer impeachment evidence when the defendant testifies than when the defense offers that same type of evidence involving statements by third-parties.

First, the appellate court noted that a proper foundation had been laid before the defendant attempted to offer the inconsistent statements. Hayes was confronted with claims of his cell mates and he denied them. On the question of using impeachment as a ruse, the court noted that the government should seldom be permitted to approach this because the unfair prejudice to someone whose liberty is at stake will substantially outweigh the probative value. On the other hand, when the defendant impeaches with the same evidence, the risks of jury misuse may be equivalent but the consequences are not the same. No one will be convicted without a fair opportunity to test the evidence through the effective cross-examination of the declarant. *United States v. Buffalo*, 2004 WL 235202 (8th Cir. 2004).

V. HEARSAY THAT IS NOT HEARSAY — ADMISSIONS OF A PARTY OPPONENT

A. PRINCIPLES

Under the common law, admissions were the most common form of hearsay admitted at trial. This was true because the only limitation on their admissibility was (and still is) that they had to be made by the party opponent. Because their admissibility was premised on the adversarial nature of the litigation process, not on the inherent reliability of the statement, they did not have to be based on personal knowledge or made under circumstances that guaranteed their reliability. Under both the common law and the Federal Rules of Evidence, one speaks at his own risk, and must explain his own statements when they are used against him.

Fundamentally, the rationale behind the admissibility of admissions under the common law and the Federal Rules of Evidence remains the same. One general difference does exist between the common law and the Federal Rule regarding their admissibility: the common law classified admissions as an exception to the hearsay rule while the Federal Rules excludes admissions from the definition of hearsay.

RULE 801 FRE
Definition

The following definitions apply under this article:

. . . .

(d) Statements which are not hearsay. A statement is not hearsay if —

. . . .

(2) Admission by party-opponent. The statement is offered against a party and is (A) the party's own statement, in either an individual or a representative capacity or (B) a statement of which the party has manifested an adoption or belief in its truth, or (C) a statement by a person authorized by the party to make a statement concerning the subject, or (D) a statement by the party's agent or servant concerning a matter within the scope of the agency or employment, made during the existence of the relationship, or (E) a statement by a co-conspirator of a party during the course and in furtherance of the conspiracy. The contents of the statement shall be considered but are not alone sufficient to establish the declarant's authority under subdivision (C), the agency or employment relationship and scope thereof under subdivision (D), or the existence of the conspiracy and the participation therein of the declarant and the party against whom the statement is offered under subdivision (E).

43 PRACTICES

They don't have to be against interests. Admissions do not have to be against the party's interests when they were made.[83] Admissions are often confused with declarations against interest and erroneously called "admissions *against interest.*"

44 PRACTICES

An admission must be used against the party who made it. Admissions have no limitations other than the fact that the party against whom they are used must be the party who made the statement. They need not be based on personal knowledge and can state opinions and conclusions that the declarant has not been shown to be qualified to make. One party, however, cannot offer his own admissions against another party. Otherwise, litigants could manufacture evidence for themselves by repeating their story to numerous individuals before trial and calling each as a witness.

45 PRACTICES

Admissions do not require personal knowledge. Fed. R. Evid. 602 does not expressly exclude admissions from the requirement of personal knowledge, as it does expert witness opinion testimony in Rule 703. Nevertheless, courts have carried forward the common law practice of requiring parties to explain their own statements and have permitted the admission of all prior statements regardless of their demonstrated basis.[84] This relaxation of the personal knowledge requirement has also been extended to vicarious admissions by agents of a party opponent.[85] The only apparent exception to this is the

---

[83] *See, e.g.,* United States v. Turner, 995 F.2d 1357, 1363 (6th Cir. 1993) ("Rule 801(d)(2) does not limit an admission to a statement against interest.").

[84] *See* Pau v. Yosemite Park & Curry Co., 39 F.3d 1187, 1994 WL 609421 at *4 (9th Cir. 1994) (unpublished opinion) ("Admissions of a party opponent need not be based upon personal knowledge and are not subject to rule 701.") *See also* 4 JACK WEINSTEIN ET AL., WEINSTEIN'S FEDERAL EVIDENCE § 801.30[1][a] (2002); Fed. R. Evid. 801(d)(2) (A) advisory committee's note (stating that admissions are free "from the restrictive influences of the opinion rule and the rule requiring first hand knowledge").

[85] *See* Brookover v. Mary Hitchcock Mem'l Hosp., 893 F.2d 411, 415-18 (1st Cir. 1990) (finding that the personal knowledge requirement does not apply to an admission under Rule 801(d)(2)(D)). As discussed above, there also is no need for personal knowledge of statements when made by a co-conspirator. *See* United States v. Lindemann, 85 F.3d 12342, 1237-38 (7th Cir. 1996).

adoptive admission by silence. For this concept to be applicable, it must first be demonstrated that the party possessed a sufficient basis in fact to allow him to contest an accusation that called for a response.[86]

46 PRACTICES

Vicarious admissions by agents authorized to speak — a dead-letter provision. For vicarious admissions, the common law distinguished between agents who were hired to speak for the principal and agents who were only hired to act. Actors could not make statements about what they did for the principal that could be used against the principal.[87] They could not make vicarious admissions.

Though Rule 801(d)(2)(C) still recognizes vicarious admissions by those who are "authorized by the party to make a statement," subsection (D) radically changes the common law by recognizing vicarious admissions made by a party's agent "concerning a matter within the scope of the agency or employment." Since all agents who are "authorized to make statements" and do so within the scope of that agency are making statements "concerning matters within the scope of [their] agency," subsection (C) has little value and, correspondingly, is somewhat of a dead-letter.

47 PRACTICES

Vicarious admissions by experts and attorneys. Admissions that are usable against the employer are not limited to statements made by regular employees. The expert witness retained for the limited purpose of trial is no different from the expert retained for a particular project outside a litigation context. Both are no less agents of the employer than the experts who are on the company's permanent payroll. Retained experts are like retained lawyers. Retained lawyers are like in-house counsel. Statements by each that are within the scope of employment are admissible as vicarious admissions, even though the individual may be speaking recklessly without adequate information or personal knowledge.[88]

---

[86] *See* United States v. Monks, 74 F.2d 945, 953 (9th Cir. 1985) (finding, for purposes of analysis under the Confrontation Clause, that the reliability of statements made by a codefendant to a third party in the defendant's presence implicating him in bank robbery as an adoptive admission depends upon four factors: "1) whether the statements are assertions of past fact; 2) whether the declarant had *personal knowledge* of the facts he related; 3) the possibility of faulty recollection; and 4)whether the circumstances suggest that the declarant misrepresented the defendant's role.") (emphasis added).

[87] *See* Rudzinski v. Warner Theaters, Inc., 114 N.W.2d 466, 469 (Wis. 1962).

[88] *See* Lightning Lube, Inc. v. Witco Corp., 4 F.3d 1153, 1198 (3d Cir. 1995) (stating, in relying upon Hanson v. Waller, 888 F.2d 806, 814 (11th Cir. 1989), that "[c]ourts have applied [rule

Courts, however, have limited the reach of vicarious admissions to those over whom the employer has "control."[89] This "control" standard ignores the fact that many professionals earn substantial incomes performing services for particular clients. It also ignores the transient nature of the "permanent" work force. Temporary employees often prove to be more permanent than "permanent" employees, and "control" has little to do with the length of the employment contract and the benefit that the employer gains from that service. Having gained that benefit, the employer should have to take responsibility for the statements those individuals make about the subject of what they have been retained to do. Once a proponent can demonstrate that the expert is an agent of a party, that expert's statements made during that relationship should be admitted as admissions.[90]

When courts focus exclusively on the factor of "control," they intolerably elevate form over substance. The anticipated length of an agents employment should only be a factor that goes to the weight that the finder of facts gives to the agent's statement.

If an employer can be held responsible for an employee's negligent conduct, or can be bound by a contract entered into by that employee, the employer should similarly be required to answer for that employee's statements about those same matters.

As employers are increasingly bringing outside consultants into their attorney-client circle of confidentiality, and claiming privilege for their communications with legal counsel on the theory that they are "virtual employees" of "functional employees,"*see* **PRACTICES NO. 133**, *infra*, there should be a

---

801(d)(2)(C)] to admit evidence of statements made by attorneys in a representational capacity."). *See also* United States v. McKeon, 738 F.2d 26, 30-33 (2d Cir. 1984) (holding that to admit opening statements made by attorneys as admissions superceding pleadings in civil litigation, the following requirements must be satisfied: 1) the prior statement must involve an assertion of fact inconsistent with similar assertions in the subsequent trials; 2) the inconsistency should be clear and of a quality that obviates any need for the trier of fact to explore other events at the prior trial; 3) some participatory role of the client must be evident; and 4) at a hearing under Rule 104(a), the court should determine that the inference being drawn from the inconsistency is a fair one and that an innocent explanation for the inconsistency does not exist).

[89] *See, e.g.*, Kirk v. Raymark Ind., Inc., 61 F.3d 147, 164 (3d Cir. 1995) (finding that because Rule 801(d)(2)(C) requires the declarant to be an agent of the party-opponent against whom the admission is offered, it "precludes the admission of the prior testimony of an expert witness [when] the expert has not agreed to be subject to the client's control in giving his or her testimony."); Sanford v. Johns-Manville Sales Corp., 923 F.2d 1142, 1150-51 (5th Cir. 1991) (rejecting a doctor's report as an admission that the plaintiff had asbestosis, because "it is highly doubtful, not impossible, that a physician would be subject to the control of nine asbestos manufacturers.").

[90] *See* H.E. Collins v. Wayne Corp., 621 F.2d 777, 781-82 (5th Cir. 1980) (allowing the admittance of an expert's deposition because Wayne Corp. claimed it had employed the expert to investigate and analyze a bus accident). *See also* In re the Chicago Flood Litigation, 93 C 1214, 1995 WL 437501 at *10 (N.D. Ill. July 21, 1995); Stanton & Hawthorne, Inc. v. Sierra Blanca Dev. Ltd., 82 Civ. 1914 (SWK), 1986 WL 6156 at *3 (S.D.N.Y. May 30, 1986).

corresponding increase in the degree to which courts recognize that those same employers must take responsibility for the vicarious admission of those "virtual" or "functional" employees.

48 PRACTICES

Denial of agency for vicarious admissions may have broad implications. When a client objects to the use of an independent contractor's or expert witness' statements as vicarious admissions, even though the subject of the statements is within the scope of work that such an individual has been retained to perform, this denial of agency that is sufficient to create vicarious admissions should be used against the client as a basis for denying any attorney-client privilege claims made for confidential communications shared with those employees. It is inconsistent for a client to claim, on the one hand, that a relationship is not close enough to produce vicarious admission, but, on the other hand, is still close enough to permit the client to share its most confidential communications without waiving the privilege protection.

B. Applications — Admissions

ONE

The plaintiff claimed that he was improperly discharged after an election. Testimony offered to establish that party affiliation played a role in the hiring practices of the new administration was a statement allegedly made by Ms. Pinero to Ms. Morales. Ms. Pinero was married to the mayor. It was claimed that this alleged statement was a vicarious admission by an agent of the mayor admissible under Rule 801(d)(2)(D) because she was part of his inner circle and was conducting interviews for him. The court concluded that insufficient evidence had been presented to establish an agency relationship between the mayor and Ms. Pinero because there was no independent evidence to corroborate the claimed agency. While the determination of whether foundation facts are established is usually left to the sound discretion of the trial judge, that discretion is not boundless and demands more than an intuitive judgment emanating from broad generalities. The fact that someone is married to another and has influence over him does not translate into an agency relationship between them. *Gomes v. Rivera Rodriguez*, 344 F.3d 103 (1st Cir. 2003).

TWO

An African-American woman, White, suffered abuse from co-workers. They used epithets like "jackass," "asshole," and "little black bitch." When her complaints were related to Megarry by union representatives, Megarry replied, "If the dumb nigger doesn't like it she can sign out." In her trial for constructive discharge the company, Honeywell, objected to the admission of these statements because they were hearsay and the last statement by management was made by a person who had died. The court concluded that they were not hearsay because they were vicarious admissions under Rule 801(d)(2)(D) and that the unavailability of the declarant was irrelevant. The court characterized the statement by Megarry as a "smoking gun." Honeywell also objected to the evidence claiming it was unfairly prejudicial. The court acknowledged that it was probably prejudicial in the context of a typical racial discrimination case, but the prejudice was fair. "The statement, if believed, demonstrates that management may have failed to take action on White's frequent complaints out of a discriminatory animus, and it helps to define the general work atmosphere, or the totality of the circumstances, so it matters little that White did not hear Megarry's statement. The statement also could have been used to explain why Megarry took no action on the complaints White says she made directly to him. The statement is also relevant in resolving the ultimate question of constructive discharge — whether the workplace was so racially abusive and hostile that a reasonable employee would have felt compelled to quit." *White v. Honeywell, Inc.*, 141 F.3d 1270 (8th Cir. 1989).

C. Co-Conspirator Admissions

PRINCIPLES

Admissions by co-conspirators are a classical form of vicarious admissions. Like statements by employees about matters within the scope of their employment or by partners relating to the joint enterprise of the partnership, those who have hired the employees or entered into a joint venture with the partners must bear the burden of explaining statements made by those representatives. They are admissible against all principles to the same extent as the principals' own statements. Like all other admissions, demonstrated personal knowledge by the declarant is not a precondition to the admissibility of such statements.

For co-conspirator admissions to be admissible, the proponent must prove (1) that the statements were made by a co-conspirator — one who has joined with another to commit a crime that could have been accomplished alone, (2) during the conspiracy — while it is still ongoing (before the objective has been accomplished), and (3) in furtherance of the conspiracy — more than just idle chatter.[91]

---

[91] *See* Bourjaily v. United States, 483 U.S. 171, 175-76 (1987) ("There must be evidence that there was a conspiracy involving the declarant and the nonoffering party, and that the statement was made 'during the course and in furtherance of the conspiracy.'").

RULE 801 FRE
Definition

The following definitions apply under this article:

. . . .

(d) Statements which are not hearsay. A statement is not hearsay if —

. . . .

(2) Admission by party-opponent. The statement is offered against a party and is . . . (E) a statement by a co-conspirator of a party during the course and in furtherance of the conspiracy. The contents of the statement shall be considered but are not alone sufficient to establish the declarant's authority under subdivision (C), the agency or employment relationship and scope thereof under subdivision (D), or the existence of the conspiracy and the participation therein of the declarant and the party against whom the statement is offered under subdivision (E).

49 PRACTICES

Existence of the conspiracy must be corroborated by independent evidence. Under the common law the existence of the conspiracy and the defendant's participation in it had to be established by evidence independent of the statement in question. That limitation was not explicitly incorporated into Rule 801(d)(2)(E). Therefore, the Supreme Court held that the content of the statement in question could be considered in determining whether these requirements are satisfied.[92] In response, Rule 801(d)(2)(E) was amended to *require* independent evidence of the elements of the co-conspirator admission in order to avoid the statement "pulling itself up by its own bootstraps." The statement in question can still be considered by the court, but is not sufficient by itself to support the finding.

50 PRACTICES

No charge of conspiracy necessary. To use the conspiracy admission theory a charge of conspiracy is not required.[93] This permits parties in both criminal and civil proceedings to surprise the opposition with evidence generated by third parties.

---

[92] *Bourjaily* at 182.

[93] *See* United States v. Peralta, 941 F.2d 1003, 1007 (9th Cir. 1991) (citing cases); United States v. Gil, 604 F.2d 546, 549-50 (7th Cir. 1979) ("[O]nce the existence of a joint venture of an illegal pur-

51 PRACTICES

Scope of co-conspirator admissions is broad. When the evidentiary foundation has been established by the proponent of the co-conspirator admissions, the conspiracy theory permits a far greater range of statements to be admitted than most appreciate. It permits every statement made by co-conspirators *before the defendant joined* the conspiracy to be used against him, as well as those made while he was a member.[94] During the conspiracy, it permits statements made by co-conspirators *after the defendant's apprehension* to be used against him if he does not take affirmative steps to withdraw from it — like turning government witness.[95] The theory in both instances is that the defendant affirmed all that preceded him by joining, and continues to benefit by all that follows, unless he demonstrates otherwise.

52 PRACTICES

The declaration against interest option. If the co-conspirator admissions rule is inapplicable, the statement of a third party will constitute hearsay when offered to prove the truth of the matter asserted and will be inadmissible unless it falls within an exception to the hearsay rule. If the declaration-against-interest exception is applicable because the statement was against the declarant's interest when it was made, and the declarant is available to testify,[96] the Sixth Amendment Confrontation Clause may be an insurmountable hurdle.

This Right of Confrontation announced by the Supreme Court in *Lilly v. Virginia*[97] precluded that use of declarations against the declarant's interests

---

pose, or for a legal purpose using illegal means, and a statement made in the course of and in furtherance of that venture have been demonstrated by a preponderance of the evidence, it makes no difference whether the declarant or any other 'partner in crime' could actually be tried, convicted and punished for the crime of conspiracy.").

[94] *See* United States v. United States Gypsum, Co., 333 U.S. 393, 364 (1948); United States v. Brown, 943 F.2d 1246, 1255 (9th Cir. 1991); United States v. Coe, 718 F.2d 830, 839 (7th Cir. 1983).

[95] *See* United States v. Ascarrunz, 838 F.2d 759, 762 (5th Cir. 1988); United States v. Taylor, 802 F.2d 1108, 1117 (9th Cir. 1986); and United States v. Disbrow, 768 F.2d 976, 982 (8th Cir. 1985).

[96] *See, e.g.,* Blackburn v. United Parcel Service, Inc., 179 F.3d 81, 96 (3d Cir. 1999) (stating the hearsay testimony therein may be admissible under Rule 801(d)(2)(A), Rule 801(d)(2)(D), or Rule 803(19) (reputation evidence concerning family history) but not 803(b)(4) because the proponent presented no evidence that the statements were against pecuniary, proprietary or penal interest of the declarant and made no showing that the declarant was unavailable). *See also* Copsey v. Swearingen, 36 F.3d 1336, 1348 (5th Cir. 1994) (finding a hearsay statement that did not fall under Rule 801(d)(2)(E) because it was not made during the course of the conspiracy inadmissible under Rule 804(b)(3) due to the declarant's availability); United States v. Myers, 892 F.2d 642, 644 (7th Cir. 1990) (noting that the hearsay statements inadmissible through Rule 801(d)(2)(A) were likely inadmissible under 804(b)(3) due to the declarant's availability).

that only collaterally inculpated the criminal defendant. The continued validity of that decision is in doubt after the Supreme Court's subsequent *Crawford* decision that radically altered the definition of the Right of Confrontation.[98] Under the most recent interpretation of the right, hearsay is only excluded if it was "testimonial" in nature when it was uttered. Since many declarations against interest are not (1) made under oath, or (2) made to authorities in a setting where the declarant could reasonably anticipate they would be used against someone in a judicial proceeding, collaterally inculpatory portions of declarations against interest may again pass constitutional muster. Under the declarations against interest rule in Fed. R. Evid. 804(b)(3), the Supreme Court has held that the rule (rather than the constitutional right) precludes collaterally inculpatory portions from being used against criminal defendants. Consequently, the evolving constitutional standard will not effect admissibility in federal courts unless the language of Rule 804(b)(3) is changed, or the existing language's interpretation (like the Confrontation Clause) is altered.

The older interpretation of the Right of Confrontation in the *Lilly* decision, that excluded collaterally inculpatory statements, was applicable only when hearsay was used against criminal defendants. The Sixth Amendment Confrontation Right creates the right only for criminal defendants. Therefore, the decision had no application to declarations against interest a criminal defendant might have used against the government, or to any hearsay that may have been used in civil proceedings. Therefore, even if the Court's new interpretation of the Confrontation Right in *Crawford* is construed as not changing the *Lilly* restriction, these other applications will still be available options when the co-conspirator admission rule is found to be inapplicable.

53 PRACTICES

How and when is the foundation established? Evidence must be presented to establish the factual foundation for the admission of co-conspirator admissions. If this is not resolved pretrial through a motion *in limine*, there are three general approaches to how this unfolds during a trial:

(1) *Structuring case.* The proponent can put her case into evidence so the foundation is established before efforts are made to elicit testimony from third parties about admissions by co-conspirators.

(2) *Evidentiary hearing.* If trial strategy dictates that the case begin with the admissions of co-conspirators, the presiding judge can exclude the jury from the courtroom and hold an evidentiary hear-

---

[97] Lilly v. Virginia, 527 U.S. 116, 144 L.Ed. 2d 117, 119 S. Ct. 1887 (1999).

[98] Crawford v. Washington, 541 U.S. 36, 124 S. Ct. 1354, 158 L. Ed. 2d 177 (2004). *See* **PRACTICES NO. 54**, *infra*.

ing. This may be the least favored approach because it delays the trial and results in testimony having to be presented twice — once to the judge and then again to the jury if the decision is favorable to the proponent.

(3) *Proffer of evidentiary foundation.* The most common procedure is for the proponent to make an oral proffer to the presiding judge regarding the evidence that will be presented. If the judge finds this evidence facially adequate, the proponent will be permitted to continue with the use of the co-conspirators' admissions based on his promise.[99] If the proponent fails to produce the evidence as described, there will be serious consequences:

- the co-conspirators' admissions will be held inadmissible;

- because the jury has already heard the damning evidence, there is no way to stuff the rabbit back into the hat. Consequently, a mistrial must be declared;

- the proponent will not be trusted in future trials when asked to accept evidence on a promise of connecting it up later.

D. Relationship of Admission Rules to Other Rules[100]

Rule 104(b). Preliminary Questions — Relevancy Conditioned on Fact. When an admission is offered, the proponent must authenticate that it was made by the opposing party or by one of that party's authorized agents. This issue is one of conditional relevance.[101] The same is true of the question of whether the elements of an implied admission by silence have been satisfied — (1) that the person to whom the admission is attributed heard the statement in question, (2) that he understood it, (3) that the statement's content was such that, had it not been true, a reasonable person would have responded to it, and (4) that there were no mental, physical, or emotional impediments that would have prevented the person to whom the admission is attributed from responding. Courts have consistently held that the elements are questions of conditional relevance for the jury, subject to the judge's preliminary determination that a reasonable jury could find that the proponent has fulfilled the requirements for admissibility.[102]

---

[99] *See generally* United States v. Vinson, 606 F.2d 149, 152-53 (6th Cir. 1979).

[100] PAUL R. RICE & ROY A. KATRIEL, EVIDENCE: COMMON LAW AND FEDERAL RULES OF EVIDENCE § 5.04 [A][3] (LEXIS 5th ed. 2005)

[101] United States v. Goichman, 547 F.2d 778, 784 (3d Cir. 1976).

[102] United States v. Moore, 522 F.2d 1068, 1075-76 (9th Cir. 1975).

The same is not true of the elements of the co-conspirators' admission. The Supreme Court, in *Bourjaily v. United States*,[103] held that these preliminary factual questions raise an issue of competence that must be determined by the trial judge pursuant to Rule 104(a). When making this decision, the Court in *Bourjaily* directed that the preponderance standard was to be employed.

Rule 105. Limited Admissibility. Rule 105 provides that when evidence is admissible for a limited purpose or against one party but not another, the court, upon request, must "restrict the evidence to its proper scope and instruct the jury accordingly." The timing of such a limiting instruction, however, is left to the trial judge's discretion. In *United States v. Garcia*,[104] two defendant co-conspirators requested that the trial judge give "contemporaneous" limiting instructions each time co-conspirator statements were admitted against some, but not all, of the eleven defendants. The court noted that "although there is some support for the proposition that Rule 105 mandates a contemporaneous limiting instruction, the weight of authority is to the contrary."[105] The court in *Garcia* upheld the trial judge's denial of the defendants' request for contemporaneous instructions.

Rule 407. Subsequent Remedial Measures

Rule 408. Compromise and Offers of Compromise

Rule 409. Payment of Medical and Similar Expenses

Rule 410. Inadmissibility of Pleas, Plea Discussion and Related Statements. The messages communicated by subsequent remedial measures, offers of compromise, payment of medical expenses and plea negotiations can logically be interpreted as admissions of certain prior conduct. All would be admissible as admissions except for the fact that they are expressly made privileged so that such conduct is encouraged.

Rule 611. Mode and Order of Interrogation and Presentation. The presiding judge is to resolve preliminary fact questions upon which the admissibility of a co-conspirator's statement will turn under Rule 104(a), but courts must resolve the proper timing for this determination. Must the proponent establish the factual conditions for admissibility before the co-conspirator's statement can be introduced? This has been left to the discretion of the court. *See*, **PRACTICES NO. 53** *supra*.

Rule 613. Prior Statements of Witnesses. A party opponent's prior statements are freely admissible against the opponent as admissions.[106] Foundations

---

[103] 483 U.S. 171, 175 (1987).

[104] 848 F.2d 1324, 1334-35 (2d Cir. 1988), *overruled on other grounds*, Gomez v. United States, 490 U.S. 858 (1989).

[105] *Id*. at 1335.

[106] *See, e.g.*, Owen v. Patton, 925 F.2d 1111, 1113 n.1 (8th Cir. 1991) (noting that the district court, allowing rebuttal testimony from Owen's investigator regarding McGee's inconsistent statement, may have admitted the testimony as a party admission due to proof that McGee was a former employee at Patton's tavern).

do not have to be laid, and personal knowledge does not have to be shown to have been possessed. If the party testifies, and his prior out-of-court admissions are inconsistent with his trial testimony, the requirements of Rule 613 — confronting the witness with the prior statement and giving him a chance to explain — are not applicable. If a witness' prior inconsistent or consistent statements are admissible under any exception to the hearsay rule, their admissibility is not influenced by what the witness does at the trial.

Rule 701. Opinion Testimony by Lay Witness. Rule 701 abolished the lay opinion rule. However, even when it was still active under the common law, it was not a limitation to using a party's statements against him. One will not be heard to object to either the form or basis of his own statements. He can explain the statements if he believes that they are misleading or inaccurate. Although the fairness of this practice is somewhat attenuated (particularly with former employees), the same is true of vicarious admissions of the agents of the party opponent.

Rule 702. Testimony by Experts. Any statement by an expert employed to assist a party in either business or litigation can be used against the party. So long as the statement is within the scope of the agent's responsibilities, and made while in the employ of the party, it constitutes a vicarious admission within Rule 801(d)(2)(D), regardless of where, when and to whom it was uttered. Statements made in an expert's report, during his deposition, or informally during a casual conversation are all vicarious admissions. *See* **PRINCIPLES NO. 88**, *supra*.

Rule 801(c). Hearsay. A statement is not hearsay if it is relevant to the action, independent of the truth of the matter asserted. In a conspiracy action, this can often arise if the government is establishing the existence of the conspiracy between certain individuals, independent of the conspiratorial admissions being offered for truth. Proving that an individual uttered certain words to another establishes that there was a relationship between the individuals, independent of the truth of the words that were uttered; it is the fact of the conversation that is important.[107] In another context, the Supreme Court made this same point in *Anderson v. United States*.[108] In *Anderson* the defendant was prosecuted for conspiracy to cast fictitious votes in an election. The Court held that testimony about what two of the defendants had previously stated in an election contest hearing was not hearsay because it was being proven only to establish that the statements were made. Through other evidence the prosecution was establishing that the statements were false.

Rule 801(d)(2). Admissions by Party-Opponent. Though statements by a codefendant do not fall within the co-conspirator's admissions provision of 801(d)(2)(E), they may still be admissible under other subsections of the admissions rule. If, for example, the statements were made after the conspiracy had

---

[107] *See* United States v. Calaway, 524 F.2d 609, 613 (9th Cir. 1975).

[108] 417 U.S. 211, 219 (1974).

ended, thereby precluding its use against other co-conspirators, it may still be used against the party who made the statement as an admission under Rule 801(d)(2)(A).[109] In addition, if a statement introduced against a party does not meet the requirements for a co-conspirator admission, it may still be admissible as an adoptive admission under Rule 801(d)(2)(B) if that party, through words or conduct, either affirmatively responds or fails to object to the assertion of a co-conspirator when he reasonably should have.[110]

Rule 803(2). Excited Utterance. Rule 801(d)(2)(E) requires exclusion of statements by co-conspirators not made "during and in furtherance of the conspiracy". Accordingly, statements made by co-conspirators after the conspiracy has ended (e.g., after all have been arrested) will not be admissible under 801(d)(2)(E). Such a statement, uttered by a co-conspirator after his arrest, however, still may be admissible under the excited utterance exception to the hearsay rule. For example, if after being arrested, a co-conspirator makes a relevant statement "while under the stress of excitement caused by a startling event or condition," the statement would be admissible as an excited utterance pursuant to Rule 803(2). In *United States v. Vazquez*[111] the defendant's post-arrest conduct after being implicated in the conspiracy by his "friend" was held admissible as an excited utterance.

Rule 901(a). Requirement of Authentication or Identification. An admission, whether oral or written, must be authenticated before it is admissible; the proponent must offer evidence that connects the statement to the party against whom it is offered. This can be accomplished in a number of ways. A witness who heard and saw the party make the statement can testify to its utterance by that party.[112] If no one heard the utterance or saw it written, someone familiar with the party's handwriting can identify it.[113] If someone heard the statement but was not with the party at the time (for example during a telephone conversation with him) that witness could testify that he recognized the other party's voice.[114] Finally, the circumstances surrounding the statement's utterance can serve to identify the speaker during a telephone conversation if the witness cannot recognize the speaker's voice. For example, the substance of the conversation may have been such that only a particular indi-

---

[109] *See, e.g.*, United States v. Copple, 827 F.2d 1182, 1189 (8th Cir. 1987).

[110] *See, e.g.*, United States v. Townsley, 843 F.2d 1070, 1084 (8th Cir. 1988).

[111] 857 F.2d 857, 864 (1st Cir. 1988).

[112] *See, e.g.*, Cuddy v. Wal-Mart Super Center, Inc., 993 F. Supp. 962, 967 (W.D. Va. 1998) (finding that the plaintiff's sworn averment that a tape recording contained a conversation between the plaintiff and an employee satisfied Rule 901(b)(1)).

[113] *See* FED. R. EVID. 901(b)(2) (allowing the opinion of a lay witness to authenticate handwriting).

[114] *See* United States v. Lopez, 758 F.2d 1517, 1520 (11th Cir. 1985), *cert. denied,* 474 U.S. 1054 (1986) (holding that the circumstances surrounding a taped telephone conversation can substantiate a claim that the recorded voice belonged to the defendant).

vidual or group of individuals with access to the information discussed could have been the speaker. The speaker also may have been returning a previous telephone call that the witness had made to him. If the call is returned and the speaker identifies himself as the one previously called, this is accepted as sufficient circumstantial evidence to authenticate the call for the purposes of admissibility.[115] It must be remembered, however, that the jury will make the ultimate determination of authenticity. Therefore, even though evidence of the admission is sufficiently authenticated to be admissible (there being sufficient evidence upon which a reasonable jury *could* find that it is authentic) the jury could still conclude that it was never made, or, if made, was not made by the person against whom it was offered.[116]

An admission can also be authenticated if it is part of business records produced in response to discovery demands. The opposing party's response authenticates the materials as being what the demanding party sought.[117]

A special problem of authentication arises if the caller who returned a previous telephone call could have been any one of multiple opposing parties, because neither the circumstances surrounding the call nor the content of the conversation specifically points to one of them. If the statement of one cannot bind the others, under some theory of vicarious admissions, is the authentication inadequate and the evidence therefore inadmissible? Borrowing from the new tort concept of group liability, the Second Circuit held that once the admission can be authenticated to the point of connecting it to a limited group of adversaries, the burden shifts to each of those adversaries to prove that he was not the one who engaged in the conversation (assuming, of course, that the jury believes that the conversation occurred in the first place).[118]

---

[115] *See* United States v. Kahn, 53 F.3d 507, 516 (2d Cir. 1995) (finding authenticity satisfied when the caller left a message and received a return telephone call); Noriega v. United States, 437 F.2d 435, 436 (9th Cir.), *cert. denied*, 402 U.S. 908 (1971) (finding that the call made by defendant was properly authenticated when the defendant provided the witness with a telephone number, after which the witness left a message for the defendant and the defendant returned the call). Courts have questioned, however, whether self-identification alone will satisfy the authenticity requirement. *Cf.* United States v. Puereta Restrepo, 814 F.2d 1236, 1239 (7th Cir. 1987) (finding self-identification by the speaker alone is not sufficient authentication); O'Neal v. Morgan, 637 F.2d 846, 850 (2d Cir. 1980), *cert. denied*, 451 U.S. 972 (1981) (holding self-identification sufficient when the person is called at a place where he reasonably could be expected to be); United States v. Orozco-Santillan, 903 F.2d 1262, 1266 (9th Cir. 1990) (determining when self-identification is coupled with additional circumstantial evidence demonstrating the person who answers the telephone to be the person who actually called, sufficient authentication exists).

[116] *See* United States v. Parker, 133 F.3d 322, 328 (5th Cir.), *cert. denied*, 523 U.S. 1142 (1998) (noting that once the government established a foundation through circumstantial evidence that the person on the telephone was the defendant, "it became the province of the jury to decide whether Mr. Parker was indeed the man on the phone and whether he made the threats.").

[117] *See, e.g.,* Ameropan Oil Corp. v. Monarch Air Serv., 92 C 3450, 1994 WL 86701, *3 (N.D. Ill. Mar. 16, 1994) ("[T]he [business] records [qualifying under 803(6)] are admissions by Monarch since they were produced pursuant to discovery demands.").

[118] *See* O'Neal v. Morgan, 637 F.2d 846, 852 (2d Cir. 1980).

VI. APPLICATIONS — HEARSAY RULE

The following are illustrations of the application of the hearsay rule. The only question being answered is whether it is hearsay, not whether it may still be admissible under an exception to the hearsay rule, discussed in the next section of the book.

Federal   Common
<u>**Rules   Law**</u>

YES NO YES NO
  X   X   1. On the issue of Michael's consciousness after the accident, Michael's statement, "The blue car ran the red light and hit me!"

<u>Explanation</u>: The statement is relevant because the declarant was able to utter it. The speaking of the words establishes consciousness. The content of the statement, and particularly the truth of the explicit message conveyed, is unimportant to the purpose for which it is being used. Consequently, the statement is not hearsay under either the common law or the federal rules.

YES NO YES NO
  X   X   2. To prove that Agnes shot her husband Fred, the fact that Agnes was seen fleeing their house at 4:14 p.m., fifteen minutes before his body was found in the bedroom. This is offered as an implied admission of her guilt by her conduct.

<u>Explanation</u>: The act of leaving the house immediately after the commission of the crime is relevant for two reasons. First, it proves that the defendant was present at the scene and, therefore, had the opportunity to commit the crime. Had the act been offered for this purpose it would not have been hearsay under either the common law or the federal rules. This conduct is also relevant because of the way the defendant fled. This suggests a consciousness of guilt on the part of the defendant and a need for her to flee. If offered as an implied admission of guilt, it is being offered for the truth of the matter impliedly asserted, and therefore is hearsay under the common law.

Under the Federal Rules of Evidence, the defendant would not have intended her act of fleeing to be an assertion of anything to anyone. Consequently, the conduct would have been nonassertive under Rule 801(a) and therefore not a "statement" within the definition of hearsay.

YES NO YES NO
X   X   3. As tending to prove Frank's insanity, the fact that he was committed to an insane asylum.

<u>Explanation</u>: The act of committing Frank to the asylum is relevant to proving his sanity only because it represents an implied assertion by those responsible for it that Frank needed the institutionalization — i.e., that Frank is insane. In

the problem, that implied assertion is being offered to prove the truth of the message it conveys. Consequently, it is hearsay under the common law. This act is also hearsay under the Federal Rules of Evidence because the act of committing someone to an asylum is an intentional assertion to the hospital by the attending physician that the patient should be committed.

YES NO YES NO
  X   X   4. In Baker's criminal trial for witness intimidation, the prosecution alleges that Baker intimidated a witness, Calhoun, who testified in a previous civil trial, with threats against his children. When called as a witness in the subsequent criminal trial, the prosecution elicits testimony from Calhoun as to Baker's statement to him the night before the civil trial to the effect, "If you testify against me, I'm going to break your children's legs."

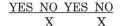

Explanation: The statement by Baker is an operative fact of the intimidation. The utterance of the words is actionable. The statement is not being offered to prove that Baker actually would have broken the legs of Calhoun's children. Consequently, it is not hearsay under either the common law or the federal rules.

YES NO YES NO
  X   X   5. At the criminal trial of Baker for aggravated battery on Calhoun's child, Calhoun is asked to repeat the threat that Baker made in the preceding problem, and this testimony is offered to prove that Baker was responsible for the child's injuries.

Explanation: Unlike Problem No. 4, the statement is now being offered to prove the truth of what Baker asserted — that he intended to harm Calhoun's children if certain events occurred. Thus, in this problem, the offer constitutes common law hearsay, but is nonhearsay as an admission under the federal rules.

YES NO YES NO
  X   X   6. Ralph observed Jim stop his car at a traffic light. On the issue of whether the light was red in the direction that Jim was traveling, Ralph's testimony describing his observation is offered at a subsequent civil action between two individuals who collided in the intersection.

Explanation: Jim's conduct is relevant to proving the color of the light only because we read the implied statement into it: "The light is red." The evidence of his conduct is being offered to prove the truth of this implied communication and, therefore, is hearsay under the common law.

Because Jim probably did not intend to communicate what is being read into his conduct, that conduct is nonassertive and therefore nonhearsay. The conduct would not constitute a "statement" under Federal Rule 801(a).

YES NO YES NO
  X   X   7. Jim stopped his car at a traffic light. As he did he commented to Ralph, a passenger reading a newspaper in the back seat, "I don't believe it. I've hit every one of these things wrong this evening." At the same moment, cars going in opposite directions collide as they enter the intersection. At the subsequent civil trial, Ralph is asked to repeat what Jim had said for the purpose of establishing that the light was red in the direction that he was traveling.

Explanation: The statement by Jim indirectly states what his conduct did in Problem No. 6 and is being offered to prove the truth of what he asserted. The only difference from Problem No. 6 is that Jim intended the implication that his words conveyed. This is not significant under the common law. Under the assertive/nonassertive distinction of the Federal Rules of Evidence, however, this would make the statement assertive, therefore a "statement" under Rule 801(a), and ultimately hearsay under Rule 801(c).

YES NO YES NO
  X   X   8. To prove that Esther was suffering from exhaustion, the fact that Dr. Barnes treated her for exhaustion.

Explanation: The conduct of Dr. Barnes is relevant because of his implied assertion through it that Esther has the condition for which he treated her. That assertion is being offered for its truth. Therefore, it is hearsay under the common law.

Inasmuch as Esther went to Dr. Barnes for treatment, Barnes probably intended his conduct in treating her as a statement to Esther that she had the condition for which he treated her. Therefore, his conduct would be assertive conduct that is hearsay under the federal rules as well as under the common law. The court could, however, reasonably find that the doctor had no intention of communicating anything through his treatment, in which case the conduct would not constitute a "statement" under 801(a).

YES NO YES NO
    X   X   9. To prove that Bobby and Pam are married, a witness will testify that she heard their exchange of nuptial vows.

Explanation: The vows are verbal acts. They are operative facts of a marriage. Their utterance, not the truth of their content, is what is important to proving the existence of the legal relationship. Therefore, the testimony regarding the vows is not hearsay either under the common law or the federal rules.

YES NO YES NO
 X   X   10. Jim was driving his car and had stopped at a traffic light. After waiting for a period of time, the driver in the car behind him honked his horn. Immediately after this occurred, cars going in opposite directions collided in the intersection. Ralph, a passenger in the car with Jim, who did not see the color of the light, is asked to testify about what the driver behind Jim had done, for the purpose of proving that the light had turned green in the direction that Jim was traveling.

Explanation: This is hearsay by conduct. By honking his horn, the driver in the car behind Jim was asserting that the light was green and that Jim should move through the intersection. That implied assertion is being offered for its truth. This conduct was also assertive under Rule 801(a) because the driver intended the communication conveyed by his conduct.

YES NO YES NO
 X   X   11. To prove that the insured died from accidental causes, the wife offers the death certificate in which that conclusion is stated.

Explanation: The certification is a written assertion of the cause of death by the individual who filled it out. It is being offered to prove the truth of what was asserted.

YES NO YES NO
 X   X   12. The plaintiff claims that the defendant manufacturing company should have punitive damages assessed against it because it failed to correct the defect in its product in a timely manner. The defendant claims it did not have notice of the defect prior to the time it took corrective actions. To prove this, it offers the testimony of the corporate president, who had one of his assistants review the customer letters that the defendant had received. The president will testify that the assistant's review failed to disclose a single complaint about the defect in question.

Explanation: The customers' silence presents no hearsay issue because it is not being used to prove anything that might be inferred from the silence, like the absence of any reason to complain. However, the president is aware of the absence of complaints only because one of his subordinates searched the files and told him that there were no complaints. This report from the subordinate is being offered for its truth and, therefore, is hearsay under both the common law and the federal rules.

YES NO YES NO
  X   X   13. To establish the time of an explosion, Susan will testify that immediately after witnessing the explosion she noted that the bank clock read 3:13 p.m.

Explanation: Although the clock reading technically is hearsay, courts have held that machines do not make statements within the scope of the hearsay rule. If properly authenticated through a sponsoring witness such as Susan, the hearsay dangers are resolved because the reliability of the information it provides is assured. Consequently, courts do not consider Susan's testimony as to the time of the explosion to be hearsay.

YES NO YES NO
  X   X   14. Ben is on the witness stand prepared to testify that Larry, the defendant's neighbor, told him that he (Larry) robbed the gas station attendant. Larry is in the courtroom.

Explanation: Larry's out-of-court statement is being offered for its truth. The fact that he is in the courtroom, subject to being called as a witness and cross-examined under oath does not influence the application of the hearsay rule. Consequently, the statement is still hearsay.

YES NO YES NO
     X X   15. To prove that the defendant committed the crime, the prosecution offers a confession that the defendant made to police.

Explanation: Under the common law, the confession is hearsay because the prosecution is offering the defendant's prior statement to prove the truth of what he admitted. Under the Federal Rules of Evidence, admissions by a party have been excluded from the definition of hearsay.

YES NO YES NO
  X   X   16. Lewis' widow has sued the Continental Insurance Company to collect the proceeds under her husband's life insurance policy. He fell from a window in the hospital where he was being treated for a gunshot wound. Continental denied the claim on the ground that the policy is ineffective because Lewis took his own life. To disprove suicide the widow offers the testimony of Baker. Baker is asked to repeat what Lewis had said to him the day before his death — that he, Lewis, was "anxious to get back to work" and that he was "looking forward to being with his friends again."

Explanation: His statements are relevant to proving that he had a desire to live only if they are believed for the truth of what he asserted about his feelings. Consequently, when offered in this action, the statements are hearsay. This is not an admission that is excluded from the definition of hearsay under Rule

801(d)(2) because a party cannot offer his own statement under that provision. Besides, it is not clear that the dead husband is the party plaintiff in this action.

YES NO YES NO

 X   X   17. Larry, Glenn, and Ben drive to a gas station. Glenn and Ben get out of the car then rush back minutes later ordering Larry to speed away. Larry asks Ben, "Did you get the dough?" To prove that Ben robbed the attendant, Larry offers to testify that Ben nodded his head in the affirmative in response to Larry's question.

Explanation: Ben's nod is equivalent to his having acknowledged through words that he robbed the gas station attendant. This acknowledgment is being offered to prove the truth of what he asserted and, therefore, is hearsay under the common law. It is also hearsay under the federal rules because Ben intended to communicate his affirmative acknowledgment to Larry. His nod, therefore, constitutes assertive conduct under the federal rules and is subject to the hearsay rule. Of course, if Ben were the defendant in the action in which this testimony was offered, it would not be hearsay under the Federal Rules of Evidence because it would constitute an admission.

YES NO YES NO

      X   X   18. Jane testified that she saw Sally steal a package of steaks.

Explanation: Jane's testimony as to what she saw Sally do is relevant to the issue of Sally's culpability for larceny independent of any communication that might be read into the conduct. Consequently, Jane's testimony is not hearsay.

YES NO YES NO

 X   X   19. After testifying that she saw Sally steal a package of steaks, Jane offers to testify: "I told Dick within one hour after the event that I had seen Sally take the steaks." Jane's statement is offered to prove that Sally stole the meat.

Explanation: Even though the hearsay dangers do not exist with a witness repeating his own prior consistent statement after having testified from memory to the same facts, courts at common law have stubbornly insisted on a wooden application of the rule that all out-of-court statements offered in court to prove the truth of what was previously asserted are hearsay. Under the federal rules, Jane's prior consistent statement would be hearsay unless offered to rebut a charge of recent fabrication.

YES NO YES NO

      X X   20. To prove that her husband was an alcoholic, Jeanette offers to testify that he attended Alcoholics' Anonymous meetings regularly for three years. The husband is a party to the action.

Explanation: His conduct is being interpreted as an admission of his alcoholism, and that admission is being offered for its truth. Thus, it is hearsay under the common law.

The husband obviously intended his membership in the organization as an admission of his condition inasmuch as treatment of alcoholism is the purpose of the organization. Therefore, his conduct would be an assertion under the Federal Rules of Evidence (assertive conduct) and, as a consequence, subject to the hearsay rule. However, admissions are excluded from the hearsay rule under Rule 801(d)(2).

If the husband is <u>not a party</u>, then the answer is Yes, Yes.

YES NO YES NO
   X   X   21. To prove that her husband severely punished their children, Katherine offers to testify that the buttocks and legs of her children were usually covered with bruises.

Explanation: The facts were known to Katherine from personal observation. Those facts are independently relevant because they are evidence of the physical abuse that the children suffered. Consequently, Katherine's testimony is not hearsay.

YES NO YES NO
   X   X   22. On the issue of Jameson's adverse possession of Blackacre, Aaronson testifies that Jameson stated to him many times: "I paid $10,000 for this piece of land."

Explanation: To establish title to property under a claim of adverse possession, the adverse possessor must possess under a color or claim of title. This statement fulfills that requirement by its mere utterance. Therefore, its utterance is an operative fact of adverse possession.

YES NO YES NO
   X   X   23. The Government seized certain carrier pigeons from Borg. To prove that the carrier pigeons were stolen, the Government offers testimony that when the pigeons were released they flew back to the various owners from whom pigeons had been stolen.

Explanation: A court will not interpret the pigeons' conduct as a statement. Through a proper foundation explaining the conduct of pigeons, a court will interpret the pigeons' actions as circumstantial evidence of who their rightful owners are.

YES NO YES NO
  X   X   24. To prove that Mavis is insane, her children testify that she built a large bird's nest in the tree in front of their house and sits in it during the day.

Explanation: The act of building a bird's nest proves insanity only if we read into the act the assertion that the builder <u>believes</u> that she is a bird. If she were building it as a project for her ornithology class to demonstrate the complexities of the undertaking, it would probably have no relevance to her sanity. If offered to prove that Mavis is insane, the proponent is interpreting Mavis' conduct as a sincere statement of what she believes she is. Many courts, however, will ignore the subtle hearsay implications of this evidence of Mavis' conduct and will admit the conduct as circumstantial evidence of her insanity on the belief that the act of building the nest is an act of insanity independent of any communication inferred from it. Under the Federal Rules of Evidence, a court would likely interpret this conduct as nonassertive and therefore not a statement within the definition of hearsay.

YES NO YES NO
  X   X   25. In a sex discrimination action, the defendant testifies that he discharged Gloria Bean because he had been told that she had been arrested for selling classified documents to a foreign government.

Explanation: As an explanation of the reason for his conduct, the defendant is not repeating the story that he had been told about Ms. Bean for the purpose of proving the truth of what was asserted — that she had sold classified documents to foreign governments. Regardless of whether she actually committed the act of which she was accused, the defendant could have discharged her for this reason and not be guilty of sex discrimination. Because the story has relevance independent of the truth of the matter asserted, it is not hearsay under either the common law or the federal rules.

YES NO YES NO
X   X   26. Jacoby sues Morris for the conversion of Jacoby's car. To establish the car's value, Jacoby offers the receipt that he received from the dealer when he purchased the car the week preceding the alleged conversion.

Explanation: This is a written statement by the dealer of what the purchaser paid for the car. It is being offered into evidence for the truth of what the dealer wrote. Thus, it is hearsay.

YES NO YES NO
X   X   27. On the issue of whether Danny struck Paul, Paul offers the testimony of Sarah that she heard Ross say that Danny had confessed that he had hit Paul.

Explanation: Under the common law this is double hearsay. Danny's admission is being offered to prove the truth of what he acknowledged. We only know that he made an admission, however, because Ross told Sarah. Consequently, Ross's statement about what Danny uttered is also hearsay. Sarah does not have first-hand knowledge of what Ross heard or of what Danny did. When offered against Danny, only his part of the hearsay chain would be eliminated under the Federal Rules of Evidence because it is an admission.

YES NO YES NO
  X   X   28. On the issue of whether Danny struck Paul in self-defense (under a reasonable belief that his safety was endangered), Sarah testifies that she heard Tom say to Danny shortly before the fight, "You better watch out, Paul is out to get you."

Explanation: The statement that Tom made to Danny is relevant to the defense of self-defense because having heard it, Danny is justified in reacting in a certain way. The truth of what Tom said is irrelevant. Consequently, the statement is not hearsay.

YES NO YES NO
  X   X   29. In the above question, the testimony is offered on the issue of whether Paul was the first aggressor in the fight with Danny.

Explanation: Unlike Problem No. 28, the statement is now being offered to prove the truth of what Tom said — that Paul was out to get Danny, and therefore that Paul was likely the first aggressor. Under these circumstances, the statement is hearsay.

YES NO YES NO
  X   X   30. To prove that the defendant was a participant in an illegal demonstration, the prosecution offers into evidence a photograph of the demonstration that shows the defendant carrying a placard.

Explanation: Photographs are not assertions by cameras. Once the camera and its product are properly authenticated by a sponsoring witness, the photograph will be admitted as demonstrative evidence.

YES NO YES NO
  X   X   31. In an action in which the plaintiff claimed inheritance rights in the estate of Peter Hooper, the plaintiff testifies that his great-great-great grandfather was the brother of Hooper's great-great-grandfather.

Explanation: Although the plaintiff is stating the fact as if he had first-hand knowledge of it, he obviously does not. The plaintiff clearly obtained his information about family history from other sources. Because the plaintiff is offering this information for its truth, it is hearsay under both the common law and the federal rules.

YES NO YES NO
 X   X 32. Anderson hits Brown with his car. Brown dies from the injuries received. While in the ambulance after the accident, Brown said to the attendant, "Anderson finally carried through on one of his threats." Brown's estate sues Anderson for his negligence and/or willful conduct that resulted in Brown's death. On the issue of damages resulting from his consciousness and the pain and suffering that he therefore experienced, the estate offers Brown's statement to the attendant.

Explanation: Brown's statement is relevant to the issue of damages because the mere utterance of it established his consciousness. Consequently, it is not hearsay. In some instances, the court may limit the attendant's testimony to the fact that Brown was conscious and spoke, rather than letting in the full statement.

YES NO YES NO
 X X   33. The police raid the Price residence on a tip that it is a betting establishment. The local Baptist minister observes the raid and calls the telephone number listed for Price. When an unfamiliar voice answers, the minister assumes it is the police and states, "I'm glad you people finally realized that Price's place is a betting establishment. Good work!" The prosecution subsequently offers the minister's statement at Price's trial to prove the establishment's nature.

Explanation: The minister's statement is being offered to prove the truth of what he asserted — that Price's home was a betting establishment. Thus, it is hearsay both under the common law and the federal rules.

YES NO YES NO
 X X   34. Arnett and Block live in a jurisdiction where there is a "good Samaritan" statute which requires citizens to render aid to those in emergency need. Arnett had an accident and was in such need. He said to Block, who happened to be passing by, "My side hurts; I feel like my chest is crushed. Please help me!" Because Block failed to render assistance, Arnett later sued him. To establish that Block was aware of Arnett's condition, Arnett offers the testimony of Walls, who saw but did not hear the interchange between Arnett and Block and whom Arnett later told what he had said to Block.

Explanation: Although Arnett's statement to Block is being offered for a non-hearsay purpose — notice of need — Walls does not have personal knowledge of what Arnett said. He only saw a verbal interchange. His testimony is only as reliable as Arnett's assertion to him. Consequently, any testimony by Walls as to what Arnett said is hearsay.

YES NO YES NO

  X   X

35. While Anderson is driving his car with Baker and Carr as passengers, Baker looks over at the speedometer and remarks to Anderson, "You know, I'm in no hurry!" This statement is offered in a tort action by Carr against Anderson for injuries that Carr suffered in an accident that occurred immediately after the remark. The statement is offered on the issue of proximate cause.

Explanation: This statement is an implied assertion by Baker that Anderson was speeding. Baker intended the implied message, and it is being offered to prove the truth of what he intended to assert. Therefore, it is hearsay under both the common law and the Federal Rules of Evidence.

YES NO YES NO

  X   X

36. To prove that Bobby and Pam are married, a witness will testify that she received a wedding announcement in the mail.

Explanation: The announcement is only a statement of the couple's intention of getting married. Unlike the utterance of the wedding vows, this is not an operative fact of the marriage. It tends to prove the marriage only if it is accepted as an accurate statement of the declarants' intent. Consequently, the testimony concerning the wedding announcement is hearsay. Of course, if this evidence were offered against either Bobby or Pam, it would not be hearsay under the Federal Rules of Evidence because it would constitute an admission.

YES NO YES NO

       X   X

37. To prove that John is David's father, Mary offers evidence that John often referred to David as "my son."

Explanation: His acknowledgment that the child is his son is being offered for the truth of that acknowledgment. Thus, testimony of the acknowledgment is hearsay. As an admission it would not be hearsay under the Federal Rules of Evidence.

YES NO YES NO

  X   X

38. To prove that Danny was selling marijuana, an undercover policeman offers to testify that when he answered the phone at Danny's apartment, a voice asked, "At a nickel a bag — can I get fifty?"

Explanation: The attempt to place the order for marijuana with Danny implies that Danny sells marijuana and is being offered to prove the truth of what the caller believed and impliedly asserted. The reliability of the evidence turns on the untested accuracy of that belief. Not only may the caller's source of information be unreliable, he may have dialed the wrong number. Thus, the call is hearsay under the common law. Because the evidence is inferred from a verbal communication, it should also be considered assertive under Rule 801(a). Many courts and commentators, however, have required that the declarant (here the caller) intend to communicate the indirect message being inferred from the speech before considering the speech to be "assertive." Because the caller in this problem probably did not intend the inferred message, courts adopting this interpretation of the assertive/nonassertive distinction would not classify this call as hearsay.

YES NO YES NO
  X   X   39. After a plane crash, on the issue of survivorship, a rescue worker will testify that twenty minutes after impact, one of the victims cried: "I am alive!"

Explanation: The statement is relevant to prove that a passenger survived the crash by the fact that it was uttered. The fact that the statement's content is identical to what it is being offered to prove is simply coincidental. Regardless of what was said, the utterance would still have proven that someone survived the crash. Because the statement is relevant regardless of the truth of the matter asserted, it is not hearsay.

YES NO YES NO
 X   X   40. To prove that the defendant committed the act upon which the plaintiff's claim of liability is premised, the plaintiff offers into evidence a certified copy of a prior judgment of conviction for the same offense.

Explanation: This is a written account of the entry of judgment in a prior criminal case based either on a plea or on a verdict of guilty by the finder of facts. It represents an implied assertion of guilt because it is premised on such a conclusion, and it is being offered to prove the truth of the matter impliedly asserted. Thus, it is hearsay.

YES NO YES NO
 X   X   41. To prove that the defendant committed the act forming the basis of a plaintiff's cause of action, the plaintiff offers a witness to testify that he was present and observed the jury return a verdict of guilty in a prosecution of the defendant for a similar prior offense.

Explanation: The previous verdict that the witness observed being returned represents a collective assertion by the jury that the defendant was proven guilty of the offense charged beyond a reasonable doubt. That collective assertion is now being offered to prove the truth of the matter asserted — factual guilt. Therefore, it is hearsay.

YES NO YES NO
   X   X   42. In an action to enjoin the display of a nativity scene on the steps of the city building because it is an uncon-

stitutional use of public property as a place of worship, the plaintiff testifies that the leader of the group gathered around the scene and stated: "This is Jesus Christ, the Son of the living God, who was sent by God to save the world." This is offered to establish the nature of the use.

Explanation: The nature of the use is determined by what people did and said while around the scene. The words spoken establish the purpose for which the scene was used independent of the truth of what was said. Thus, the words are not hearsay.

YES NO YES NO
  X   X   43. Jackson gives a detailed demonstration of how he committed a crime. This is recorded on video tape. The tape is later offered at Jackson's trial to prove that he was the assailant.

Explanation: Jackson is confessing through his conduct. He is asserting that he committed the crime in the manner in which he acted it out, and that assertion is being offered to prove that what he described through his conduct was true. Thus, it is hearsay under the common law. Even though Jackson intended to describe the way he committed the crime, this conduct would not be hearsay under the Federal Rules of Evidence because it would be an admission under Rule 801(d)(2).

YES NO YES NO
  X   X   44. The police found contraband wrapped in a shirt that contained a label with the defendant's name on it. The prosecution offers this label at the defendant's criminal trial to establish his ownership of the shirt and possession of the contraband.

Explanation: The prosecution is proving ownership of the shirt (and, in turn, possession of the contraband wrapped in it) through the written assertion of ownership that is attached to the shirt. The reliability of that tag as an indication of ownership is dependent upon the perception, memory, and sincerity of the individual who placed it there. Therefore, its use as evidence of ownership makes it common law hearsay, though it is an admission under the federal rules.

Interestingly, Wigmore would call this nonhearsay by labeling it a "mechanical trace" that shows that at a previous time a certain act was or was not done. 1 WIGMORE ON EVIDENCE § 25 (3d ed. 1940). *See United States v. Snow*, 517 F.2d 441 (9th Cir. 1975). This description, however, is as meaningless as McCormick's label "the verbal part of an act" to characterize the telephone calls to the betting establishment as nonhearsay evidence of the establishment's character. In both instances the distinguished professors are trying to hide the hearsay dangers created by the use of the evidence behind the screen of a descriptive label. In this sense the label "mechanical trace" is also like the ploy of correctly labeling hearsay evidence circumstantial evidence because of the indirect manner in which it proves the proposition to which it is directed and then concluding that such evidence must not be hearsay because of that characterization.

YES NO YES NO
   X   X   45. Sheriff Vinson was accused of taking bribes. Undercover agents set up a payoff through one of the complainants and made payment to an intermediary for the sheriff in an envelope marked "Sheriff Charles Vinson." This envelope was later found in the Sheriff's possession and offered at his trial to establish his receipt of the payment.

Explanation: The substantive message that might be conveyed by the words placed on the envelope (i.e., ownership by Sheriff Charles Vinson) is irrelevant to the purpose for which the evidence is being used. The words are nothing more than identifying markings that allow the police to trace the possession of the envelope and the bribe money it contained. The fact that the name and the identity of the individual ultimately found with the envelope are the same is simply coincidental. The use of the evidence would have been no different had the identifying mark been a picture of a duck instead of the name of the defendant. By contrast, an example of when the introduction of evidence of a name would constitute hearsay is where the name is on a laundry label in a shirt, and the label is being offered to prove that the shirt belonged to the person whose name appears on it. Unlike in the above problem, the reliability of the evidence then depends on the perception of ownership by the person responsible for placing the name in the shirt and the sincerity with which he performed that act.

YES NO YES NO
   X   X   46. To prove that the defendant was aware of his faulty automobile brakes, the plaintiff introduces evidence of the defendant's past attempts to have the brakes repaired.

Explanation: One cannot complain about a condition without possessing knowledge about the condition of which he is complaining. The defendant's prior conduct proves that he had knowledge of the faulty brakes without any message being read into it. Thus, the conduct is not hearsay.

YES NO YES NO
   X   X   47. On the issue of whether David struck Paul, Willis testifies that he saw David strike Paul.

Explanation: The testimony is not hearsay because Willis is testifying to an act that he personally observed and that has independent relevance to the cause of action.

YES NO YES NO
  X   X

48. In an action for personal injuries by a guest in an automobile against the automobile's owner, the owner's defenses are contributory negligence and assumption of the risk. At the trial a second passenger offers to testify that an hour before the accident, in the presence of the plaintiff, a mechanic said: "The front axle on your car is in bad shape. It could break any time." This statement is offered to prove that the axle was defective.

Explanation: The utterance of the mechanic is being offered to prove the truth of what he told the driver of the car — that the axle was defective. Thus, the statement is hearsay.

YES NO YES NO
     X   X

49. The same facts as in Problem No. 48, except that the testimony is offered to prove assumption of the risk.

Explanation: Unlike Problem No. 48, the mechanic's statement is being offered here to prove only that the mechanic uttered it. Having been uttered in the plaintiff's presence, the plaintiff would have had notice of the potential defect, and if he stayed in the car despite this notice, he would have assumed the risk of the defect that was there. Thus, the statement is not hearsay when offered for this purpose. Of course, other evidence would have to have been presented in the case to establish that the axle was defective and that it was the cause of a subsequent wreck.

YES NO YES NO
  X   X

50. Shawna is a five-year-old child. While attending kindergarten her teacher noticed a red mark on her neck that resembled what is commonly referred to as a "hickey." When questioned about it she responded that her stepfather had "sucked on it [her neck]." This aroused a suspicion of sexual abuse, and the teacher summoned the school psychologist. When Shawna later talked with this psychologist and the teacher she could not explain what had been done to her by her stepfather, so the psychologist had Shawna demonstrate on an anatomically correct doll the various acts. In a later judicial proceeding against the stepfather, would testimony by the psychologist or teacher regarding what they observed Shawna demonstrating be hearsay?

Explanation: The answer depends on the purpose for which the testimony is offered. If offered to explain why there was probable cause to issue a warrant for the stepfather's arrest, it would not be hearsay. The issue upon which it is being offered in these two instances would not require that the story being told by Shawna be accepted for its truth. The issue is simply the reasonableness of the action taken by the magistrate who issued the warrant, which turns solely on the reasonableness of the conclusions that could have been reached by him based on what he was told the school officials observed, totally independent of what was actually true. If, on the other hand, the child's demonstration were being repeated to prove that she was actually abused in the ways that she demonstrated, the testimony would be hearsay. Even though the child did not orally describe what she had experienced, her conduct spoke as clearly as her words could have, and the reliability of the communication depends on the quality of her perception, memory, and sincerity. *State v. McCafferty*, 356 N.W.2d 159 (S.D. 1984).

YES NO YES NO
  X   X   51. In a prosecution for conspiracy to grow massive amounts of marijuana indoors, the government offered into evidence two notes that were discovered during a search for a warehouse. These contained instructions regarding maintenance of the plants.

Explanation: The relevance of the notes does not turn on the truth of their content. They are being offered because they are relevant to establishing the purpose for which the warehouse was being operated by those who sent and received the communications.

VII. EXCEPTIONS TO THE HEARSAY RULE — FORMER TESTIMONY

A. PRINCIPLES

The former testimony exception allows a party to use the testimony of a witness who testified in a previous proceeding but is unavailable when his testimony is needed at a subsequent trial. From the extreme position of requiring that both *the parties and the issues* in the former and subsequent proceedings be *identical* before the exception was applicable, courts have permitted both the parties and the issues to vary, if the party against whom the testimony was first offered had the *same interest and motive to develop the testimony* as the party against whom it is proposed to be offered.[119] This is true, however, *only in civil proceedings*. In criminal cases, the testimony from a prior proceeding can only be used against the same party in a subsequent proceeding.[120]

---

[119] *See* New Jersey Turnpike Auth. v. PPG Indus., Inc., 197 F.3d 96, 110 n.21 (3d Cir. 1999) (noting merely "a shared interest in the material facts and outcome of the case" will suffice to establish a predecessor in interest relationship). *Compare* Lloyd v. American Expert Lines, Inc., 580 F.2d 1179, 1187 (3d Cir. 1978).

[120] It has generally been believed that this result is compelled by the Sixth Amendment Right of Confrontation. In addition, the language of Rule 804(b)(1) compels this result in federal courts. *See* United States v. Salerno, 505 U.S. 317, 322 (finding the defendants could admit under Rule 804(b)(1) grand jury transcripts of witnesses who invoked their Fifth Amendment privilege against

In the previous proceeding, the now unavailable witness must have been under oath, and the party against whom the testimony is now offered (or a predecessor in a civil action or proceeding) must have had an *opportunity* to cross-examine.

RULE 804 FRE
Hearsay Exceptions: Declarant Unavailable

. . . .

(b) Hearsay exceptions. — The following are not excluded by the hearsay rule if the declarant is unavailable as a witness.

(1) Former testimony. — Testimony given as a witness at another hearing of the same or a different proceeding, or in a deposition taken in compliance with law in the course of the same or another proceeding, if the party against whom the testimony is now offered, or, in a civil action or proceeding, a predecessor in interest, had an opportunity and similar motive to develop the testimony by direct, cross, or redirect examination.

54 PRACTICES

Misapplication of confrontation right? Historically, prior testimony has not been admissible against a criminal defendant unless he was the person against whom it was previously used. It was believed that the criminal defendant's right to confront his accuser compelled this restriction. As that right has been interpreted and reinterpreted in Supreme Court decisions over the past several decades, the use of prior testimony against a different criminal defendant may not have violated his Confrontation right. The Court's recent decision in *Crawford v. Washington,*[121] however, creates uncertainty about the continued validity of all prior Confrontation decisions.

The broadest reading of the Confrontation Right was in *Ohio v. Roberts,*[122] when the Court held that the right imposed two obligations on the government: (1) to use reasonable efforts to obtain the presence of the declarant as a witness; and (2) to use only hearsay statements of the declarant that have some indicia of reliability. Since *Roberts*, the Court has consistently cut back

---

self-incrimination only upon a specific showing of similar motive); United States v. DiNapoli, 8 F.3d 909, 913 (2d Cir. 1993) (en banc) (precluding the admission of grand jury transcripts because "the situation is not necessarily the same [when] the two proceedings are different in significant respects, such as their purposes or the applicable burden of proof.").

[121] 541 U.S. 36, 124 S. Ct. 1354, 158 L. Ed. 2d 177 (2004).

[122] 448 U.S. 56, 66 (1980).

on its interpretation of what obligations this right imposes.[123] Therefore, the restriction in criminal cases may be unwarranted. If a verbatim transcript of the prior proceedings is available, and the former party against whom it was offered had the same interest and motive to develop the testimony (and, in fact, did so) there is no compelling reason for excluding the evidence, other than the fact that Rule 804(b)(1) still requires it.

In *Crawford* the Court shifted the focus of the Confrontation Right from the government's obligation to use best efforts to physically produce the witness at trial, to the "testimonial" nature of the hearsay statement when it was uttered. If the statement was of a "testimonial" nature (a term that the Court did not define with any particularity), the criminal defendant appears to have an absolute right to confront the witness. Consequently, the right afforded to criminal defendants in Rule 804(b)(1), which may not have been compelled under *Roberts*, may now be compelled under *Crawford* because prior testimony is unquestionably of a "testimonial" nature. Whether that translates into an absolute right to cross-examine, or whether the cross-examination by another who shares the same interest and motive to develop the testimony will suffice, is yet to be determined.

Even if the restriction on prior testimony offered against the criminal defendant is not constitutionally compelling, the restriction on the criminal defendant's right to offer prior testimony *against the government* has no constitutional basis. Only the criminal defendant, and not the government, is given the right of confrontation in the Bill of Rights. In addition, precluding a criminal defendant from offering exculpatory testimony from a state prosecution simply because the prosecution was previously a state, and now is the federal government, probably violates the defendant's right to due process of law.[124] To avoid the restrictions in Rule 804(b)(1), parties should offer the prior testimony under the residual exception in Rule 807. Courts have held that if the proponent can demonstrate circumstantial guarantees of trustworthiness, there is no reason for excluding the evidence.[125]

---

[123] *See, e.g.*, White v. Illinois, 502 U.S. 346 (1992) (finding the right to confrontation does not prevent admission of spontaneous declarations and statements made in the course of receiving medical care because "such out-of-court declarations are made in contexts that provide substantial guarantees of their trustworthiness."); *Bourjaily* 483 U.S. at 182 (1987) (holding the Sixth Amendment right to confrontation does not require a showing of independent indicia of reliability in order to admit the hearsay statement of the out-of-court declaration of a co-conspirator); United States v. Inadi, 475 U.S. 387, 394-96 (1986) (rejecting the proposition that the right to confrontation requires a showing of unavailability before admitting the hearsay statements of a co-conspirator.).

[124] *See* Chambers v. Mississippi, 410 U.S. 284, 295-97 (1973) (correctly interpreting an established rule followed nationwide that restricted the defendant from using reliable declarations against interest against the government violated his right to due process of law because the rule precluded him from presenting reliable witnesses in his defense).

[125] *See, e.g.*, United States v. Guinan, 836 F.2d 350, 353-54 (7th Cir. 1988).

55 PRACTICES

Two levels of hearsay with most prior testimony. When prior testimony is being offered in a judicial proceeding, usually two levels of hearsay need to be addressed: (1) the testimony at the former trial and (2) the transcript through which the testimony is established. Only the first level is resolved by the prior testimony exception. The second level can be resolved with several different exceptions:

(1) *Present sense impression, 803(1) FRE* — because the transcription was created simultaneously with the testimony.

(2) *Recorded recollection, 803(5) FRE* — if the reporter appears as a sponsoring witness, identifies the transcript, authenticates its accuracy when made and testifies that he cannot fully and adequately recall all that the witness said.

(3) *Business records — records of regularly conducted activity, 803(6) FRE* — if it is established that the transcript was made from personal knowledge, pursuant to a business duty, at or near the time of the event and that the court relies on the transcript.

(4) *Public records and reports, 803(8)(B) FRE* — if the court reporter is considered a government employee, the transcript was made from personal knowledge and it was made pursuant to a public duty.

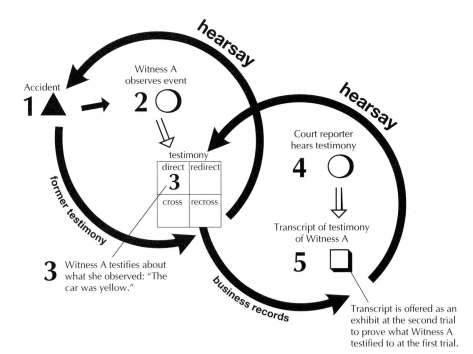

56 PRACTICES

Objections to the form of the question. Under Fed. R. Evid. 611(c), the party calling the witness generally should not use leading questions on direct examination. If such questions are asked and answered without an objection by the opposing party, the objection will not be heard when the transcript of that testimony is being offered in a later proceeding. The failure to object serves as a waiver of objections to the form of the question. This rule is based on fairness to the proponent who will not be in a position at a later time to rephrase the question. The same is not true of *substantive* objections — for example, that the testimony calls for inadmissible hearsay. Although the objection is belatedly interposed, the proponent is in no worse position than he would have been in had the objection been made timely.

57 PRACTICES

Failure to cross-examine a witness when he first testified. If a party was given an opportunity to cross-examine a witness at the first trial and chose to waive it, like failing to object to the form of a question, *see above*, it is waived for the subsequent trial as well. The only exception to this rule is when the party against whom the prior testimony is being offered can show that he does not have the same interest and motive to cross-examine at the first trial as he does at the second. This argument seldom succeeds when the second trial is the product of a reversal and remand. Because both the parties and the issues are usually the same, fairness dictates that the proponent of the prior testimony not be deprived of the evidence because of a tactical decision at the first trial.

If, however, the prior testimony was from a different civil action that involved different parties, it is easier to establish that the interests and motive may not have been the same. Even if the parties and issues were substantially similar in the prior civil action (for example arising from the same nucleus of operative facts), the fact that the witness was not cross-examined, and the need for cross-examination is apparent in the context in which it is subsequently being used, establishes a *prima facie* case of different interests and motives.

B. Relationship of Prior Testimony to Other Rules[126]

Rule 801(d)(1)(A). The Available Witness — Prior Inconsistent Testimony. When a witness has given prior inconsistent testimony that has been

---

[126] Paul R. Rice & Roy A. Katriel, Evidence: Common Law and Federal Rules of Evidence § 5.03[A][3] (LEXIS 5th ed. 2005)

recorded, that testimony can be introduced for its truth even though the declarant is available. Rule 801(d)(A) is the flip side of 804(b)(1), former testimony, where the declarant must be shown to be unavailable before his testimony is admissible. Unlike former testimony in Rule 804(b)(1), former testimony in Rule 801(d)(1)(A) need not have been made in a previous action involving the same issues or parties with a similar interest and motive to develop the testimony. The reliability of this evidence derives from the fact that it is used while at, so to speak, the horse's mouth.

Rule 801(d)(2). Admission by Party Opponent. When the former testimony of a party opponent is being offered, none of the conditions of Rule 804(b)(1) has to be satisfied.

Rule 807. Other Exceptions. Even though the limitations of Rule 804(b)(1) have not been satisfied, prior testimony before a grand jury (where the defendant has no right to cross-examine) has been admitted against a criminal defendant when there has been a demonstration that the testimony was trustworthy.[127] Such a use does not violate the broadest contemporary interpretation of the Confrontation clause in *Ohio v. Roberts*.[128] The residual exception was not discussed as a possibility when the defendant attempted to use grand jury testimony against the government. Although the same government was subsequently prosecuting the accused, the Court was not convinced that the government had the same interest and motive to develop the testimony for the grand jury that they had had during the defendant's trial.[129]

Rule 902. Self-Authentication. If the court reporter's transcript is certified, it will be self-authenticating under Rule 902(8).[130] This will satisfy the bottom level of hearsay — proving that the testimony was actually given. To satisfy the top link of hearsay — the testimony to prove the truth of what was previously testified about — the proponent must establish the elements of prior testimony exception. If the party against whom the testimony is being offered is not a party involved in the previous litigation, and it is not being offered on the same issue, the introduction of this evidence might involve an extensive evidentiary hearing on the issue of whether the previous party had the same interest and motive to develop the testimony.

C. Applications — Prior Testimony Exception

ONE

Acosta is charged with conspiracy to distribute marijuana. At his preliminary hearing his wife testifies in his defense. Despite her testimony, Acosta is bound

---

[127] *See* United States v. Guinan, 836 F.2d 350, 353-54 (7th Cir. 1988).

[128] 448 U.S. 56 (1980).

[129] United States v. Salerno, 505 U.S. 317 (1992).

[130] *See, e.g.,* Airlie Found, Inc. v. United States, 826 F. Supp. 537, 546 (D.D.C. 1993) (finding "[c]ertified transcripts of prior testimony may be used [on] a motion for summary judgment").

over to the grand jury, which indicted him. At his subsequent trial he claims that his wife is unavailable to testify because her child is ill, and she has to stay home to care for him. Acosta, therefore, offers the transcript of her prior testimony at the preliminary hearing. The burden of proving unavailability of a witness under Rule 804(a) rests on the proponent of the hearsay. Here the defendant has not carried that burden. He has offered no evidence that he requested his wife to testify or that she had refused to do so. There was no medical testimony as to the nature or severity of the child's illness or that the child's health would be jeopardized by the mother's absence. Moreover, there was no pretrial motion for a continuance in order to produce the witness at a later time. Therefore, because the defendant has failed to establish his wife's unavailability, her prior testimony at the preliminary hearing is not admissible at the defendant's subsequent trial under the former testimony exception to the hearsay rule. *United States v. Acosta*, 769 F.2d 721 (11th Cir. 1985).

TWO

Peter Tecott testified before the grand jury during the criminal investigation of James Huxtable's gambling activities. The grand jury subsequently indicted Huxtable for income tax evasion. After Huxtable's indictment, but before trial, Tecott died in an automobile accident. As part of his case-in-defense, Huxtable seeks to introduce Tecott's exculpatory grand jury testimony that was provided him by the prosecution. Having testified before the grand jury prior to his death, Tecott is an unavailable declarant under Rule 801(b) and 804(a)(4). Thus, his testimony before the grand jury is potentially admissible as former testimony under FRE 804(b)(1). However, to be admissible under this exception, the former testimony must have been offered against a party who had an opportunity and similar motive to develop the testimony in the previous proceeding. If offered against the defendant in a criminal action, the former testimony must actually have been used against the defendant in the prior proceeding. Had the Government offered Tecott's grand jury testimony against the accused, it would not have been admissible, because even though it was offered against the defendant and he had the same motive to develop it, he had no opportunity to do so because only the Government is present during the grand jury proceedings. In this case, however, the defendant is seeking to have the grand jury testimony admitted *against* the *Government*. Consequently, Tecott's testimony may be admissible under the former testimony exception if the Government had an opportunity and similar motive to develop the testimony. In *United States. v. Salerno*, 505 U.S. 317, 120 L. Ed. 2d 255, 112 S. Ct. 2503 (1992) the Supreme Court held that simply because the government presented the testimony in the grand jury proceedings does not automatically mean that the testimony is admissible against the government at a subsequent trial. The proponent of the evidence must demonstrate how the government had a similar motive to test the testimony in the grand jury proceedings and the court must specifically make a factual finding on this issue. In *Salerno* the testimony was excluded.

VIII. EXCEPTIONS TO THE HEARSAY RULE — DECLARATIONS AGAINST INTEREST

A. PRINCIPLES

Declarations against interest are statements made by non-agent third parties and offered against someone other than the persons who made them. Unlike admissions, their admissibility is premised on their inherent reliability because it is thought that the person would not have made the statement unless it were true. Therefore, these statements are admissible only if certain conditions are satisfied:

Guarantees of reliability

1. The statement must have been against the interest of the person who made it when it was made; and

2. The declarant must have known it was against his interest at the time it was made.

Creating a necessity

3. The declarant must be shown to be unavailable to be called as a witness when the statement is offered at trial.

RULE 804 FRE
Hearsay Exceptions: Declarant Unavailable

. . . .

(b) Hearsay exceptions. The following are not excluded by the hearsay rule if the declarant is unavailable as a witness:

. . . .

(3) Statements against interest. A statement which was at the time of its making so far contrary to the declarant's pecuniary or proprietary interest, or so far tended to subject the declarant to civil or criminal liability, or to render invalid a claim by the declarant against another, that a reasonable person in the declarant's position would not have made the statement unless believing it to be true. A statement tending to expose the declarant to criminal liability and offered to exculpate the accused is not admissible unless corroborating circumstances clearly indicate the trustworthiness of the statement.

58 PRACTICES

Directly inculpatory portions only. Only the portions of the statements that are against the interests of the declarant are admissible under this exception. Therefore, in federal courts, Fed. R. Evid. 804(b)(3) has been interpreted as excluding the portion of an acknowledgment of guilt that names a third party.[131]

While states have the right to interpret their declarations against interest exception as encompassing the portions of the statements held inadmissible in *Williamson* (because that decision represented only a rule interpretation), the Supreme Court subsequently held that the portions of declarations against interest that are not against the interests of the declarant or made while the declarant was in custody are not sufficiently reliable to satisfy the Sixth Amendment Confrontation Right.[132]

Lilly was applying the definition of the Confrontation Right announced in *Ohio v. Roberts*[133] where a two-prong test was created. First the government had to demonstrate that it had made good faith efforts to produce the witness at trial. Second, once that demonstration had been made, the hearsay that was being used in lieu of live testimony had to be shown to possess an "indicia of reliability." It was the second prong of the *Roberts* decision that prompted the *Lilly* Court to reject declarations against interest that were made in custody and that only collaterally inculpated the defendant. After the *Lilly* decision, states still had the right to employ a broadly interpreted declaration against interest exception when evidence was offered *against the government* in a criminal case, and against *all parties in civil cases.*

Since the *Lilly* decision the Supreme Court has changed its interpretation of the Confrontation Right. Critical of the "indicia of reliability" test because it was so unpredictable, the Court created a new "testimonial" test that is equally unpredictable because inexplicably the Court didn't provide a definitive definition of "testimonial." It appears to encompass statements that were made to authorities with the expectation that it would be used in a criminal prosecution.

---

[131] Williamson v. United States, 512 U.S. 594, 600-01 (1994) (holding Rule 804(b)(3) "does not allow admission of non-self-inculpatory statements, even if they are made within a broader narrative that is generally self-inculpatory.").

[132] Lilly v. Virginia, 527 U.S. 116, 137 (1999) ("[T]he historical underpinning of the confrontation clause and the sweeping of our prior confrontation cases offer one cogent reminder: It is highly unlikely that the presumptive unreliability that attaches to accomplices' confessions that shift or spread blame can be effectively rebutted when the statements are given under conditions that implicate the core concerns of the old ex parte affidavit — that is, when the government is involved in the statements' production, and when the statements describe past events and have not been subjected to adversarial testing.").

[133] Ohio v. Roberts, 448 U.S. 56, 65 L. Ed. 2d 597, 100 S. Ct. 2531 (1980).

If the hearsay statement is "testimonial" in nature when it is uttered, the government cannot use it against a criminal defendant. In contrast, the Confrontation Clause apparently imposes no restricts on the government's use of non-testimonial hearsay. Therefore, under the new *Crawford* definition of the Confrontation Right, it is possible that declarations against interest that are not "testimonial" in nature, but only collaterally inculpate the accused, can again be used by the government against a criminal defendant. Whether this proves to be true will have to await the Court's explanations of the dimensions of the right in future decisions.

59 PRACTICES

All declarations against interest can be admissions, but all admissions will not be declarations against interest. A declaration against interest will be an admission when offered against the declarant. An admission is any statement that the opposing party has said that is offered against that opposing party. Therefore, all declarations against interest can be admissions. The converse, however, is not true. All admissions will not be declarations against interest. Unlike the admission, which has no restrictions, the declaration against interest is admissible only if the statement was against the declarant's interests when it was made, he knew it was against his interests, and the declarant is unavailable when the statement is offered. Because admissions do not need to be against the interests of the declarant when spoken (the admissibility of admissions is premised on the adversarial nature of the process — you speak at your own risk — not on its inherent reliability), they may not be admissible against third parties because there are insufficient guarantees of trustworthiness.

B. Relationship of Declarations Against Interest Exception to Other Rules[134]

Rule 602. Lack of Personal Knowledge. Although Rule 804(b)(3) does not explicitly require that the declarant have personal knowledge of the facts he related, such knowledge is required by Rule 602.[135] The rule directs that "a witness may not testify to a matter unless evidence is introduced sufficient to support a finding that the witness has personal knowledge of the matter." If the declarant is not shown to have personal knowledge, his hearsay statement will be relating another hearsay statement. An exception will be needed for both levels of hearsay if it is to be admissible.

---

[134] PAUL R. RICE & ROY A. KATRIEL, EVIDENCE: COMMON LAW AND FEDERAL RULES OF EVIDENCE § 5.03 [C][3] (LEXIS 5th ed. 2005)

[135] *See, e.g.*, United States v. Lang, 589 F.2d 92, 98 (2d Cir. 1978) ("In a hearsay situation, the declarant is, of course, a witness, and neither [Rule 803] nor Rule 804 dispenses with the requirement of firsthand knowledge.").

Rule 807. Other Exceptions. If corroborating circumstances do not clearly show that an exculpatory or inculpatory declaration against interest is trustworthy, or if a court determines that the statement is not sufficiently against the declarant's interest to provide sufficient assurances of reliability, these same factors will usually result in there not being sufficient circumstantial guarantees of trustworthiness to bring the statement within the coverage of the discretionary exception contained in Rule 807.[136]

C. Applications — Declarations Against Interest Exception

After personal items stolen from Duran were found in the possession of an individual in another country, a relative of Duran expressed remorse about having stolen the items and sold them. In litigation in the United States to obtain the stolen items, the third party who had acknowledged stealing them was in Panama and could not be convinced by other family members to come to the United States to testify. Therefore, relatives who heard the apology were called to testify about the substance of what was said, to prove the truth of the theft acknowledged. The court accepted the testimony under Rule 804(b)(3) because the declarant was demonstrated to be unavailable (outside the subpoena power of American courts), uncooperative (in that he would not voluntarily come to testify after having been asked) and the substance of the statement tended to expose the declarant to both civil and criminal liability. *United States v. Samaniego*, 2003 WL 22158772 (11th Cir. 2003).

IX. EXCEPTIONS TO THE HEARSAY RULE — FORFEITURE BY WRONGDOING

A. PRINCIPLES

Unlike most other exceptions, this one has no ancient common law history. It was recently adopted in Fed. R. Evid. 804(b)(6) to address the problem of parties making adverse witnesses unavailable, and thereby precluding the opponent from proving his case.[137] This exception permits the opposing party to offer *any* prior statement that the unavailable witness made.

---

[136] *See* United States v. Love, 592 F.2d 1022, 1026 (8th Cir. 1979)(holding "[t]he same circumstances which lead us to conclude that the statement was not admissible under 804(b)(3) because it cannot be said 'that a reasonable man in his position would not have made the statement unless he believed it to be true' requires us to reject the government's contention that the statement was admissible under [Rule 807].").

[137] *See* United States v. Emery, 186 F.3d 921, 926 (8th Cir. 1999), *cert. denied* 120 S. Ct. 968 (2000) (holding a trial court is not required to hold a hearing pursuant to Rule 804(b)(6), but instead can admit the evidence at trial "contingent upon proof of the underlying murder by a pre-

Prior to the adoption of Rule 804(b)(6), many circuits had recognized a waiver-by-misconduct rule. Like Rule 804(b)(6), the waiver rule was premised on the maxim that "the law [will not] allow a person to take advantage of his own wrong."[138] Under the judicially created waiver rule courts applied a "clear and convincing" evidence standard comparable to what they were following under Rule 404(b) when prior bad acts were offered against a party. After the clear and convincing evidence standard used in Rule 404(b) was abandoned for the lower preponderance standard,[139] Rule 804(b)(6) also adopted a preponderance of the evidence standard for determining whether a defendant through his own misconduct in procuring the unavailability of a witness, has waived his right to object to evidence on hearsay grounds.[140]

RULE 804 FRE
Hearsay Exceptions; Declarant Unavailable

. . . .

(b) Hearsay Exceptions. The following are not excluded by the hearsay rule if the declarant is unavailable as a witness:

. . . .

(6) Forfeiture by wrongdoing. A statement offered against a party that has engaged or acquiesced in wrongdoing that was intended to, and did, procure the unavailability of the declarant as a witness.

60 PRACTICES

Exception premised on necessity, not reliability. Like the ancient document rule, this exception is premised on nothing more than *necessity*. Once the proponent of the evidence establishes the factual foundation: (1) wrongdoing by party, (2) intent to cause unavailability, and (3) unavailability, there is *no requirement* that the prior statement be shown to have been made under conditions of apparent *sincerity* or otherwise possess some *indicia of reliability*.[141] Because of the absence of any assurance of reliability, one might

---

ponderance of the evidence."); United States v. Houlihan, 92 F.3d 1271, 1280 (1st Cir. 1996) (rejecting the argument that the government must prove through clear and convincing evidence that the defendant caused a potential witness' unavailability).

[138] Diaz v. United States, 223 U.S. 442, 458 (1912), quoted in United States v. Mastrangelo, 693 F.2d 269 (2d Cir. 1982).

[139] Huddleston v. United States, 485 U.S. 681, 99 L. Ed.2d 771, 108 S. Ct. 1496 (1989) .

[140] United States v. Ochoa, 229 F.3d 631, 639 n.2 (7th Cir. 2000).

[141] *But see* United States v. Thevis, 665 F.2d 616, 633 n.17 (5th Cir.), cert. denied, 459 U.S. 825 (1982) (holding, before enactment of Rule 804(b)(6), that even when clear and convincing evidence demonstrates the objecting party caused the unavailability of the witness, "the trial court should scrutinize the proffered statements to ensure that the evidence is not unreliable.").

expect efforts to exclude many statements offered under the provision because its potential unfair prejudice substantially outweighs its probative value.[142] Depending on how courts modify the application of this rule under Rule 403 when indicia of reliability are absent, this rule may accomplish little more than to allow the admission of the same evidence that a presiding judge has the discretion to admit under the residual exception in Rule 807 when there are "equivalent circumstantial guarantees of trustworthiness."[143]

61 PRACTICES

Breadth of "acquiescence" provision unknown. The intriguing question that the rule leaves unaddressed, and the Advisory Committee's Notes do not comment upon, is how broadly the "acquiescence" provision should be interpreted. Hypothetically, both of the following scenarios could lead to the admissibility of all of the prior statements made by a witness:

(1) A gang member is arrested for the murder of an individual and his compatriots kill the single eye-witness. Has the defendant acquiesced in the killing because it is common gang practice and he has *refused to assist the police* in either apprehending those who helped him, or stopping the gang violence?

(2) A defendant is told that a key government witness, without prompting from either himself or his friends, is planning to leave the jurisdiction. Is the defendant acquiescing in wrongdoing by *not notifying authorities* so that the flight can be stopped?

It is unclear how the courts will interpret this provision.[144] What is clear, however, is that the arguments for forfeiture of the right to complain about a lack of demonstrated reliability of hearsay statements used in lieu of the murdered witness' testimony become progressively less compelling as less involvement of the defendant is interpreted as justifying "acquiescence." All issues of reliability (many of which will have to speculated about) cannot always be relegated to the question of weight. At some point due process must compel a demonstration of reliability, not

---

[142] *See* FED. R. EVID. 403 and United States v. Thevis, *supra* (discussing Rule 403).

[143] *See* United States v. Thevis, *supra* (discussing the residual exception).

[144] Prior to the adoption of the forfeiture by wrongdoing exception, the Second Circuit concluded that a waiver was effected by the defendant possessing knowledge of a plot to kill the witness and failing to warn appropriate authorities. United States v. Mastrangelo, 693 F.2d 269, 273-74 (2d Cir. 1982). Participation in a conspiracy can result in a waiver of the right of confrontation if (1) the wrongdoing leading to the unavailability of the witness was in furtherance of and within the scope of the conspiracy, and (2) such wrongdoing was reasonably foreseeable as a natural or necessary consequence of the conspiracy. United States v. Cherry, 217 F.3d 811, 820, 2000 U.S. App. LEXIS 26830, *25-26 (10th Cir. May 2, 2000); United States v. White, 838 F. Supp. 618 (D.D.C. 1993), *aff'd*, 325 U.S. App. D.C. 282, 116 F.3d 903 (D.C. Cir. 1997).

just because it is necessary for fundamental fairness for the defendant (who has so much at stake), but also because it is essential to the preservation of the perceived credibility of the criminal justice system.

Rule 804(b)(6) has been held inapplicable to statements made by a victim when the assailant killed out of personal animosity, rather than for the purpose of making the person unavailable as a witness. The wrongful conduct must have been intended to make the person unavailable as a witness.[145]

B. Relationship of Forfeiture by Wrongdoing Exception to Other Rules[146]

Rule 804(b)(1). Former testimony. The former testimony exception makes prior testimony offered against a partner in crime inadmissible against another partner whose trial has been severed. This creates a virtual "open season" on key government witnesses between those trials. Without revising this sacrosanct limitation on the prior testimony exception, the Advisory Committee has done an end-run around it — getting around the limitation with another exception. The important characteristic of this new exception is that once its conditions have been met (and the gravity of those conditions is yet to be decided), it will pre-empt all other exceptions. Therefore, if the act of getting rid of the witness occurs after he testified at an accomplice's trial, even though the transcript of that testimony could not be used against the defendant under Rule 804(b)(1), because that exception restricts its use in criminal cases to the same defendant, this exception will permit the introduction of the transcript.

C. Applications — Forfeiture by Wrongdoing Exception

ONE

The defendant was charged with mail fraud and wire fraud relating to her receipt of insurance proceeds following the deaths of her second husband and a former paramour. At her trial the government offers several statements made by Robert Gray, the defendant's second husband, months preceding his murder by the defendant and her current paramour. These statements were in several contexts and all related to acts of violence against him by his wife and her lover, Goode. Although there was ample evidence to establish that Robert Gray was killed by his wife and lover to eliminate the only witness to her previous killing of her first husband for insurance proceeds, the defendant claims that the doctrine of forfeiture by wrongdoing was not applicable because there was no

---

[145] United States v. Emery, 186 F.3d 921, 926 (8th Cir. 1999), *cert denied*, 528 U.S. 1130, 120 S. Ct. 968, 145 L. Ed..2d 839 (2000). *Cf.* Commonwealth v. Levanduski, 2005 Pa Super 117 2005 Pa. Super. LEXIS 497 *See*, Commonwealth v. Laich, 566 19, 28 n.4, 777 A.2d 1057, 1062 n.4 (2001).

[146] PAUL R. RICE & ROY A. KATRIEL, EVIDENCE: COMMON LAW AND FEDERAL RULES OF EVIDENCE § 5.05 [B][3] (LEXIS 5th ed. 2005)

evidence that the defendant intended to make her husband unavailable in *this* trial. The court rejected this interpretation of Rue 804(b)(6), holding that the rule only requires that the defendant intend to render the declarant unavailable "as a witness." "The text does not require that the declarant would otherwise be a witness at any *particular* trial, nor does it limit the subject matter of admissible statements to events distinct from the events at issue in the trial in which the statements are offered. Thus, we conclude that Rule 804(b)(6) applies *whenever* the defendant's wrongdoing was intended to, and did, render the declarant unavailable as a witness against the defendant, without regard to the nature of the charges at the trial in which the declarant's statements are offered. . . . [O]ur interpretation of Rule 804(b)(6) ensures that a defendant will not be permitted to avoid the evidentiary impact of statements made by his victim, whether or not he suspected that the victim would be a witness at the trial in which the evidence is offered against him. A defendant who wrongfully and intentionally renders a declarant unavailable as a witness in any proceeding forfeits the right to exclude, on hearsay grounds, the declarant's statements at that proceeding and any subsequent proceedings." *United States v. Gray*, 405 F.3d 227, 241-42 (4th Cir. 2005).

TWO

While the defendant was incarcerated, he was made aware of the intentions of gang members to eliminate the witness to the crime for which he stood charged. When he was tried, the witness had been killed by members of the gang and the prosecution offered prior statements that the victim had made about the culpability of the defendant under the doctrine of forfeiture by wrongdoing in Rule 804(b)(6). The defendant objected, claiming (1) that the government had to establish his involvement in the efforts to make the witness unavailable by more than a preponderance of evidence and (2) that it was improper to impute to him the wrongdoings of others.

The court rejected both arguments. On the burden of persuasion issue, the court joined the ranks of the majority of circuit courts in holding that evidentiary foundations need only be established by a preponderance of evidence. On the second ground the court noted that the language of the rule only requires that a party be shown to have either engaged in "or acquiesced in" wrongdoing that was intended to, and did, procure the unavailability of the declarant as a witness." The court went on to explain the breadth of "acquiescence."

> Acquiescence consists of 'the act or condition of acquiescing or giving tacit assent; agreement or consent by silence or without objection.' . . . In other words, the plant language of the Rule supports the district court's holding that a defendant need only tacitly assent to wrongdoing in order to trigger the Rule's applicability. Active participation or engagement, or, as Rivera would have it, the personal commission of the crime, is not requires.

The court went on to cite other circuits that have imputed co-conspirators' actions to a defendant and held the forfeiture rule applicable when the defendant had knowledge of a plot to kill the victim and gave no warning to appropriate authorities. *United States v. Rivera*, 412 F.3d 562, 566-67 (4th Cir. 2005).

X. EXCEPTIONS TO THE HEARSAY RULE — PRESENT SENSE IMPRESSION

A. PRINCIPLES

Studies have shown that some of the most accurate, and therefore reliable, descriptions of an event are those made while the event is occurring. More accurate still are statements describing an event that is interesting, but not so exciting that the observer's reflective thought processes are overwhelmed. With all of her senses focused on the occurrence, the observer experiences the greatest detail with the greatest accuracy. This experience is the foundation for the present sense impression exception to the hearsay rule. This is a new exception under the Federal Rules of Evidence. Therefore, there is no common law history, although in the latter part of the 19th century commentators like Professor Thayer advocated the adoption of the exception.[147]

RULE 803 FRE
Hearsay Exceptions; Availability of Declarant Immaterial

The following are not excluded by the hearsay rule, even though the declarant is available as a witness:

(1) Present Sense Impression. A statement describing or explaining an event or condition made while the declarant was perceiving the event or condition, or immediately thereafter.

62 PRACTICES

Temporal proximity is crucial. The only guarantee of reliability possessed by statements made admissible through the present sense impression exception is the temporal proximity of the statement to the event being described or explained. Therefore, courts should construe the requirement of "immediately thereafter" strictly — consistent with a statement designed to be

---

[147] Thayer, *Bedingfield's Case — Declarations as a Part of the Res Gestae*, 15 Am. L. Rev. 1 (1881). *See also* Houston Oxygen Co. v. Davis, 139 Tex. 1, 161 S.W.2d 474 (Comm'n App. 1942).

made "while . . . perceiving the event or condition." Unfortunately, this has not been the history of the exception.[148]

Courts have begun to relax the contemporaneity requirement with the present sense impression in the same way they did with excited utterances, which originally had to be made simultaneously with or "immediately after" the exciting event. This was prompted by the fact that the new present sense impression exception borrowed not only the "immediately thereafter" language from the common law excited utterance exception, but also that exception's limitation to "statements describing or explaining an event of condition." Further contributing to the inappropriate expansion of the exception is the close factual similarities between the circumstances giving rise to the use of the two different exceptions. It is critical, however, for courts to remember that only excited utterances (not present sense impressions), have the added indicia of reliability created by the exciting nature of the event described.

63 PRACTICES

The potential for gutting other exceptions. The present sense impression exception does not require that the observed event be exciting. This is why the exception is so useful. Because the exception, theoretically, applies to all contemporaneous statements, if the scope of its application is not appropriately limited — perhaps to objectively observed events or conditions — it could render meaningless many of the limitations in other exceptions, like present physical condition, present state of mind, and past recollection recorded — all of which would theoretically also be present sense impressions under a literal interpretation of the words of the exceptions.

The greatest danger is posed for the exception for present state of mind in Fed. R. Evid. 803(3). Except for statements relating to the execution, revocation, identification, or terms of a will, Rule 803(3) addresses the admissibility of statements that would be admissible under the present sense impression exception because they have to be made contemporaneously with the condition being described. Therefore, Rule 803(1) virtually consumes Rule 803(3) unless it is limited to statements about *observed events*, rather

---

[148] Courts have struggled to define the time limitations of the contemporaneity requirement. *See* United States v. Blakey, 607 F.2d 779, 785 (7th Cir. 1979), *overruled on other grounds,* United States v. Harty, 930 F.2d 1257 (7th Cir. 1991) (finding substantial contemporaneity is still satisfied even though time lapse may have been up to twenty-three minutes); United States v. Cain, 587 F.2d 678, 680-81 (5th Cir.), *cert. denied,* 440 U.S. 975 (1979) (determining a CBer's transmission was not made immediately after perceiving the defendants because, otherwise, the defendants would have walked five miles within a few minutes after being seen); Hilyer v. Howat Concrete Co., Inc., 578 F.2d 422, 426 n.7 (D.C. Cir. 1978) (holding that a fifteen to forty-five minute interval does not conform to the contemporaneity requirement as contemplated by Rule 803(1)).

than subjective conditions experienced by declarant and which cannot be corroborated by the person hearing the statement.[149] No courts, however, appear to have followed this approach.

To the extent that courts use the exceptions interchangeably, they must be conscious of the state of mind exception's limitation — excluding statements of memory or belief when introduced to prove the facts remembered or believed. Failing to observe this limitation could jeopardize the very existence of the hearsay rule itself, because everything we say reveals what we currently believe about what we say.[150]

B. Relationship of Present Sense Impression Exception to Other Rules[151]

Rule 604. Interpreters. Interpreters produce classical present sense impressions by simultaneously uttering what they are perceiving.[152]

Rule 803(2). Excited Utterances. The present sense impression exception differs from the excited utterance exception in three ways. First, it does not need to be in response to an exciting event. Second, it must be made much closer in time to the event perceived (more contemporaneous with the event). Third, it must describe or explain the event as opposed to simply "relate" to it.[153] The excited utterance is presumed to be reliable because of the overwhelming nature of the perceived event. In contrast, the present impression is thought to be reliable because of the reflexive nature of the declarant's statement in response to his perceiving the event.

Rule 803(5). Past Recollection Recorded

Because Rule 801(a) defines a "statement" as an "oral or written assertion," written present sense impressions would appear to be within the scope of Rule 803(1). Therefore, the present sense impression exception potentially consumes the past recollection recorded exception in Rule 803(5) — depending on the

---

[149] *See* Trustees of the Univ. of Penn. v. Lexington Ins. Co., 815 F.2d 890, 905 (3d Cir. 1987) (observing the Advisory Committee's Note to Rule 803(3) that the "state of mind exception is [a] specific example of Rule 803(1) exception for present sense impression.").

[150] Shepard v. United States, 290 U.S. 96, 104 78 L.Ed. 196, 54 S. Ct. 22 (1933). *See* **PRACTICES NO. 65**, *infra*.

[151] PAUL R. RICE & ROY A. KATRIEL, EVIDENCE: COMMON LAW AND FEDERAL RULES OF EVIDENCE § 5.05 [B][3] (LEXIS 5th ed. 2005)

[152] United States v. Kramer, 741 F. Supp. 893, 896 (S.D. Fla. 1990).

[153] *See* United States v. Moore, 791 F.2d 566, 572 n.4 (7th Cir. 1986), *overruled on other grounds*, 865 F.2d 149 (7th Cir. 1989) ("It may be more precise in the present context to state that the present sense impression exception requires that the statement be made contemporaneously, or almost contemporaneously, with the event that prompted it. The excited utterance exception, on the other hand, requires only that the statement be made contemporaneously with the excitement resulting from the event, not necessarily with the event itself.").

degree to which courts relax the contemporaneity requirement in Rule 803(1). Rule 803(1) requires that the "statement" have been made "while the declarant was perceiving the event or condition, or immediately thereafter." In contrast, Rule 803(5) requires that the "writing" have been "made or adopted by the witness when the mater was fresh in the witness' memory."

Tactically, the proponent of such hearsay should always attempt to admit the written statement under the present sense impression exception in Rule 803(1) because it avoids all of the restrictions in Rule 803(5) — (1) the declarant being available as a witness, (2) a required loss of memory by the declarant, (3) the authentication of the writing by the declarant, and (4) it must be read into evidence because it is not admissible as an exhibit unless offered by the opposing party.

C. Applications — Present Sense Impression Exception

ONE

Darrell Brookins and Harvey Peacock were involved in an arson scheme that lasted nearly two years, from 1982 to 1984. In December 1984, Brookins received a phone call from Peacock in which Peacock informed Brookins that the police were on to them and that Brookins should get out of town. Immediately after the phone call, Brookins turned to his wife, informed her of the gist of Peacock's statements, and then fled. Brookins was subsequently killed in a high-speed car chase with the police. At Peacock's trial for numerous counts of arson, the Government introduced Peacock's comments to Brookins through the testimony of Brookins' widow for the purpose of proving the truth of what Peacock directly and impliedly admitted to Brookins. This was upheld on appeal. Under the common law, this problem creates two levels of hearsay — what Peacock said to Brookins and what Brookins, in turn, related to his wife. The first level, between Peacock and Brookins, is admissible under the admission exception. Of course, under the federal rules there is only one level of hearsay because admissions have been excluded from the definition of hearsay in Rule 801(d)(2). The remaining level of hearsay is a present sense impression. Brookins repeated Peacock's comments immediately after talking with Peacock on the phone. There was little time for him to consciously manipulate the truth, and his subsequent conduct corroborated the sincerity of his statement. Thus, the comments are sufficiently contemporaneous to the phone call to be admissible as present sense impressions. *United States v. Peacock*, 654 F.2d 339, 350 (5th Cir. 1981), *vacated in part on other grounds*, 686 F.2d 356 (1982), *cert. denied*, 464 U.S. 965 (1983).

TWO

While repossessing a rental car that Peter Phelps had leased, police officers conducted a routine search of the car in Phelps' presence. During this search, the police discovered a pound of cocaine in a gym bag located in the trunk of the car. When the officers discovered the cocaine in the gym bag, Phelps stated, "That's not mine; Taylor put it in the trunk." In Phelps' and Taylor's subsequent joint prosecution for possession of cocaine, Phelps seeks to introduce this statement through the testimony of one of the police officers present during the search. The court held that Phelps' statement was not admissible as a present sense impression because it was not made substantially contemporaneously with an event being perceived. "The proffered statement could not be considered a present sense impression under Rule 803(1) because the subject matter of the statement offered was not what the declarant was presently perceiving when the statement was made, but rather something which had occurred at a remote previous time, namely whenever the gym bag was placed in the trunk." *United States v. Phelps*, 572 F. Supp. 262, 265 (E.D. Ky. 1983).

The *Phelps* court also held that the statement was not admissible as an excited utterance. The trustworthiness of the excited utterance is predicated on the statement's spontaneity. One of the factors that courts consider in determining whether a statement is an excited utterance is the subject matter of the utterance itself. Because Phelps' statement described a previous event and not the discovery of the bag containing the cocaine, the event that allegedly gave rise to Phelps' statement, a court did not believe that the statement was truly spontaneous. The court concluded that the statement at issue was not an excited utterance because a significant amount of time elapsed between the police officers' declaration of intent to search the rental car and the actual search giving the declarant an opportunity to fabricate an explanation for the cocaine's presence in his car. *Phelps*, 572 F. Supp. at 266. This logic is inappropriately premised on an assumption that the declarant is guilty.

XI. EXCEPTIONS TO THE HEARSAY RULE — EXCITED UTTERANCES

A. PRINCIPLES

Statements made under the stress of excitement are thought to be reliable because the danger of insincerity is reduced when the declarant's reflective thought processes are overwhelmed. Additionally, memory problems are minimized when the statement describes or explains an event or condition while its effects were being experienced. The excitement that overwhelms thought processes, however, also negatively affects the accuracy of one's perception. Nevertheless, a hearsay exception is recognized because two of the four hearsay dangers are thought to be adequately addressed. Courts see the declarant as little more than the mouthpiece for the event — it is the event itself speaking through him.

Under Fed. R. Evid. 803(2), the reliability of the exception is further lost with the relaxation of the necessary content of the statement. Under the Rule

803(2), the statement only needs to "relate" to the startling event. Consequently, the statement may not be describing what is being seen or otherwise experienced.[154]

RULE 803 FRE
Hearsay Exceptions; Availability of Declarant Immaterial

The following are not excluded by the hearsay rule, even though the declarant is available as a witness:

. . . .

(2) Excited utterances. A statement relating to a startling event or condition made while the declarant was under the stress of excitement caused by the event or condition.

64 PRACTICES

Theory and practice not consistent. If the theory of the exception were believed — that when overwhelmed, one speaks with sincerity — the courts would not allow the declarant to be impeached through evidence of bias and prior convictions. Presumably, what the declarant may be inclined to do upon reflection would not be relevant to what he does spontaneously. Rule 806, however, permits all hearsay declarants, without exception, to be impeached with all means of impeachment available when the witness testifies in person.

RULE 806 FRE
Attacking and Supporting Credibility of Declarant

When a hearsay statement, or a statement defined in Rule 801(d)(2)(C), (D), or (E), has been admitted in evidence, the credibility of the declarant may be attacked, and if attacked may be supported, by any evidence which would be admissible for those purposes it the declarant had testified as a witness. Evidence of a statement or conduct by the declarant at any time, inconsistent with the declarant's hearsay statement, is not subject to any requirement that the declarant may have been afforded an opportunity to deny or explain. If the party

---

[154] *See* Murphy Auto Parts Co. v. Ball, 249 F.2d 508, 511 (D.C. Cir. 1957), *cert. denied*, 355 U.S. 932 (1958) (determining that because the logic of the admission of an excited utterance rests on the premise that the startling nature of the event and the inability of the declarant to reflect upon it together ensure the statement's sincerity, the fact the utterance only indirectly relates to the subject matter of the event perceived should only be a factor in the analysis of whether the description was truly spontaneous).

against whom a hearsay statement has been admitted calls the declarant as a witness, the party is entitled to examine the declarant on the
statement as if under cross-examination.

B. Relationship of Excited Utterance Exception to Other Rules[155]

Rule 104(a). Preliminary Questions. Rule 104(a) provides that the court
should rule on preliminary questions of admissibility. In applying Rule 803(2),
therefore, the court should decide (1) whether there was a startling event, (2)
whether the declarant was under the stress of excitement caused by the event
when the statement was made, and (3) whether the statement "related" to the
event. For example, in a personal injury case, suppose the defense wishes to
introduce the statement of someone who did not see the actual collision but who
saw plaintiff's car run a red light and heard a sudden crash. After hearing the
crash, the declarant said, "They shouldn't 'a run that light." Before the statement could be admitted, the court would have to decide whether the running of
the red light and the hearing of a crash comprised a sufficiently startling event
to have stilled the declarant's reflective capacity while he was making the statement and whether the statement about the light related to the collision.

Rule 602. Lack of Personal Knowledge. While Rule 803(2) does not explicitly mandate that the declarant have observed the exciting event that overwhelms him, it is clear under Rule 602 that the declarant must have had
firsthand knowledge of the facts recited in her excited utterance.[156] Generally,
the proponent must present enough direct or circumstantial evidence to allow
the jury to infer that the declarant observed the startling event.[157] Proving
firsthand knowledge can often be difficult. Courts have approached the issue
with a good deal of flexibility and common sense. Consequently, if witnesses are
not available to substantiate firsthand knowledge, courts have looked to the
statement's content, the declarant's emotional state and the circumstances surrounding the utterance as circumstantial proof of the declarant's firsthand
knowledge.[158]

---

[155] PAUL R. RICE & ROY A. KATRIEL, EVIDENCE: COMMON LAW AND FEDERAL RULES OF EVIDENCE
§ 5.05 [A][3] (LEXIS 5th ed. 2005)

[156] *See* United States v. Mitchell, 145 F.3d 572, 576 (3d Cir. 1998) (citing the requirement that
the declarant must "personally perceived the event or condition about which the statement is
made").

[157] *See* 6 WIGMORE, EVIDENCE §1751, at 222 (Chadbourn rev. 1976); McCORMICK ON EVIDENCE
§272 (4th ed. 1994).

[158] *See* McLaughlin v. Vinzant, 522 F.2d 448, 451 (1st Cir. 1975) (stating "it was permissible to
draw an inference not only from the force of the statement itself but from the fact that she was
accompanying McLaughlin and was somewhere in the immediate vicinity of the fatal event, that
she possessed first-hand knowledge of the killing.").

Rule 806. Attacking and Supporting Credibility of Declarant. If the theory of the excited utterance were actually believe in by courts, they would not permit the declarant to be impeached with evidence of something like bias, because the reflective thought processes of the declarant are overwhelmed. Because they don't actually believe the theory, such impeachment is permitted.

C. Applications — Excited Utterance Exception

ONE

The victim was shot by an individual while he was sitting in his car. When the police arrived he spoke little, but noted that his gold Gucci chain had been stolen. At the hospital it was discovered that the victim was paralyzed from the neck down and could not speak due to a tracheotomy. The following day, while his sister was visiting he uttered the word "T" in an apparent attempt to identify his attacker. Officers also testified that he identified his attacker by blinking at the photograph of the defendant when it was placed in an array in front of him. The defendant did not testify at the trial and his "statements" were brought into court through the sister and police officers. Over a hearsay objection the court excluded the statements as excited utterances and this decision was upheld on appeal. The court believed too much time had elapsed for the statements to fairly be said to have been made under the stress of excitement caused by the shooting. The fact that he waited until the following day to try to identify the assailant suggested to the court that the statements were the product of deliberation. *United States v. Lawrence*, 2003 WL 22697997 (3d Cir. 2003).

TWO

The victim assaulted this girlfriend with a gun. A short time thereafter the victim made a 911 call to the police from a neighbor's house. Her voice sounded scared and nervous to the dispatcher. She also appeared excited to the officer who responded. The court held that the victim's statements were excited utterances because (1) they were not made in response to suggestive questions, (2) made a short time after the event causing her excitement, and (3) she was visibly excited to those who saw and heard her. "To determine whether the declarant was still under the stress of excitement caused by the assault when he made the statement, we must consider the lapse of time between the startling event and the statement, whether the statement was made in response to an inquiry, the age of the declarant, the physical and mental condition of the declarant, the characteristics of the event, and the subject matter of the statement." *United States v. Phelps*, 163 F.3d 1052 (8th Cir. 1999).

XII. EXCEPTIONS TO THE HEARSAY RULE — STATE OF MIND

A. PRINCIPLES

When the state of mind of the declarant is an issue, a present state of mind exception to the hearsay rule admits the declarant's contemporaneous statements about such a state. Because it is the declarant's personal state of mind, there are minimal perception problems; because the statement must be contemporaneous with the existence of the state of mind, no memory problems exist; and because the statement must be made under conditions of apparent sincerity, that hearsay problem is minimized. This may be the least understood, and most often misapplied, exception to the hearsay rule.

RULE 803 FRE
Hearsay Exceptions; Availability of Declarant Immaterial

The following are not excluded by the hearsay rule, even though the declarant is available as a witness:

. . . .

(3) **Then existing mental, emotional, or physical condition.** A statement of the declarant's then existing state of mind, emotion, sensation, or physical condition (such as intent, plan, motive, design, mental feeling, pain, and bodily health), but not including a statement of memory or belief to prove the fact remembered or believed unless it relates to the execution, revocation, identification, or terms of declarant's will.

65 PRACTICES

Independent relevance. The state of mind exception can only be employed when the state of mind of the declarant has independent relevance.[159] In other words, the mere existence of the state of mind, *independent of the reason for its existence*, must be why it is relevant to the cause of action. The reason for this is quite simple — when only the existence of the state of mind is at issue, only the declarant's perception of that state is implicated. In contrast, when the reasonableness of that state is involved, the declarant's per-

---

[159] *See, e.g.,* United States v. Tokars, 95 F.3d 1520, 1535 (11th Cir. 1996), *cert. denied,* 520 U.S. 1151 (1997) (allowing admission of evidence concerning the victim's state of mind when relevant to show the defendant's motive to kill); United States v. Kelly, 722 F.2d 873, 878 (1st Cir. 1983), *cert. denied,* 465 U.S. 1070 (1984) (finding in an extortion prosecution based upon fear of economic loss, the state of mind of the victim of extortion becomes highly relevant).

ception and memory of other acts, events and conditions come into play, thereby multiplying hearsay concerns with no assurances of trustworthiness.

Example

A child expresses her unhappiness because her classmates are not being nice to her. The statement could be repeated in court by a third party who heard it if it were offered to prove that the child was unhappy, and therefore, might not thrive in that environment, but it could not be repeated for the purpose of proving why she was unhappy — her treatment by the classmates.

66 PRACTICES

Forward and backward continuity. The declarant's state of mind will control what the declarant does in the future. It has independent relevance to that conduct. Therefore, when the declarant says today that he intends to go to the farm tomorrow, the current state of mind is relevant to events in the future and will be admitted under the present state of mind exception.[160] This is illustrated in the following diagram:

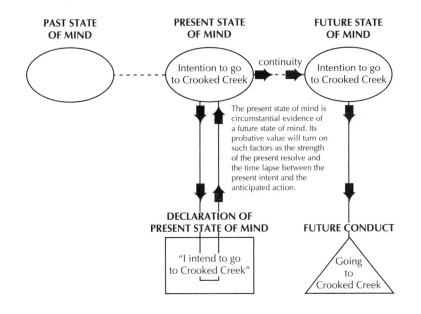

---

[160] *See* Mutual Life Ins. Co. v. Hillmon, 145 U.S. 285, 295-96 (1892) ("The letters in question were competent not as narratives of facts communicated to the writer by others, nor yet as proof that he actually went away from Wichita, but as evidence that, shortly before the time when the other evidence tended to show that he went away, [Walters] had the intention of going, and of going with Hillmon, which made it more probable both that he did go and that he went with Hillmon than if

In a similar fashion, but on a higher level of complexity, the present state of mind can be taken as circumstantial evidence of the *declarant's past conduct*. Because the declarant holds a certain attitude toward something today, it is circumstantial evidence that he held the same attitude in the recent past. If that attitude could have prompted certain conduct, this statement is circumstantial evidence that the declarant engaged in that conduct.[161] If, for example, I say that I despise a certain individual and would like to see him dead, that is circumstantial evidence I held the same attitude toward him yesterday. If other evidence demonstrates I had the opportunity to injury that individual, my statement of hostility would be admissible under the state of mind exception to prove that I was the one who battered him. This is illustrated in the following diagram:

67 PRACTICES

Can't be used to prove a past observed fact. What the state of mind exception *cannot* be used to prove is a *past fact observed* by the declarant.[162] The declarant's state of mind has no independent relevance. No matter how earnestly the declarant wants to see a particular fact, her state of mind does not control the factual occurrence. If, for example, the declarant states that the car that hit the child in the parking lot was yellow, her state of mind does not control the color of the car. Therefore, the state of mind exception cannot be used to admit the statement to prove the color of the car. If this were permitted, it would destroy the hearsay rule. Everything that an individual says reflects that individual's state of mind about what has been described. If the existence of that state of mind could be used as circumstantial evidence of the occurrence described, nothing would ever be excluded under the hearsay rule.[163] If the logic of the past event led *to* the creation of the state of mind, rather than resulted *from* the state of mind, the state of mind exception is inapplicable. This is illustrated in the following diagram.

---

there had been no proof of such intention.") (note, however, that the comment about the letters being used to show that "he went with Hillmon" was *dicta* because the letter was being used only to prove the writer's conduct — that Walters went to Crooked Creek , not the conduct of the third party, Mr. Hillmon).

[161] *See* United States v. Miller, 874 F.2d 1255, 1264-65 (9th Cir. 1989) (finding that the trial court did not abuse its discretion in disallowing the admission of evidence to prove the past state of mind of the defendant because the court allowed other statements to show the defendant's then state of mind).

[162] *See* Shepard v. United States, 290 U.S. 96, 104 (1933) (disallowing the statements given by the dying victim under evidence of a state of mind exception because the government "did not use the declarations by Mrs. Shepard to prove her present thoughts and feelings, or even her thoughts and feelings in times past . . . [but rather] used the declarations as proof of an act committed by some one else, as evidence that she was dying of poison given by her husband.").

[163] *Shepard,* 290 U.S. at 106.

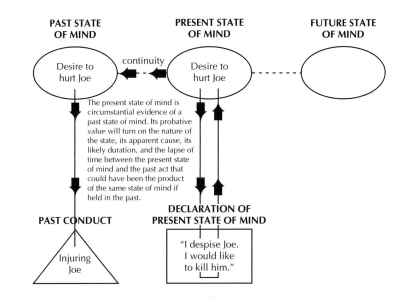

68 PRACTICES

Proving the conduct of third parties. When the declarant expresses a state of mind to engage in certain conduct *with a third party*, can the statement be used as circumstantial evidence that the declarant did what he intended to do (engage in that conduct), and did it with the third party? If the declarant says "I'm going out with Frank tonight," could that statement be used to prove that Frank went out with her? In the famous case of *People v. Alcade*[164] the court held that the statement could be used to prove that the victim went out with Frank. Federal courts have followed the lead of *Alcade*.[165] More recently, courts have held that one individual's statement of intention to act with another may be used as evidence that both acted together so long as there is "independent evidence connecting the declarant's statement with the non-declarant's activities."[166] The corroboration requirement makes a

---

[164] 24 Cal.2d 77, 187-88, 148 P.2d 627, 632 (1944).

[165] *See* United States v. Pheaster, 544 F.2d 353, 377-80 (9th Cir. 1976).

[166] United States v. Delvecchio, 816 F.2d 859, 863 (2d Cir. 1987). *See also* United States v. Nersesian, 824 F.2d 1294, 1325 (2d Cir.), *cert. denied*, 484 U.S. 958 (1987) ("[D]eclarations of intentions or future plans are admissible against a nondeclarant when they are linked with independent evidence that corroborates the declaration."); United States v. Jenkins, 579 F.2d 840, 842-43 (4th Cir.), *cert. denied,* 439 U.S. 967 (1978) (rejecting the admission of a declarant's statement of state of mind to prove a third party's subsequent conduct of third party, but admitting the statement to establish why third party acted as he did when independent evidence exists demonstrating that the third party did engage in the alleged conduct.). *But see* United States v. Houlihan, 871 F. Supp. 1495, 1501 (D. Mass. 1994) (holding, in adopting the Ninth Circuit's approach, Rule 803(3) does not require corroborating, independent evidence before evidence of state of mind may be admitted regarding the future conduct of a third party).

lot of sense. The declarant's state of mind does increase the probability that she would have waited for Frank to pick her up and rejected other alternatives that may have become available. It establishes her availability and his opportunity.

B. Relationship of State of Mind Exception to Other Rules[167]

Rule 104(a). Preliminary Questions. Before a court will admit a statement under the state of mind exception, the proponent must show that the declarant's state of mind is independently relevant to some issue in the case. The trial judge will make this determination of relevance before accepting the evidence.[168] Because the law considers the written instrument controlling, what one of the parties intended, but did not place in writing, is irrelevant to the proceedings.

Rule 803(1). Present Sense Impression. Rule 803(1) admits statements "describing or explaining [a] . . . condition made while the declarant was perceiving the . . . condition" as an exception to the hearsay rule. By its terms, this rule renders Rule 803(3) superfluous because all statements of one's "then existing state of mind, emotion, or sensation" would also constitute descriptions or explanations of those same conditions. The focus of Rule 803(1), however, appears to be on observed events rather than subjective states of mental or physical condition, because the trustworthiness of statements of present sense impression turns on the fact that the declarant had made the statement simultaneously with the described event to one who has an equal opportunity to observe it and thereby check the accuracy of the statement.[169] Thus, the existence of corroboration for the statement appears to have been an underlying assumption of the drafters of Rule 803(1).[170] While courts frequently allude to a requirement of corroboration,[171] it is not clear that the statements would have been excluded in the absence of corroboration.[172]

---

[167] PAUL R. RICE & ROY A. KATRIEL, EVIDENCE: COMMON LAW AND FEDERAL RULES OF EVIDENCE § 5.05 [C][3] (LEXIS 5th ed. 2005)

[168] *See* Prather v. Prather, 650 F.2d 88, 90 (5th Cir. 1981) (concluding that the plaintiff's state of mind was not relevant to the construction of a written contract that was unambiguous).

[169] *See* Houston Oxygen Co. v. Davis, 139 Tex. 1, 5-7, 161 S.W.2d 474, 476-477 (1942).

[170] *See* Waltz, *The Present Sense Impression Exception to the Rule Against Hearsay: Origins and Attributes*, 66 IOWA L. REV. 869 (1981).

[171] *See, e.g.,* In re Japanese Elec. Prod. Antitrust Lit., 723 F.2d 238, 303 (3d Cir. 1983), *rev'd on other grounds*, 475 U.S. 574 (1986).

[172] *See* State v. Flesher, 286 N.W.2d 215, 217 (Iowa 1979) ("Obviously, corroboration, or the lack of it, will affect the weight given to the declaration. We find nothing, however, in either the wording of the exception of its underlying rationale which requires corroboration as a condition of its admissibility."); *see also Comment, the Need for a New Approach to the Present Sense Impression Hearsay Exception After* State v. Flesher, 67 IOWA L. REV. 179, 191-200 (1981); Comment, *The Present Sense Impression Hearsay Exception: An Analysis of the Contemporaneity and Corroboration Requirements,* 71 NW. U. L. REV. 634 (1976).

If courts permit parties to use Rule 803(1) as a substitute for Rule 803(3), they must not allow parties to use it to prove a state of mind, if that state is relevant only to prove the truth of a fact remembered or believed. Judicial laxity in this regard will jeopardize the survival of the hearsay rule itself. See **PRACTICE NO. 66**, supra.

C. Applications — State of Mind Exception

ONE

In an action to determine the rightful owner of personal property in the possession of the defendant, witnesses are called to testify that another individual expressed remorse for having stolen the items from Mr. Duran. It is argued that these statements are admissible under the present state of mind exception to the hearsay rule. While the court acknowledged that the statements could be used to prove the then existing remorse of the declarant at the time of the utterance, it could not be used to prove the truth of the cause of the state of mind — the past act of having stolen the items. The court noted that this limitation is necessary to avoid the virtual destruction of the hearsay rule. *United States v. Samaniego*, 2003 WL 22158772 (11th Cir. 2003).

TWO

James Kelly, a state senator, was indicted for extortion induced under color of authority. To establish that the victims of Kelly's alleged extortion scheme feared official retribution should they have failed to comply with Kelly's requests, an essential element of the crime charged, the Government sought to introduce a letter that one of the victims had written to his business associate in which the victim explained: "Kelly seems to have us over a barrel on this one. If we don't give his nephew a job, we may have several of our contracts with the state canceled, or worse. You know these Irish people, they don't get mad, they just get even." The letter is admissible under the state of mind exception to the hearsay rule, for it establishes the victim's presently existing fear of official retribution, a requirement of the federal extortion statute. *United States v. Kelly*, 722 F.2d 873 (1st Cir. 1983), *cert. denied*, 465 U.S. 1070 (1984).

THREE

Pando was charged with intent to distribute cocaine. After his arrest, Pando made a tape recorded statement to police officers. In this statement, Pando claimed he *had been* "coerced and threatened" into transporting the cocaine. Defense counsel offered the statement to show Pando's state of mind at the time he was captured with the drugs in his possession. The state of mind exception to the hearsay rule is recognized because it is a contemporaneous statement of one's state of mind. There is no perception problem because it is your state of mind, and there is little memory problem because it is your *present* (then existing) state of mind. The defendant is attempting to do through the state of mind exception what he cannot do through the admission exception — make statements that he can later use in his own behalf. Here, however, the statement does not fit within the elements of the exception because it refers to his *past* state of mind. If, when interrogated by the police, Pando had said, "They'll kill me and my son if I say anything!" the statement would be admissible to prove then existing fear, which would be circumstantial evidence of previous fear when the crime was committed. *United States v. Rodriguez-Pando*, 841 F.2d 1014 (9th Cir. 1988).

XIII. EXCEPTIONS TO THE HEARSAY RULE — PRESENT PHYSICAL CONDITION

A. PRINCIPLES

When an individual makes a statement about a then existing physical condition, an exception to the hearsay rule allows a third party to repeat what was said because: the condition being described is subjective (therefore no perception problems); the condition currently exists (therefore no memory problem); and, if the statements are made under conditions of apparent sincerity (which can be probed through the witness who heard and is repeating it), little reason remains for keeping the statements from the fact-finder.

When a patient makes statements to a medical doctor for treatment, the patient often needs to describe symptoms not being experienced at that very moment. Despite the lack of contemporaneity (required when such statements are made to non-medical personnel), courts have permitted the physicians to repeat what the patient said for the purpose of proving the truth of the symptoms being described. As the Supreme Court of the United States stated, "a statement made in the course of procuring medical services, where the declarant knows that a false statement may cause misdiagnosis or mistreatment, carries special guarantees of credibility that a trier of fact may not think replicated by courtroom testimony."[173]

The common law exception, however, only permitted the doctor to repeat for truth the patient's statements about present and past symptoms for the current illness for which treatment was sought. Statements of medical history, while important to treatment, were thought to be fraught with memory problems. Statements of causation were fraught with sincerity problems because the patient would know that this knowledge generally is unimportant to accurate

---

[173] White v. Illinois, 502 U.S. 346, 356 (1992) (finding the Confrontation Clause does not require the declarant to be unavailable before a witness may testify to spontaneous utterances and statements made by the declarant in the course of seeking medical advice). *See* United States v. Tome, 61 F.3d 1446, 1449 (10th Cir. 1995) ("this exception is premised on the theory that a patient's statements to her physician are likely to be particularly reliable because the patient has a self-interested motive to be truthful: She knows that the efficacy of her medical treatment depends upon the accuracy of the information she provides to the doctor.").

diagnosis and treatment by the doctor. If, however, the patient's statements of medical history and causation were *crucial* to the doctor's diagnosis and treatment, the exception allowed the doctor to repeat what the patient had told him, but the jury received instructions that the information could not be accepted for its truth — only to explain the doctor's conclusions.

Under Fed. R. Evid. 803(4), some of the guarantees of reliability are lost because the physician can repeat the patient's statements about symptoms, medical history and causation even though treatment is not sought — the patient can simply be seeking a diagnosis for litigation purposes. Relative to statements of history and causation, Rule 803(4) vastly expanded their admissibility. The doctor now may repeat for their truth all statements made by the patient relating to symptoms, medical history and causation, so long as the history and causation are *reasonably pertinent* to diagnosis or treatment. Rule 803(4) probably incorporated more changes from its common law precursor than any other common law hearsay exception that was codified.

RULE 803 FRE
Hearsay Exceptions; Availability of Declarant Immaterial

The following are not excluded by the hearsay rule, even though the declarant is available as a witness:

　. . . .

(3) Then existing mental, emotional, or physical condition. A statement of the declarant's then existing state of mind, emotion, sensation, or physical condition (such as intent, plan, motive, design, mental feeling, pain, and bodily health), but not including a statement of memory or belief to prove the fact remembered or believed unless it relates to the execution, revocation, identification, or terms of declarant's will.

(4) Statements of purposes of medical diagnosis or treatment. Statements made for purposes of medical diagnosis or treatment and describing medical history, or past or present symptoms, pain or sensations, or the inception or general character of the cause or external source thereof insofar as reasonably pertinent to diagnosis or treatment.

Changes from the common law:

(1) *Either diagnosis or treatment.* The patient can go for diagnosis *or* treatment. While statements given solely for developing testimony for trial are less trustworthy, this relaxation is premised on the belief the doctor can detect subtle exaggerations, or they can effectively be revealed during the cross-examination of the physician.

(2) *To anyone for treatment — not only medical doctors.* When a patient is in need of treatment, statements are often made to non-medical personnel. The rule now recognizes that those statements are as reliable as the ones made to a medical doctor, so long as the purpose of diagnosis or treatment is established.

(3) *By anyone for treatment.* The rule does not limit the exception to statements by the patient being treated. So long as the individual relating the facts had personal knowledge of another's symptoms (for example, a mother aware of her child's symptoms), or of the patient's complaints (for example, the trainer of an athlete hearing her complaints of dizziness before she became unconscious) that individual may be the source of the information upon which the physician acted.

(4) *Medical history is admissible for truth.* Previously, medical history was only admissible for the purpose of explaining the doctor's diagnosis and treatment.

(5) *Statements about causation are admissible for truth.* Previously, causation, like medical history, was only admissible if *necessary* to explain the doctor's conclusions.

(6) *Pertinent, not crucial to diagnosis or treatment.* The standard for admitting medical history and causation was reduced from "crucial" to "reasonably pertinent to diagnosis or treatment."

69 PRACTICES

Medical doctors repeating statements about medical history and causation — the origin of a broad illogical practice. Allowing medical doctors to repeat, for explanatory purposes only, otherwise inadmissible statements by the patient upon which the physician relied (i.e., medical history and causation), was the origin of the current practice under Rule 703 of permitting *all experts* to rely on otherwise inadmissible evidence so long as the evidence is of a type "reasonably relied upon by experts in the particular field in forming opinions or inferences on the subject."

RULE 703 FRE
Bases of Opinion Testimony by Experts

The facts or data in the particular case upon which an expert bases an opinion or inference may be those perceived by or made known to the expert at or before the hearing. If of a type reasonably relied upon by experts in the particular field in forming opinions or inferences upon the subject, the facts or data need not be admissible in evidence in order for the opinion or inference to be admitted. Facts or data that are otherwise inadmissible shall not be disclosed to the jury by the proponent of the opinion or inference unless the court determines their probative value in assisting the jury to evaluate the expert's opinion substantially outweighs their prejudicial effect.

This practice was illogical when it was limited to medical doctors and is no less so when extended to all expert witnesses. If a statement is crucial to a conclusion being offered for its truth, that conclusion cannot be accepted for its truth without also accepting the conclusion's basis. Under Rule 703, the inadmissible evidence only has to be "reasonably relied upon." Theoretically, it may be easier to accept the conclusion without accepting the entire basis (both admissible and inadmissible evidence), but it requires mental gymnastics that jurors may not appreciate or be capable of doing. *See* **PRACTICES NO. 105**, *infra*.

A paradox here is that as this illogical practice was extended from medical doctors to all expert witnesses by Rule 703, it was eliminated for medical doctors in Fed. R. Evid. 803(4), which made such statements admissible for their truth.

B. Relationship of Present Physical Condition Exception to Other Rules[174]

Rule 602. Lack of Personal Knowledge. Rule 602 requires that all witnesses speak from firsthand or personal knowledge. This means that all declarants of hearsay statements must have firsthand knowledge of the facts about which they speak because their statements are, in effect, presented as witnesses. Consequently, if persons other than the ones seeking treatment relate symptoms to doctors to facilitate treatment, Rule 602 requires that the declarant have personally observed those symptoms.[175] This excludes from Rule 803(4) statements of symptoms known to the declarant solely because the patient had previously mentioned them to the declarant. In this circumstance, because only the declarant has firsthand knowledge of what the patient said, the doctor's testimony concerning the patient's symptoms creates a double hearsay problem. To rectify these hearsay statements, the proponent must first show that the prior statement from the patient to the declarant is independently admissible under a hearsay exception. Usually, this is not difficult because the patient will have made the statements as spontaneous statements of present physical condition, and these statements fall within the scope of either Rule 803(1) (statements of present sense impression) or Rule 803(3) (statements of

---

[174] PAUL R. RICE & ROY A. KATRIEL, EVIDENCE: COMMON LAW AND FEDERAL RULES OF EVIDENCE § 5.05 [D][3] (LEXIS 5th ed. 2005)

[175] *See, e.g.,* Taylor v. Cameron Coca-Cola Bottling Co., Inc., No. 96-1122, 1997 WL 719106, *7 (W.D. Pa March 27, 1997) (admitting the statements of an affiant under Rule 803(4) when they were based on personal knowledge).

then existing physical condition). In addition, because under Rule 803(4) a patient may make statements for the purpose of medical treatment to non-physicians, the prior statement to the one who spoke to the physician may also be admissible under the rule. This is illustrated in the following diagram, which shows how a mother's statements, relating a child's complaints, may be admissible through the physician.

Rule 703. Bases of Opinion Testimony by Experts. Rule 703 allows experts to base their opinions on otherwise inadmissible facts or data, so long as those facts or data are of the type reasonably relied upon by experts in the particular field. Unlike Rule 803(4), the text of Rule 703 does not address whether such facts or data are admissible into evidence, and if so, for what purpose. Under Rule 803(4), the statements of symptoms, medical history, and causation are all admissible for truth if reasonably pertinent to diagnosis or treatment. This expanded admission of statements of medical history under the Federal Rules allows a criminal defendant to avoid taking the stand and yet still manage to tell his version of events by merely retaining a psychiatric expert to examine the defendant. The defendant can then relate to the medical expert his entire life history (or selected elements of it) and the psychiatrist can then use this information to form a diagnosis about the defendant. Rule 803(4) now allows all such statements to come in for their truth, thereby allowing the defendant to avoid the rigors of cross-examination and still tell his side of the story by putting his psychiatric expert witness on the stand.[176]

Rule 803(6). Records of Regularly Conducted Activity. Often the only available evidence of what a patient said to the attending physician will be hospital records or the records of the doctor's office because physicians, like other people, often forget or are not available as witnesses at trial. To prove the truth of the statement through these records produces a double hearsay problem. The records are "testifying" that the person that created them "told" them what the patient had said. The admission of these records will require the employment of the business records exception under Rule 803(6) as well as Rule 803(4). Through the business records exception, the proponent can establish the fact that the patient uttered certain words. Once it is established that the patient actually made the statement in question, Rule 803(4) allows a court to admit the statement into evidence for the truth of what was asserted if the declarant were seeking medical diagnosis or treatment. Using the hypothetical from the previous diagram regarding the mother who repeated to the doctor what the child had said to her, the following diagram illustrates how a triple hearsay problem is created and resolved.

---

[176] *See* United States v. Madoch, 935 F. Supp. 965 (N.D. Ill. 1996).

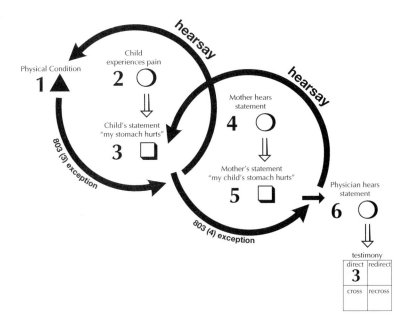

C. Applications — Present Physical Condition Exception

ONE

Roy Roberts brought an action against two police officers for police brutality. As part of his case-in-chief, Roberts seeks to introduce the diagnosis of the doctor who treated him. In his written diagnosis, the doctor stated that Roberts suffered "multiple contusions and hematoma, consistent with patient's claim of excessive force." Roberts seeks to introduce the diagnosis through the hospital record in which the diagnosis was logged. This statement was not admissible through the statements to doctors for diagnosis or treatment.

The evidence presents two levels of hearsay, the patient's statement to the doctor, and the doctor's written account of what he had been told. The second level, created by the attempt to introduce the doctor's diagnosis through the written hospital record rather than the doctor's live testimony, is resolvable by the business records exception to the hearsay rule. So long as the written reports were made in the routine of business based on personal knowledge by someone with a duty to make the record and for the purpose of furthering business ends, they are admissible to prove the truth of what was asserted in them. Therefore, any statements that the doctor made in the diagnosis based on his personal observation are admissible for their truth. Such statements would include his observation that Roberts suffered multiple contusions and hematoma (as well as what Roberts said about those injuries). The first level of hearsay, Roberts' statement concerning the cause of his injuries in the written diagnosis, presents a more difficult problem. Even though the doctor's records could prove that he made statements about the cause of his injuries, such statements are not admissible to prove their truth because Rule 803(4) makes admissible a patient's statements to his doctor only if the statements were pertinent to diagnosis or treatment. Statements regarding fault for the injuries treated, however, do not fall within this limitation. Therefore, Roberts' statement about excessive force would not be admissible under the exception. *Roberts v. Hollocher*, 664 F.2d 200, 204-05 (8th Cir. 1981).

TWO

Elizabeth Bulthius sued Eli Lilly & Company for the injuries that she received from having allegedly developed cancer after her mother ingested the drug diethylstilbesterol (DES) while she was pregnant with Elizabeth. The defendant moved for summary judgment. In opposition, the plaintiff presented her mother's deposition testimony in which her mother stated that in 1952 her attending doctor told her that she was being given DES. The judge refuses to consider this deposition because the mother's testimony would not have been admissible at trial. The decision was correct. The mother's testimony repeated what the doctor told her, and the doctor's statement was being offered to prove the truth of what he said. It is hearsay and not admissible under the common law present physical condition exception codified in Rule 803(4) because that exception is only applicable to statements made to the physician by the patient. Here the statement was being made in a deposition. *Bulthuis v. Rexall Corp.*, 789 F.2d 1315, 1316 (9th Cir. 1985).

THREE

The defendant is charged with aggravated sexual abuse of minor children. Waters, the social worker, questioned the children several times using a forensic interview protocol required by the State of Michigan. Both children revealed various incidences of sexual abuse by the defendant. The victims were also interviewed by two physicians and these interviews revealed the same type of abuse. The defendant objected to the admission of the social workers interviews with the children because Rule 803(4) is limited to statements from the patient for the purpose of medical diagnosis or treatment. The admission of this testimony was upheld on appeal because Waters testified that her primary purpose in interviewing the children was to diagnosis their mental health. Developing testimony was not the primary motive or even a major purpose of the interviews. She concluded that they were suffering from post-traumatic stress disorder and anxiety. *United States v. Kappell*, 2005 WL 1875516 (6th Cir. 2005).

XIV. EXCEPTIONS TO THE HEARSAY RULE — PAST RECOLLECTION RECORDED

A. PRINCIPLES

When a writing was made or adopted by a witness about that witness' perceptions, during or immediately after the event perceived, and the witness subsequently testifies that (1) he has no memory of the matter observed; (2) the writing is authentic; and (3) that the writing was accurate when made, the writing may be offered in lieu of his testimony.[177] The rationales for the exception involve both necessity and assurances of reliability. The necessity arises from the declarant's complete loss of memory. Reliability is insured, somewhat, by the age of the writing and timing of its creation. Having been created closer to the time of the event observed, memory problems are reduced. A contemporaneity requirement may reduce some sincerity problems arising from litigation resulting from disputes about the observed event.

Moving away from the underlying rationale, Rule 803(5) diminishes the necessity rationale because the witness no longer needs to have completely forgotten the event. He only needs to be unable to testify fully and accurately. Reliability is somewhat reduced by the fact that the writing no longer needs to be made "simultaneous with or immediately after" the event observed. Rule 803(5) only requires that it be made "when the matter was fresh in the witness' memory." What is fresh? How is it calculated? Decisions diverge significantly. Some have permitted months to pass and subsequent writings admitted as recorded recollection.[178]

---

[177] *See* United States v. Porter, 986 F.2d 1014, 1016-17 (6th Cir.), *cert. denied*, 510 U.S. 933 (1993) ("A document may be read to a jury under the rule as past recorded recollection if (1) the witness once had knowledge about the matters in the document; (2) the witness now has insufficient recollection to testify fully and accurately; and (3) the record was made at a time when the matter was fresh in the witness' memory and reflected the witness' knowledge correctly."). *See also* United States v. Patterson, 678 F.2d 774, 778 (9th Cir.), *cert. denied*, 459 U.S. 911 (1982); United States v. Edwards, 539 F.2d 689, 691-92 (9th Cir.), *cert. denied*, 459 U.S. 911 (1982). For an extensive discussion of the past recollection recorded exception to the hearsay rule, *see* Newell H. Blakely, *Past Recollection Recorded: Restrictions on Use as Exhibit and Proposals for Change*, 17 HOUS. L. REV. 441, 446-63 (1980).

[178] *See* United States v. Smith, 197 F.3d 225, 231 (6th Cir. 1999) (finding that a fifteen month delay satisfied the freshness requirement when the defendant could not demonstrate why the matter was not "fresh" when recorded); United States v. Patterson, 678 F.2d 774, 779 (9th Cir. 1982) (accepting a ten month delay between observation and recordation); United States v. Senak, 527 F.2d 129 (7th Cir. 1975) (determining that a three-year delay satisfied the rule).

RULE 803 FRE
Hearsay Exceptions; Availability of Declarant Immaterial

The following are not excluded by the hearsay rule, even though the declarant is available as a witness:

. . . .

(5) Records recollection. A memorandum or record concerning a matter about which a witness once had knowledge but now has insufficient recollection to enable the witness to testify fully and accurately, shown to have been made or adopted by the witness when the matter was fresh in the witness' memory and to reflect that knowledge correctly. If admitted, the memorandum or record may be read into evidence but may not itself be received as an exhibit unless offered by an adverse party.

70 PRACTICES

Avoid this exception when possible. The past recollection recorded exception has several restrictions: (1) The declarant must be called as a witness to authenticate the written instrument; (2) the witness must not have sufficient recollection to testify fully and accurately; and (3) the writing must be read into evidence, and cannot be offered as an exhibit by its proponent.[179] Because none of these limitations apply to the present sense impression exception in Rule 803(1), Rule 803(5) should be avoided, unless the written statement was recorded so long after the event that the statement cannot be considered to have documented the described event "immediately after" its occurrence, and therefore, is not within the scope of Rule 803(1).

Under the Federal Rules of Evidence the present sense impression is the oral equivalent of the common law past recollection recorded, except for the fact that the present sense impression exception is not limited to oral statements.[180]

---

[179] *See* Newton v. Ryder Transp. Serv., Inc., 206 F.3d 772, 774 (8th Cir. 2000).

[180] *See* United States v. Mitchell, 145 F.3d 572, 577 (3d Cir. 1998) (finding an anonymous note inadmissible under Rule 803(1) when no evidence demonstrated that the writer had no time to "reflect and fabricate.").

RULE 803 FRE
Hearsay Exceptions; Availability of Declarant Immaterial

The following are not excluded by the hearsay rule, even though the declarant is available as a witness:

(1) Present Sense Impression. A statement describing or explaining an event or condition made while the declarant was perceiving the event or condition, or immediately thereafter.

The new present sense impression exception borrowed language from the common law definition of past recollection recorded when it required that the statement have been made "simultaneously with or immediately after" the event being described. This, coupled with the absence of an explicit limitation in the rule, prompts many courts to admit written statements, previously admitted as past recollection recorded, as a present sense impression. Present sense impression has advantages over past recollection recorded: (1) the declarant need not be the witness called to authenticate it; (2) lost memory by the declarant is irrelevant (both his testimony and the writing can be offered into evidence); and (3) the writing can be offered into evidence as an exhibit and taken to the jury deliberation room (past recollection recorded will not be received as an exhibit unless offered by the opposing party).

B. Relationship of Past Recollection Recorded Exception to Other Rules[181]

Rule 612. Writing Used to Refresh Memory. One should clearly distinguish between the hearsay exception of past recollection recorded, through which a writing is offered into evidence for the truth of the matter asserted therein, and present recollection revived, which involves a proponent's use of that same writing to refresh a witness' exhausted memory but is not offered into evidence. Under the concept of present recollection revived, the writing is not used as evidence because the witness who examined it is able to testify to the relevant facts based on the present recollection which the examination of the writing revived. Consequently, a proponent's limited use of a writing to revive a witness' recollection poses no hearsay problem.

A common tactic of trial attorneys in using a writing to refresh the recollection of a witness involves reading the damaging portions to the witness and then asking whether they refresh his recollection. This tactic operates to place before the jury the substance of the writing even though it is not being offered into evidence. The hope, of course, is that the jury will use it improperly, even though explicitly instructed to do otherwise. Before the writing has not been qualified

---

[181] PAUL R. RICE & ROY A. KATRIEL, EVIDENCE: COMMON LAW AND FEDERAL RULES OF EVIDENCE § 5.05 [E][3] (LEXIS 5th ed. 2005).

under one of the exceptions to the hearsay rule, the court should only permit counsel to show the document to the witness. Neither the witness nor counsel should be permitted to read it aloud in front of the jury.[182]

Rule 901. Requirements of Authentication or Identification. The authentication of a document containing a past recollection recorded must either be through the testimony of the person who authored that document or the person who adopted it after it was prepared by another. Generally, only these persons can establish the elements of the exception, because the exception applies only if the proponent has shown that one of these persons had firsthand knowledge of the event recorded, that this person currently has "insufficient recollection to enable him to testify fully and accurately," that the writing was made while the witness' memory was fresh, and that the writing was accurate when it was made or adopted.

Rule 1002. Requirement of Original. Although Rule 803(5) will not allow the introduction of the writing as an exhibit unless the adverse party offers it, the proponent is not relieved of the requirement of producing the original of the writing if its contents are being proved, pursuant to the best evidence or original writing rule that is codified in Rule 1002. Although the proponent is not offering the writing into evidence as an exhibit, he is still proving its contents — it is only being filtered through oral testimony.

C. Applications — Past Recollection Recorded Exception

An individual was involved in a severe car accident with another car. While lying in the hospital the next day, the injured driver described the accident in his diary. The injured party subsequently died. To establish the defendant's negligence in a wrongful death action, the deceased's estate seeks to introduce the his diary. Objected to as hearsay, the diary is excluded. It was not admissible under the past recollection recorded exception because it is only applicable to the recorded recollection of a witness who is present to authenticate the accuracy of the writing. *Zenith Radio Corp. v. Matsushita Electrical Industrial Co.*, 505 F. Supp. 1190, 1228 n.48 (E.D. Pa. 1980).

---

[182] *See* Goings v. United States, 377 F.2d 753, 760-61 (8th Cir. 1967).

XV. EXCEPTIONS TO THE HEARSAY RULE — BUSINESS RECORDS

A. PRINCIPLES

Business records are any regularly maintained records relied upon by the individual or entity that maintains them. For the business records exception to apply, the proponent must establish the following elements:

(1) The records were regularly maintained and relied upon;

(2) The records were maintained by individuals with personal knowledge;

(3) The individual with personal knowledge made the entries pursuant to a business duty to the entity keeping the records;

(4) The entries were made at or near the time of the transaction or event recorded.

(5) These elements must be established by someone with personal knowledge of how the records are maintained.[183]

RULE 803 FRE
Hearsay Exceptions; Availability of Declarant Immaterial

The following are not excluded by the hearsay rule, even though the declarant is available as a witness:

. . . .

(6) Records of regularly conducted activity. A memorandum, report, record, or data compilation, in any form, of acts, events, conditions, opinions, or diagnoses, made at or near the time by, or from information transmitted by, a person with knowledge, if kept in the course of a regularly conducted business activity, and if it was the regular practice of that business activity to make the memorandum, report, record, or data compilation, all as shown by the testimony of the custodian or other qualified witness, of by certification that complies with Rule 902(11), Rule 902(12), or a statute permitting certification, unless the source of information or the method or circumstances of preparation indicate lack of trustworthiness. The term "business" as used in this paragraph includes business, institution, association, profession, occupation, and calling of every kind whether or not conducted for profit.

---

[183] *See, e.g.,* United States v. So, 105 F.3d 667, 1996 WL 734863, *2 (9th Cir. 1996) (unpublished opinion) (stating the elements of 803(6) as records (1) made at or near the time of the event, (2) recorded by a person with knowledge, and (3) kept in the regular course of business, as cited in United States v. Bland, 961 F.2d 123, 127 (9th Cir.), *cert. denied,* 506 U.S. 858 (1992)).

RULE 902 FRE
Self-authentication

Extrinsic evidence of authenticity as a condition precedent to admissibility is not required with respect to the following:

. . . .

(11) Certified domestic records of regularly conducted activity. The original or a duplicate of a domestic record of regularly conducted activity, which would be admissible under Rule 803(6), if accompanied by a written declaration of its custodian or other qualified person, in a manner complying with any Act of Congress or rule prescribed by the Supreme Court pursuant to statutory authority, certifying that the record —

(A) was made at or near the time of the occurrence of the matters set forth, by or from information transmitted by, a person with knowledge of those matters;

(B) was kept in the course of the regularly conducted activity; and

(C) was made by the regularly conducted activity as a regular practice.

A party intending to offer a record in evidence under this paragraph must provide written notice of that intention to all adverse parties, and must make the record and declaration available for inspection sufficiently in advance of their offer in evidence to provide an adverse party with a fair opportunity to challenge them.

(12) Certified foreign records of regularly conducted activity. In a civil case, the original or a duplicate of a foreign record of regularly conducted activity, which would be admissible under Rule 803(6), if accompanied by a written declaration by the custodian or other qualified person certifying that the record —

(A) was made at or near the time of the occurrence of the matters set forth, by or from information transmitted by, a person with knowledge of those matters;

(B) was kept in the course of the regularly conducted activity; and

(C) was made by the regularly conducted activity as a regular practice.

The declaration must be signed in a manner which, if falsely made, would subject the maker to criminal penalty under the laws of the country where the declaration is signed. A party intending to offer a record into evidence under this paragraph must provide written notice of that intention to all adverse parties, and must make the record and declaration available for inspection sufficiently in advance of their offer into evidence to provide an adverse party with a fair opportunity to challenge them.

71 PRACTICES

Sponsoring witness — what he doesn't know won't necessarily hurt you. The sponsoring witness establishes the relevance of an item — providing the factual foundation to prove that the item is what the proponent claims. If the item is a written record that has been classified as hearsay and the proponent claims that it falls within the business records exception to the hearsay rule, the proponent must lay the factual foundation for that classification through the sponsoring witness. To accomplish this, the sponsoring witness need not be the official custodian that was required by the early common law. The sponsoring witness may be anyone within the company who knows how, when and why the company maintains the records.[184]

The sponsoring witness *must know*:

(1) the basis upon which the records are maintained — personal knowledge by the entrant;

(2) that the records were made pursuant to a duty to the enterprise;

(3) that they regularly made entries into the record;

(4) at or near the time of the event recorded; and

(5) that the enterprise relies upon those records.

The sponsoring witness does *not need to know*:

(1) the identify of the specific individual who made the entry; or

(2) anything about the substance of what was recorded.

72 PRACTICES

Foundation witness no longer needs to appear. The foundation for admitting the business record no longer has to be established by live testimony from a custodian or other qualified person. Under Rules 902(11) & (12), an affidavit of a qualified person will suffice. This affidavit will be made by the same individual who otherwise could be called to testify and it must establish the same foundation facts — the only difference is that the foundation will no

---

[184] *See* United States v. Turner, 189 F.3d 712, 720 (8th Cir.), *cert. denied,* 524 U.S. 909 (1999) (stating the "sponsoring witness need not possess or even see the records in question before trial").

longer be subject to cross-examination. Therefore, the factual foundation for all challenges must be developed in the pretrial discovery process.

This procedure may be problematic for the opposing party in jurisdictions with "rocket dockets" and limited discovery probes. When there is limited time and limited discovery probes available to the opposing party, it is unlikely that they will be used to fish for potential deficiencies in business records, unless those records are central to the cause of action.

This problem, however, may never arise because the conditions for using the self-authentication provision in Rule 902(11) may make it unattractive to many parties. Rule 902(11) requires the party using the affidavit procedure to make the records being authenticated *available to the opposing party prior to trial*.

A party intending to offer a record in evidence under this paragraph must provide written notice of that intention to all adverse parties, and must make the record available for inspection sufficiently in advance of its offer in evidence to provide an adverse party with a fair opportunity to challenge it.

This requirement may compel the pretrial disclosure of records that otherwise would not be sought by the opponent through discovery demands. Consequently, the procedure may benefit the opposing party more than the party offering the records. This is particularly true in civil litigation where executives of a company will be testifying on other matters and can be used as the sponsoring witness for the company's internal records. Therefore, this new self-authentication procedure may prove to be less efficient and more costly because it can be more intrusive. Consequently, for the reasons discussed in **PRACTICES NO. 73,** *infra,* the use of the new authentication procedure may be reserved for records that have already been produced or records of third parties that will be offered into evidence by third parties at trial.

73 PRACTICES

The upside and downside of certification. The *upside* of certification is the increased efficiency and reduced costs associated with bringing witnesses to the location of the trial, solely to go through the formality of establishing the elements of the business records exception. This would be particularly true when individuals would have to be brought from foreign countries. There are, however, *several downsides* to the use of certifications:

(1) *Free discovery.* As discussed above, when using certifications, the proponent is required to disclose the records to the opposing side sufficiently in advance of trial to give the opposing party a reasonable opportunity to prepare to challenge it. The downside is that if you use the certification with your own business records you may be providing *free discovery* to the

opposing side. You are giving access to your evidence without forcing the adversary to use one of its often restricted numbers of its discovery probes. Increasingly, rocket dockets are being employed, and with these shortened pretrial processes, limitations are being placed on the number of discovery demands parties are permitted to employ. Consequently, certification may generally be used only when a party is offering the business records of a third party or his own records that have already been discovered.

(2) *Additional time to find grounds for objection.* By giving the opposing party your business records in advance of trial, you needlessly give that party extra time to find reasons to object to its admissibility. This is unnecessary if the foundation for such records can be laid at trial by corporate executives who will otherwise be called to testify on substantive matters.

(3) *Out on a limb when objections are raised.* If you have used the certification, and therefore do not call a witness to sponsor the records, when concrete concerns are raised by the opposing party (after having been given time to examine them), you may have no one on your witness list who can adequately respond to the problems. Since the opposing party need not give you the same notice of its objections that you have been required to give that party of your intentions to use the certification, this may catch you totally by surprise. As a consequence, you may find yourself unprepared to meet the specific challenges.

74 PRACTICES

My business records can become your business records. A business record is maintained by an employee with personal knowledge of the matters recorded therein pursuant to a business duty. The form and appearance of this record is irrelevant to its status as the company's record. Therefore, when a receiving clerk checks a bill of lading against the products that were delivered, his initialing of each entry in the bill of lading that contains the letterhead of the vendor becomes the business record of the receiving company by adoption. Regardless of the company's name appearing at the top of the piece of paper, to the extent the bill reflects the employee's personal knowledge, it is that company's business record. The employee does not have to create a new piece of paper with a consistent form, size, color and heading in order to activate the business records exception. That would intolerably be elevating form over substance by requiring a meaningless act to be performed for the sake of consistency.[185]

---

[185] *See, e.g.,* United States v. Ullrich, 580 F.2d 765, 771 (5th Cir. 1978) (finding the document of one business integrated in another business when the second corroborated the contents of the report); United States v. Pfeiffer, 539 F.3d 668, 671 (8th Cir. 1976) (noting that the custodian "was

75 PRACTICES

Where business records begin and what they can prove. The business record begins at the point when an individual possesses *personal knowledge and a business duty* to make a record of the facts perceived. This point of coalescence marks when the reliability of the record begins because of the enterprise's reliance. The records containing those entries can prove the truth of what the employee recorded. As these records are successively used within the enterprise to develop additional records, based on additional personal knowledge and duty by other employees, those additional records are equally admissible to prove the truth of all entries.

Example

A clerk in the receiving department of a company checks the quantity and quality of goods received by rail at the back gate. He notes this delivery and places the note in his ledger. Because a shipping clerk checked the quantity and quality of the materials that were received, he has personal knowledge of those facts. He also has a business duty to record those facts and maintain a ledger. Therefore, the company can offer his ledger under the business records exception to the hearsay rule to prove what was received on any particular day. See Diagram A below.

Diagram A

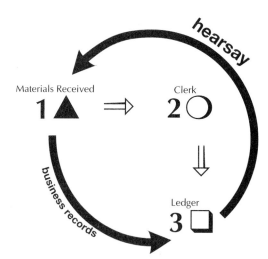

familiar with these shipping invoices and the same delivery slips were checked by [him] against [the] bills of lading for accuracy and proper freight payments."). *See also* United States v. Childs, 5 F.3d 1328, 1333-34 (9th Cir. 1993) (relying on *Ullrich*).

For the ledger (3) to be used to prove the delivery (1), the quality of the evidence depends on the perception, memory, sincerity of the clerk (2), who is not a witness. Because the clerk (2) made the ledger (3) from both personal knowledge of (1) and a duty to report it, (3) is admissible as a business record to prove (1).

76 PRACTICES

Multiple levels of hearsay — one exception. Within a single company, numerous uses might be made of an entry after it is originally recorded. The single business records exception takes care of the multiple levels of hearsay that may follow the use of that original entry. The final accounting statements generated from thousands of those entries going through multiple steps in the accounting process are also made admissible by the single business records exception.[186]

Example

An employee in the receiving department of a company checks the quantity and quality of goods received at the back gate. Making a note of this delivery he places the original note in his ledger and sends copies to other departments within the company — accounts payable, inventory, and the shop where the order originated (and where the materials will be used to fabricate other products). This is a daily procedure through which thousands of deliveries are documented. At the end of an accounting period the accounting department prepares a cost-of-goods-sold statement based on the accumulated records sent to it by the receiving department and the fabrication shop where the raw materials are used and a commercial product is manufactured. Because a shipping clerk checked the quantity and quality of the materials received at the back gate, he has personal knowledge of those facts. He also has a business duty to record those facts and send that information to other department. Therefore, not only can his ledger be offered under the business records exception to the hearsay rule to prove what they received on any particular day, the accounting department can rely on that ledger, as well as the records of the fabrication shops (that also relied on the receiving department notes) to produce a cost of goods sold statement that can be introduced to prove the truth of what it reports. See Diagram B:

---

[186] As the Fifth Circuit in United States v. Ismoila, 100 F.3d 380, 392 (5th Cir. 1996) noted:

Double hearsay exists when a business record is prepared by one employee from information supplied by another employee. If both the source and the recorder of the information, as well as every other participant in the chain producing the record, are acting in the regular course of business, the multiple hearsay is excused by Rule 803(6). However, if the source of the information is an outsider, Rule 803(6) does not, by itself, permit the admission of the business record. The outsider's statement must fall within another hearsay exception to be admissible because it does not have the presumption of accuracy that statements made during the regular course of business have.

Diagram B

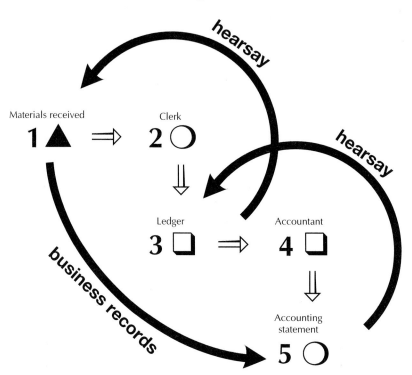

As illustrated in Diagram A, the ledger (3) may be used to prove the delivery (1), under the business records exception. In the same fashion, the accounting statement (5) can be offered under the business records exception to prove the accumulation of thousands of entries at stage (1). Because the accountant (4) has personal knowledge of what the receiving clerk reported to him, and the accountant has a business duty to report that information in cost-of-good-sold statements, those statements are as admissible as the individual ledger entries in (3). Because the accountant (4) made the statement (5) from both personal knowledge of (3) and a duty to report it again with the additional information he has acquired on his own or from another employee, the accountant's records and reports are admissible business records to prove all recorded fact from (1) forward.

77 PRACTICES

"Regularly maintained" is not synonymous with "routinely made." A common misunderstanding is that the business records must be routinely made to come within the 803(6) hearsay exception for business records. Inappro-

priately, they equate systematic with routine.[187]

Systematic means that the records are not made haphazardly, but that they are regularly made as part of an organized practice. Routine, on the other hand, connotes entries that are repetitive in nature. If entries had to be routine to be admissible, the records of construction costs of a new foundry in a plant that is rebuilt every 30 years would not be admissible. Such a result, of course, would be absurd. The lack of "routineness" should not be dispositive. So long as the other elements of the exception are established, there are sufficient indicia of reliability.

This is not to say, however, that the absence of routineness should not factor into the court's assessment of the reliability of the records. Indeed, a non-routine record should raise red flags for the court — prompting an inquiry into the nature, reasons and use being made of the unusual entries. It should not, however, be seen as a preclusive factor. Lack of routineness should be seen as another factor that the court should consider when assessing whether "the source of information or the method or circumstances of preparation indicate lack of trustworthiness," such as when documents are prepared primarily in anticipation of litigation — the *Palmer v. Hoffman*[188] reservation in Rule 803(6).

78 PRACTICES

Expert opinions in business records. The expert opinions contained in business records are *presumed* to meet the requirements of the expert opinion rules — Rules 702 and 703. The opponent of the business records is given the burden of challenging those qualifications and the challenge generally will be limited to the question of weight.[189]

---

[187] *See, e.g.,* Pierce v. Atchison Topeka & Sante Fe R.R. Co., 110 F.3d 431, 444 (7th Cir. 1997) (finding that the district court did not abuse its discretion in not admitting a file memorandum, despite the fact the sponsoring witness "testified that he maintained personal files in the ordinary course of business and that he drafted memoranda in order to record 'unique' dealings with employees, but that it was not usual for him to draft such memoranda," because the memorandum had not been made routinely.)

[188] 318 U.S. 109 (1943).

[189] *See* United States v. Locavoli, 604 F.2d 613, 622-23 (9th Cir. 1979), *cert. denied,* 446 U.S. 935 (1980) ("We see no reason to adopt an inflexible rule that every case requires the proponent of a business record containing expert opinion to affirmatively establish the qualifications of the person forming the opinion. Rule 803(6) expressly provides for the exclusion of a business record if the source of information indicates a lack of trustworthiness."). *But see* Forward Comm. Corp. v. United States, 608 F.2d 485, 510 (Ct. Cl. 1979) ("[U]nless Rule 803(6) is deemed to override the opinion rules, it should not be construed to allow the introduction of expert opinions without opportunity to ascertain the qualifications of the maker, the extent of his study or for other reasons to cross-examine him. Otherwise, the report of every appraiser would be admissible upon the mere showing that the preparer was in the business of making such appraisals, without more.").

This places another burden on the parties in the pretrial discovery process that is constantly being restricted in time and scope as "rocket dockets" become more prevalent. Even without such restrictions, the burden is often impossible to meet because the admissibility of business records does not require the identification by the sponsoring witness of the individuals who made particular entries. Over an extended period, many individuals may have been responsible for any given entry. The consequence of eliminating the foundation otherwise required by Article VII may be that entries of questionable reliability are being accepted in court under the assumption that businesses wouldn't tolerate unqualified employees.

79 PRACTICES

Business records — admissions by those who maintain them. When a party's own business records are offered against him, the proponent can employ either the business records exception in Rule 803(6) or the vicarious admissions exclusion from the definition of hearsay in Rule 801(d)(2)(C) & (D). The proponent need only establish the statement was made by an employee who communicated on matters that were within the scope of his employment responsibilities.[190]

RULE 801 FRE
Definition

The following definitions apply under this article:

. . . .

(d) Statements which are not hearsay. A statement is not hearsay if —

. . . .

(2) Admission by party-opponent. The statement is offered against a party and is (A) the party's own statement, in either an individual or a representative capacity or (B) a statement of which the party has manifested an adoption or belief in its truth, or (C) a statement by a person authorized by the party to make a statement concerning the subject,

---

[190] *See, e.g.,* United States v. Smith, 609 F.2d 1294, 1301 n.7 (9th Cir. 1979) ("Since the [business] records contain [the defendant's] signature, they may more appropriately be regarded as non-hearsay admissions under Rule 8011(d)(2)(A) and 801(d)(2)(B). If so, compliance with the requirement of Rule 803(6) is irrelevant. We need not decide whether the documents were admissions, however, since they are admissible under the business records exception."). *See also* United States v. Emenogha, 1 F.3d 473, 484 n.14 (7th Cir. 1993).

or (D) a statement by the party's agent or servant concerning a matter within the scope of the agency or employment, made during the existence of the relationship, or (E) a statement by a co-conspirator of a party during the course and in furtherance of the conspiracy. The contents of the statement shall be considered but are not alone sufficient to establish the declarant's authority under subdivision (C), the agency or employment relationship and scope thereof under subdivision (D), or the existence of the conspiracy and the participation therein of the declarant and the party against whom the statement is offered under subdivision (E).

Establishing a vicarious admission can be as cumbersome as establishing the business records exception — especially with the new methods of authentication in Rules 902(11) and (12). Nevertheless, the admissions route may offer an advantage in that the admission rule does not contain a provision that permits it to be excluded if personal knowledge of the employee is not demonstrated or "the source of information or the method or circumstances of preparation indicate lack of trustworthiness."

80 PRACTICES

Absence of business records proving a negative — an unnecessary exception. If a business record is established to record certain events and conditions observed by employees, and that report fails to include a reference to certain facts when describing the event (facts, which if seen, would have been reported), by negative implication, the report would be evidence that the particular event did not occur or that a particular fact was not true. The same should be true if no report exists describing a particular event in the business record and such a report normally would be made and filed in a particular record if the event had occurred. If the regularity of the practice of reporting, and reliance on that report by the enterprise keeping it, give assurances that the events or conditions mentioned are accurately described, the same logic gives assurances of accuracy for the events or conditions not mentioned or described.[191]

Nevertheless, Rule 803(7) recognizes a hearsay exception for the absence of a record. This absence may prove the nonoccurrence or nonexistence of the matter that would have been reported. This exception, and its sister exception addressing the absence of entries in public records, 803(10), are logically unnecessary. To come within the coverage of 803(7), the record must first comply with the requirements of Rule 803(6). The same is true for Rules 803(10) and (8). Having complied with the requirements of the business and public

---

[191] *See* Armstead v. HUD, 815 F.2d 278, 282 n.3 (3d Cir. 1987) (noting that the admission of business records to show the absence of an entry requires the proponent to lay a proper foundation and that such evidence may be excluded if the records indicate a lack of trustworthiness).

records rules, these "absence" exceptions simply allow what logic has already permitted.

RULE 803 FRE
Hearsay Exceptions; Availability of Declarant Immaterial

The following are not excluded by the hearsay rule, even though the declarant is available as a witness:

. . . .

(7) Absence of entry in records kept in accordance with the provisions of paragraph (6). Evidence that a matter is not included in the memoranda, report, records, or data compilations, in any form, kept in accordance with the provisions of paragraph (6), to prove the nonoccurrence or nonexistence of the matter, if the matter was of a kind of which a memorandum, report, record, or data compilation was regularly made and preserved, unless the sources of information or other circumstances indicate lack of trustworthiness.

. . . .

(10) Absence of public record or entry. To prove the absence of a record, report, statement, or data compilation, in any form, or the nonoccurrence or nonexistence of a matter of which a record, report, statement, or data compilation, in any form, was regularly made and preserved by a public office or agency, evidence in the form of a certification in accordance with Rule 902, or testimony, that diligent search failed to disclose the record, report, statement, or data compilation, or entry.

All that Rule 803(10) adds is the acknowledgment that a failure to find after a "diligent search" can be certified under Rule 902. That certification possibility, however, exists without Rule 803(10), and the requirement of a "diligent search" failing to disclose the report is a logical imperative of this means of proving nonoccurrence through Rules 803(6) and (8).[192]

---

[192] One court has held that when the government files a "Certificate of Nonexistence of Record" demonstrating the record does not exist within its files, once this certificate satisfies Rule 902, it *ipso facto* satisfies Rule 803(10). United States v. Mateo-Mendez, 21 F.3d 1039, 1043 (9th Cir. 2000).

B. Relationship of Business Records Exception to Other Rules[193]

Rules 401 and 402. Relevant Evidence. When the relevance of evidence and of test results from that evidence require the evidence to remain unaltered from the time it was seized, the proponent of the evidence and test results must establish a *chain of custody* dispelling possibilities of alteration and misidentification. If, for example, blood were extracted from one alleged to have been an intoxicated driver, the results of blood/alcohol tests would usually be admissible only after the proponent had adequately traced the chain of individuals who had access, custody, or control over the extraction, and provided assurances through their testimony that the blood remains the original unaltered substance.

If the blood specimen were taken in the regular course of business, such as in a hospital, the tests were conducted pursuant to that same regular business practice, procedures were in place to keep the blood from being contaminated, and all of this were established pursuant to Rule 803(6), the equivalent of a chain of custody has been established. A further chain of custody is probably unnecessary.[194]

Rule 602. Lack of Personal Knowledge. Because Rule 602 requires that witnesses testify from personal knowledge, a business record cannot begin until there is a coalescence in a single person of (1) personal knowledge of relevant information and (2) a business duty to report or record that information. The personal knowledge satisfies Rule 602 and the business duty to record or report ensures that the written account is a reliable substitute for the testimony of that person. While the official custodian or other qualified person must establish these requirements, that individual need not have personal knowledge of each entry. Therefore, the personal knowledge of the original entrant will be established from business custom. See **PRACTICES NO. 71**, *supra*.

Rule 803(8). Public Records and Reports. Rule 803(8) does not permit the government to use records or reports of law enforcement personnel against criminal defendants to the extent that such records or reports include either matters observed or facts otherwise found after authorized investigations. Can

---

[193] PAUL R. RICE & ROY A. KATRIEL, EVIDENCE: COMMON LAW AND FEDERAL RULES OF EVIDENCE § 5.05 [F][3] (LEXIS 5th ed. 2005)

[194] Pieters v. B-Right Trucking, Inc., 669 F. Supp. 1463 (N.D. Ind. 1987) (finding such evidence is admissible under Rule 803(6) "if transmitted by a declarant (such as a doctor or a nurse) who reports to the recordkeeper as part of a regular business . . . [if it] was kept in the course of a regular conducted business activity, and if it was the regular practice of the business to make the record, as shown by the witness"). While records of doctors and nurses kept in the ordinary course of business satisfy the rule, statements by a patient relating his own medical history will not. *See* Cook v. Hoppin, 783 F.2d 684, 689 (7th Cir. 1986).

a court admit public documents not admissible under Rule 803(8) as business records under Rule 803(6), if the documents comply with the elements of that provision? The majority of courts have held that 803(8) is not preclusive — 803(6) remains a possibility.[195]

Rule 803(17). Market Reports, Commercial Publications. Rule 803(17) recognizes "Market quotations, tabulations, lists, directories, or other published compilations, generally used and relied upon by the public or by persons in particular occupations." Although courts at common law did not generally recognize the materials listed in Rule 803(17) as exceptions to the hearsay rule, there was a growing trend to admit a limited class of reports, journals, directories, and tabulations that were commonly used in trades or businesses and widely accepted as being accurate and reliable. Such materials included, for example, price listings, market quotations, telephone directories, and mortality tables. This provision, therefore, represents a codification of the common law trend. The types of publications classified under this rule are those widely circulated, generally relied upon, and that deal with compilations of relatively straightforward objective facts that do not require subjective analysis.[196]

In many instances, Rule 803(17) and the business records exception in Rule 803(6) will overlap. In *United States v. Grossman*,[197] for example, the prosecution introduced into evidence, for the purpose of proving the value of items stolen, a catalog that a wholesaler published each year for distribution to retail establishments. Because a purchasing agent who was familiar with the catalog's preparation and use authenticated it, the court concluded that it was properly qualified as an exception under both the business records provision and Rule 803(17).[198] The value of Rule 803(17), of course, arises when the custodian or other qualified person of the materials is not available as a sponsoring witness: the evidence can still be admissible because it will be self-authenticating under Rule 902(6) as printed material purporting to be a periodical, or under Rule 902(7), because of the inscriptions, signs, tags, or labels indicating ownership, control, or origin that would have been affixed in the course of business.

Rule 1006. Summaries. The best evidence rule requires that the original of documents be used at trial when their contents are being proved. If such documentary evidence is too voluminous to be conveniently presented and examined in court, Rule 1006 allows a proponent to present it in summary form, so long

---

[195] *See* McGarry v. United States, 388 F.2d 862 (1st Cir. 1967). *See also* United States v. Metzger, 778 F.2d 1195, 1201 (6th Cir. 1985) (finding Rule 803(8)(C) not preclusive); United States v. King, 613 F.2d 670, 673 (7th Cir. 1980) (same). *But see* United States v. Oates, 560 F.2d 45, 78 (2d Cir. 1977) (holding that when rule 803 (8)(B) or (C) bars admission of hearsay evidence, the proponent may not then use Rule 803(6)).

[196] *See* White Industries v. Cessna Aircraft Co., 611 F. Supp. 1049, 1068-69 (W.D. Mo. 1985).

[197] 614 F.2d 296 (1st Cir. 1980).

[198] *Id.* at 297.

as the underlying documents are available to the opponent for examination.[199] If the proponent offers the contents of these summarized documents for their truth and the summary is written rather than orally presented through the testimony of the individual who examined the voluminous materials, the proponent creates a double hearsay problem. The first layer stems from the underlying documents, and the second layer is the summary itself. Note that the summary rule is only an exception to the best evidence rule. The rule is not an exception to the hearsay rule. To be admissible, therefore, the proponent must find an applicable exception for each hearsay level. *See* **PRINCIPLES NO. 96**, *infra.*

If the summarized documents constitute regularly maintained business records, Rule 803(6) satisfies the first level of hearsay. The same exception satisfies the second level of hearsay if the summaries were created in the regular course of business — for instance, summary financial statements like income statements, cost of goods sold statements and cash-flow statements. If, however, the summaries were created specifically for the litigation, as is often the case, they do not qualify as business records under the Supreme Court's holding in *Palmer v. Hoffman*.[200] The exceptions most likely to satisfy this hearsay link are present sense impression, Rule 803(1), and past recollection recorded, Rule 803(5). For either of these exceptions to apply, of course, the person who prepared the summary would have to be called to authenticate it. If, as is most often the case, the summary is created by a computer, no hearsay problem would be created because only individuals can be declarants and create hearsay under Rule 801. The program used to create the summary, however, would have to be authenticated.

C. Applications — Business Records Exception

ONE

There was a heated exchange between the plaintiff and his superior, during which the superior made a comment about Jews. The plaintiff is Jewish. The plaintiff claims that he reacted strongly to the comment, the superior apologized and the plaintiff commented to the superior "You're done!" Following this exchange two things happened. First, the plaintiff was fired. Second, before the firing the superior wrote a memo memorializing his version of the event. It was considerably different from the plaintiff's version that was testified to in the subsequent trial for retaliatory firing. When the defendant tried to introduce the memo as a business record it was rejected by the court for two reasons. First, the court did not believe it was prepared in the ordinary course of business. The testimony on this point was sketchy and contradictory. Second, the circumstances

---

[199] *See* United States v. Strissle, 920 F.2d 1162-64 (4th Cir. 1990) (finding that the underlying evidence supporting the summaries does not need to be admitted into evidence so long as the supporting documents were admissible and available to the defendant).

[200] 318 U.S. 109 (1943).

under which the memo was prepared made it untrustworthy. It was prepared when the superior thought he was going to fire the plaintiff. *Hertz v. Luzenac American, Inc.*, 370 F.3d 1014 (10th Cir. 2004)

TWO

Plaintiff sued for gender discrimination. In the trial the company offers letters of complaint from customers to establish the poor "people skills" of the plaintiff. The defendant contended that the letters were not hearsay, and even if they were, they were admissible under the business records exception. The trial court admitted them and was reversed on appeal. The letters were hearsay because their only relevance in the trial was the truth of their content. They did not fall within the business records exception because the authors of the letters, while basing their complaints on personal knowledge, did not write the letters pursuant to a regularly conducted business activity. The requirements of duty and personal knowledge did not coalesce in these individuals. The business records of the company could prove that the complaint letters were received, but another exception needs to be found for the letters themselves. *Rowland v. American General Finance, Inc.*, 2003 WL 21912173 (4th Cir. 2003).

XVI. EXCEPTIONS TO THE HEARSAY RULE — PUBLIC RECORDS

A. PRINCIPLES

The public records exception represents the public equivalent of the private business records exception. Sufficient indicia of reliability presumably exists when the records are maintained pursuant to a public responsibility.

Unlike business records, however, the public records are not limited to those made by a public official shown to have possessed personal knowledge of the transaction or event being recorded.[201] Furthermore, there is no requirement that entries be made at or near the time of the transaction being recorded.

RULE 803 FRE
Hearsay Exceptions; Availability of Declarant Immaterial

The following are not excluded by the hearsay rule, even though the declarant is available as a witness:

. . . .

---

[201] *See* United States v. Koontz, 143 F.3d 408, 411-12 (8th Cir. 1998) (finding that Rule 602 did not apply to Rule 803(8) because the report itself constituted the relevant evidence and the federal drug agent only needed to authenticate the report).

(8) Public records and reports. Records, reports, statements, or data compilations, in any form, of public offices or agencies, setting forth (A) the activities of the office or agency, or (B) matters observed pursuant to duty imposed by law as to which matters there was a duty to report, excluding, however, in criminal cases matters observed by police officers and other law enforcement personnel, or (C) in civil actions and proceedings and against the Government in criminal cases, factual findings resulting from an investigation made pursuant to authority granted by law, unless the sources of information or other circumstances indicate lack of trustworthiness.

81 PRACTICES

Broader than the business records exception. The public records exception is broader than the business records exception in Rule 803(6) because subsection (C) of Rule 803(8) permits the introduction of "factual findings resulting from an investigation made pursuant to authority granted by law." Unlike business records, this permits the introduction of the results of an investigation in which the government investigators have no personal knowledge of the matter about which findings have been made. The language also permits the admission of government agency findings even though they were the product of an administrative process in which the rules of evidence were not closely followed.[202]

82 PRACTICES

Narrower than the business records exception. While in one respect the public records exception is broader than the public records exception, see above, the public records exception remains *narrower than the business records exception* because it contains restrictions that do not appear in Rule 803(6). In subsection (B), the public records exception permits the introduction of "matters observed pursuant to duty imposed by law, as to which matters there was a duty to report." The provision excludes "in criminal cases matters observed by police officers and other law enforcement personnel."

If applied as written, however, the restriction in (B) precludes both the prosecution and the defense from offering such entries against the other. The rule, however, has not been applied as it is written. The restriction in subsection (B) has been construed to be the equivalent of the restriction in subsection (C), which only precludes factual findings from being used against

---

[202] *See generally* Chandler v. Roudebush, 425 U.S. 840, 863 n.39 (1976).

criminal defendants.[203] They are admissible against the government and in all civil actions and proceedings.

83 PRACTICES

Public records exception is not preclusive for public records. Simply because records are public records does not mean that they can only be introduced into evidence under the public records exception. Therefore, the restrictions of Rule 803(8) can be circumvented by offering the public records under other exceptions like the business records exception, Rule 803(6), or the past recollection recorded exception, Rule 803(5).[204]

84 PRACTICES

Admissibility of supporting evidence. The findings made admissible in subsection (C) are not limited by the literal terms of the provision — "factual findings." In *Beech Aircraft Corporation v. Rainey,*[205] the Supreme Court concluded that the fact/opinion distinction is intractable, because all findings of past facts, by definition, are nothing more than an adjudicator's opinion about those facts. In addition, because Rule 803(8) makes *"Records . . . setting forth . . . factual findings"* admissible for their truth, the Court held that normative judgments based upon "factual findings" (*e.g.,* that the accident occurred because of the negligence of the pilot) are also admissible for their truth because they are part of the content of the "record" that the literal terms of the rule make admissible.[206]

The logic of the Supreme Court's decision in *Beech Aircraft* may haunt the Court. The decision rests on a broad reading of Rule 803(8), which provides for the admission of *"reports . . . setting forth . . . factual findings."* Because the rule is not limited to "factual findings" themselves, but encompasses the *entire report* that merely contains such "findings," this reading opens a Pandora's Box relative to the range of things that can be found in agency reports. The language raises the possibility that all of the evidence heard, relied upon and delineated in the agency's "report" can be admitted for

---

[203] United States v. Smith, 521 F.2d 957, 965-66 (D.C. Cir. 1975).

[204] Circuit courts that have addressed the preclusive effect of Rule 803(8) have uniformly rejected the idea. *See, e.g.,* United States v. Hayes, 861 F.2d 1225, 1229-30 (10th Cir. 1988); United States v. Wilmer, 799 F.2d 495, 500-01 (9th Cir. 1985) *cert. denied,* 481 U.S. 1004 (1986); United States v. Quezada, 754 F.2d 1190, 1193-94 (5th Cir. 1985); United States v King, 613 F.2d 670 (7th Cir. 1980); United States v. Sawyer, 607 F.2d 1190, 1193 (7th Cir 1979).

[205] 488 U.S. 153, 163-64 (1998).

[206] *Id.* at 166.

its truth too. Courts may attempt to avoid this result by defining the "report" as something more limited than the entire manuscript, but it is not apparent how they can do that consistent with the logic in *Beech Aircraft*.

The following summarizes the arguments that could be made for admitting or excluding the basis of agency reports:

Admitting the Factual Basis
Through the Agency Report

Arguments

| *Pros* | *and* | *Cons* |

+ Agency opinions can assist the finder of facts in arriving at independent conclusions only if the agencies reveal their bases and they give the jury an opportunity to evaluate them. Without a basis for assessing reliability, the role of the jury as independent finder of facts becomes compromised.

– The FRE Advisory Committee never intended the government records exception to be construed so broadly. It is a pure fiction to believe that the jury can limit its use of such evidence. Consequently, the public records must be limited to agency findings.

– To permit the basis to be heard by the jury, in substance creates an open-ended exception to the hearsay rule through the public records exception.

+To permit the jury to hear an agency conclusion premised on the truth of the underlying facts permits the indirect use of those underlying facts. If, however, the court believes that such a distinction is logical, the evidence could be introduced, and the jury instructed, under Rule 105 to limit its use to assessing the weight to be given to the findings, not for the truth of the matter asserted.

– If the proponent of the public record is permitted to offer those portions of the agency record delineated in the agency's report, for the purpose of evaluating the agency's findings, the opponent should be permitted to introduce those portions of the same public record upon which the agency *did not rely*. Only through the revelation of both can the jury fully assess the quality of the findings. Admissibility of the underlying facts should not be allowed to turn on the fortuity of what the agency chooses to mention in its report. This distorts the judicial process by giving an unfair advantage to the party who prevailed before the agency.

+Permitting the introduction of otherwise inadmissible evidence through expert opinion testimony was an accepted practice under the common law. It permitted medical doctors to testify to patients' statements of medical history and causation so long as these statements were crucial to the doctors' diagnosis and treatment.

The jury, however, was instructed that the patients' statements were only being offered as a basis for evaluating the doctors' testimony, not for truth.

85 PRACTICES

A solution to the unfairness created by admission of the entire public report. If Rule 803(8)(C) is interpreted as admitting the entire report of the public agency because the basis for the agency's factual findings can only be assessed through an examination of the evidence presented to it, this creates a distinct unfairness for the party against whom the agency ruled. Probabilities are that the report will be heavily weighted with recitations of the evidence that the agency felt compelled its conclusions, with only passing references to the evidence presented by the losing side. Since this may be only a fraction of the record before the agency, fairness requires that the entire record be available to the finder of fact when the agency's findings are offered. One might argue that the common law rule of completeness, codified in Fed. R. Evid. 106, compels this result. *See* **PRACTICES NO. 7**, *supra*.

86 PRACTICES

Does not encompass judicial findings. Rule 803(8)(C) makes findings of fact resulting from administrative agency investigations admissible for their truth, even if the administrative agency did not follow any rules of evidence in the proceeding. Inadmissible evidence may, therefore, have formed the basis of the findings. Judicial findings are not admissible under Rule 803(8)(C) because courts are not considered "government agencies."[207] Judicial findings are admissible under Rule 803(22), which creates an exception for judgments. Judgments are admissible to prove "any fact essential to sustain the judgment," but the Rule admits only judgments from criminal felony convictions. No civil judgments are admissible even though due process was afforded and the rules of evidence were followed. Rule 803(22), therefore, is grossly inconsistent with the logic of Rule 803(8)(C). *See* **PRACTICES NO. 88**, *infra*.

87 PRACTICES

What appears in the Rule is not the way it is being applied. Rule 803(8) provides for the admissibility of three types of public reports — reports addressing (A) the activities of the office or agency (the type of materials that can be found in the Code of Federal Regulations (CFR); (B) matters observed pursuant to a duty imposed by law; and (C) factual findings resulting from an investigation authorized by law. For "matters observed," the rule totally excludes the observations of law enforcement personnel in criminal cases. This not only excludes evidence offered against an accused, but also excludes evidence the accused may wish to offer against the government. Factual findings resulting from an investigation, however, are excluded in criminal cases only when offered against the accused.

Since matters observed may be more trustworthy than conclusions drawn after an investigation in which the rules of evidence are not followed, it is strange that the more reliable entries in a public report have the most restrictions. This, coupled with the fact that the statements by law enforcement personnel could be vicarious admissions by agents of the government raises the question of whether excluding such evidence, when offered by the criminal defendant, violates the defendant's right to due process of law.[208] Accordingly,

---

[207] *See, e.g.,* Nipper v. Snipes, 7 F3d 415, 417-18 (4th Cir. 1993).

it has been held that since the limitations in (B) were placed in the Rule by Congress after the Evidence Code had been promulgated and without the same input and deliberations that preceded the limitation in (C), the two subsections should be read as being modified by the single limitation in (C).[209] Since concerns about the Right of Confrontation drove both limitations, the result in *Smith* is justified because the Sixth Amendment does not guarantee that right to the government.

B. Relationship of Public Records Exception to Other Rules[210]

Rule 104. Preliminary Questions. As a preliminary question of fact under Rule 104(a), the judge will have to decide if a public record contains "factual findings" and, if challenged by the opponent as untrustworthy, whether the sources of information (*i.e.*, firsthand knowledge of the government official, testimony of witnesses, or hearsay) or other circumstances relating to the investigation (such as the qualifications of the persons involved and the procedures that were followed) indicate that the findings may not be reliable.

Rule 403. Exclusion of Relevant Evidence on Grounds of Prejudice, Confusion, or Waste of Time. Even if an official report technically complies with the terms of Rule 803(8), courts will still be required to assess the evidence's probative value against the unfair prejudice, confusion, and delay that will result from introducing findings and conclusions that may be given more weight than they deserve. If use of the report will cause many time-consuming evidentiary disputes about the background data and the method by which the finder of facts will assess the findings' probative value, the court is also justified in excluding it. In all instances under Rule 403 the dangers of unfair prejudice must substantially outweigh the probative value. This is a discretionary decision that appellate courts are loath to second-guess.[211] Claims of unfair prejudice are made more often in jury trial cases because of the possibility that jurors will tend to give such findings preclusive effect (despite cautionary instructions from the presiding judge).[212]

Rule 803(5). Past Recollection Recorded. An official trial transcript is a public record of a matter observed by one with a duty to report and therefore is within the scope of Rule 803(8)(B). If a proper foundation is laid through the tes-

---

[208] *See* Chambers v. Mississippi, 410 U.S. 284, 35 L.Ed. 2d 297, 93 S. Ct. 1038 (1973).

[209] United States v. Smith, 521 F.2d 957, 962 (D.C. Cir. 1975).

[210] PAUL R. RICE & ROY A. KATRIEL, EVIDENCE: COMMON LAW AND FEDERAL RULES OF EVIDENCE § 5.05 [G][3] (LEXIS 5th ed. 2005)

[211] *See* Barfield v. Orange County, 911 F.2d 644, 650 (11th Cir. 1990); Johnson v. Yellow Freight System, 734 F.2d 1304, 1309 (8th Cir. 1984), cert. denied, 469 U.S. 1041 (1984); Walton v. Eaton Corp., 563 F.2d 66, 74-75 (3d Cir. 1977); Cox v. Babcock & Wilcox Co., 471 F.2d 13, 15 (4th Cir. 1972).

[212] *See, e.g.*, Pearce v. E.F. Hutton Group, Inc., 653 F. Supp. 810, 816 (D.D.C. 1987).

timony of the court reporter (*i.e.*, the court reporter has insufficient recollection to testify fully, but has firsthand knowledge, and the transcript was accurate when made and made at the time of the event recorded), the transcript will also be admissible as past recollection recorded under Rule 803(5).[213] The transcript may also fall within the business records exception of Rule 803(6).

Rule 803(9). Records of Vital Statistics. Records of vital statistics are simply a specific kind of public record, the admissibility of which is generally addressed under Rule 803(8). Although Rule 803(9) may seem unnecessary, it encompasses a source of information not covered by either Rules 803(8)(B) or (C) — information *reported to* public officials by individuals who are not public officials.

Rule 803(10). Absence of Public Record or Entry. The absence of entries in a public record has its own hearsay exception. This directly admits what is impliedly admissible anyway through the public records exception. *See generally* **PRACTICES NO. 80**, *supra*.

Rule 902. Self-Authentication. If documents offered into evidence under Rule 803(8) are public records or reports on file in a public office, these documents are self-authenticating under Rule 902(4) if proven by certified copy. If the report is not on file, but is an official publication, it is self-authenticating under Rule 902(5) when issued by public authority.

Rule 1002. Requirement of Original

Rule 1005. Public Records. Although proving the content of a writing generally gives rise to a best evidence problem, thereby necessitating the production of the original, Rule 1002, public records or reports on file in a public office are excepted from this rule under Rule 1005. If the public record or report is in the form of a published opinion, all copies of it would be an original and the fact that one copy may be on file in a public office would become meaningless. Rule 1006(3).

C. Applications — Public Records Exception

ONE

In an action against Inusu for the death of a driver who was ejected from the automobile upon impact, the plaintiff offered a memorandum written by staff members of the National Highway Traffic Safety Administration (NHTSA). This was written in response to a congressman's request that standards be established for the stability of certain kinds of passenger vehicles. The staff memo relied on the work of Leon Robertson, who was called as an expert witness at the trial on the stability issue. The NHTSA did not accept the staff's peti-

---

[213] *See* United States v. Arias, 575 F.2d 253 (9th Cir. 1978).

tion and its supporting memo that set forth Robertson's methods as well as the plaintiff's stability theories. The court rejected the memo as inadmissible hearsay. It was not admissible under Rule 803(8)(A) because it set forth more than just the activities of the agency. It was not admissible under Rule 803(8)(C) because it did not "reflect 'factual findings' of the NHTSA. Rather [the conclusions] embody the positions and opinions of individual staff members, which the agency ultimately declined to accept. Our conclusion is in accord with other circuits that have held that interim agency reports or preliminary memoranda do not satisfy Rule 803(8)(C)'s requirements." *Smith v. Isuzu Motors Ltd.*, 1998 WL 119610 (5th Cir. 1998).

TWO

The defendants were charged with conspiring to defraud the town of Cicero through a partnership involving the mayor of the town and other members of the town's Board of Trustees. The mayor presided over meetings of the Board. In January, several months after the fraud became public knowledge, the Board met. The minutes of this meeting contained a false statement that the Town had made no payments to SRC since October 1996. A week later the minutes were amended to reflect that the Mayor had twice asked whether any payments had been made to SRC since October when the board directed no further moneys to be paid unless the Board approves. Neither the minutes of either the October meeting or the January meeting mentioned any such direction. The records were excluded as inadmissible hearsay under Rule 803(8) because they were untrustworthy. The inference of doctoring was strong. The record keeper was a member of the conspiracy and had a strong motive to falsify them. Therefore, they were untrustworthy and excluded under the language of 803(8) because "the method or circumstances of preparation indicate lack of trustworthiness." *United States v. Spano*, 421 F.3d 599 (7th Cir. 2005).

XVII. EXCEPTIONS TO THE HEARSAY RULE — JUDGMENTS

A. PRINCIPLES

A judgment is admissible to prove the truth of facts essential to sustain that judgment. This exception is limited, however, to final judgments from *criminal felony prosecutions*.

RULE 803 FRE
Hearsay Exceptions; Availability of Declarant Immaterial

The following are not excluded by the hearsay rule, even though the declarant is available as a witness:

. . . .

(22) Judgment of previous conviction. Evidence of a final judgment, entered after a trial or upon a plea of guilty (but not upon a plea of nolo contendere), adjudging a person guilty of a crime punishable by death or imprisonment in excess of one year, to prove any fact essential to sustain the judgment, but not including, when offered by the Government in a criminal prosecution for purposes other than impeachment, judgments against persons other than the accused. The pendency of an appeal may be shown but does not affect admissibility.

88 PRACTICES

Administrative findings versus judicial decisions — is the different treatment justified? As previously noted, even though civil judgments result from proceedings in which procedural processes are afforded to all participants, and the rules of evidence screen the basis for judgments based on the reliability of the evidence, no civil judgment is admissible to prove the facts essential to that judgment.[214]

This result is perverse because findings of fact are admissible under Rule 803(8) from government investigations in which the rules of evidence may not be followed. Consequently, the findings by many state public utility commissions, and the Federal Communications Commission, for example, after hearing on the reasonableness of rates being charged, are admissible to prove the truth of what they concluded about the anti-competitive nature of AT&T's proposed telephone rates. Nevertheless, findings of fact concerning the same rates after a year of trial in the government's divestiture case against AT&T, could not be proven through the judgment entered by the court.[215]

Whatever expertise government agency personnel may possess does not guarantee that they will arrive at more accurate conclusions regarding matters within their narrow bailiwick than will judges and lay jurors. Though judges and jurors may consider less evidence, because of the rules of evidence, Rule 703 permits them to hear expert witness testimony that may be premised on the same additional evidence considered by the government agency. *See* **PRACTICES NOS. 104 & 105**, *infra*. Consequently, the rationale for the distinction is not apparent.

---

[214] *See* Nipper v. Snipes, 7 F.3d 415, 417-118 (4th Cir. 1993) (noting a "judge in a civil trial is not an investigator, rather a judge").

[215] *See* United States v. AT&T, 461 F. Supp. 1314 (D.D.C. 1978).

B. Applications — Judgments Exception

A motorist filed a complaint against a driver and his employer, alleging that the driver negligently operated his motor vehicle, causing a collision with the plaintiff motorist. Before trial the defendant driver made a motion *in limine* to prohibit the plaintiff from introducing into evidence the driver's misdemeanor conviction for leaving the scene of the accident giving rise to the law suit. The court held that conviction, which was based on a guilty plea by the driver, was not admissible under Rule 803(22), since it was not a felony, but the guilty plea was admissible under Rule 801(d)(2) because it was a personal admission. The court noted that while this creates a conflict between Rule 803(22) and Rule 801(d)(2) this should not result in a per se rule of exclusion of guilty please for misdemeanors. Instead, the court held that the issue should be address under Rule 403 when determining whether the probative value of the admission is substantially outweighed by the danger of unfair prejudice. *Hinshaw v. Keith*, 645 F.Supp. 180, 181-82 (D. Me 1986).

XVIII. HEARSAY AND THE RIGHT TO CONFRONTATION

PRINCIPLES

The Supreme Court has struggled to define the Right of Confrontation guaranteed to criminal defendants in the Sixth Amendment to the U.S. Constitution. Facially, the guarantee appears to require the Government to call witnesses whose testimony will incriminate the defendant. Such an obligation, however, would appear to be inconsistent with hearsay exceptions that made the availability of the declarant immaterial to admissibility, which was recognized long before the Star Chamber proceedings (the 16th century persecutions in England of King Henry VIII's political enemies) and the confrontation right that was created in response to abuses in those proceedings.

The Supreme Court has consistently rejected attempts to construe the Right to Confrontation as a constitutionally-mandated prohibition against hearsay. While the hearsay rule and the Confrontation Right arose from the same concerns about reliability, the two rights have never been equated. At the same time, the Court has never clearly defined the Confrontation Right in a way that permits the two rights to co-exist with any level of predictability. The concept has gone through three stages of evolution.

First Stage. Initially, the Court resolved each confrontation issue on the basis of the particular facts of each case. Factors that proved to be significant to those determinations were (1) the gravity of the evidence in question, (2) the possibility of the jury's misuse of the evidence, (3) the hearsay statement's inherent reliability, as reflected by the circumstances under which it was made, (4) whether the evidence involved perception and memory problems that could be exposed through cross-examination, and (5) the availability of other evidence demonstrating the guilt of the accused and the reliability of the evidence in question. *Dutton v. Evans*, 400 U.S. 74 (1970).

Second Stage. The second stage provided the broadest, and perhaps the clearest, definition of the Right to Confrontation. In *Ohio v. Roberts*,[216] the Court held that the right imposed two obligations on the government: (1) to use reasonable efforts to obtain the presence of the declarant as a witness; and (2) to use only hearsay statements of the declarant that have some indicia of reliability. The clarity of the *Roberts* decision was short lived. Since its pronouncement, the Court consistently cut back on its interpretation of what obligations this right imposes on the government.[217] Despite repeated opportunities to do so, the Court never required the government to produce a hearsay declarant or show the declarant's unavailability before introducing any hearsay made admissible under Fed. R. Evid. 803 (which considers the declarant's unavailability immaterial).[218] This made the Right of Confrontation turn on the legislative classification of hearsay exceptions under Rule 803, where availability is immaterial, and Rule 804, where unavailability is material. This was perverse because those classifications came predominantly from the common law and were premised on little more than historical accident — the factual context of the cases in which the exceptions were initially recognized. Because these classifications were arbitrary, reliance on them to define the Right of Confrontation was nothing less than absurd.

Third Stage. In the latest stage of its evolution, the Court pinned the application of the Right of Confrontation on whether the hearsay declaration was "testimonial" in nature. In *Crawford v. Washington*, 541 U.S. 36, 124 S. Ct. 1354, 158 L. Ed. 2d 177 (2004) the Court invented this test after an historical analysis of the context from which the Right of Confrontation arose — principally the Star Chamber proceedings in which individuals were charged, convicted, and sentenced to death on false statements from out-of-court hearsay declarants.

---

[216] 448 U.S. 56, 66 (1980).

[217] *See, e.g.*, White v. Illinois, 502 U.S. 346 (1992) (finding the right to confrontation does not prevent admission of spontaneous declarations and statements made in the course of receiving medical care because "such out-of-court declarations are made in contexts that provide substantial guarantees of their trustworthiness."); *Bourjaily* 483 U.S. at 182 (1987) (holding the Sixth Amendment right to confrontation does not require a showing of independent indicia of reliability in order to admit the hearsay statement of the out-of-court declaration of a co-conspirator); United States v. Inadi, 475 U.S. 387, 394-96 (1986) (rejecting the proposition that the right to confrontation requires a showing of unavailability before admitting the hearsay statements of a co-conspirator.).

[218] *See, e.g.*, Idaho v. Wright, 497 U.S. 805 (1990) (residual exception) and White v. Illinois, 502 U.S. 346 (1992) (excited utterance exception).

89 PRACTICES

Not seeing the forest for the trees. Curiously, the majority opinion in *Crawford* declined to articulate a definition of "testimonial," even though the test is supposedly compelled by centuries-old practices. Nevertheless, the majority suggested that the term encompassed "statements that were made under circumstances which would lead an objective witness to reasonably believe that the statement would be available for use at later trial."

By focusing the definition of the Right of Confrontation on the type of hearsay the government relies upon, rather than the fact that its historical unreliability often stemmed from the fact that it was fabricated, the Court relegates the right to one that addresses the symptom of the problem exposed in the Star Chamber proceedings, rather than the problem itself. By focusing only on the type of hearsay, it ignores the more fundamental problem of fabrication. If, for example, an excited utterance were not considered "testimonial" because of the circumstances under which it was allegedly made, a government willing to fabricate evidence could avoid the restrictions of the Confrontation Clause by fabricating an excited utterance, rather than another type of hearsay exception that would be considered "testimonial." If falsification is the driving force behind the Confrontation Right, the nature of the created hearsay should be irrelevant to when the right is applicable.

90 PRACTICES

Does Crawford *reverse all* Roberts *progeny?* There has been a quarter of a century of case precedent under the *Ohio v. Roberts* two prong test (unavailability and indicia of reliability). Does the new *Crawford* testimonial test overrule all prior decisions under that two-prong test that turned on whether the hearsay possessed sufficient indicia of reliability? Specifically, this would include the cases of *Lilly v. Virginia*, 527 U.S. 116, 144 L. Ed.2d 117, 119 S. Ct. 1887 (1999) (declarations against interest that collaterally inculpated third parties), and *Idaho v. Wright*, 497 U.S. 805, 111 L. Ed.2d 638, 110 S. Ct. 3139 (1990) (residual exception that relied on corroborating evidence to demonstrate reliability), where the Court held that the Confrontation Clause was violated because the statements did not possess sufficient indicia of reliability.

While the *Lilly* result might be upheld because the statements that were made could be classified as testimonial, the statements made in *Wright* by a child victim of sexual abuse may not be testimonial. Does *Crawford* therefore overrule *Wright*, thereby permitting corroborating evidence to influence the assessment of reliability? The answer may lie in the Due Process Clauses of the Fifth and Fourteenth Amendments.

The two part *Roberts* test appears to have merged two constitutional rights — the right to be confronted by your accuser and the right to due process of law — in the characterization of the single right to confrontation. If demonstrating that good faith, albeit unsuccessful, efforts to bring the witness forward satisfied the government's obligation to the criminal defendant under the Confrontation Clause, the second prong — indicia of reliability — could be interpreted as addressing what the government must use in lieu of that live testimony to satisfy the right to due process. Certainly, if the issue of confrontation were not involved (perhaps because the witness had testified), the Supreme Court could overrule a conviction if the additional evidence that was employed created a fundamental unfairness. This is similar to what the Court did in *Chambers v. Mississippi*, 410 U.S. 284, 35 L. Ed.2d 297, 93 S. Ct. 1038 (1973) where the state prohibited a criminal defendant from offering a third party's declarations against interest to exonerate himself because the third party was available as a witness (thereby not satisfying the unavailability requirement of that hearsay exception). If the Court were willing to concede that it had collapsed two rights into one in its *Roberts* decision, much of the case law under that precedent would still be viable after *Crawford* through the Due Process Clauses of the Fifth and Fourteenth Amendments.

Chapter 5

WRITINGS

I. ORIGINAL WRITING/BEST EVIDENCE RULE

A. PRINCIPLES

Because of the special importance of writings in our jurisprudence — the more important events in our lives having to be witnessed by writings — the best evidence rule (or more recently called the original writing rule) requires the proponent of the writing to produce the original writing when proving the writing's content. Fear of fraud drives this requirement.

When a proponent seeks to prove the content of a writing, and the writing is material to the litigation, the proponent must offer the original of that writing unless it is shown to be unavailable through no serious fault of the offering party.

The original writing requirement embodies five exceptions:

(1) *Materiality.* When the writing is not material to the litigation the best evidence rule is ignored;[219]

(2) *Lost or Destroyed.* When the original has been lost or destroyed through to no serious fault of the party offering secondary evidence, the proponent can turn to secondary evidence;[220]

(3) *Public Record.* When the original document is on public record its content can be proven with either a certified copy or a compared copy;[221]

(4) *Possession of Adversary.* When the original writing is in the possession of the opposing party, that party will not be heard to complain about the failure of the proponent to produce the original in

---

[219] *See* McCormick on Evidence § 234, at 710 (5th ed. 1999) (explaining there are three factors that generally play a role in determinations of materiality for purposes of the best evidence rule: the centrality of the writing to the principal issues of the litigation; the complexity of the relevant features of the writing; and the existence of a genuine dispute as to the contents of the writing.).

[220] *See* Pendley v. Murphy, 122 Ga. App. 33, 143 S.E.2d 674 (1965) (outlining the general standard of diligence).

[221] *See* Amoco Production Co. v. United States, 619 F.2d 1383 (10th Cir. 1980) (noting that most judicial decisions and statutes commonly hold that no explanation is needed for failure to produce the original of a public record). Although degrees of secondary evidence are generally not recognized, public records is an exception to that rule. When the original is on public record, Rule 1005 requires a certified or compared copy, or both be shown to be unavailable (perhaps because the courthouse burned) before testimony as to content is admissible.

his possession, so long as adequate notice was given to the party that the contents of the document would be proven at the trial;

(5) *Summaries.* When the original writings are so voluminous that they cannot conveniently be used at trial, judges can allow summaries to be used in lieu of bringing the voluminous original to court.[222]

ARTICLE X. CONTENTS OF WRITING, RECORDINGS AND PHOTOGRAPHS

RULE 1002 FRE
Requirement of Original

To prove the content of a writing, recording, or photograph, the original writing, recording, or photograph is required, except as otherwise provided in these rules or by Act of Congress.

RULE 1004 FRE
Admissibility of Other Evidence of Contents

The original is not required, and other evidence of the contents of a writing, recording, or photograph is admissible if —

(1) Originals lost or destroyed. — All originals are lost or have been destroyed, unless the proponent lost or destroyed them in bad faith; or

(2) Original not obtainable. — No original can be obtained by any available judicial process or procedure; or

(3) Original in possession of opponent. — At a time when an original was under the control of the party against whom offered, that party was put on notice, by the pleadings or otherwise, that the contents would be a subject of proof at the hearing, and that party does not produce the original.

(4) Collateral matters. — The writing, recording, or photograph is not closely related to a controlling issue.

After the proponent has demonstrated that the original is unavailable, the common law generally recognized degrees of secondary evidence. First, written copies had to be offered, and only in their absence was testimony about content accepted. Under Rule 1004 no degrees of secondary evidence are recognized. Therefore any proof of content is admissible.

---

[222] *See generally* 4 WIGMORE, EVIDENCE § 1230, at 535 (Chadbourne rev. 1972).

91 PRACTICES

A legal and practical aspect to the rule. Obviously, if a witness testifies to the content of a written contract, the witness is describing the content of a writing. To support this testimony, the proponent must comply with the best evidence rule by producing the original or showing that it is unavailable through no serious fault of the proponent of the testimony. The contract witnessed by the writing may have been entered into before the creation of the writing. Nevertheless, because the writing was created, it prevails over previous agreements. Therefore, proving the terms of the contract is proving the content of the writing, thereby creating a best evidence issue.

Oral contracts are equally enforceable unless the subject of the contract falls within the statute of frauds, requiring the contract to be in writing to be enforceable (e.g., conveyances of real property and contracts that cannot be performed within one year from the date of the contract). Why then must the proponent of the testimony bear this added burden simply because the enforceable contract is put in writing? This result constitutes the *legal aspect* to the rule. The writing acquires added legal significance because of the parol evidence rule. Even though either party to the contract could have testified to its terms before it was reduced to writing, once that formality is taken, the content of the writing is what is being proven, not the contract it witnesses.[223]

The *practical aspect* of the best evidence rule arises when the witness acquired the information about which she is testifying from a writing. Using the contract example, if the witness is a third party who had read the written instrument after it was executed, rather than a party to the contract, that witness is proving the terms of the contract. The same thing, of course, is true of an attesting witness to a will.

92 PRACTICES

Basis of expert witness testimony is an implied exception. Rule 703 provides that if the facts or data upon which an expert relies in forming an opinion are of a "type reasonably relied upon by experts in the particular field in forming opinions or inferences upon the subject, the facts or data need not be admissible in evidence." This raises the question whether Rule 703 supersedes the best evidence requirement in Rule 1002 and allows a witness to testify to

---

[223] *See* Richardson v. Payton, 20 F. Cas. 725 (1807) (refusing to admit parol evidence concerning the contents of a letter written by the defendant); Herzig v. Swift & Co., 146 F.2d 444 (2d Cir. 1945) (noting the one partner's testimony concerning a deceased partner's share of the earnings probably violated the best evidence rule because the testimony concerned the content of the partnership agreement, a written contract).

the content of documents indirectly without producing the documents themselves.

For example, if a doctor testifies to a diagnosis that is based on an X-ray, must the proponent produce the X-ray (which is considered a "photograph" under Rule 1001(2), and therefore a "writing" under Rule 1001(1)) in its original form because she is proving the X-ray's contents? The answer appears to be no. Rule 703 supersedes the best evidence rule in this instance. The Advisory Committee's comments following Rule 703 as well as Rule 1002 both compel this conclusion. In its Note to Rule 703 the Committee stated:

> The third source contemplated by the rule consists of presentation of data to the expert outside court and other than by his own perception. In this respect the rule is designed to broaden the basis for expert opinions beyond that current in many jurisdictions and to bring the judicial practice into line with the practice of the experts themselves when not in court. Thus a physician in his own practice bases his diagnosis on information from many sources and of considerable variety, including statements by patients and relatives, reports and opinions from nurses, technicians and other doctors, hospital records, and *X-rays*. Most of them are admissible in evidence, but only with the expenditure of substantial time in producing and examining various authenticating witnesses.[224]

Similarly, following Rule 1002, the Advisory Committee commented:

> It should be noted, however, that Rule 703 allows an expert to give an opinion based on matters not in evidence, and the present rule must be read as being limited accordingly in its application. Hospital records which may be admitted as business records under Rule 803(6) commonly contain reports interpreting X-rays by the staff radiologist, who qualifies as an expert, and these reports need not be excluded from the records by the instant rule.[225]

93 PRACTICES

Business records are an implied exception to the best evidence rule, too. Financial statements produced within most businesses are summaries of numerous materials produced or received in the daily operation of the enterprise. Are these financial statements and the documents upon which they were based subject to the best evidence rule? Are these statements admissible only if the underlying records are also admitted or shown to be

---

[224] Fed. R. Evid. 703 Advisory Committee's Note, 56 F.R.D. 183, 283 (1972) (emphasis added).

[225] Advisory Committee's Note to Rule 1002, 56 F.R.D. 183, 343 (1972).

unavailable? In *United States v. Draiman*,[226] the Seventh Circuit supported the view that summaries prepared in the regular course of business (and therefore business records within the scope of Rule 803(6)) are admissible independent of the original writing rule and the summaries exception to it. The *Draiman* court concluded:

> Rule 1006 contemplates the admission of a summary, prepared for trial, as *secondary* evidence of "voluminous writings, recording or photographs" that could not conveniently be introduced at trial. . . . The entries on a business record, however, are considered the original entries, and therefore the business record is admissible without regard to the availability of the underlying documents.[227]

94 PRACTICES

When proving absence of content are you proving the content? In Rule 803(7), Absence of Entry in Business Record, and Rule 803(10), Absence of Public Record or Entry, a hearsay exception is recognized for proof that certain things cannot be found in a record after diligent search. Does such proof give rise to a best evidence problem relative to the collection? Are you proving the content by evidence that there is no content? It has been held that the absence of content is not proving the content of what is present.[228] This decision may make sense for the absence of particular distinctive types of things easily recognized if present. It may not when the presence or absence may turn on one's interpretation of what is there. For example, if it were claimed that a set of regulations in a handbook did not give someone the authority to do what he is being sued for not doing, the entirety of the content of the book of regulations must be seen in order to ascertain the accuracy of the negative conclusion about content.

II. BEST EVIDENCE RULE — THE SUMMARIES EXCEPTION

A. PRINCIPLES

When summaries are used at trial because the underlying documents being explored are so voluminous the jury cannot conveniently use them, the originals

---

[226] 784 F.2d 248, 256 n.6 (7th Cir. 1986).

[227] *Id. See also* United States v. Catabran, 836 F.2d 453, 456-57 (9th Cir. 1988) (affirming defendant's convictions for violating 18 U.S.C. § 152 where computer printouts fell into business records exception).

[228] *See* United States v. Scales, 594 F.2d 558, 562-63 (6th Cir. 1979), *cert. denied*, 441 U.S. 946 (1979) noting that if records are admitted under Fed. R. Evid. 803(7) to show what their contents did not include, there is no reason why Rule 1006 would not apply to a summary of their contents).

do not have to be offered at trial unless the judge requires it. A summary may be used in lieu of the originals.

To use the summaries rule the proponent of the evidence must prove the following:

(1) The underlying documents are *too voluminous* to use conveniently in the courtroom;

(2) The underlying documents are *admissible*;

(3) The underlying documents were made *available to the opposing party* for examination;

(4) The summary is *properly authenticated* — shown to produce a reliable result.[229]

RULE 1006 FRE
Summaries

The contents of voluminous writings, recordings or photographs which cannot conveniently be examined in court may be presented in the form of a chart, summary, or calculation. The originals, or duplicates, shall be made available for examination or copying, or both, by other parties at [a] reasonable time and place. The court may order that they be produced in court.

95 PRACTICES

Pretrial notification. If the proponent of a summary must make the underlying documents available to the opposing party for examination, the right to inspect is meaningful only if the rule is interpreted as imposing a *notification requirement*. Aside from the right to inspect implicitly imposing the notice requirement, there is an equally compelling reason to provide it. If the opposing party recognizes the hearsay problem created by the summary, advanced notice will permit the residual exception in Rule 807 to be used when no other delineated exception is applicable. *See* **PRACTICES NO. 96**, *infra*.

In addition to giving notice of an intention of offering the summary, a wise attorney will provide both the underlying documents and the summary to the opposing side for examination. This disclosure allows an added check

---

[229] *See, e.g.,* United States v. Campbell, 845 F.2d 1374, 1381 (6th Cir. 1988); AMPAT/Midwest, Inc. v. Illinois Tool Works Inc., 896 F.2d 1035 (7th Cir. 1990); United States v. Johnson, 594 F.2d 1253, 1255 (9th Cir.), *cert. denied*, 444 U.S. 964 (1979); United States v. Smyth, 556 F.2d 1179 (5th Cir. 1977).

on the accuracy of the summary, which enhances the chances that the presiding judge will recognize the summary as substantive evidence admissible in lieu of the voluminous underlying documents. See **PRACTICES NO. 97**, *infra*.

96 PRACTICES

The hearsay problem. Because the summary is offered to prove the truth of the content of the voluminous underlying documents, the offer creates a theoretical hearsay problem.[230] This issue, however, is often overlooked and may not be present when a computer is used to prepare the summary because under Rule 801, only individuals can be declarants and create hearsay.[231] The proper authentication of the computer software addresses the hearsay concerns of perception, memory and sincerity.

Hearsay is involved when the proponent creates the summary by hand. To resolve the hearsay concerns with non-computer-generated summaries, the proponent should employ the residual exception in Rule 807, provided the opposing party has been given the notification and opportunity to prepare to meet it required in Rule 807.

RULE 807 FRE
Residual Exception

A statement not specifically covered by Rule 803 or 804 but having equivalent circumstantial guarantees of trustworthiness, is not excluded by the hearsay rule, if the court determines that (A) the statement is offered as evidence of a material fact; (B) the statement is more probative on the point for which it is offered than any other evidence which the proponent can procure through reasonable efforts; and (C) the general purposes of these rules and the interests of justice will best be served by admission of the statement into evidence. However, a statement may not be admitted under this exception unless the proponent of it makes known to the adverse party sufficiently in advance of the trial or hearing to provide the adverse party with a fair opportunity to prepare to meet it, the proponent's intention to offer the statement and the particulars of it, including the name and address of the declarant.

---

[230] *See* United States v. Johnson, 594 F.2d 1253, 1255 (9th Cir. 1979) (noting that Rule 1006 is not an exception to the hearsay rule).

[231] *See, e.g.,* City of Phoenix v. COM/Systems, Inc., 706 F.2d 1033 (9th Cir. 1983); Ford Motor Co. v. Auto Supply Co., 661 F.2d 1171 (8th Cir. 1981); United States v. Smyth, 556 F.2d 1179 (5th Cir. 1977).

Other hearsay exceptions that might apply are present sense impression, Rule 803(1), and past recollection recorded, Rule 803(5).

97 PRACTICES

Evidentiary status of summaries. Although the summary rule is an exception to the best evidence requirement and, therefore, should be accepted at trial *in lieu of* the originals, many courts do not employ the summary rule in this fashion. Instead, these courts have restricted the use of summaries to pedagogical devices — suggestions to the fact-finder on how the voluminous originals produced at trial should be summarized. When so restricted, the summaries receive no evidentiary status, and are not permitted to be taken to the jury deliberation room.[232] This practice relegates summaries to the status of demonstrative evidence controlled by Rule 611, which gives the trial judge broad discretion to control the mode and order of the presentation of evidence at trial.

RULE 611 FRE
Mode and Order of Interrogation and Presentation

(a) Control by court. The court shall exercise reasonable control over the mode and order of interrogating witnesses and presenting evidence so as to (1) make the interrogation and presentation effective for the ascertainment of the truth, (2) avoid needless consumption of time, and (3) protect witnesses from harassment or undue embarrassment.

In effect, this practice nullifies the broad use that was intended for summaries under Rule 1006.

B. Applications — Summaries Exception

ONE

State Farm was sued for breach of contract and bad faith dealing. When claims files were sought in pretrial discovery, State Farm objected, and based on assurances that it was not going to go through its claims files one-by-one to demonstrate what Medical Claims Review Service recommended and whether or not those recommendations were followed by the company, discovery was denied. At trial, State Farm attempted to introduce the testimony of Dr. Juola

---

[232] *Compare* Pierce v. Ramsey Winch Co., 753 F.2d 416 (5th Cir. 1985) (jury not permitted to take summary to deliberation); United States v. Gardner, 611 F.2d 770, 776 (9th Cir. 1980) (same) *with* United States v. Pinto, 850 F.2d 927, 935 (2nd Cir. 1988) (permitting jury use of summary during deliberation); United States v. Smyth, 556 F.2d 1179 (5th Cir. 1977) (same).

and a study (summary) of references between MCRS and State Farm. The study was offered to show that State Farm often paid more on claims than MCRS recommended. Plaintiff objected under Rule 1006 because the original underlying files had not been made available to the plaintiff. The objection was sustained and the summary and testimony of Dr. Juola were excluded. Production under Rule 1006 operates independently of the discovery rules. "In order to substantiate the relevance and accuracy of the statistical information offered by State Farm, [Rule] 1006 required production to [the plaintiff] of the entire claims file for each claim from which statistical information was extracted in order to determine if, in fact, State Farm relied upon something other than the reviews of MCRS in settling those claims." *Robinson v. State Farm Mutual Automobile Ins. Co.*, 2000 WL 1877745 (Idaho 2000).

TWO

During an extended trial for conspiracy the government displayed time-line and organizational charts on poster boards. On these boards the government mounted photographs of each one of the defendants corresponding to their roles in the conspiracies. With the photographs they also attached summaries of the evidence presented to the jury. The government never introduced the charts into evidence. The defendants objected to the use of the charts because the government failed to comply with the requirements of Rule 1006. The court disagreed because the government did not rely on the charts as an evidentiary substitute for putting into evidence large numbers of underlying original writings. Therefore Rule 1006 was not controlling. The charts were nothing more than pedagogical devices controlled by Rule 611, graphically representing the complex story reflected in the admitted evidence. *United States v. Posada-Rios*, 1998 WL 736317 (5th Cir. 1998).

III. BEST EVIDENCE RULE — THE PUBLIC RECORDS EXCEPTION

A. PRINCIPLES

The public records exception to the best evidence rule permits the original of a document recorded on a public record to stay on the public record for notice purposes. In lieu of the original, the proponent may use either a certified or compared copy (a copy made and compared to the original by the witness who is testifying) of the recorded document. In the absence of either of these types of copies, testimony can be used.

98 PRACTICES

Scope of public records exception. The public records exception applies whenever the public record contains the original of a writing, the content of which is being proven. The public record can contain the original in two distinct ways, both of which can be illustrated with the transfer of real property through a deed of conveyance.

(1) The first instance arises when there is a dispute between the grantor and grantee over what was conveyed by the grantor. If the original deed was recorded on the public record, the public records exception permits the deed's content to be proven either by a certified copy of what is on the record or a compared copy authenticated by the person who made it. If, as is usually the case, only a copy of the deed was recorded on the public record, and the original was returned to the grantee, the original in the possession of the grantee must be produced when its content is being proven in the cause of action.[233]

(2) The second instance occurs when a dispute exists between either the grantor or the grantee and a third party who claims title through an additional conveyance after the first deed. The third party has a right to rely on the public records for notice of ownership. Therefore, if the first conveyance included a reservation of mineral rights on the property, for example, and that reservation was not recorded with the deed, the bona fide purchaser has the right to rely on what is recorded, regardless of whether the original or a copy was recorded on the public record. For notice purposes, *whatever information is on the public record becomes the original.* Therefore, when the litigation involves an innocent third party — the party for whom the notice statutes were enacted — the third party must prove the content of whatever is on the public records.[234]

IV. RELATIONSHIP OF THE BEST EVIDENCE RULE TO OTHER RULES[235]

Rule 103. Rulings on Evidence. Rule 103(a)(1) provides that error may not be predicated upon a ruling that admits or excludes evidence unless the ruling affects a party's substantial rights, and the opponent made a timely objection or

---

[233] Amoco Production Co. v. United States, 619 F.2d 1383, 1389 (10th Cir. 1980) (noting that since the deed in question was returned to the parties after recording, it was not a public record as contemplated by Rule 1005).

[234] Amoco Production Co. v. United States, 619 F.2d 1383, 1389-91 (10th Cir. 1980) (indicating that third party bona fide purchasers may rely on the contents of the public record, and therefore, must prove the contents of the public record on which they rely).

motion to strike, specifically stating the ground of objection (assuming that the specific ground was not apparent from the context). Because a ruling on a best evidence issue will usually not affect substantial rights, a party's failure to object on specific best evidence grounds will likely waive that objection. In *Sumitomo Bank of California v. Product Promotions, Inc.*,[236] for example, defense counsel objected to the plaintiff's use of summaries of inventory accounting calculations based on shipping and receiving records on the ground that the summary used an erroneous inventory analysis commencement date. The court held that defense counsel's failure to inspect the underlying records beforehand, subsequent examination of which revealed discrepancies in the summaries and the records allegedly summarized, waived whatever objection the defendant may have had under Rule 1006. Similarly, in *Zenith Radio Corporation v. Matsushita Electrical Industrial Company*,[237] a party introduced duplicates of documents under Rule 1003 that were objectionable because the documents were public records, which, under Rule 1005, a party must prove through certified or compared copies. The opponent, however, failed to raise the point at the time the proponent offered the duplicates. Consequently, the court held the opponent had waived the issue.

Rule 104. Preliminary Questions. Except for conditional relevance issues, the presiding judge resolves preliminary questions of fact upon which the admissibility of evidence depends. Under Rule 104(b), if the relevance of evidence depends upon the fulfillment of a condition of fact, the jury is to decide whether the proponent has satisfied that condition. Relative to the application of the best evidence rule, Rule 1008 specifically delineates three issues that courts should consider to be questions of conditional relevance and, therefore, questions that the jury should resolve. They include: "(a) whether the asserted writing ever existed, or (b) whether another writing, recording, or photograph produced at the trial is the original, or (c) whether other evidence of contents correctly reflects the contents . . . ." The presiding judge resolves all other issues arising under the best evidence rule.

Rule 611. Mode and Order of Interrogation and Presentation. Adding to the confusion over whether Rule 1006 summaries can be offered into evidence as exhibits and viewed by the jury during deliberations, a split of authority has developed over whether Rule 1006 even applies when summaries are used at trial to summarize other evidence and not offered as an exhibit.[238] The court in *Posada-Rios* explains that the proponent's limited use, and the presiding judge's admonitions to the jury regarding that limited use, determine which rule controls admissibility.[239]

---

[235] Paul R. Rice & Roy A. Katriel, Evidence: Common Law and Federal Rules of Evidence § 7.01 [C] (LEXIS 5th ed. 2005)

[236] 717 F.2d 215 (5th Cir. 1983).

[237] 505 F. Supp. 1190, 1227 (E.D. Pa. 1980).

Rule 613. Prior Statements of Witnesses

Rule 1002. Requirement of Original. A party may offer a witness' prior inconsistent statement into evidence for impeachment purposes only after that party complies with the requirements of Rule 613(b). Rule 613(b) requires that the witness be given an opportunity, at some time during the trial, to explain or deny the statement. Contrary to common law, however, this no longer needs to be done before proving the utterance of the inconsistent statement. If this inconsistent statement is in written form, the best evidence rule applies. Because the proponent of the prior inconsistent statement is proving the content of the writing containing the statement, Rule 1002 requires the proponent to use the original or explain its unavailability.

Rule 901. Requirement of Authentication or Identification. Tangible evidence, including writings, is not relevant to a cause of action until the evidence is authenticated or identified. If a proponent offers copies or duplicates of a writing instead of the original, the proponent must authenticate both the original and the copy that she is using in the original's stead. Pursuant to Rule 901, the proponent will usually fulfill this requirement through a sponsoring witness who has personal knowledge of the original and copies. In *United States v. Gipson*,[240] for example, the defendant was charged with stealing barbed wire from the United States Government. To establish the Government's ownership of the wire, the prosecution introduced two original forms used to order the wire and two photocopies of those same forms indicating the receipt of the ordered wire. The prosecution called the person who signed the forms to authenticate both the originals and the copies under Rule 901(b)(1).

Often the original of the document will be self-authenticating under Rule 902. For example, it may be commercial paper under Rule 902(9), an acknowledged document under Rule 902(8), or an official publication under Rule 902(5). In these instances, only the authenticity of the copy or duplicate must be established through other evidence. The proponent could accomplish this through testimony as to the manner in which the copy or duplicate were reproduced. If reproduction were accomplished through photocopying, and if the copy offered can be identified as the one reproduced, that will be sufficient to authenticate the copy as a true and accurate reproduction of the self-authenticating original. Occasionally both the original and the copy will be self-authenticating. This would be true, for example, if the original were a public record and the official

---

[238] *Compare* State v. Winn, 948 F.2d 145, 158-59 (5th Cir. 1991) *cert. denied* 503 U.S. 976 (1992) (finding charts summarizing admitted evidence admissible under Rule 1006) and United States v. Pinto, 850 927, 935-36 (2nd Cir.) *cert. denied* 488 U.S. 932 (1988) *with* United States v. Posada-Rios, 158 F.3d 832, 869 (5th Cir. 1998) (the admissibility of charts not offered into evidence is not governed by Rule 1006, but by Rule 611) and United States v. Baker, 10 F.3d 1374, 1411 (9th Cir. 1993) (declining to use Rule 1006 to admit summaries into evidence).

[239] *See* Fauci v. Mulready, 337 Mass. 532, 150 N.E.2d 286 (1958) (delegating responsibility of all preliminary questions concerning the admissibility of evidence). Fed. R. Evid. 104 codifies the principle set forth in *Fauci*.

[240] 609 F.2d 893, 895 (8th Cir. 1979).

custodian certified the copy as accurate. Under Rule 902(4), this certification will serve to authenticate both the original and the copy.

Note that a document's self-authenticating nature only establishes a *prima facie* case of authenticity, enough to get it passed the judge's screening and into evidence. The jury, pursuant to Rule 104(b), becomes the final arbiter of whether the original and the copy or duplicate are authentic. *See* **PRACTICES NO. 8**, *supra*.

V. APPLICATIONS — BEST EVIDENCE OR ORIGINAL WRITING RULE

ONE

The defendant was charged with the illegal importation of marijuana and possession with intent to sell. His boat was stopped speeding long the shoreline of Southern California. Suspicious circumstances led to the boat being boarded and marijuana being found. To prove that the boat has crossed international borders, the government offered the testimony of an officer who used the "backtrack" feature of the Global Positioning System (GPS) found on the boat to retrace the defendant's voyage from Mexico to the Coronado Islands and then to the San Diego Bay. This testimony was found to have violated the original writing rule because the content of the GPS monitor was being proven and the officer had no personal knowledge of the facts that were recorded on the device. The government did not produce the GPS device, did not show that a printout of its contents was not available. In addition, the court noted that the government failed to prove that the GPS was properly functioning and that the information it produced was necessarily accurate. *United States v. Bennett*, 2004 WL 758253 (9th Cir. 2004).

TWO

Plaintiff was a train conductor who was injured when assisting a passenger disembark from the train with an oversized footlocker. As the passenger lowered the footlocker down to the conductor on the platform, the footlocker slipped and fell on the conductor's chest, severely injuring him. Plaintiff brought an action against his employer for failure to furnish a safe place to work by failing to include within the rules that govern the use of the train, regulations with respect to taking luggage aboard a train car. At trial, the plaintiff seeks to testify that as a conductor he did not have authority to stop a passenger boarding a train with a footlocker. The court held that the conductor's testimony as to his authority relates to his authority as established by written rules and regulations. Because in this instance the conductor is attempting to prove the content of these regulations through his testimony, his testimony creates a best evidence problem. Unless he can establish that an original of the written regulations is unavailable through no serious fault of his own, the court should exclude his testimony as to his authority to stop a passenger boarding a train with a footlocker

Conway v. Consolidated Rail Corp., 720 F.2d 221, 224 (1st Cir. 1983), *cert. denied*, 104 S. Ct. 1911 (1984).

Chapter 6

OPINION TESTIMONY

I. LAY OPINION TESTIMONY

PRINCIPLES

Under the English common law, a lay witness may offer an opinion only after the witness first discloses the primary facts upon which the opinion was premised.[241] Professing to follow this precedent, American courts adopted a distorted interpretation that attempted to distinguish between fact and opinion testimony, but enforced the primary facts doctrine when opinions were allowed.

Because the distinction between fact and opinion is ephemeral,[242] the courts developed exceptions that virtually consumed the rule. Consequently, Rule 701 abolished the distinction. Now, lay opinions are freely admissible if the court determines they are rationally based on personal knowledge and helpful to a clear understanding of the witness' testimony.

RULE 701 FRE
Opinion Testimony by Lay Witnesses

If the witness is not testifying as an expert, the witness' testimony in the form of opinions or inferences is limited to those opinions or inferences which are (a) rationally based on the perception of the witness and (b) helpful to a clear understanding of the witness' testimony or the determination of a fact in issue and (c) not based on scientific, technical or other specialized knowledge.

99 PRACTICES

Did the primary facts doctrine survive codification? Under the common law, the primary facts doctrine required the facts upon which an opinion was based to be proven before a lay opinion was admissible. Rule 701 does not explicitly perpetuate the primary facts doctrine. Does this mean that the requirement has been abolished?

---

[241] *See* 7 WIGMORE ON EVIDENCE § 1917, at 2-3 (Chadbourn rev. 1978).

[242] *See* MCCORMICK ON EVIDENCE § 11, p. 20 (5th ed. 1999) and 7 WIGMORE ON EVIDENCE, § 1919, at 14-17 (Chadbourn rev. 1978).

The Supreme Court has taken the approach in its interpretation of the rules that if the rule does not explicitly adopt an element or requirement, and they otherwise are not essential to the logical application of a rule,[243] the common law has not survived codification.[244] The only language in Rule 701 suggesting that the primary facts doctrine survived is the requirement that the opinion must be helpful to "a clear understanding of *the witness' testimony*" (emphasis added). This language could be construed as suggesting that there must be other testimony that the opinion clarifies — an indirect adoption of the "primary facts" doctrine. In *Rohannan v. Pegelow*,[245] the court held that if it is shown that the witness based his testimony on personal observation, the failure to state the underlying facts supporting the opinion goes to the strength or weakness of the testimony and not to its admissibility. This reasoning appears to be consistent with Rule 705, which permits an expert witness to testify about his opinion "without first giving the underlying facts or data."

Regardless of whether the primary facts doctrine is found to have survived codification, to the extent possible, the proponent of any witness' opinion testimony (lay or expert opinion) should always explore the basis of the opinion. This practice not only enhances the credibility of the opinion, it is the only means by which the jury can fulfill its independent fact-finding role.

100 PRACTICES

Is everybody an expert now? The latest revision to Rule 701(c) adds an additional restriction to the admissibility of lay witness opinion testimony. If a lay witness offers an opinion "based on scientific, technical or other specialized knowledge," the testimony is not admissible. This addition to Rule 701 was the Advisory Committee's attempt to resolve the problem of litigants (1) failing to identify expert witnesses in the pretrial discovery process, (2) thereby not exchanging expert witness statements, and (3) avoiding depositions about their proposed testimony, and then calling the witness at trial as a lay witness under Rule 701 when they possessed personal knowledge about the matter being litigated. It is unclear why this revision was necessary. For discovery abuses judges have had the power to impose appropriate sanctions like excluding the testimony, or, if the failure was inadvertent, permitting the

---

[243] *See, e.g.,* Tome v. United Sates, 513 U.S. 150 (1995) (concluding that a prior consistent statement had to predate the motive to fabricate before it logically rehabilitates the credibility of a witness).

[244] *See, e.g.,* Bourjaily v. United States, 483 U.S. 171 (1987) (finding Congress silently revolutionized the co-conspirator admission exception by not incorporating into Rule 801(d)(2)(E) either the requirement of independent corroboration of the existence of the conspiracy and the defendant's participation in it or the prohibition against considering the content of the co-conspirator's admission in determining its admissibility)

[245] 652 F.2d 729, 732 (7th Cir. 1981).

expert to delineate the facts about which he has personal knowledge, but not let him give his credentials or give any opinions based on his expertise.

This revision may cause more problems than it will solve because the rule addresses the problem through the knowledge held by the witness rather than the level of expertise required to speak on a subject. To some extent every witness bases his opinions on differing levels of scientific, technical or other specialized knowledge from education, training or experience. If a witness testifies about the speed of a car, that conclusion will be based, in part, on the knowledge he acquired from years of experience in driving automobiles and watching them move. If a witness testifies that the item in question smelled like cucumbers, ammonia, or marijuana, or tasted like cocaine or a Merlot wine, such testimony stems from specialized knowledge acquired from experience. Are all these opinions now going to be excluded if those witnesses were not placed on the proponent's expert witness list? Surely a judge is not expected to conduct hearings to screen the qualifications of lay, as well as expert, witnesses! *See* **PRACTICES NOS. 102 and 103,** *infra.*

While this provision may become as obscure as the concept of conditional relevance under Rule 104(b) (of which most lawyers and judges are not even aware), a wise attorney might be overly cautious and list all witnesses who will be giving opinion testimony based on *any* level of special experience. This decision will establish a practice that may support claims he wishes to make against the opinions offered by the opposing party's witnesses.

II. EXPERT WITNESSES

A. Determining Expertise

PRINCIPLES

Before a witness is asked to give an opinion on a matter that requires special expertise, the proponent is required to demonstrate that the witness acquired and possesses that expertise through knowledge, skill, experience, training, or education. This preliminary examination of the expert witness is called the voir dire, the same title assigned to the preliminary examination of prospective jurors (veniremen) when they are being asked questions to determine whether they are qualified to serve on the petit jury.

RULE 702 FRE
Testimony by Experts

If scientific, technical, or other specialized knowledge will assist the trier of fact to understand the evidence or to determine a fact in issue, a witness qualified as an expert by knowledge, skill, experience, training, or education may testify thereto in the form of an opinion or otherwise if (1) the testimony is based upon sufficient facts or data, (2) the testimony is the product of reliable principles and methods, and (3) the witness has applied the principles and methods reliably to the facts of the case.

101 PRACTICES

Qualifications are presumed for expert opinions appearing in business and public records. Business records are an exception to the hearsay rule because once the elements of that exception have been satisfied, reliability is assured. The common law business records exception is codified in Rule 803(6). That provision expressly includes reports in the form of opinions. This result gives rise to the question of whether such opinions are admissible under Rule 803(6), regardless of whether the proponent established their admissibility under Rule 702. The answer appears to be that this hearsay exception *does not override* the requirements in Rule 702, but instead satisfies the Rule by presuming the requirements have been met. The practical effect of this interpreted interplay between Rules 702 and 803(6) is that the burden shifts from the proponent to establish expertise to the opponent who must now challenge it.[246] *See* **PRACTICES NO. 78**, *supra*.

Because Rule 803(6) shifts to the opponent the burden of challenging the expertise of those rendering opinions in business records, pretrial discovery is significantly more important.

Similarly, public records often contain opinions that require special expertise. Rule 803 (8)(C) admits findings resulting from an investigation authorized by law. Like business records in Rule 803(6), those findings are admissible "unless the sources of information or other circumstances indicate a lack of trustworthiness." Also like business records, admissibility of these public findings does not depend upon the demonstration of the expertise of those who rendered them.[247]

---

[246] *See* United States v. Licavoli, 604 F.2d 613 , 622-23 (9th Cir. 1979). *But see* Forward Communications Corp. v. United States, 608 F.2d 485, 510 (Ct. Cl. 1979).

[247] As the court explained in Melville v. American Home Assurance Co., 584 F.2d 1306, 1316 (3d Cir. 1978), courts presume the expertise and, therefore, the trustworthiness of the findings contained in public records:

> Official reports are admitted as an exception to the hearsay rule because they are presumed to be generally reliable. The objections permitted by Rules 702 and 705 provide a means of testing their reliability. Before these objections may be recognized, however, the party challenging the validity of an official report admitted under 803(8)(C) must come forward with some evidence which would impugn its trustworthiness . . . . To allow objections to be sustained under Rules 702 and 705 without a showing of untrustworthiness would have the practical effect of nullifying the exception to the hearsay rule provided by Rule 803(8)(C).

B. Evolved Judicial Screening

PRINCIPLES

As with all other evidence, the admissibility of opinion testimony on scientific evidence is determined by balancing the logical relevance of the evidence against the risk of unfair prejudice from the jury's unjustified reliance on the conclusions advocated without independent evaluation of the evidence. In the context of the sciences and technology, this balance becomes complicated by the complexity of the principles involved, of the methodologies by which those principles are employed, and of the circumstances to which they are applied.

In the past, courts universally employed the test enunciated in *Frye v. United States*[248] for screening opinion testimony on novel scientific evidence: the proponent was required to establish that the scientific principle supporting the evidence had gained sufficient acceptance in the field to which it belonged to have gained "general acceptance." This test was adequate when screening only novel scientific principles. The complexities of science were such, however, that not only were the principles novel, but also the means, or "methodologies," by which those principles were employed. The general acceptance test was extended to the methodologies as well. After courts accepted, generally, the principles and methodologies, they were then confronted with novel applications of those principles and methodologies. This often occurred in the toxic tort cases where causation was being proven. When a general acceptance screen was employed to screen novel applications as well, it resulted in the disproportionate exclusion of relevant evidence because these applications were so unique that no one else in the relevant sciences would have either an interest in or familiarity with them. Consequently, "general acceptance" could rarely be established.

To avoid this result, some courts began experimenting with a test that balanced the probative value of the evidence against the potential unfair prejudice from its misuse by the jury. This balance, of course, originally led to the creation of the *Frye* "general acceptance" test; but in applying the balance specifically to each case, the presiding judge could accommodate the unique situations of each admissibility decision. In the midst of this debate, the Federal Rules of Evidence were promulgated. Unfortunately, they did not explicitly address this difficult problem. Therefore in *Daubert v. Merrell Dow Pharmaceuticals, Incorporated*,[249] twenty years after their enactment the Supreme Court announced how the general principles codified in the Federal Rules of Evidence were to be used to resolve the question.

---

[248] 293 F. 1013, 1014 (D.C. Cir. 1923). Many states that have generally adopted the Federal Rules of Evidence still follow this rule even though the Supreme Court held that it was silently abandoned by the codification of the Federal Rules of Evidence. Daubert v. Merrell Dow Pharm., Inc., 509 U.S. 579 (1993).

[249] 509 U.S. 579, 589 (1993).

Initially, the court noted the testimony must be both relevant and reliable.[250] Relevance simply means that the application of the technical principles at issue would produce a result that will assist the jury. This was referred to as the "fit" between the issues and the evidence. To determine whether the principles and their application will sufficiently assist the jury, the presiding judge then must determine whether the principles and their application represented "good science," or as the Court referred to it, "scientific knowledge."[251]

To make this determination the Court decided that "general acceptance" in the relevant science *no longer constituted a prerequisite* to admissibility. Such acceptance should be only a *factor* in the ultimate determination. Other illustrative factors identified by the court included: (1) whether the principle had been tested; (2) the results of peer review in professional publications; and (3) the potential rate of error.[252]

In *Kumho Tire Co. v. Carmichael*[253] the Supreme Court extended the same judicial "gate-keeping" or screening responsibilities to technological evidence. The Court found this required by Rule 702 which conditioned the admissibility of expert testimony on whether the "scientific, technical, or other specialized knowledge" that they possess "will assist the trier of fact to understand the evidence or to determine a fact in issue."

Correctly understood, *Daubert* and its progeny are more concerned with judicial screening of the scientific, technical, and other specialized bases for expert opinions, rather than the qualification of the individuals called to give opinions as expert witnesses.

102 PRACTICES

Frye in drag. On the surface, *Daubert* and *Kumho Tire* gave trial judges broad discretion in determining the admissibility of scientific evidence. After these decisions, the factors *experts* previously considered in determining reliability and general acceptance are now weighed by the *judge*. In reality, however, trial judges lack the expertise to make these assessments. Indeed, the very factors delineated by the Court in *Daubert* require input from the same professional community that previously had to accept the scientific principles, methodologies or applications under the *Frye* test.

For example, the court must look at whether the community has tested the scientific or technological principles. What tests are adequate? How should

---

[250] *Id.*

[251] *Id.* at 590.

[252] *Id.* at 592-94.

[253] 119 S. Ct. 1167 (1999).

the tests be administered? What variations in testing protocol skew the results? A judge arguably has insufficient expertise to make these assessments except by going back to the most relevant scientific community he can define — the very community that he previously relied upon under *Frye*.

Peer review remains an important source of helpful information. Who are the peers of a scientific expert? The answer is, the members of the *same scientific community* identified and relied upon under the *Frye* test.

Without question the rate of error is central to the determination of "scientific" or "technological" reliability. What is an acceptable rate of error? How does a court go about making that determination? Not surprisingly, courts consult the very people whose general opinion, according to the Supreme Court, has ceased to be dispositive since Article VII of the Federal Rules of Evidence failed to codify the *Frye* test.

When the court gets around to considering "general acceptance" in the relevant scientific field, that field will already have influenced the judge's assessment of all of the other factors to the point where it is preordained. Consequently, *Daubert* is little more than *Frye* in drag. When we lift the crinolines the Court dressed scientific screening in, it is readily apparent that it's still *Frye* under there. As a result, decisions on admissibility of such evidence under *Frye* and *Daubert* generally have been identical.

As acknowledged by Judge Kozinski on the *Daubert* remand, the judges' responsibility is to "resolve disputes among respected, well-credentialed scientists . . . where there is no scientific consensus."[254] This is a very difficult undertaking and experience will likely show that when judges try to act like scientists they do not fare well without extensive guidance from relevant scientific disciplines. One can only wonder if when lawyers attempt to act like scientists, it is not roughly the equivalent to scientists trying to act like lawyers. The old adage that a person who represents himself at trial "has a fool for a client" may have relevance to other disciplines as well.

103 PRACTICES

How reliable must it be? In making the determination of admissibility, the *Daubert* decision directs that scientific principles must be reliable. Reliable by what standard? In the hard sciences, an acceptable rate of error may be no greater than 1% to 3%. If that standard is imposed on scientific evidence offered to establish causation in a toxic tort action (as it was when lack of general acceptance was dispositive), the standard of admissibility will be some-

---

[254] 43 F.3d 1311, 1316 (9th Cir. 1995).

thing akin to "beyond a reasonable doubt" rather than the preponderance standard that customarily governs questions of admissibility.

Members of the Advisory Committee verbally indicated at a public hearing on the recently enacted revisions that the preponderance test is the implicit standard that governs this admissibility question (thereby justifying its rejection of a proposed explicit standard of reliability). Because that preponderance standard is not explicitly stated in the rule, it remains highly probable that the *Frye* practices that still control in so many ways, influence this decision as well.

The incorporation of the *Daubert* criteria into the rule has not clarified this matter. The language merely requires that expert testimony be the product of *reliable* principles and methods . . . [and that the expert have] applied the principles and methods *reliably* to the facts of the case." The question still remains, Reliable by whose standards?

C. The Basis for Expert Opinions

PRINCIPLES

Under the common law, an experts' testimony was admissible only when there was a demonstrated need. Their role was to assist the finder of facts, and their assistance was limited to instances where that assistance was *necessary*.[255] In addition, a person could qualify as a expert only if she knew *substantially more* than the average juror by her knowledge, skill, training or education.

Because of their unique role, experts remain the only witnesses permitted to testify without personal knowledge of the relevant facts in a case. To elicit opinion testimony from an expert, the proponent may pose hypothetical questions. Traditionally, to be relevant to the issues the jurors were being asked to decide, the questions had to assume the truth of facts in evidence — facts upon which admissible evidence had been offered. Without such a limitation, the expert could be commenting on a different case than the one the jury was hearing and about which it was being asked to render a judgment. The testimony, therefore, would not assist the jurors because it would not be relevant.

Rule 703 of the Federal Rules of Evidence changes this practice. It provides that "[t]he facts or data in the particular case upon which an expert bases an opinion or inference may be those perceived by or made known to the expert at or before the hearing." This provision is consistent with the common law. The change comes in the next sentence: ". . . If of a type reasonably relied upon by

---

[255] *See* Ladd, *Expert Testimony*, 5 VAND. L. REV. 414, 418 (1952).

experts in the particular field in forming opinions or inferences upon the subject, the facts or data need not be admissible in evidence. . . ."**256**

RULE 703 FRE
Bases of Opinion Testimony by Experts

The facts or data in the particular case upon which an expert bases an opinion or inference may be those perceived by or made known to the expert as or before the hearing. If of a type reasonably relied upon by experts in the particular field in forming opinions or inferences upon the subject, the facts or data need not be admissible in evidence in order for the opinion or inference to be admitted. Facts or data that are otherwise inadmissible shall not be disclosed to the jury by the proponent of the opinion or inference unless the court determines that their probative value in assisting the jury to evaluate the expert's opinion substantially outweighs their prejudicial effect.

104 PRACTICES

Reasonably relied upon. The assumption underlying the provision that permits experts to rely on otherwise inadmissible evidence is that the expert is better qualified to evaluate the otherwise inadmissible evidence and assess its reliability.**257** This assumption is justified only when the expert witness *personally evaluated* the otherwise inadmissible evidence and applied his expertise in assessing its reliability so he can explain to the jury the reasons for concluding the evidence is reliable. Generic types of evidence "relied upon by experts" should be insufficient.**258** Only through such fact specific explanations can the jury fulfill its independent fact finding role.

---

256 For a general discussion of the problems created by Rule 703, *see* PAUL R. RICE & ROY A. KATRIEL, EVIDENCE: COMMON LAW & FEDERAL RULES OF EVIDENCE, § 8.02[B][8], pp. 1111-1129 (LEXIS 5th ed. 2005); P. R. Rice, *Inadmissible Evidence as a Basis for Expert Opinion Testimony: A Response to Professor Carlson*, 40 VAND. L. REV. 583 (1987); R. Carlson, *Policing the Basis of Modern Expert Testimony*, 39 VAND. L. REV. 577 (1986). *See also* PAUL R. RICE, THE ALLURE OF THE ILLOGIC: A COHERENT SOLUTION FOR RULE 703 REQUIRES MORE THAN REDEFINING "FACTS OR DATA", 47 MERCER L. REV. 495 (1996) and PAUL R. RICE, *Expert Testimony: A Debate Between Logic or Tradition Rather Than Between Deference or Education,* 87 N.W. L. REV. 1166 (1993).

257 United States v. Sims, 514 F.2d 147, 149 (9th Cir. 1975) ("Years of experience teach the expert to separate the wheat from the chaff and to use only those sources and kinds of information which are of a type reasonably relied upon by similar experts in arriving at sound opinions on the subject.").

258 P. R. Rice, *Inadmissible Evidence as a Basis for Expert Opinion Testimony: A Response to Professor Carlson*, 40 VAND. L. REV. 583 (1987); R. Carlson, *Policing the Basis of Modern Expert Testimony*, 39 VAND. L. REV. 577 (1986).

If the expert has not personally examined the underlying facts, and is permitted to rely on otherwise inadmissible evidence that is only the *generic type* that is reasonably relied upon, inquiry should be made during cross-examination of that expert into the various conditions and factors that could diminish the value of the evidence and, ultimately, the reliability of conclusions premised on its accuracy.

This practice of permitting experts to rely on otherwise inadmissible evidence, simply because it was done in practice, existed under the common law. The practice, however, was limited to testimony from medical experts. If a medical doctor testified that a patient's statements about his medical history or the cause of his injury was *crucial* to the doctor's diagnosis and treatment, the doctor was permitted to recite what the patent had said. Under the common law, however, the statements could not be accepted by the jurors for the truth of what was recited. Although the statements had been accepted for their truth and relied upon by the doctor in forming the conclusions the jurors were being asked to accept for their truth, the jurors were instructed that they could not use the pivotal underlying statements in the same way. The jurors were told that they could only consider the statements as a basis for assessing how much weight they should give to the doctor's conclusions.

If this paradigm makes no sense to you, and sounds like nonsense, your instincts are sound. A conclusion premised on the truth of certain facts — indeed, facts that were crucial to the conclusion — cannot itself be accepted without relying on the truth of the facts forming its basis. The practice is so ingrained, however, neither the bench nor the bar can see that the emperor is wearing no clothes. This is evidenced by the fact that Rule 703 now extends this nonsense to *all* expert testimony. Paradoxically, Rule 803(4), which now makes the doctor's statements of medical history and causation admissible for truth, eliminated the nonsensical common law practice with medical doctors that laid the foundation for Rule 703.

105 PRACTICES

Disclosure of inadmissible basis — what is its evidentiary status? Rule 703 explicitly precludes the otherwise inadmissible facts or data from being disclosed to the jury by the *proponent* of the opinion "unless their probative value substantially outweighs their prejudicial effect." This is a reverse Rule 403 burden that permits the exclusion of otherwise *admissible evidence* when the *opponent* proves that the potential unfair prejudice from admitting the evidence "substantially outweighs" its probative value.

This provision does not address the evidentiary status of the otherwise inadmissible evidence once the judge finds it admissible on the grounds that its probative value substantially outweighs the potential unfair prejudice. Historically, when the proponent of an opinion was permitted to delineate his otherwise inadmissible basis, that basis did not come in for truth — only to give the jury a basis for assessing the weight to be given to the opinion testimony. *See* **PRACTICES NOS. 104,** *supra*.

One may argue that the practice under Rule 703 differs from the common law in that the proponent *must affirmatively show* that the particular evidence has *significant value*. Under the common law practice, the value of the evidence was presumed without such a demonstration. If this new burden is satisfied, the otherwise inadmissible basis may be admitted for truth under the residual exception in Rule 807 because the evidence has circumstantial guarantees of trustworthiness equivalent to the delineated exceptions in Rules 803 and 804.[259] This result is justified, however, only if three conditions are met: (1) the expert has personally examined the otherwise inadmissible evidence, (2) applying her expertise to its evaluation has concluded that it is trustworthy, and (3) can explain the reasons for that conclusion to the presiding judge and the jury.

RULE 807 FRE
Residual Exception

A statement not specifically covered by Rule 803 or 804 but having equivalent circumstantial guarantees of trustworthiness, is not excluded by the hearsay rule, if the court determines that (A) the statement is offered as evidence of a material fact; (B) the statement is more probative on the point for which it is offered than any other evidence which the proponent can procure through reasonable efforts; and (C) the general purposes of these rules and the interests of justice will best be served by admission of the statement into evidence. However, a statement may not be admitted under this exception unless the proponent of it makes known to the adverse party sufficiently in advance of the trial or hearing to provide the adverse party with a fair opportunity to prepare to meet it, the proponent's intention to offer the statement and the particulars of it, including the name and address of the declarant.

The underlying basis should be admissible for truth because:

---

[259] *See The Evidence Project — Proposed Revisions to the Federal Rules of Evidence*, 171 F.R.D. 330, 587, 641-43 (1997), *see* www.wcl.american.edu/pub/journals/evidence, where a new exception to the hearsay rule is proposed for otherwise inadmissible evidence relied upon by experts. In this proposal, the proponent of expert testimony must demonstrate (1) that the expert has applied her expertise in assessing the reliability of otherwise inadmissible evidence and (2) that "the statements possess substantial guarantees of trustworthiness." This showing is equivalent to the demonstration required by the 2000 revision to Rule 703. Unlike the proposed revision, Rule 703 only permits the expert to *delineate* the inadmissible evidence relied upon. In contrast, the Evidence Project proposal would make the otherwise inadmissible evidence admissible for its truth when this demonstration has been made. Currently, the equivalent can be achieved only by convincing the court that the requirements of the residual exception in Rule 807 have been satisfied.

(1) the proponent has *specifically shown the reliability* of the individual pieces of otherwise inadmissible evidence, thereby assuring "equivalent circumstantial guarantees of trustworthiness" required in Rule 807;

(2) if the *expert* is qualified to assess reliability in practice, he should be *able to explain* to the judge and the jury *why the otherwise inadmissible evidence is sufficiently trustworthy* to be relied upon;

(3) the expert is *subject to cross-examination* by the opposing party about each explanation;

(4) the opposing party has been *given advance notice* of the intended use of such evidence through extensive expert witness discovery;

(5) since the *merits of the underlying factual basis can be fully explored*, the jury is in a much better position to serve as an independent finder of facts; and

(6) *logically*, if the truth of the facts is important to the expert's conclusions, the jury's *use* of the expert's conclusions *requires* a corollary *acceptance of the truth of the expert's basis.*

By giving experts the right to rely on otherwise inadmissible evidence, the jury is being precluded from being an independent finder of facts if it is given conclusions without also being given (1) their basis, (2) an opportunity to assess their truth, and (3) right to employ what they hear and assess. Otherwise, the role of the expert in trials has been radically changed from one who assists the jury in resolving difficult scientific and technological questions, to one who resembles a super-thirteenth juror who casts a vote on a different case than the jury is permitted either to hear or consider.[260]

D. Opinion Held to a Reasonable Certainty

PRINCIPLES

After an expert is properly qualified under Rule 702, the expert may testify to conclusions reached by (1) applying the demonstrated expertise to facts relevant to the case at hand, (2) employing reliable scientific, technological, or other specialized principles, (3) through methodologies shown to be trustworthy.[261] These elements having been established, experts commonly arrive at diametrically opposed conclusions, both of which may be admissible.

---

[260] *See* PAUL R. RICE & ROY A. KATRIEL, EVIDENCE: COMMON LAW & FEDERAL RULES OF EVIDENCE, § 8.02[B][14][c][ii] (LEXIS 5th ed. 2005).

[261] *See generally,* Kumho Tire Co., Ltd. v. Carmichael, 526 U.S. 137 (1999) and Daubert v. Merrell Dow Pharmaceuticals, Inc., 509 U.S. 579 (1993). *See also* **PRACTICES NO. 102 & 103,** *infra.*

106 PRACTICES

Certainty not required. When attorneys elicit conclusions from retained experts at trial, it is common to hear a question phrased as follows: "Dr. Johnson, based on the studies that you have just outlined, do you have an opinion *to a medical certainty* about the nature of Jennifer Meglio's spinal injury?" Indeed, this type of question is so common, some judges have mistakenly concluded that expert conclusions are not admissible unless they are held to a scientific or technological *certainty*.[262] This is wrong. No testimony, expert or otherwise, should be required to pass such a high admissibility threshold.[263] Despite its strong influence on the jury, even the voluntariness of a criminal defendant's confessions need only be shown to be voluntary by a *preponderance of the evidence* standard.[264]

The concern of trial judges, of course, is that experts, with their elevated influence over lay jurors, will foist upon the jury unjustified, albeit influential, opinions that are actually little more than speculation. While this concern is legitimate, a broad range of valuable and helpful opinions exist between speculation (a calculated guess) on the one hand, and certainty on the other. If parties have adequately established the basis upon which an expert opinion can be formed, the level of certainty a witness is willing to claim should only be a factor that influences the weight given to the evidence.[265]

E. Hypothetical Questions

PRINCIPLES

Rule 602 generally requires witnesses to have personal knowledge of the facts recounted in their testimony. Unlike all other witnesses, however, experts are explicitly exempted. Helpful testimony may be elicited from such experts through hypothetical questions. After facts have been proven (or acceptably proffered), the proponent may pose a hypothetical question to an expert, asking

---

[262] *See, e.g.,* Lanza v. Poretti, 537 F. Supp. 777, 785 (E.D. Pa. 1982) ("Absent direct physical evidence of smoking or elimination of all other possible causes *with reasonable scientific certainty,* the witness' opinion amounted to nothing more than mere speculation and conjecture.") (Emphasis added)

[263] *See* United States v. Cyphers, 553 F.2d 1064, 1072 (7th Cir. 1977); *State v. Mitchell*, 390 A.2d 495 (Me 1978).

[264] *See* Lego v. Twomey, 404 U.S. 553 (1972).

[265] *See, e.g.,* International Adhesive Coating Co., Inc. v. Bolton Emerson International, Inc., 851 F.2d 540, 545 (1st Cir. 1988) ("[T]he fact that an expert's opinion may be tentative or even speculative does not mean that the testimony must be excluded so long as opposing counsel has an opportunity to attack the expert's credibility" and reveal the weakness of the factual underpinning of the opinion.).

if the expert is able to form an opinion based on an assumption that the facts recited are true. If the expert answers in the affirmative, the proponent may ask the expert to state that opinion.

RULE 602 FRE
Lack of Personal Knowledge

A witness may not testify to a matter unless evidence is introduced sufficient to support a finding that the witness has personal knowledge of the matter. Evidence to prove personal knowledge may, but need not, consist of the witness' own testimony. This rule is subject to the provisions of rule 703, relating to opinion testimony by expert witnesses.

RULE 703 FRE
Bases of Opinion Testimony by Experts

The facts or data in the particular case upon which an expert bases an opinion or inference may be those perceived by or *made known to the expert at or before the hearing*. If of a type reasonably relied upon by experts in the particular field in forming opinions or inferences upon the subject, the facts or data need not be admissible in evidence in order for the opinion or inference to be admitted. If the facts or data are otherwise inadmissible, they shall not be disclosed to the jury by the proponent of the opinion or inference unless their probative value substantially outweighs their prejudicial effect.

107 PRACTICES

Only admissible evidence in hypotheticals. Even though Rule 703 permits experts to be informed of facts "at *or before* the hearing" (emphasis added) and to rely on inadmissible evidence "of a type reasonably relied upon by experts in the particular field in forming opinions . . . upon the subject," courts have not permitted the use of hypothetical questions without evidentiary support for each factual assumption.[266] Despite this restriction, Rule 703 still permits experts to be given facts *before* the hearing (details of which the lawyer may exaggerate in translation) and the expert, "knowing" those facts are "true," to offer an opinion at trial that he would not be willing to give based solely on the evidence before the jury. In other words, the expert encourages the jurors

---

[266] *See* Piotrowski v. Southworth Products Corp., 15 F.3d 748, 753 (9th Cir. 1994); *Toucet v. Maritime Overseas Corp.*, 991 F.2d 5, 10 (1st Cir. 1993); Iconco v. Jensen Construction Co., 622 F.2d 1291, 1293 (8th Cir. 1980).

to draw a conclusion the expert himself would not reach if he were one of the them, and hearing only what they are being permitted to hear. This practice alters the roles of both the expert witness and the jurors. The expert no longer assists the jury in drawing conclusions from the evidence before it, and the jury no longer functions as the sole finder of facts based on that evidence.[267]

108 PRACTICES

Cross-examining in kind. Rule 703 expressly provides experts may base an opinion on facts or data "made known to the expert at . . . the hearing." Because that right applies to both direct and cross-examination, an expert can be effectively cross-examined by adding and subtracting facts from the original question to test how, and under what circumstances, the opinion changes with each changed assumption. If the expert continues to insist on the opinion he originally gave on direct, he appears biased in favor of that position, regardless of what facts may be found to be true. Therefore, his credibility is diminished. If, on the other hand, his opinion changes with degrees of change in the facts, or with added facts (proffered and later proven by the cross-examiner), the cross-examiner may acquire favorable testimony for his case from the other side's witness. At the very minimum, the jury can be thoroughly confused about the expert's opinion after several variations in the facts have produced different conclusions.

109 PRACTICES

Don't worry about exaggerations in the opposing party's hypotheticals. Jurors are told they are the finders of fact and need not find the facts stated in the hypothetical to be true simply because the expert assumed their truth. With this foundation, the opposing party can emphasize to the jurors during closing argument that the expert's opinion is based on the facts being found true as precisely characterized in the hypothetical question. If the jurors find that the facts vary from the characterizations, in either kind or degree, they should be encouraged to disregard the expert's opinion. Exaggerated characterizations in hypothetical questions can backfire on the proponent because it plays into the hand of the adversary — setting the opposition up for a more effective closing argument.

---

[267] *See generally,* PAUL R. RICE & ROY A. KATRIEL, EVIDENCE: COMMON LAW AND FEDERAL RULES OF EVIDENCE, § 8.02[B] [15][d] (LEXIS 5th ed. 2005).

F. Expert Testimony on the Inherent Dangers of Eyewitness Identification

PRINCIPLES

Generally, jurors are believed to possess the ability to assess the credibility of a witness without expert witness assistance. Under the common law, expert testimony on credibility determinations failed to satisfy the necessity standard. Experts' opinions were only admissible under the common law when their assistance was necessary to lay jurors performing their independent fact finding role. Under Rule 702, which only requires that the expert guidance be helpful to the jury in order to be admissible, the practice of excluding expert testimony on this subject continues. Courts generally have concluded that such testimony does not sufficiently "assist the trier of fact to understand the evidence or determine a fact in issue" in light of the general capability of jurors to make credibility assessments and their tendency to rely too heavily on such evidence. Absent special circumstances, such as child victims of sexual abuse testifying about those acts, courts universally reject expert testimony about the credibility of a particular witness.[268] At the other extreme, courts historically remain unreceptive to general testimony about the inherent dangers of eyewitness identification.[269]

RULE 702 FRE
Testimony by Experts

If scientific, technical, or other specialized knowledge will assist the trier of fact to understand the evidence or determine a fact in issue, a witness qualified as an expert by knowledge, skill, experience, training, or education, may testify thereto in the form of an opinion or otherwise, provided that (1) the testimony is based upon sufficient facts or data, (2) the testimony is the product of reliable principles and methods, and (3) the witness has applied the principles and methods reliably to the facts of the case.

---

[268] See, e.g., United States v. Kime, 99 F. 3d 870, 883-85 (8th Cir. 1996); United States v. Cecil, 836 F.2d 1431, 1442 (4th Cir. 1988); United States v. Barnard, 490 F.2d 907, 917 (9th Cir. 1974); United States v. Azure, 801 F.2d 336 (8th Cir. 1986); United States v. Provenzano, 688 F.2d 194, 203-04 (3d Cir.), cert. denied, 456 U.S. 1051 (1982); United States v. Samara, 643 F.2d 701, 705 (10th Cir.), cert. denied, 454 U.S. 829 (1981).

[269] See, e.g., United States v. Fosher, 449 F. Supp. 76, 77 (D. Mass.), aff'd, 590 F.2d 381 (1st Cir. 1979).

110 PRACTICES

Demonstrated relevance increases admissibility. Many factors can influence a witness' memory. While the forgetting curve with the lapse of time differs between witnesses, everyone's memory fades as time passes. Generally, forgetting occurs rapidly and then levels out.[270] Therefore, immediate identifications are more trustworthy than delayed identifications, whether by show-up or lineup, corporal or photographic. Though jurors understand these principles, many issues relating to eyewitness identification are counterintuitive. For example, stress does not increase the quality of perception and memory, but distorts it. Another common misunderstanding is that the more confident a witness is in his identification, the more accurate the identification. In fact, studies have shown there is no correlation between the two.

Other factors that effect the accuracy of recollection include: (1) "unconscious transfer" — when witnesses confuse objects or people that they observed in two different situations; (2) "subsequent incorporation" — a process by which witnesses modify their stories to incorporate post-event information; and (3) the "feedback factor"— a process by which witnesses reinforce the stories of one another and each become more confident in their conclusion.[271] Though *Chapple* led the way in appreciating the importance of expert testimony on the issue of eyewitness identification problems, many federal courts have followed suit.[272]

The more general the testimony, the less relevant, helpful and admissible the assistance appears. Similarly, the more specific the conclusion about the credibility of a particular witness, the more the testimony interferes with the independent role of the jury. If, however, the proponent of the expert testimony demonstrates that the particular problems being discussed by the expert are present in the case at hand, particularly when the information is inconsistent with popular beliefs about eyewitness identification, courts have tended to admit such evidence.

---

[270] *See* Cindy J. O'Hagan, *When Seeing Is Not Believing: The Case for Eyewitness Expert Testimony*, 81 GEO. L.J. 741 (1993); Joseph Sanders, *Expert Witnesses in Eye Witness Facial Identification Cases*, 17 TEX. TECH. L. REV. 1409 (1986).

[271] *See* State v. Chapple, 660 P.2d 1208 (Ariz. 1983); Note, *Did Your Eyes Deceive You? Expert Psychological Testimony on the Unreliability of Eyewitness Identification*, 29 STAN. L. REV. 969, 1017-18 (1977). *See also* Cindy J. O'Hagan, *When Seeing Is Not Believing: The Case for Eyewitness Expert Testimony*, 81 GEO. L.J. 741 (1993) and Joseph Sanders, *Expert Witnesses in Eyewitness Facial Identification Cases*, 17 TEX. TECH. L. REV. 1409 (1986).

[272] *See* United States v. Moore, 786 F.2d 1308, 1312-13 (5th Cir. 1986); United States v. Sebetich, 776 F.2d 412, 419 (3d Cir. 1985); United States v. Smith, 736 F.2d 1103, 1105-06 (6th Cir. 1984); United States v. Serna, 799 F.2d 842, 850 (2d Cir. 1986).

G. Opinion on Ultimate Issue

PRINCIPLES

In addition to the common law restriction on lay opinion testimony, both lay-men and experts were generally prohibited from giving opinions on ultimate issues. The problem with the rule arose through the widely varying definitions of "ultimate issue." Because Rule 701 relaxed the admissibility of lay opinion testimony, and Rule 702 reduced the standard for the admissibility of expert opinion testimony from "necessary" to merely "helpful," the ultimate issue rule became obsolete. Therefore, Rule 704 eliminated the restriction: "[T]estimony in the form of an opinion or inference otherwise admissible is not objectionable because it embraces an ultimate issue to be decided by the trier of fact." After John Hinckley shot President Reagan, Congress reacted negatively to the psy-chiatric testimony presented at his trial and enacted Rule 704(b).

RULE 704 FRE
Opinion on Ultimate Issue

(a) Except as provided in subdivision (b), testimony in the form of an opinion or inference otherwise admissible is not objectionable because it embraces an ultimate issue to be decided by the trier of fact.

(b) No expert witness testifying with respect to the mental state or condition of a defendant in a criminal case may state an opinion or inference as to whether the defendant did or did not have the mental state or condition constituting an element of the crime charged or of a defense thereto. Such ultimate issues are matters for the trier of fact alone.

Subsection (b) revived a facet of the ultimate issue rule in criminal cases rel-ative to the state of mind of the criminal defendant. No expert witness testify-ing with respect to the mental state or condition of a defendant in a criminal case may state an opinion or inference about whether the defendant did or did not have the mental state or condition constituting an element of the crime charged or of a defense thereto.

111 PRACTICES

Who is restricted by the rule? Rule 704(b) does not clearly articulate whether the subsection applies only to "expert witnesses," as indicated in the first sen-tence, or to all witnesses, as suggested in the last sentence where the issue is reserved exclusively for the trier of fact — "the trier of fact *alone.*" (Empha-sis added) The admissibility of a lay witness' opinions that the defendant "was acting crazy" and "didn't seem to know what he was doing" is at stake. The new revision to Rule 701 further complicates this ambiguity problem because it precludes lay opinion testimony "based upon scientific, technical or other specialized knowledge." Is the conclusion about "crazy" and "not knowing what he is doing" the product of specialized knowledge? If the testimony is not otherwise excluded under Rule 704(b), it may be excluded under Rule 701. *See* **PRACTICES NO. 100**, *supra*.

112 PRACTICES

Meaningless impact of rule. Rule 704(b) was a Congressional response to the psychiatric witnesses who appeared at the trial of John Hinckley for the attempted murder of President Ronald Reagan. The trial and its parade of experts was likened to a circus and its clown acts. Subsection (b) was an attempt to stop the circus. It failed.

Psychiatric experts may still be called as witnesses and testify to (1) psychiatric disorders; (2) the symptoms of the defendant that suggest that he has the disorder; (3) how the disorder could effect an individual's ability to form specific intentions or understand the consequences of his conduct. The only testimony that the rule precludes the expert from offering is testimony that relates the psychiatric testimony to the defendant's personal state of mind at the time the crime was committed. The expert cannot testify as to whether he thought the defendant was insane or probably possessed a certain state of mind at the time he committed a particular act — perhaps the most helpful portion of the potential testimony of psychiatric experts because it bridges the science and the legal/societal standards of insanity or specific intent by the most qualified individuals (those who are part of both the science and society). So we still have the clowns and they are still dropping their pants. We have only prevented them from honking their horns as they leave.

113 PRACTICES

"Unexplored legal criteria" ruse. Courts have excluded opinions because they were stated in terms of "unexplored legal criteria."[273] They have not explained, however, why exploring that standard with the witness giving the opinion and instructing him to employ that legal culture does not suffice to cure whatever problem they find with the conclusion.

This practice, unfortunately, has been loosely elevated to a general exclusion of expert opinions on conclusions of law — the application of the relevant

---

[273] *See* Andrews v. Metro North Commuter R. Co., 882 F.2d 705, 770 (2d Cir. 1989).

facts to the controlling legal principles.[274] This result is inappropriate. If the proponent of the expert establishes that the expert correctly used the applicable legal standard in forming a conclusion, the only legitimate basis for excluding qualified opinions is that the opinions do not "assist the trier of fact."[275] Because most ultimate issues are stated in legal terminology, this practice translates into little more than a resuscitation of the ultimate issue rule.

At the same time, if Rule 704 was *not* intended to permit the admission of expert conclusion on mixed issues of law and fact — applying relevant facts to controlling legal principles — then there was no need for the addition of subsection Rule 704(b) after the attack on President Reagan, which explicitly excludes experts from giving opinions on the mental state of a criminal defendant — specifically on whether from the facts adduced whether the defendant was "insane" (a legal concept) at the time the crime was committed.

H. Relationship of Expert Opinion Rules to Other Rules[276]

Rule 104(a). Preliminary Questions of Admissibility Generally. Under Rule 104, the presiding judge will decide whether the use of expert testimony on a particular issue is appropriate, and whether the individual called to testify has the necessary expertise to assist the jury. The trial judge's discretion is quite broad in this regard. An appellate court will not reverse a trial judge's decisions unless the appellant can demonstrate that the decision was "clearly" or "manifestly" erroneous.[277] Appellate courts give such broad discretion to trial judges in the area of expert witnesses because the resolution of these issues is based on factors that vary from case to case and that involve the balancing of

---

[274] *See* Berry v. City of Detroit, 25 F.3d 1342, 1350 (6th Cir. 1994); A.E. by and through Evans v. Independent School Dist. No. 25, 936 F.2d 472, 446 (10th Cir. 1991); Montgomery v. Aetna Cas. & Sur. Co., 898 F.2d 1537, 1541 (11th Cir. 1990); Specht v. Jensen, 853 F.2d 805 (10th Cir. 1988); Matthew v. Ashland Chemical, Inc.,770 F.2d 1303, 1311 (5th Cir. 1985); and Owen v. Kerr-McGee Corp., 698 F.2d 236, 240 (5th Cir. 1983).

[275] In Specht v. Jensen, 853 F.2d 805, 810 (10th Cir. 1988) this point was made by dissenting Judge Seymour to the majority decision that upheld the exclusion of a lawyer's testimony about the unreasonableness of a search.

The majority opinion in this case makes these very mistakes. Although the opinion pays lip service to the Federal Rules of Evidence by recognizing that expert opinions on the ultimate issue are admissible if helpful to the fact-finder, it condemns the expert testimony here as embodying inadmissible legal conclusions, a characterization that does not explain why the testimony is not helpful or is otherwise inadmissible. Labeling testimony as a legal conclusion in and of itself provides not meaningful guidance on either its admissibility of any resulting prejudice.

[276] PAUL R. RICE & ROY A. KATRIEL, EVIDENCE: COMMON LAW AND FEDERAL RULES OF EVIDENCE § 8.02 [C] (LEXIS 5th ed. 2005).

[277] General Electric Co. v. Joiner, 522 U.S. 136, 142 (1997).

conflicting facts and equitable considerations.[278] Consequently, if reasonable opposing equitable or factual considerations exist, the appellate court will not substitute its judgment for that of the trial court.[279]

Rule 201. Judicial Notice of Adjudicative Facts. Rule 201 empowers courts to take judicial notice of facts not subject to reasonable dispute. Accordingly, a court may take judicial notice that certain kinds of information are of the type experts in a particular field reasonably rely. In *United States v. Lawson*,[280] for example, the appellate court took judicial notice of the fact that psychiatrists customarily use staff reports, interviews with other physicians, and background information from the Marine Corps and the U.S. Attorney's Office to diagnose mental illness. The appellate court was required to take judicial notice of this fact because the trial court had not made such a finding based upon information supplied by the testifying psychiatrist.

Rule 403. Exclusion of Relevant Evidence on Grounds of Prejudice, Confusion, or Waste of Time. After the court determines that a qualified person is addressing a proper subject of expert testimony, but before admitting the testimony, it must consider the potential prejudice that may arise upon the introduction of such evidence. If the evidence's prejudicial effect *substantially outweighs* its probative value, the court must exclude it under Rule 403. In making this determination, the judge will consider a variety of factors including: (1) the importance of the issue on which the expert testimony is offered, (2) whether the testimony would be cumulative or repetitive of evidence already admitted, (3) whether other less prejudicial evidence is available, and (4) whether such testimony might tend to confuse rather than assist the jury.[281] The court may also consider (5) the degree to which the expert opinion was based on inadmissible evidence, even though such evidence is generally relied upon by experts in the particular field.[282]

In criminal cases in which the prosecution uses scientific evidence against the defendant, this balance takes on particular importance because of the aura surrounding expert testimony. Failure to balance probative value and prejudicial effect properly resulted in reversal on appeal in *United States v. Green*[283] even though the standard of review for such determinations is manifest error. In *Green,* the defendant was convicted of conspiracy to manufacture a controlled substance. His conviction was based in part on extensive expert testimony concerning both the physical effects resulting from usage of the substance

---

[278] *See* Walsh v. Centeio, 692 F.2d 1239, 1242 (9th Cir. 1982).

[279] For instances of appellate courts' overruling the trial judge, *see* Davis v. Freels, 583 F.2d 337 (7th Cir. 1978), and Young v. Illinois Central Gulf Railroad Co., 618 F.2d 332 (5th Cir. 1980).

[280] 653 F.2d 299, 302 n.7 (7th Cir. 1981).

[281] *See United States v. Fosher*, 590 F.2d 381, 382 (1st Cir. 1979).

[282] *See Barrel of Fun, Inc. v. State Farm Fire & Cas. Co.*, 739 F.2d 1028, 1033 (5th Cir. 1984) (noting that Rule 703 does not guarantee the admissibility of all expert testimony satisfying its criteria if such testimony runs afoul of other evidentiary requirements).

[283] 548 F.2d 1261, 1268-70 (6th Cir. 1977).

and the drug's economic value to those who sell it. On appeal, the court found the admission of this expert testimony to be reversible error because the evidence served only to prejudice the jury. With regard to such background evidence, the court warned "trial courts should exercise greater care in drug cases [because such evidence] may be capable of subliminally inciting or confusing the jury."[284]

Rule 602. Lack of Person Knowledge. Lay witnesses may not testify to either facts or opinions unless they have personal knowledge of the matter about which they speak. Rule 701 codifies this requirement in the context of lay opinions.[285] In contrast, expert witnesses are excepted from this requirement of personal knowledge because of their special knowledge and skill. Thus, experts are explicitly excluded from Rule 602, which states "[t]his rule is subject to the provisions of Rule 703, relating to opinion testimony by expert witnesses."

Rule 56(e) of the Federal Rules of Civil Procedure allows the court to consider affidavits and deposition testimony in support of a motion for summary judgment only if they are based on "personal knowledge." In *Shearing v. Iolab Corporation*[286] the court held that the language of Rule 56(e) controlled, thereby precluding an affidavit of an expert not based entirely on personal knowledge. The court stated Rule 56(e) does not differentiate between affidavits by experts and non-experts. The court's conclusion probably is incorrect. Rule 56(e) was promulgated before Rule 703 of the Federal Rules of Evidence, which explicitly exempts expert testimony from Rule 602, allowing experts to rely on facts outside their personal knowledge when testifying.[287]

Rule 608. Evidence of Character and Conduct of Witness. Opinions on the credibility of witnesses are expressly made admissible in Rule 608(a): "The credibility of a witness may be attacked or supported in the form of opinion . . . for truthfulness or untruthfulness." Although Rule 608(a) does not establish prerequisites for admissibility, Rule 701 that requires all lay opinions rationally be based on the perceptions of the individual offering them and helpful to the determination of a fact in issue. In *United States v. Dotson*[288] the Fifth Circuit held that when a party objects to the factual basis of an opinion as to credibility, the court "should require that the witness identify the basis or source of his opinion," and should then assess whether the opinion was rational, given those delineated perceptions. In *Dotson,* the court concluded that the trial court erred

---

[284] *Id.* at 1270.

[285] *See* United States v. Hoffner, 777 F.2d 1423, 1426 (10th Cir. 1985).

[286] 712 F. Supp 1446, 1453-54 (D. Nev. 1989).

[287] *See* Huber v. Howard County, MD., 56 F.3d 61, 1995 WL 325644, *4-5 (4th Cir. 1995); Doe v. Cutter Biological, Inc., 971 F.2d 375, 384-85 (9th Cir. 1992); Colgan v. Fisher Scientific Co., 935 F.2d 1407, 1423 n15 (3d Cir. 1991).

[288] 799 F.2d 189, 193 (5th Cir. 1986).

in admitting the opinions of police officers whose conclusions were based on nothing more than the fact that they had investigated the defendant.

The Eighth Circuit held that it was inappropriate to allow a pediatrician, established as an expert in child sexual abuse, to testify he "could see no reason why [Wendy, the alleged victim of the abuse] would not be telling the truth."[289] The court stated that this was not admissible under Rule 608(a)(1) because it went beyond the general character for truthfulness of Wendy's story. On a more general level, the court held that the expert testimony was inappropriate because it put the expert's stamp of credibility on Wendy's story (essentially telling the jury that Wendy was telling the truth and that Azure was guilty of sexually abusing her), thereby creating too great a risk that the jury would surrender its own common sense in weighing the evidence. The circuit courts agree about the inadmissibility of expert testimony on the credibility of a particular witness.[290] One should be careful, however, not to confuse those cases excluding expert testimony on the credibility of particular witnesses, with those addressing the admissibility of expert testimony on more general topics that relate to credibility, such as the inherent dangers of eyewitness identifications, which some courts have accepted. *See* **PRACTICES NO. 110**, *supra.*

Rule 615. Exclusion of Witnesses. Rule 615 provides for the sequestration of witnesses — their exclusion from the courtroom during the testimony of other witnesses so that they are unable to hear and adjust their testimony to the stories told by one another. Under this rule, however, the court has discretion to exempt certain witnesses from sequestration. Under Rule 615(3), the court may allow any witness to remain in the courtroom "whose presence is shown by a party to be essential to the presentation of his cause."

Under this provision, courts have exempted expert witnesses whose presences were essential to the trial because of the complex nature of the issues being litigated (for example, a patent infringement action), or who would be offering opinions based on the facts presented through the testimony of others. The latter exemption is justified on two grounds. First, because the expert is not a transaction witness in many cases, and, therefore, does not offer factual testimony that must conform to the stories of others. Therefore, the principal reason for the rule of exclusion is not present. Second, because the expert will base his testimony on the substance of what other witnesses will establish, hearing the testimony of those witnesses in the same way as the jury puts them in the same position as the jurors. Allowing the expert to hear other witnesses' testimony would eliminate the need to use hypothetical questions through which the facts otherwise would be brought to the expert's attention.[291]

---

[289] United States v. Azure, 801 F.2d 336, 339 (8th Cir. 1986).

[290] *See, e.g.,* Nimely v. City of New York, 414 F.3d 381, 398 (2d Cir. 2005); Morris v. Burnett, 319 F.3d 1254, 1277 (10th Cir. 2003); United States v. Cecil, 836 F.2d 1431, 1442 (4th Cir. 1988); United States v. Provenzano, 688 F.2d 194, 203-04 (3d Cir.), *cert. denied,* 459 U.S. 1051 (1982); United States v. Jackson, 576 F.2d 46, 49 (5th Cir. 1978).

[291] *See* Morvant v. Construction Aggregates Corp., 570 F.2d 626, 630 (6th Cir. 1978).

Following the lead of *Morvant*, the Second Circuit has also held the trial court should have accepted the representations of counsel that the presence of the expert was required for the effective management of the case.[292] In *Malek*, the opposing side's expert testified to a specific finding that was not in his report. Because this finding was important to the determination of arson, the appellate court concluded the sequestered expert's presence in the courtroom "was important to the presentation of the Maleks' case, and a ten-minute recess [following the testimony] was not an adequate substitute for his presence." In these opinions, the courts come very close to making an absolute exception from sequestration for expert witnesses in trials where there is a battle of the experts. Courts make such an exception because a trial judge cannot know in advance what a witness will say, and therefore, cannot gauge how necessary the presence of the opposing expert will be. Thus, the standard practice will likely be to except experts from sequestration absent compelling reasons to do otherwise.

Rule 802. Hearsay Rule. Whenever a party offers an out-of-court statement in a judicial proceeding to prove the truth of the matter asserted, the statement constitutes hearsay and should be excluded unless it falls within a recognized exception to the hearsay rule contained in Rules 803 and 804 or within an exclusion from the definition in Rule 801(d). In determining whether a party is offering a statement for the truth of its content, the critical question that must first be answered is "Why is the statement relevant?" If the statement is relevant only because of the truth of its content, then its introduction will necessarily give rise to hearsay problems. *See* **PRACTICES NO. 27**, *supra*.

Under Rule 703, an expert can rely upon information and data about which he has no first-hand knowledge. The expert can rely upon reports and opinions prepared by other experts if experts in the particular field reasonably rely upon these types of reports and opinions. If an expert relies on such reports, a hearsay issue is created because the party who called the expert is *indirectly* offering the reports for the truth of their content if the party is offering the expert's opinion for its truth. The general acceptance by experts in the field of the kind of hearsay reports on which an expert has based his opinion provides an assurance of reliability and trustworthiness that is equivalent to that which must be present when an exception to the hearsay rule is recognized. It is unclear, therefore, whether Rule 703 creates an *implicit* exception to the hearsay rule that would allow the expert to testify to the hearsay basis of his opinion and allow the jury to accept this basis for its truth. *See* **PRACTICES NOS. 104-105**, *supra*.

If the testifying expert has *not* relied on another expert's report, one cannot read from it when cross-examining him with it, because such conduct gives rise to a hearsay problem. This complication arises because the report's only relevance is the truth of its contents. Because the witness neither produced nor

---

[292] Malek v. Federal Ins. Co., 994 F.2d 49, 53-55 (2d Cir. 1993).

relied upon the report, its mere existence, aside from its truth, does not serve to impeach as a prior inconsistent statement.[293] If a party can undercut a witness' testimony only by arguing the substantive correctness of the conclusions in another expert's report, that report is hearsay.[294]

Rule 803(18). Learned Treatises. Prior to the adoption of the Federal Rules of Evidence, most jurisdictions only allowed learned treatises to be used during the cross-examination of an expert witness and it was only admissible for impeachment purposes. If the expert recognized the treatise as authoritative and, in many jurisdictions, relied upon it in forming her opinions, a cross-examining party could read a passage from it to show an inconsistency. The court treated the statement in the treatise as the expert's own statement because she was considered to have adopted it through her reliance on it. Theoretically, therefore, the statement's truth or falsity was irrelevant because its value sprang solely from its inconsistency with the testimony. The reality of the use of such a treatise, however, was that jurors accepted it for its substantive truth, even though cautioned against it by limiting instructions. Acknowledging this fact, the Federal Rules of Evidence recognized a new exception to the hearsay rule, admitting the treatise for its truth if brought to an expert's attention on direct or cross-examination and established as authoritative, either through an expert witness' recognition or through judicial notice.

Rule 1002. Requirement of Original: The Best Evidence Rule. Pursuant to Rule 1002, if a party is proving the content of a writing, and it is material to the litigation, that party must produce the original of that writing unless the court excuses this requirement under Rules 1003, 1004, and 1005. If an expert bases an opinion on a written report, is he indirectly proving its content by giving his opinion and directly proving its content by testifying to the basis of his opinion? Despite its potential applicability, apparently the best evidence rule does not apply in this context. Directly addressing this issue, the Advisory Committee stated:

> It should be noted, however, that Rule 703 allows an expert to give an opinion based on matters not in evidence, and the present rule [Rule 1002] must be read as being limited accordingly in its application. Hospital records which may be admitted as business records under Rule 803(6) commonly contain reports interpreting X-rays by the staff radiologist, who qualifies as an expert, and these reports need not be excluded from the records by the instant rule.[295]

See **PRACTICES NO. 92**, *supra*.

---

[293] *See* Bobb v. Modern Products, Inc., 648 F.2d 1051, 1055-56 (5th Cir. 1981), overruled on other grounds, 107 F.3d 331 (5th Cir. 1997).

[294] Bryan v. John Bean Division of FMC Corp., 566 F.2d 541, 546-547 (5th Cir. 1978).

[295] Fed. R. Evid. 1002 Advisory Committee's Note, 56 F.R.D. 183, 343 (1972).

III. APPLICATIONS — LAY AND EXPERT OPINION RULES

ONE

After an installed knee prosthesis malfunctioned, the plaintiff sued the manufacturer on theories of negligence and design defect. It was claimed that the knee's deterioration was caused by the defendant's method of sterilization and the implant's time on the shelf. To prove his theory the plaintiff offered the testimony of James Pugh, a litigant consultant specializing in metallurgy, biomedical engineering, and polyethylene failure. The trial judge found that he possessed the requisite credentials to be an expert witness, and his testimony was acceptable under *Daubert* because his analysis was based on a scientific reason for the failure of the polyethylene that was laid out and explored at his deposition. The judge, however, never identified what the articulated scientific reason was, or how it measured up to *Daubert's* indicia of reliability. On appeal the court held that the judge's gate-keeping role had not been satisfied. The expert's theory about causation (1) had never been published, and (2) had not been tested, either by himself or by his peers. (3) His theory that the causation he supports results in an appearance distinctive from delamination from other causes — leaving a readily identifiable signature or hallmark — had not received any, let alone general, scientific acceptance. (4) His testimony was developed for the litigation. (5) Alternative causes of the implant's failure may not have been adequately discounted. (6) His testimony about sterilization through gamma radiation was wholly unfounded and without any adherents. *Fuesting v. Zimmer, Inc.*, 421 F.3d 528 (7th Cir. 2005).

TWO

In a sexual harassment action against the police department, the plaintiff called another female officer in the department as a witness. Her testimony was: "After reading about the plaintiff's claims, I told another officer how I felt that it was unfair and how the plaintiff was not being given a chance to show her potential. This was just like my experience with the department. I think it's the old-boy network and that conclusion is shared by other officers, one of whom said to me that the plaintiff's potential was being squashed by the men in the department." The court ruled the testimony inadmissible because the witness had no actual knowledge of what had happened to the plaintiff. She was not qualified as an expert on anything and her assessments were not the limited kind of opinion testimony deemed helpful to a jury. It was simply argument offered from the witness stand that incorporated hearsay. *Bandera v. City of Quincy*, 2003 WL 22111107 (1st Cir. 2003).

THREE

After being shot by the police, who used excessive force after entry into the plaintiff's home, a civil rights action was filed. In the trial the plaintiff called a Certified Public Accountant to testify as an expert to the damages he has suffered from his reduced work capacity as a result of the shooting. The CPA, using his pre-shooting tax returns and client invoices estimated the dollar amount of his loss. The expert witness relied upon the plaintiff's "best guess" as to the impairment of his capacity to work rather than on a doctor's analysis. The defendant objected to the admissibility of his testimony. It was held that once the court determined that the witness is competent to testify as an expert, challenges to the expert's testimony goes to weight rather than admissibility. The fact that he relied upon the plaintiff's representations, rather than scientific evidence, goes to the credibility of the testimony, and it is up to the opposing party to expose deficiencies in the factual basis on cross-examination and criticize them in closing argument. Such expert testimony should be excluded only if it is unsupported by evidence. Here his mathematical calculations were derived from standard accounting procedures based on the plaintiff's estimation. To the extent the jury did not believe the plaintiff's estimation they could reduce their reliance on the expert's testimony that was premised on its accuracy. *Doran v. Eckold*, 362 F.3d 1047 (8th Cir. 2004).

FOUR

In an action for public nuisance because of odors emanating from the plaintiff hog confinement facilities, the plaintiff called expert witnesses who testified that they constituted a nuisance. The experts based their testimony in part on answers to questionnaires sent to individuals around the plaintiffs' property. Defendant objected to the admissibility of these opinions because they were based on hearsay, and to the admission of the results of the questionnaires. Plaintiffs claimed that Rule 703 permits the expert to rely on otherwise inadmissible evidence so long as it is of the type reasonably relied upon by experts in the particular field in forming opinions or inferences upon the subject. The question posed was whether the expert testimony was inadmissible because its acceptance required the finder of facts to accept the truth of the representations in the questionnaires. Stated differently, are the inadmissible hearsay questionnaire results made admissible if the experts permissibly relied upon them?

Rule 703 permits the otherwise inadmissible basis of an expert's opinions to be used and delineated only for the purpose of showing the *basis* for the opinions. This assumes an independent basis in the record for the experts' conclusions. The hearsay results of the questionnaires are not admissible for substantive truth of the facts asserted therein simply because the experts relied upon them. Therefore, use of the expert's basis to establish facts essential to the opinion is inappropriate. Since the primary dispute here was the character and extent of the odor problem emanating from the defendant's facilities, the admission of the answers to the questionnaires was prejudicial error because it was necessarily offering them for the truth of their contents. *Gacke v. Pork XTRA, LLC,* 2004 WL 1344974 (Iowa 2004). The court did not address the possibility that the questionnaire results could be admissible under the residual exception in Rule 807.

FIVE

In an action for the defective design of a stand-up power lift truck, the plaintiff called an engineer to opine that the truck was defectively designed in that it (1) had an open cockpit with no safety restraints, (2) the lift failed to display warning notices about likely dangers, and (3) the truck had no fail-safe design. The expert witness admitted that he was not an expert in the design or engineering of stand-up power lift trucks, but had knowledge of engineering principles that have universal application. Defendant moved to exclude the expert testimony because the engineer was not an expert in lift-truck design.

While some principles are universal in their application, the court struck the testimony of this expert because (1) he had never designed or consulted on a design of stand-up lift trucks, (2) had never designed a component of a stand-up lift truck, and (3) had neither operated nor seen a stand-up lift truck before testifying in this case. The exclusion of this testimony by the trial judge was not an abuse of discretion. *Anderson v. Raymond Corp.*, 2003 WL 21919577 (8th Cir. Aug. 2003).

SIX

In a slip-and-fall case the plaintiff called a chiropractor to give expert testimony on the cause of the plaintiff's pain and discomfort. His testimony was based on a number of factors. First he ruled out alternative sources, such as infection, since the plaintiff did not have fever and did not have redness in her back. He ruled out arthritis through x-rays that did not show any signs of arthritis. He ruled out genetic etiology after taking a medical history. He testified that he followed normal procedures for chiropractors in evaluating and treating the plaintiff. After treatment did not result in improvement, this expert referred the plaintiff back to her medical doctor for further examination and evaluation. The doctor found nothing further and referred the plaintiff back to the chiropractor. Defendant claimed that the expert testimony was based entirely on the plaintiff's word and cited no published study to support his position and therefore should be excluded.

The testimony is admissible. First, the chiropractor based his opinion on more than simply crediting the plaintiff's statements to him. He performed tests and relied upon physical observations in coming to his conclusions. Second, publications do not always have to be cited in order to draw reliable conclusions about causation. Peer-reviewed studies do not exist to confirm physicians' diagnoses. The defendants cross-examination of the chiropractor and challenge to his credentials provided adequate assurances that the finder of fact would give appropriate weight to his conclusions. *Kudabeck v. Kroger Co.*, 338 F.3d 856 (8th Cir. 2003).

Chapter 7
IMPEACHMENT AND CROSS-EXAMINATION

I. IMPEACHMENT — BIAS

A. PRINCIPLES

The credibility of a witness is directly linked to the quality of his perception and memory. Though the quality of perception and memory depends upon a variety of factors (*e.g.*, one's vantage, physical circumstances, elapsed time, and mental disease or defect), it can be heavily influenced by the bias that a witness brings to his perception and recollection. The old expression that people see things through differently colored glasses rings true. People are biased both for and against things, ideas and people, and they might perceive or misperceive many things according to their mind-set.

Bias represents the broadest basis for introducing impeachment evidence. Biases for and against things can be reflected in what we say and do to others, what others say and do to us, relationships (familial and emotional), and interests (*e.g.*, economic, political and religious). The ranges of biases and the means by which the parties can prove them is infinite — restricted only by logic and a balancing of probative value against the potential for unfair prejudice.

While no federal rule directly addresses the issue of bias evidence, courts have considered it an inherent part of a party's right to confront and cross-examine witnesses.[296]

114 PRACTICES

Is there a foundation required before extrinsic evidence of bias is admissible? Under the common law, most jurisdictions required that a foundation be laid before extrinsic bias evidence — evidence that required the calling of additional witnesses — could be introduced. This foundation required that the

---

[296] United States v. Abel, 469 U.S. 45, 49-50 (1984). "It is permissible to impeach a witness by showing his bias under the Federal Rules of Evidence. Just as it was permissible to do so before their adoption. In this connection, the comment of the Reporter for the Advisory Committee which drafted the Rules is apropos: 'In principle, under the Federal Rules no common law of evidence remains. "All relevant evidence is admissible, except as otherwise provided. . . ." In reality, of course, the body of common law knowledge continues to exist, through in the somewhat altered form of a source of guidance in the exercise of delegated powers.'" Cleary, *Preliminary Notes on Reading the Rules of Evidence*, 57 Neb. L. Rev. 908, 915 (1978) (footnotes omitted).'" *See* United States v. Manske, 186 F.3d 770, 777 (7th Cir. 1999); United States v. Spencer, 25 F.3d 1105, 1109 (D.C. Cir. 1994);

allegedly biased witness be confronted with the accusation of bias and be given a fair opportunity to admit and explain the evidence that would be presented, or to deny bias. Only if the witness denied the bias was the cross-examiner permitted to offer additional evidence on the subject.

In the absence of a controlling rule, federal courts have been divided over the foundation requirement. Most circuits have followed the common law practice of requiring the foundation.[297] A few courts, however, have refused to impose a foundation requirement on the belief that if a foundation requirement is not required in the evidence code, the courts should not impose it.[298] Interestingly, some of the courts imposing the requirement have done so in an apparent attempt to draw a parallel with the impeachment tool of prior inconsistent statements (where a foundation requirement was imposed under the common law); they have made reference to Rule 613, the rule that controls the admissibility of inconsistent statements.

Relying on Rule 613 may be a bit perverse because Rule 613 appears to have *abolished* the foundation requirement for the presentation of extrinsic evidence of inconsistent statements. Therefore, abolition of the same requirement for the presentation of bias evidence is the only action that Rule 613 supports.[299] Nevertheless, circuit courts have split over this issue,[300] and most have perpetuated the common law foundation requirements.

RULE 613 FRE
Prior Statements of Witnesses

(a) **Examining witness concerning prior statement.** In examining a witness concerning a prior statement made by the witness, whether written or not, the statement need not be shown nor its contents disclosed to the witness at that time, but on request the same shall be shown or disclosed to opposing counsel.

---

[297] United States v. Elkins, 70 F.3d 81, 84 (10th Cir. 1995); United States v. Johnson, 965 F.2d 460 (7th Cir. 1992); United States v. Devine, 934 F.2d 1325 (5th Cir. 1991); United States v. Cutler, 676 F.2d 1245 (9th Cir. 1982); Hilyer v. Howat Concrete Co., 578 F.2d 422 (D.C. Cir. 1978); United States v. Di Napoli, 557 F.2d 962 (2d Cir. 1977); United States v. Truslow, 530 F.2d 257 (4th Cir. 1975); Felix v. Virgin Islands, 2005 WL 3077599, at 8 (D.V.I. Nov. 3, 2005).

[298] *See, e.g.,* United States v. McCabe, 131 F.3d 149, 1997 WL 753348, at *6 (9th Cir. Nov. 26, 1997); United States v. Diggs, 522 F.2d 1310, 1331 (D.C. Cir. 1975) (not imposing the requirement in a case of alleged racial bias).

[299] *See* United States v. Hudson, 970 F.2d 948 , 955-565(1st Cir. 1992); United States v. Lynch, 800 F.2d 765, 770 (8th Cir. 1986); Wammock v. Celotex Corp., 793 F.2d 1518, 1522-23 (11th Cir. 1986) *withdrawn* 835 F.2d 990 (11th Cir. 1988).

[300] *Compare* United States v. Leslie, 759 F.2d 366, 380 (5th Cir. 1985) (foundation required) and United States v. Harvey, 547 F.2d 720 (2d Cir. 1976) (foundation required) *with* United States v. McCabe, 131 F.3d 149, 1997 WL 753348, at *6 (9th Cir. Nov. 26, 1997);and United States v. Diggs, 522 F.2d 1310, 1331 (D.C. Cir. 1975) (no foundation required).

(b) Extrinsic evidence of prior inconsistent statement of witness. Extrinsic evidence of a prior inconsistent statement by a witness is not admissible unless the witness is afforded an opportunity to explain or deny the same and the opposite party is afforded an opportunity to interrogate the witness thereon, or the interests of justice otherwise require. This provision does not apply to admissions of a party-opponent as defined in Rule 801(d)(2).

Because the Federal Rules of Evidence have established no foundation requirement for the introduction of extrinsic evidence of bias, it has been argued that Rule 402 precludes courts from perpetuating whatever foundation requirement may have existed at common law?[301] Rule 402 provides that relevant evidence is admissible unless excluded by "the Constitution . . . , by Act of Congress, by these rules, or by other rules prescribed by the Supreme Court. . . ."

B. Relationship of Bias Rule to Other Rules[302]

Rule 403. Exclusion of Relevant Evidence on Grounds of Prejudice, Confusion, or Waste of Time. As with all other logically relevant evidence, prior to the admission of bias evidence courts must balance the evidence's probative value against the potential unfair prejudice that may result to the party against whom it is being offered. This is particularly true in criminal cases when the Government uses bias evidence against the defendant. However, as the Supreme Court explained in *United States v. Abel,*[303] before a court is required to exclude bias evidence on these grounds, it must determine that the evidence is "unduly" prejudicial.

Abel involved a prosecution for bank robbery. Ehle, a cohort of the defendant who had pleaded guilty, testified for the Government and implicated Abel. To impeach Ehle, the defense called one of Abel's fellow prison inmates, Mills, who testified that Ehle had admitted to him that he intended to implicate Abel falsely. To impeach Mills, the Government, in its case-in-rebuttal, recalled Ehle as a witness and elicited from him information about the membership of Mills and Abel in a secret prison gang that was sworn to perjury and self-protection on each member's behalf. On appeal, the defendant claimed the trial court abused its discretion in allowing the Government to introduce this evidence. The appellate court rejected this claim. "The attributes of the Aryan Brotherhood — a secret prison sect sworn to perjury and self-protection — bore directly not only on the *fact* of bias but also on the *source* and *strength* of Mills' bias. The tenets

---

[301] *See* Imwinkelreid, *Federal Rule of Evidence 402: The Second Revolution*, 6 REV. LIT. 129, 149 (1987) (arguing that Rule 402 repeals prior decisional admissibility rules that have not been codified).

[302] PAUL R. RICE & ROY A. KATRIEL, EVIDENCE: COMMON LAW AND FEDERAL RULES OF EVIDENCE § 6.06 [D] (LEXIS 5th ed. 2005).

[303] 469 U.S. 45 (1984).

of this group showed that Mills had a powerful motive to slant his testimony towards respondent or even commit perjury outright."[304]

Rule 411. Liability Insurance. Rule 411 renders evidence of liability insurance coverage inadmissible on the issue of whether a person acted negligently on a particular occasion. The rule, however, explicitly provides that this evidence is admissible if probative of a witness' prejudice or bias. This situation usually arises if the witness either is an employee of the insurance company that is financing the insured's defense (the claims agent, for example) or has been retained by the insurance company to give expert testimony at the trial.

Rule 610. Religious Beliefs or Opinions. Evidence of a witness' religious beliefs or opinions are inadmissible under Rule 610 for the purpose of showing that these beliefs or opinions have an effect on the witness' character for truthfulness. Nevertheless, the witness' affiliation with a particular religious denomination or congregation may be admissible as evidence of his bias if, for example, that congregation were a party to the litigation. As the Advisory Committee explicitly stated: "an inquiry [into a witness' religious beliefs] for the purpose of showing interest or bias because of them is not within the prohibition."[305]

C. Applications — Bias

ONE

In a civil rights action against a county judge for allegedly undertaking a racially-motivated campaign to discredit and damage the plaintiff and have him dismissed from his job, the plaintiff offers evidence of the judge's prior conduct in judicial proceedings involving the plaintiff. This conduct included racially derogatory remarks, the issuance of judicial process without justification, and the release of false information to the press. The defendant/judge objects to the introduction of this evidence of his prior acts. The court held that the evidence is admissible under Rule 404(b) as proof of the judge's racially discriminatory motive. Whenever evidence of past conduct is otherwise admissible under Rule 404(b) because it establishes or contravenes a material element of the claim or defense, Rule 608(b) is inapplicable and provides no basis for exclusion. *Harris v. Harvey*, 605 F.2d 330, 337 (7th Cir. 1979), *cert. denied*, 445 U.S. 938 (1980).

TWO

Alexander Dardi was indicted for various criminal violations of the federal securities laws. As its principal witness, the Government called Peter Brann, an unindicted accomplice of Dardi's, who testified extensively as to the alleged

---

[304] *Id.* at 470.

[305] Fed. R. Evid. 610 Advisory Committee's Note, 56 F.R.D. 183, 272 (1972).

securities fraud scheme. To counter Brann's testimony, Dardi called Ian McCollom, a financial analyst from Switzerland who had dealt extensively with Brann. McCollom testified on direct that Brann's reputation for truth and veracity in Geneva, Switzerland, "was just as poor as it could possibly be." On cross-examination, the Government seeks to question McCollom about an arrest warrant for embezzlement outstanding against him in Switzerland. Brann had brought the embezzlement charge against McCollom. Upon objection by defense counsel, the court ruled that even though the questioning might not permit the cross-examination pursuant to Rule 608(b), because the substance of what is alleged does not substantively relate to truthfulness, the inquiry is permissible on cross-examination because it reflects McCollom's potential bias and hostility toward Brann. *United States v. Dardi*, 330 F.2d 316, 330 (2d Cir.), *cert. denied*, 379 U.S. 845 (1964).

II. IMPEACHMENT — CHARACTER EVIDENCE AND CONDUCT OF WITNESS

A. PRINCIPLES

When a witness testifies, he silently prefaces each of his answers with "You can believe me when I say . . . ." Therefore, each witness' credibility is placed in issue. As a consequence, each witness' character trait for truth and veracity can be explored. Character witness can be called who testify to a preceding witness' *reputation* for truth and veracity in the community (the only method of proof under the common law) and to the character witness' personal opinion of the previous witnesses same character trait (the expanded method of proof under Rule 608(a)). While each witness may be asked about his prior conduct that reflect on his character trait for truth and veracity, the interrogator is stuck with the answer. If the conduct is denied, it may not be proven with extrinsic evidence.

RULE 608 FRE
Evidence of Character and Conduct of Witness

(a) **Opinion and reputation evidence of character**. The credibility of a witness may be attacked or supported by evidence in the form of opinion or reputation, but subject to these limitations: (1) the evidence may refer only to character for truthfulness or untruthfulness, and (2) evidence of truthful character is admissible only after the character of the witness for truthfulness has been attacked by opinion or reputation evidence or otherwise.

(b) **Specific instances of conduct.** Specific instances of the conduct of a witness, for the purpose of attacking or supporting the witness' character for truthfulness, other than conviction of crime as provided in Rule 609, may not be proved by extrinsic evidence. They may, however, in the discretion of the court, if probative of truthfulness or untruthfulness, be inquired into on cross-examination of the witness (1) concerning the witness' character for truthfulness or untruthfulness, or (2) concerning the character for truthfulness or untruthfulness of another witness as to which character the witness being cross-examined has testified.

The giving of testimony, whether by an accused or by any other witness, does not operate as a waiver of the accused's or the witness' privilege against self-incrimination when examined with respect to matters which relate only to character for truthfulness.

115 PRACTICES

Taking the answer — a perverse limitation on character attacks. If a person takes the witness stand at trial, he opens for examination his credibility or character trait for truthfulness. A cross-examiner may attack a witness' credibility in a number of different ways. One of these methods of impeachment is provided for in Rule 608(b). The cross-examiner may inquire about specific instances of the witness' conduct that reflected on his credibility. For example, he may have filed false travel vouchers with his former employer. For fear of distraction and delay, courts have placed a significant limitation on this method of impeachment: if the witness denies the conduct, the cross-examiner must *take the answer* — the cross-examiner may not prove by extrinsic evidence that the witness actually participated in the conduct inquired about and denied.

This is perverse. The credibility of many witnesses is often central to the resolution of disputes. If, in the past, a witness committed acts that casts a shadow on his truthfulness, proof of those acts may not reflect sufficiently on his credibility to justify the distraction that will be involved in bringing additional witnesses forward to prove them, not to mention the additional witnesses who will be called in response. When, however, the witness has denied those acts during cross-examination, the witness may have lied under oath in the presence of the individuals attempting to assess credibility. What better evidence of lack of credibility could be presented? If this doesn't justify whatever delay and distraction may be involved, it is difficult to imagine what would.

Prior convictions, Rule 609(a), is an exception to the requirement of "taking the answer." If the witness' prior conduct reflecting negatively on this character trait for truthfulness also resulted in a conviction, the cross-examiner may prove that conviction through extrinsic evidence, even if the witness denies the conduct underlying the conviction. If the conviction is older than ten years, however, the evidence is inadmissible under Rule 609(b) unless the court determines, in the interests of justice, that the value of the conviction relative to the witness' credibility substantially outweighs its prejudicial effect. The same 10 year restriction does not apply when inquiry is made into the underlying conduct under Rule 608(b).[306]

B. Relationship of Witness' Character to Other Rules[307]

Rule 404(a). Character Evidence Generally. Parties can offer character evidence under both Rule 404(a) and Rule 608(a). The purpose for which a party offers the evidence will dictate which rule controls the offer. Rule 404(a) controls the use of character evidence if an accused in a criminal case offers evidence of one of her character traits that is pertinent to the charge that has been made against her, for the purpose of convincing the finder of facts that she is not guilty. The focus of such character evidence is on past conduct. This rule is limited to *criminal cases* and it requires that *the defendant* initiate the use of evidence on the issue. In contrast, Rule 608(a) will govern the offer of character evidence when any witness testifies in any litigation. The focus of this evidence is on the witness' present credibility and the likelihood that the witness' testimony will be truthful. The opposing party must first attack a witness' credibility before the proponent may offer character evidence supporting the witness' credibility. *United States v. Danehy*, 680 F.2d 1311 (11th Cir. 1982).

Rule 404(b). Other Crimes, Wrongs, or Acts. Rule 608(b) prohibits the admission of extrinsic evidence to prove the truth of the witness' alleged specific instances of conduct. Evidence that is not admissible under 608(b), however, may still be admissible under 404(b) for other purposes, such as proving intent. *See, e.g., United States v. Horton*, 847 F.2d 313, 324 (6th Cir. 1988). Horton was charged with mail fraud. During the course of the direct examination of him in his case-in-defense, Horton testified that he entered into a manufacturer's representation agreement with Gagnier Fiber Products while he was still employed at Ford in an effort to have an established client base in the event that he lost his job at Ford. In rebuttal the government called the owner of Gagnier who testified that he paid Horton a commission not because he needed a manufacturer's representative, but because he would not get any business from Ford if he refused to pay the kickback. In response to the defendant's claim that the admission of this evidence violated Rule 608(b)'s ban on the admission of extrinsic evidence of specific acts in order to attack credibility, the Court of Appeals held that the evidence was properly admitted under Rule 404(b) to establish the defendant's intent to defraud. *See also United States v. Smith*

---

[306] *See* United States v. Callaway, 938 F.2d 907, 911-12 (8th Cir. 1991).

[307] PAUL R. RICE & ROY A. KATRIEL, EVIDENCE: COMMON LAW AND FEDERAL RULES OF EVIDENCE § 6.03 [C] (LEXIS 5th ed. 2005).

Grading and Paving Inc., 760 F.2d 527 (4th Cir.), *cert. denied*, 474 U.S. 1005 (1985).

If the evidence is only inquired about on cross-examination as a reflection on the witness' credibility, the pretrial notice requirement of Rule 404(b) is inapplicable. This is illustrated in *United States v. Tomblin*, 46 F.3d 1369 (5th Cir. 1995), where the defendant was charged with bribery, extortion and related offenses. When Tomblin took the witness stand, the government, during its cross-examination of him, inquired about an alleged bribery of a foreign government official and bankruptcy fraud that allegedly occurred when the witness skimmed money from his bankrupt business and fled to another state. Addressing the defendant's contention that the government violated Rule 404(b) by failing to provide advance notice of its intention to inquire about these matters, the court stated that because the questioning was proper under Rule 608 "the provision of Rule 404(b) that requires the prosecutor to give notice of his intention to use other-acts evidence does not apply here."

Rule 611(b). Scope of Cross-Examination. Under Rule 611(b), courts generally limit the scope of cross-examination to the scope of direct. Only subjects that a proponent raises explicitly or by implication on direct can be explored on cross. This rule does not apply to the issue of a witness' credibility. Consistent with the common law, Rule 611(b) provides: "Cross-examination should be limited to the subject matter of the direct examination and matters affecting credibility of the witness."

Rule 701. Opinion Testimony by Lay Witnesses. Rule 608(a) allows a witness to give an opinion about the credibility of another witness (stating whether she would believe the other witness under oath), and imposes no prerequisite that the witnesses be long acquainted or that the testifying witness be aware of any recent information on the other witness. Rule 608(a), however, must be read in conjunction with Rule 701, the lay witness opinion rule. For lay opinions to be admissible under Rule 701, the opinion must rationally be based on the perception of the witness and helpful to a clear understanding of the evidence and the determination of a fact in issue. In *United States v. Dotson*, 799 F.2d 189, 193 (5th Cir. 1986), the testimony of eight police officers that in their opinion the defendant and his witnesses were not truthful was held to be inadmissible because the only basis shown for their opinions was the fact that the officers had taken part in an investigation of the defendant.

Reputation testimony is the reputation witness' personal opinion of what others in the community believe about a particular individual. Courts require this reputation evidence to be based on interactions with people in the community. The basis of reputation evidence under Rule 405 is usually personal acquaintance with those who know the individual whose character is being proven. It is unnecessary that such knowledge be acquired informally and fortuitously. It has been held that knowledge of what others believe can be admissible if it was acquired from surveys conducted for the purpose of the litigation where the testimony is offered. *See United States v. Pacione*, 950 F.2d 1348

(7th Cir. 1991) (holding that reputation witness who spoke with approximately 400 of defendant's former customers had an adequate foundation to present reputation testimony). Knowledge of an individual acquired in this manner is not an adequate basis for the witness to give her personal opinion of the individual's character. It would be inadequate because the witness has no personal knowledge of the individual.

C. Applications — Witness' Character

ONE

In his trial for murder-for-hire the defendant's defense was that he believed that his conversations with the agent he allegedly hired to kill his wife were part of a role-playing exercise. He claimed that he was not planning to divorce his wife and that he had lied about his wife's failure to sign the divorce papers as a "trigger" for going ahead with the plan. During cross-examination of the defendant the government pointed out inconsistencies in the testimony and argued that the defendant's story was not credible. To give weight to his defense, the defendant responded with testimony about his good character for truthfulness under Rule 608(a). The court held that the reinforcing testimony was inadmissible.

Reinforcing character evidence for a witness is only admissible after the character trait for truthfulness has been attacked. Pointing out inconsistencies and arguing lack of credibility is not an attack on the accused's character trait for truthfulness. *United States v. Drury*, 2003 WL 22038921 (11th Cir. 2003).

TWO

A civil action was filed against police officers for false arrest and malicious prosecution. During her opening statement at trial the plaintiff argued that the jury should not believe the testimony of Trooper King when he claimed that the plaintiff, Renda, told him that she had lied. She claimed that the evidence would show that King was a corrupt police officer. When King tried to offer evidence of his good character for truthfulness in his case in defense the trial judge excluded it. On appeal, that decision was reversed.

The evidence should be admitted because the nature of the plaintiff's challenge to the defendant's credibility goes beyond a direct attack on the witness' veracity in the particular case and rose to the level of general corruption, opening the door for good character evidence. The court distinguished this evidence from bias that relates to a motive to lie in the particular case and not a general predisposition to lie. Consequently, it generally does not give rise to the right to present responsive character evidence. Similarly, inconsistent statements do not open the door to good character evidence because there can be a number of reasons for the error and a general character trait for untruthfulness is only one. *Renda v. King*, 347 F.3d 550 (3d Cir. 2003).

THREE

The defendant was charged with various offenses relating to a conspiracy to help foreign citizens to gain illegal admission into the United States. During the cross-examination of the defendant the government began asking her about signing a legal document attesting to the genuineness of a sham marriage which she knew the parties were going through solely to get around U.S. immigration laws. The court held this line of questioning appropriate under Rule 608(b).

The fact that the defendant was willing to help others evade the law plainly bore on her truthfulness. "Her willingness to engage in these acts shows Defendant was willing to engage in deceptive practices to avoid immigration laws. The evidence was especially relevant as it bore significant similarities to the conduct at issue in the trial." *United States v. Thiongo*, 2003 WL 22119712 (1st Cir. 2003).

FOUR

Defendant was charged with filing false tax returns. During the cross-examination of him the government asked: "Isn't it a fact that your contact with Pratt & Whitney was canceled because Pratt & Whitney determined that you had violated their gratuity policy by giving gifts to one of its employees?" The defendant admitted the act, but explained that it was a wedding gift and it was made to an employee who was not involved in choosing customers. After his conviction, the appellate court found that this line of questioning was inappropriate under 608(b) because the conduct inquired about did not involve untruthfulness. *United States v. Simonetti*, 237 F.3d 19 (1st Cir. 2001).

III. IMPEACHMENT — PRIOR CONVICTIONS

A. PRINCIPLES

Under the early common law, witnesses who had been convicted of certain types of crimes were disqualified from testifying. Over the centuries, the standards of disqualification were converted to standards for impeachment. People convicted of criminal offenses were permitted to testify, but could be impeached by the introduction of evidence of their felony convictions and of their misdemeanor convictions involving moral turpitude.

Because the standard of "moral turpitude" was so ambiguous, and therefore unpredictable, Rule 609 rejected the standard. Though perpetuating the felony/misdemeanor distinction for impeachment purposes (subject to different balancing tests for criminal defendants and all other witnesses), misdemeanors are admissible only when the crimes involved "dishonesty or false statement." Evidence of the witness' convictions for crimes of dishonest or false statement, regardless of whether a felony or misdemeanor, is *automatically admissible*.

RULE 609 FRE
Impeachment by Evidence of Conviction of Crime

(a) General rule. For the purpose of attacking the credibility of a witness,

(1) evidence that a witness other than an accused has been convicted of a crime shall be admitted, subject to Rule 403, if the crime was punishable by death or imprisonment in excess of one year under the law under which the witness was convicted, and evidence that an accused has been convicted of such a crime shall be admitted if the court determines that the probative value of admitting this evidence outweighs its prejudicial effect to the accused; and

(2) evidence that any witness has been convicted of a crime shall be admitted if it involved dishonesty or false statement, regardless of the punishment.

This rule creates a different standard for the admission of prior convictions against government witnesses than it does prior convictions of the criminal defendant. Against government witnesses, felony convictions are admissible unless the potential unfair prejudice substantially outweighs probative value. Against the criminal defendant, the felony conviction comes in only if the government demonstrates that the probative value outweighs the "prejudicial effect."[308] Presumably this mean *unfair* prejudicial effect to the defendant since the purpose of presenting any evidence against the defendant is to prejudice the him and his case.

116 PRACTICES

Dishonesty or false statement—a factual standard. The category of crimes that involve dishonesty or false statement is determined on a factual, rather than a legal, basis. The crime need not require an element of dishonesty or false statement — instead, the factual circumstances of the crime are controlling. Consequently, there have been different rulings on the admissibility of the same types of offenses, like narcotics.[309]

Of course, when the circumstances of prior convictions are not available, the elements of the crime must be relied upon by default. Perjury, embezzlement, and obtaining property by false pretenses are obvious examples of crimes that involve dishonesty or false statement.

---

[308] *See* United States v. Tse, 2004 WL 1622053 (1st Cir. 2004).

[309] *Compare* United States v. Hayes, 553 F.2d 824, 827-28 (2d Cir. 1977) *with* United States v. Lewis, 626 F.2d 940, 946 (D.C. Cir. 1980).

117 PRACTICES

Subject of conviction does not have to relate to credibility to be admissible. In contrast to Rule 608, which permits a witness to be asked about his own prior conduct that reflects on his credibility, if a witness' prior conduct resulted in a conviction, Rule 609 does *not require* the substance of the witness' conviction to relate to credibility in any way! Whether convicted of perjury, assault and battery or possessing marijuana, if the conduct giving rise to the conviction is subject to a potential penalty of imprisonment in excess of one year, it constitutes a felony and is admissible. The penalty need not have been imposed as a sentence.

Initially, the question of admissibility under Rule 609 is based solely on whether the crime is a felony. If the *witness is not a criminal defendant*, the felony conviction is admissible, unless the *opposing party can demonstrate* that the potential prejudice substantially outweighs its probative value, a Rule 403 type balance. If the *witness is the criminal defendant*, the equation changes. The felony conviction is admissible only if the *government can demonstrate* that the probative value of the evidence outweighs the potential for unfair prejudice. Through this balance, the nature of the act gets factored into the admissibility question.

If the substance of the crime for which any witness was convicted does involved conduct reflecting on credibility — defined in the rule as involving "dishonesty or false statement" — the conviction becomes *automatically admissible* in all civil and criminal proceedings. No discretion is given to the judge to exclude such convictions under Rule 403 because the specific balance incorporated into the rule supersedes the general balance codified in that rule.[310]

118 PRACTICES

Other uses of felony convictions. Specific instances of conduct are admissible under Rule 404 if they are relevant to the defendant's mind-set at the time of the commission of an act and, therefore, probative beyond general predisposition. Rule 404(b) makes such evidence admissible to establish such things as the defendant's motive, intent, knowledge, common scheme, and design. Therefore, regardless of whether a prior felony conviction is admissible for impeachment purposes under Rule 609, it may be admissible as evidence of the prior conduct that gave rise to the convictions through which something like intent or knowledge could be inferred. For example, if a defendant were charged with the possession of stolen goods, and raised as a defense his lack

---

[310] For an excellent discussion of both the impact of the rule and its legislative history, *see* United States v. Smith, 551 F.2d 348, 356-64 (1976).

of knowledge that the goods were stolen, the government could present evidence of his prior convictions for possession of stolen goods for the purpose of proving he had knowledge of the nature of the goods that he was most recently found to have possessed.[311]

The use of prior convictions for the purpose of proving the conduct giving rise to them creates a hearsay problem. The government would be offering them to prove the truth of the matter asserted through them. The hearsay exception in Rule 803(22) for judgments of previous convictions resolves this problem, but only if the prior convictions were for a felony grade offense.

RULE 404(b) FRE
Character Evidence Not Admissible to Prove Conduct; Exceptions; Other Crimes

(b) **Other crimes, wrongs, or acts.** Evidence of other crimes, wrongs, or acts is not admissible to prove the character of a person in order to show action in conformity therewith. It may, however, be admissible for other purposes, such as proof of motive, opportunity, intent, preparation, plan, knowledge, identity, or absence of mistake or accident, provided that upon request by the accused, the prosecution in a criminal case shall provide reasonable notice in advance of trial, or during trial if the court excuses pretrial notice on good cause shown, of the general nature of any such evidence it intends to introduce.

119 PRACTICES

You have to testify to create a ground of error — an offer of proof is not sufficient. Rule 103(a)(2) provides that if a court erroneously excludes evidence and this exclusion affects a substantial right of the objecting party, the exclusion will constitute reversible error only if the substance of the excluded evidence was made known to the court by an offer of proof or was apparent from the context within which the excluded question was asked. If the defendant, through a motion *in limine* prior to testifying, objects to the introduction of his prior conviction for impeachment purposes, and the court overrules this objection and admits the conviction, the defendant must place his testimony on the record. This will allow both the trial and appellate courts to meaningfully balance the challenged conviction's probative value against the potential prejudice its use will create for the defendant. Would an offer of proof through either a proffer by defense counsel or through the defendant's actual examination outside the presence of the jury adequately make this showing if a court required the defendant to make it?

---

[311] *See* Huddleston v. United States, 485 U.S. 681, 685 (1988).

Initially the circuits were split over whether an offer of proof was even required to establish a basis for the prejudice/probative balance. Needless to say, courts did not envision that such an offer, if made, would be inadequate to preserve the defendant's objection to the introduction of the prior conviction. In *Luce v. United States*,[312] however, the Supreme Court held that a defendant who did not testify at trial because the trial court had determined the defendant's prior convictions were admissible for impeachment purposes was not entitled to appellate review of the trial court's determination admitting the conviction even if the defense made an offer of proof concerning the defendant's testimony.

Though widely criticized in the criminal defense bar, the decision was essential. Without the criminal defendant's actually taking the witness stand, there is no assurance that the defendant ever planned to take the witness stand in his own defense. Consequently, the motion to suppress and offer of proof permitted the defendant to set up a straw man for the purpose of making error for appellate review purposes in case he was convicted. Equally important, the mere fact the prosecution was given permission to use the prior convictions for impeachment purposes does not mean that evidence of the convictions actually would have been used. Prosecutors often abandon evidence when it is not needed, particularly when use of it will only create potential grounds of error for appeal.

B. Relationship of Prior Conviction Rule to Other Rules[313]

Rule 104. Preliminary Questions. The determination of the nature of prior offenses (whether the crimes in question involved dishonesty or false statement) and the balancing of probative value against prejudicial effect are preliminary questions that the presiding judge will decide by a preponderance of the evidence standard under Rule 104(a).

Rule 105. Limited Admissibility. Pursuant to Rule 105, if evidence is admissible for one purpose and inadmissible for another, the court, if a party requests it, must instruct the jury on the evidence's proper use. If a criminal defendant testifies and the prosecution offers evidence of his prior convictions for impeachment purposes, the court, either upon request or *sua sponte*, may instruct the jury that it cannot use the convictions as substantive evidence of the defendant's guilt in the present proceeding.[314] This instruction is particularly necessary if the defendant's prior crimes are similar to the one for which he is currently being tried. It is assumed that jurors are capable and willing to do this.

---

[312] 469 U.S. 38, 422-43 (1984).

[313] PAUL R. RICE & ROY A. KATRIEL, EVIDENCE: COMMON LAW AND FEDERAL RULES OF EVIDENCE § 6.04 [C] (LEXIS 5th ed. 2005)

[314] *See* United States v. Diaz, 585 F.2d 116, 118 (5th Cir. 1978).

Rule 404. Character Evidence Not Admissible To Prove Conduct;

Rule 405. Methods of Proving Character. Under Rule 404(a), evidence of a person's relevant character trait is admissible to prove that he acted in the past in conformity with that character trait only in criminal cases, and then only if the defendant opens the issue by presenting such evidence. If the defendant offers such character evidence and the government responds in kind, Rule 405(a) limits the kind of proof that either party may present to opinion or reputation testimony. Rule 405(b) specifically precludes character from being proven by specific instances of conduct unless it constitutes an essential element of the charge, claim, or defense.

Rule 609(a) is an exception to both of these rules. Courts consider prior convictions to be relevant to a witness' credibility because the convictions reflect a predisposition on his part to be dishonest or to disregard the truth (crimes involving dishonesty or false statement, Rule 609(a)(2)) or to generally disregard his legal, moral, or ethical obligations to society (all other felony convictions, Rule 609(a)(1)). These convictions, however, constitute nothing more than character evidence. They are distinguishable from character evidence offered under Rule 404(a) only in that parties offer prior convictions to prove present conduct (fabricating testimony) rather than past conduct. Rule 609 is an exception to Rule 404(a)'s prohibition on the use of character evidence to prove propensity because prior conviction evidence is admissible to impeach all witnesses in all kinds of litigation — civil as well as criminal. Rule 609 is an exception to Rule 405 because it constitutes evidence of prior specific conduct.

Rule 410. Inadmissibility of Pleas. Rule 410 precludes the use of a plea of nolo contendere against the defendant who entered it. This preclusion does not prevent the use of convictions entered on the plea if offered for impeachment purposes pursuant to Rule 609. As Judge Joiner explained in *United States v. Dennis*[315] Rule 410 has no effect on the use of the conviction in this instance.

Rule 607. Who May Impeach. The government, like all other parties in litigation, may impeach its own witnesses. This possibility, however, can give rise to a special problem when the witness is a codefendant who previously was convicted of the offense for which the defendant is being tried. Although this most recent conviction may be admissible under Rule 609 for impeachment purposes, the possibility exists that when used for that limited purpose the jury will inappropriately give it a broader use, construing it as evidence of the defendant's guilt. Accordingly, every circuit has adopted the rule that evidence that is inadmissible for substantive purposes may not be purposely introduced under the pretense of impeachment.[316] As one court has observed:

> [I]t would be an abuse of [Rule 607], in a criminal case, for the prosecution to call a witness that it knew would not give it useful evidence,

---

[315] 532 F. Supp. 625, 627 (E.D. Mich. 1982).

[316] *See* United States v. Peterman, 841 F.2d 1474, 1479 n.3 (10th Cir. 1988).

just so it could introduce hearsay evidence against the defendant in the hope that the jury would miss the subtle distinction between impeachment and substantive evidence — or, if it didn't miss it, would ignore it.[317]

The rule adopted by the *Peterman* court was that the prosecution "may not introduce evidence 'under the guise of impeachment for the *primary* purpose of placing before the jury substantive evidence which is not otherwise admissible.'"[318] *See* **PRACTICES NO. 38,** *supra.*

C. Applications — Prior Convictions

ONE

The defendant was charged with attempting to enter the United States illegally. At his trial his defense was that he was on drugs and didn't realize what he was doing. When cross-examined by the government he objected to attempts to impeach him with testimony about a six year old conviction for possessing marijuana for sale. The court found the evidence admissible because the conviction was recent and credibility was a central issue in the case. To accommodate the defendant's concerns about unfair prejudice the court sanitized the conviction by allowing the government to refer to it only as "a felony conviction." *United States v. Martinez-Martinez*, 369 F.3d 1076 (9th Cir. 2004).

TWO

In Joe Walker's trial for possession of heroin with the intent to distribute, the Government called Lynn Trout, Walker's roommate, as its principal witness in its case-in-chief. To impeach Trout's credibility, Walker sought to cross-examine Trout as to her two convictions for prostitution in Louisiana. The first conviction was in 1978, and the second was in 1983. In Louisiana, the first conviction for prostitution is a misdemeanor. The second conviction for prostitution, however, is considered a felony punishable by imprisonment for up to five years. Trout was given a suspended sentence with regard to both convictions. Upon Walker's proffer of the two prostitution convictions, the Government objected. The court did not permit cross-examination as to the first conviction because it was neither a felony nor a crime involving dishonesty of false statement. Courts uniformly have held that prostitution does not involve dishonesty or deceit. *United States v. Walker*, 613 F.2d 1349, 1352 (5th Cir.), *cert. denied*, 446 U.S. 944 (1980).

The second conviction was more problematic. Under the common law it would be admissible simply because it was a felony grade offense (despite the fact that it was for the same conduct that gave rise to the first inadmissible misde-

---

[317] United States v. Webster, 734 F.2d 1191, 1192 (7th Cir. 1984).

[318] 841 F.2d at 1479.

meanor grade offense). It would be excluded only if the opponent could convince the court that its prejudicial effect substantially outweighed its probative value under the balancing test discussed in such cases as *Luck v. United States*, 348 F.2d 763 (D.C. Cir. 1965), and *Gordon v. United States*, 383 F.2d 936 (D.C. Cir. l967). This is a difficult, if not impossible burden to satisfy when the criminal defendant is offering the impeaching evidence, even though the probative value of the conviction is insignificant. For an acknowledged prostitute, the unfairness is either insignificant or nonexistent.

IV. IMPEACHMENT —— WRITINGS USED TO REFRESH RECOLLECTION

A. PRINCIPLE

When a writing is used to refresh a witness' recollection *while testifying*, the opposing party must be given an opportunity to review the writing and to cross-examine the witness with it. The same is true of writings used to refresh witnesses' recollection *before* testifying; however, in that situation, production is only required if the court finds it is "necessary in the interests of justice."

RULE 612 FRE
Writings Used to Refresh Memory

Except as otherwise provided in criminal proceedings by section 3500 of title 18, United States Code, if a witness uses a writing to refresh memory for the purpose of testifying, either —

(1) while testifying, or

(2) before testifying, if the court in its discretion determines it is necessary in the interests of justice, an adverse party is entitled to have the writing produced at the hearing, to inspect it, to cross-examine the witness thereon, and to introduce in evidence those portions which relate to the testimony of the witness. If it is claimed that the writing contains matters not related to the subject matter of the testimony, the court shall examine the writing *in camera*, excise any portions not so related, and order delivery of the remainder to the party entitled thereto. Any portion withheld over objections shall be preserved and made available to the appellate court in the event of an appeal. If a writing is not produced or delivered pursuant to order under this rule, the court shall make any order justice requires, except that in criminal cases when the prosecution elects not to comply, the order shall be one striking the testimony or, if the court in its discretion determines that the interest of justice so require, declaring a mistrial.

120 PRACTICES

Production of documents used to refresh. If a lawyer refreshes a witness' recollection while the witness testifies, opposing counsel is entitled to review the writing. Because the potential impact of that writing on the witness' testimony is so great, this obligation to produce is only fair. A difficult problem arises, however, when documents are used to refresh recollection *before* testifying. Witnesses commonly review all of their correspondence on a particular subject matter before appearing as a witness at either a deposition or trial.

The "necessary in the interests of justice" standard governs the obligation to give these documents to opposing counsel. The meaning of this standard, however, will vary with each judge. In making this determination, the court will consider the sensitive nature of the document (*i.e.*, business communications, proprietary information about such things as trade secrets, customer lists and sales data, or communications protected by the attorney-client privilege) but such properties will not be dispositive. The most influential factor will be the importance of the communication to the testimony already rendered. This is a very difficult determination for the presiding judge to make because an informed witness will seldom, if ever, acknowledge that he could not have testified without the assistance he obtained from the documents that he reviewed.

Courts have attempted to promulgate rules for determining when reliance is sufficient to justify production, but all of them are flawed. Some courts require a particularized showing of necessity that is hard to satisfy.[319] These restrictive standards may be appropriate because disclosure of documents reviewed in preparation for testifying gives an unfair advantage to companies that constantly churn communications and keep their employees' memories fresh about past events.

Of all the standards devised, the assessment of whether the witness' testimony "discloses a significant portion of the substance of that material" is the most curious. By that test, if a witness had nearly perfect recollection before reviewing the writing, he will always reveal significant portions of the documents examined, regardless of how they influenced his testimony. The better his recollection, the greater the probability he will disclose the content of documents describing the same thing, regardless of whether he examined them.

---

[319] *See* Sporck v. Peil, 759 F.2d 312, 317-18 (3d Cir. 1985) (requiring disclosure only if the proponent demonstrates that the witness "relied upon" the document, in that the document "influenced" his testimony); Baker v. CNA Ins. Co., 123 F.R.D. 322, 327 (D. Mont. 1988) (mandating disclosure only where the witness, after refreshing his recollection, "discloses a significant portion of the substance of [the reviewed] material."). *See also* Prucha v. M & N Modern Hyradulic Press Co., 76 F.R.D. 207 (W.D. Wis. 1977); Joseph Schlitz Brewing Co. v. Muller & Phipps (Hawaii), Ltd., 85 F.R.D. 118 (W.D. Mo. 1980).

121 PRACTICES

Privileges can be waived by pretrial review. Under the common law, privileges like the attorney-client privilege were not waived by examining confidential communications in preparation for giving testimony. Waiver only occurred when memory was refreshed *while testifying*. Rule 612 has changed that practice. Presiding judges are now given discretion to order the production of the documents reviewed prior to testifying if, in the judge's discretion, she determines it to be necessary in the interests of justice.[320] Interestingly, the courts that have found waiver have failed to mention that the House Committee on the Judiciary explicitly noted with regard to Rule 612 and the privilege issue that "The Committee intends that nothing in the rule be construed as barring the assertion of a privilege with respect to writings used by a witness to refresh his memory."[321] This expressed intent appears to have been ignored because legislative intent is not controlling over the explicit language of the rule, and no protective language was incorporated into the rule.

Why is it so important for the opposing side to see these documents? What unfairness would result if the protection were not waived for documents reviewed prior to testifying and the documents were not available for inspection? The cases state that an opponent's examination of these documents allows it to gauge the quality of the witness' recollection by comparing the writing and the direct testimony. But how will making this comparison reflect the quality of the recollection? If there were discrepancies between the writing and the testimony, would this cast doubt on the witness' credibility or the accuracy of the testimony? Clearly not, because a proponent can use anything to refresh a witness' recollection; it need not be accurate or even related to the testimony given. That the detection of discrepancies between the writing and the testimony says nothing about the quality of the witness' recollection is particularly evident in the situation where the writing was prepared by someone other than the witness. The existence of discrepancies between the writing and the testimony, therefore, could establish nothing regarding the reliability of the testimony unless the writing were accepted for the truth of its content, a hearsay use that Rule 612 does not sanction merely because the document has been used to refresh recollection. The only time discrepancies between a document used to refresh a witness' recollection and the testimony that the witness actually gave would seem to have any probative value relative to testing the accuracy of the witness' professed recollection is if the

---

[320] *See* Sporck v. Peil, 759 F.2d 312 (3d Cir. 1985); Wheeling-Pittsburgh Steel Corp. v. Underwriters Labs., Inc., 81 F.R.D. 8 (N.D. Ill. 1978); Berkey Photo, Inc. v. Eastman Kodak Co., 74 F.R.D. 613 (S.D.N.Y. 1977).

[321] House Comm. On Judiciary, Fed. Rules of Evidence, H.R. Rep. No. 650, 93d Cong., 1st Sess., p. 13 (1973).

witness were responsible for the writing. In this instance, if the writing varied from the testimony, the variance itself would reflect on the witness' credibility independent of the truth of its content.

Would the document impeach the testimony if its content were identical to the testimony? It may, but only if the proponent used the document to refresh the witness' recollection at trial, not if the proponent used it prior to the witness' testimony. If the witness, while testifying, had indicated he suffered a memory loss, and then, after examining the document, gave testimony that was identical to it, one might reasonably conclude he was simply repeating what he had read. If, however, the witness had examined the document prior to trial and there was no indication the witness had a loss of memory before that examination, the fact that the two accounts are identical may indicate little more than consistency and accuracy, depending on the length and complexity of the witness' testimony. This would be particularly true if the witness had authored the document.

122 PRACTICES

Admitting the document produced. If the adverse party is given the right to examine the communication, Rule 612 explicitly gives the examining party the right to "cross-examine the witness thereon," and to "introduce in evidence those portions which relate to the testimony of the witness." The rule, however, does not specify or limit the *purpose* for which it may be offered.

This absence is particularly troublesome because anything can be used to refresh recollection — it doesn't have to be authenticated, doesn't have to be true, doesn't even have to have been created by the witness whose memory is being refreshed.

If the document is neither authenticated nor established as reflecting the truth, it makes no sense for the court to permit the writing to be offered for its truth. This fact, coupled with the context of the right's creation — within Rule 612 — requires that the use of the writing on cross-examination be *restricted to impeaching the witness.* Even this use, however, is somewhat problematic. Its value for impeachment is necessarily limited to writings the witness has created. If that witness is not responsible for the writing's creation, inconsistencies between the writing and the testimony do not impeach unless the fact-finder believes the writing's content — a hearsay use that should be forbidden due to a lack of reliability.

B. Applications — Refreshing Recollection

ONE

The defendant was charged with embezzlement. To rebut evidence of her sudden financial improvement after the bank theft, the defendant proffered a document purporting to list the appraised value of items she claims to have sold to raise the money. After excluding it as inadmissible hearsay, defense counsel tried to refresh the defendant's recollection with the document so she could testify to its contents. The government again objected and the objection was sustained. On appeal of her conviction, the decision to prohibit the defendant from refreshing her recollection with the document was upheld. First, the defendant was able to testify at length about the property she had owned without consulting the appraisal. Second, having previously ruled that the appraisal was inadmissible hearsay, it was not unreasonable for the trial judge to avoid the potential for improper testimony based on the witness' reading of the document. *United States v. Weller*, 2001 WL 10318 (10th Cir. 2001).

TWO

Officer Bolton was testifying at the murder trial of the defendant. While being cross-examined about a confrontation involving the victim and the defendant after the shooting in which the victim said the defendant was not one of the men who attacked and robbed him, the Office claimed not to remember precisely what happened. To refresh his recollection, the defense tried to show the forgetful Officer the report of the confrontation prepared by Office Hucke. The prosecution objected to this use of the report because it had not been prepared by the officer being cross-examined. The objection was sustained. This was error. The court was confusing past recollection recorded and present recollection revived. The appellate court said this was confusing evidence and non-evidence. The former is offered in lieu of the officer's testimony. The latter is used only to refresh and the evidence is being offered through the officer's refreshed testimony. "When the writing in question is to be utilized simply 'to awaken a slumbering recollection of an event' in the mind of the witness, the writing may be a memorandum made by the witness himself — 1) even if it was not made immediately after the event, 2) even if it was not made of firsthand knowledge, and 3) even if the witness cannot now vouch for the fact that it was accurate when made. It may be a memorandum made by one other than the witness, even if never before read by the witness or vouched for by him. It may be an Associated Press account. It may be a highly selective version of the incident at the hands of a Hemingway or an Eliot. All that is required is that it ignite the flash of accurate recall— that it accomplish the revival which is sought." *Baker v. State*, 35 Md. App. 593, 371 A.2d 699 (1977).

V. IMPEACHMENT — ATTACKING AND SUPPORTING CREDIBILITY OF DECLARANT

A. PRINCIPLE

A declarant refers to a person who makes an out-of-court statement that is being repeated in court by someone who heard it, for the truth of what previously was stated. The declarant is no less a witness than the individual who appears in court to repeat what he said, taking an oath, and being examined by the participating lawyers about what he claims to know. The credibility of the declarant is no less a concern, and the declarant is subject to the same methods of impeachment as the in-court witnesses — for example, prior inconsistent statements, psychiatric disorders, biases and prior convictions. For impeachment purposes, the only difference between in-court witnesses and out-of-court declarants is their availability for examination. If the out-of-court declarant is not called as an in-court witness by the proponent of his statement, none of the foundation requirements or obligations to confront the witness with his prior statements, *see* Rule 613, or the evidence of his bias is applicable.

RULE 806 FRE
Attacking and Supporting Credibility of Declarant

When a hearsay statement, or a statement defined in Rule 801(d)(2), (C), (D), or (E), has been admitted in evidence, the credibility of the declarant may be attacked, and if attacked may be supported, by any evidence which would be admissible for those purposes if declarant had testified as a witness. Evidence of a statement or conduct by the declarant at any time, inconsistent with the declarant's hearsay statement, is not subject to any requirement that the declarant may have been afforded an opportunity to deny or explain. If the party against whom a hearsay statement has been admitted calls the declarant as a witness, the party is entitled to examine the declarant on the statement as if under cross-examination.

123 PRACTICES

Testifying without taking the witness stand — hearsay declarants can be impeached too. Criminal defense attorneys often use the ploy of having their clients speak to a psychiatrist to whom the clients reveal information to which they would have testified if they had chosen to take the witness stand at their trials. The psychiatrists, in turn, testify at trial about their opinions on conditions and disorders possessed by the defendants that could have affected their mental state at the time of the criminal offenses. In giving the reasons for their diagnoses, these psychiatrists reveal much of what the defendants told them, and that they, in turn, credited. In substance, therefore, the psychiatrists serve as conduits for the defendants' testimony. This practice permits criminal defendants to have their cake and eat it, too — testifying without being tested.

This result is only partially true. While defense counsels' clients cannot be cross-examined about the substance of their testimony, defense counsel often forget that all means of impeachment — bias, inconsistent statements, prior convictions, etc. — remain available through the testimony of third parties.

B. Applications — Attacking and Supporting Credibility of Declarant

The defendant, Carroll, was charged with the illegal possession of a firearm by a felon. At his trial, Annie McMullen testified that from inside her apartment she saw the defendant outside holding a gun and speaking with her son, Darren. McMullen explained that she dialed 911 twice to report the incident, and during one of the calls informed the 911 operator that her son had told her that Carroll previously pulled a gun on him because they were fighting about a woman. Defense counsel attempted to cross-examine Annie McMullen about her son's drug use, but was prohibited by the trial court because the judge concluded that McMullen's testimony was not hearsay. The trial judge commented, "She's just hearing something."

On appeal, the defendant contended that Rule 806 permitted him to question McMullen about her son's drug use, drug dealing and gang membership because her testimony placed her son's credibility in issue. The appellate court agreed. "It is unclear whether this testimony was offered for any reason other than its truth, but because no other reasons were offered and it was admitted without any limiting instruction, we assume that it was offered for its truth. . . . Darren's statement was therefore hearsay and the jury may have considered it as substantive evidence for establishing the essential issue at trial — whether Carroll possessed a firearm. Thus, under Rule 806, Carroll should have been allowed to attack Darren's credibility as if Darren had testified at trial. *United States v. Carroll*, 53 Fed. Appx. 785, 786-87 (7th Cir. 2002) (unpublished order).

Chapter 8
ATTORNEY-CLIENT PRIVILEGE

I. GENERAL PRINCIPLES

In its most basic application, the attorney-client privilege protects confidential communications from a client to an attorney for the purpose of obtaining legal advice or assistance. There are five elements to the privilege: (1) a client (2) making a confidential (3) communication (4) to an attorney (5) for the purpose of obtaining legal assistance.[322]

RULE 501 FRE
General Rule

Except as otherwise required by the Constitution of the United States or provided by Act of Congress or in rules prescribed by the Supreme Court pursuant to statutory authority, the privilege of a witness, person, government, State, or political subdivision thereof shall be governed by the principles of the common law as they may be interpreted by the courts of the United States in the light of reason and experience. However, in civil actions and proceedings, with respect to an element of a claim or defense as to which State law supplies the rule of decision, the privilege of a witness, person, government, State, or political subdivision thereof shall be determined in accordance with State law.

124 PRACTICES

Still under the common law. Privilege is the only area within the evidence code that explicitly was left to development under common law principles.[323] Therefore, all of the case law within the federal system is as relevant today as it was when the decisions were rendered. Since all states either follow the common law or have codified the common law principles as delineated in

---

[322] *See* United States v. United Shoe Machinery Corp., 89 F. Supp. 357, 358-59 (D. Mass. 1950). *See generally*, PAUL R. RICE, ATTORNEY-CLIENT PRIVILEGE IN THE UNITED STATES, § 2:1 (Thomson West 2d ed. 1999), acprivilege.com.

[323] Because the subject of bias was not addressed in the Rules, it also has been left to common law principles, but this result from omission rather than an explicit relegation. *See* **PRACTICES NO. 114**, *supra*.

these proposed federal rules that were not enacted by Congress, state decisions can also provide persuasive authority.[324]

125 PRACTICES

No presumptions about the privilege. When outside counsel (as opposed to in-house counsel) is consulted, some courts have used the term "presumption" relative to the elements of "confidentiality" and the "purpose of obtaining legal advice or assistance." These courts probably do not mean to use the term presumption in the technical legal sense. *See* **PRACTICES NO. 148,** *infra.* From the contexts of their discussions, these courts appear to be merely identifying logical inference or assumptions that are permissible from the facts established. They are identifying facts that suggest that each element is present, thereby justifying the recognition of the privilege unless the opposing side comes forward with evidence to the contrary. The status of the lawyer as in-house, as opposed to outside, counsel is one of those factors.[325]

The cost of legal services is such that contacts with outside counsel generally will not occur unless legal assistance is being sought. Therefore, contacts with outside counsel are assumed to be for legal advice or assistance. Similarly, because lawyers are bound by the code of professional responsibility, it is assumed that outside counsel will maintain the confidentiality of the client's communications. In contrast, in-house counsel is often involved in many facets of the organization's endeavors. They assist in business strategy, negotiate contracts, participate in labor disputes, and are often responsible for entire divisions of the company (holding vice president titles to prove that). As a consequence, it cannot be assumed that contacts with in-house counsel are primarily for the purpose of obtaining legal assistance. Often, the purposes are, at best, mixed. As a consequence, the burden is on the corporation to prove that all elements of the privilege have been satisfied without the assistance of assumptions otherwise employed. Contrary to the protestations of the corporate world, this is not discriminating against in-house counsel. It is simply reacting to the realities of the circumstances of in-house counsel's employment.

While it generally could be assumed that in-house counsel would maintain confidences to the same extent as outside counsel, the problem of confidentiality is complicated by the nonlegal roles in which the lawyer also serves. Therefore, the client has to establish with competent evidence the facts that confidentiality was intended and appropriately maintained within the company.

---

[324] The law of attorney-client privilege in the 50 states and the District of Columbia is discussed in PAUL R. RICE, ATTORNEY-CLIENT PRIVILEGE: STATE LAW (Rice Publishing 2006) (CD rom only) (available on Westlaw at ACP-STATES).

[325] *See generally,* PAUL RICE, ATTORNEY-CLIENT PRIVILEGE IN THE UNITED STATES, § 6:31 (Thomson West 2d ed. 1999)

II. THE CORPORATE CLIENT

A. PRINCIPLES

The attorney-client privilege extends to the corporate entity. It provides protection for communications between all corporate employees and corporate legal counsel on matters within the scope of their corporate responsibilities. This "subject matter" test defines which individuals (and in which of their capacities) personify the corporate client.[326] A small number of states employ a "control group" test that limits the application of the corporate privilege to communications between corporate counsel and employees who have the power to take action based on the advice being sought by the corporation.[327]

126 PRACTICES

The corporate privilege — a strained application. A corporation has no physical existence except through the individuals who personify it, and it cannot act or communicate except through those individuals. When the attorney-client privilege was extended to the corporate entity, it could not serve the privilege's purpose of encouraging open and candid communications from the client to the attorney unless it encouraged those agents to speak. Unfortunately, it provides little encouragement because the corporate privilege has been construed as belonging to the corporate entity, the legal fiction that cannot speak, and not to the individuals who speak for it. Thus the privilege gives no *direct* personal protection to those upon whom the corporate entity is dependent for both action and communication.[328]

The corporate attorney-client privilege gives protection to corporate agents only if the corporation, through its officers and directors, asserts the privilege. Unfortunately, it often is in the corporate entity's best interest to sacrifice individual agents by waiving the privilege. Corporations frequently waive their privilege protection to gain government concessions and benefits. Therefore, even if corporate officers personally do not want to sacrifice those indi-

---

[326] Upjohn Co. v. United States, 449 U.S. 383 (1981).

[327] Illinois is the most prominent example. For a discussion of the law of Illinois and the other states employing the "control group" test, *see* PAUL R. RICE, ATTORNEY-CLIENT PRIVILEGE: STATE LAW, § 4:12 (Rice Publishing 2006) (CD rom only) (available on Westlaw at ACP-STATES).

[328] *See, e.g.,* United States v. Aramony, 88 F.3d 1369, 1388-92 (4th Cir. 1996) *cert. denied* 520 U.S. 1239 (1997) (president of a corporation was not the client of the corporation's attorney); In re Bevill, Bresler & Schulman Asset Management Corp., 805 F.2d 120, 123 (3d Cir. 1986) ("[A]ny privilege that exists as to a corporate officer's role and functions with a corporation belongs to the corporation, not the officer."); United States v. Piccini, 412 F.2d 591, 593 (2d Cir. 1969) ("The [communication] claimed to be privileged, however, was given by Piccini as an officer of the corporation, so that the privilege, if any, was that of the corporation, and may not be availed of by Piccini.").

vidual agents who may be their friends, because of the fiduciary duty those officers owe to corporate shareholders, they are compelled to make the sacrifice through a waiver of the protection to avoid personal liability for the negligent mismanagement of corporate assets.

Since a corporation has economic powers through which it can compel its employees to speak with its legal counsel — the "talk or walk" ultimatum — it is not clear that the recognition of the corporate attorney-client privilege is justified.[329] Similarly, since corporate executives can be liable to shareholders for negligent mismanagement of corporate assets if they do not seek legal advice and assistance when needed, corporations cannot reasonably claim that without the privilege, corporations would not seek legal guidance.

III. THE COMMUNICATION

A. PRINCIPLES

The attorney-client privilege is designed to encourage clients to communicate more candidly with their attorneys. Motivating the privilege is the notion that if clients are assured what they say to their attorneys cannot be used against them, they will be more willing to disclose facially damning details essential to sound advice or assistance for the attorney.[330] The privilege, therefore, extends a protection to a client's communications to an attorney or an attorney's agent if those communications are in confidence and for the purpose of obtaining legal advice or assistance.

3. BASIC PROTECTION

client   attorney

Because the responsive communications of the attorney often reveal the content of the prior communications of the client, the courts have extended the scope of the privilege protection. Courts afforded a *derivative protection* to the

---

[329] *See generally*, PAUL RICE, ATTORNEY-CLIENT PRIVILEGE IN THE UNITED STATES § 4:10 (Thomson West 2d ed. 1999); John E. Sexton, *A Post-Upjohn Consideration of the Corporate Attorney-Client Privilege*, 57 N.Y.U. L. REV. 443, 464-71 (1982).

[330] *See* Commodity Futures Trading Comm'n v. Weintraub, 471 U.S. 343, 348 (1985) ("Both for corporations and individuals, the attorney-client privilege serves the function of promoting full and frank communications between attorneys and their clients. It thereby encourages observance of the law and aids in the administration of justice.").

attorney's communications with the client — a protection applicable *only to the extent that the attorney's communication disclosed the content of a prior, confidential client communication.*[331] Therefore, to establish the privilege for the responsive communication of the attorney, the client must prove two privilege communications to obtain judicial recognition of one.

3a. DERIVATIVE PROTECTION

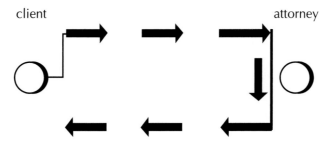

client   attorney

127 PRACTICES

Protecting "communications between" has led to misinterpretations and misapplications. On the belief that most attorney communications reveal client confidences, many courts have defined the attorney-client privilege loosely as protecting communications "between" the attorney and client.[332] This loose definition was spurred, in part, by the language in Proposed Federal Rule of Evidence 503 (not enacted), a proposal containing the same preposition.[333] This loose characterization of the privilege extends the priv-

---

[331] *See* Tax Analysts v. I.R.S., 117 F.3d 607, 611 (D.C. Cir. 1989) (holding that advice from the attorney was not protected because it did not reveal information that had been confidentially communicated by the client); Eugene Burger Management Corp. v. United States, 1999 U.S. Dist. LEXIS 22096, *23-24 (D.D.C. July 12, 1999) ("[A]ssuming the witness himself can claim the privilege, the attorney-client privilege has no application here because the communication from Narode, the lawyer, did not reveal what was told Narode in confidence by a client."); Midwest Univ. v. HBO & Co., 1999 WL 32928, *2 (N.D. Ill. 1999) ("When a lawyer gives legal advice to the client it does not automatically trigger the attorney-client privilege. Rather, statements which would reveal the substance of the confidential communication [of the client] are protected.").

[332] *See, e.g.*, Sprague v. Thorn Americas, Inc., 129 F.3d 1355, 1370 (10th Cir. 1997); In re Grand Jury Subpoena Bierman, 765 F.2d 1014, 1018 (11th Cir. 1985); United States v. Amerada Hess Corp., 619 F.2d 980, 986 (3d Cir. 1980); Softview Computer Products Corp. v. Haworth, Inc., 2000 U.S. Dist. LEXIS 9457, *5-6 (S.D.N.Y. July 10, 2000) ("[E]ven if the content of the letter [from the attorney] can be considered legal advice, it is not legal advice that reflects a client confidence, and, therefore, is not privileged.").

[333] Rule 503(b) of the Proposed Federal Rules of Evidence defined the attorney-client privilege:

A client has a privilege to refuse to disclose and to prevent any other person from disclosing confidential communications made for the purpose of facilitating the rendition of professional legal services to the client, (1) between himself or his representative and his lawyer or his lawyer's representative, or (2) between his lawyer and the lawyer's repre-

ilege's protection far beyond what is necessary to further the privilege's limited goal of encouraging candid client communications. Clients would not be less candid in communications with their attorneys if attorney communications revealing information from other sources were discoverable.

As illustrated below, the use of the preposition "between" obscures the scope of the protection. The scope of the protection could be limited to no more than its common law progenitor illustrated at 3.a. — communications to the attorney and responsive communications revealing the content of what the client originally said. On the other hand, the scope of the protection may include any other communication from the attorney, regardless of whether it reveals only the law that was communicated to the client (independent of its application to the client's circumstances), illustrated at 3.b., or facts acquired from third parties, illustrated at 3.c.

3b. "BETWEEN"

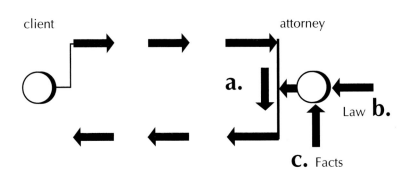

This recharacterization of the scope of the privilege protection resulted in a radical expansion of the protection. Without either acknowledging this expansion or appreciating its consequences, courts have widely adopted it. While many courts have intended the expansion to include only the responsive *advice* of the attorney, 3.b.,[334] most have given no indication of any limitation. A few courts have even gone so far as explicitly extending the

---

sentative, or (3) by him or his lawyer to a lawyer representing another in a matter of common interest, or (4) between representatives of the client or between the client and a representative of the client, or (5) between lawyers representing the client.

[334] *See, e.g.*, Upjohn v. United States, 449 U.S. 384, 389-90 (1981) ("[T]he privilege exists to protect not only the giving of professional advice to those who can act on it but also the giving of information to the lawyer to enable him to give sound and informed advice."); United States v. Defazio, 899 F.2d 626, 635 (7th Cir. 1990) ("Communications from attorney to client are privileged only if they constitute legal advice, or tend directly or indirectly to reveal the substance of a client confidence.").

privilege's coverage to *all communications* from the attorney, even those relaying only information from third parties, 3.c.[335]

This expansion of the privilege appeals to courts for two reasons. First, the expansion is roughly accurate. Most responsive communications will reveal, to some extent, the content of prior communications of the client. Second, and more importantly, the expansion simplifies the resolution process. The elimination of the derivative theory, removes the need to prove two valid claims in order successfully to assert one. All that the proponent must demonstrate under this expanded definition is that the lawyer communicated legal advice or assistance to the client in confidence.

The hidden dangers in this practice surfaced in the Ninth Circuit's decision in *United States v. Bauer*.[336] *Bauer* involved the prosecution of a bankruptcy petitioner for fraudulently failing to report all of his assets in his bankruptcy petition. In his defense, Bauer claimed he innocently withheld information about certain assets believing they did not have to be reported. Consequently, the principal focus of the trial revolved around Bauer's knowledge and intent. To establish a knowing misrepresentation, the government called the defendant's former bankruptcy attorney who, over the objections of Bauer, was required to testify that he had informed the defendant that as a bankruptcy petitioner, Bauer had a legal obligation to report all of his property in the petition, and that any false statement would constitute perjury. On the appeal of his conviction, Bauer claimed that the trial judge's order violated his attorney-client privilege. The Ninth Circuit agreed.[337]

The trial judge required the disclosure by the bankruptcy attorney on the belief that when an attorney advises the client about the rules of the court, he is not acting as an attorney, but as an officer of the court conveying public information.[338] This decision was influenced, in part, by a well-established body of law holding that when an attorney notifies a client of dates on which the client was ordered by the court to appear for sentencing, there can be no reasonable expectation on the part of the client that such communications are confidential. Consequently, when the client is later tried for

---

[335] *See, e.g.*, In re LTV Securities Litig., 89 F.R.D. 595, 602-03 (N.D. Tex. 1981) ("In theory, the client states facts and the attorney gives advice; and in theory, if the advice to the client does not reveal what the client told him it is not privileged. . . . Whatever the conceptual purity of this 'rule,' it fails to deal with the reality that lifting the cover from the advice will seldom leave covered the client's communication to his lawyer. Nor does it recognize the independent fact gathering role of the attorney. Finally, enforcement of the rule would be imprecise at best, leading to uncertainty as to when the privilege will apply. . . . A broader rule . . . protects from forced disclosure any communication from an attorney to his client when made in the course of giving legal advice. . . . [W]e think the broader rule better serves the interests underlying the attorney-client privilege and is not inconsistent with the principle that the attorney-client privilege should be applied narrowly.").

[336] 132 F.3d 504 (9th Cir. 1997).

[337] *Id.* at 506-07.

[338] *Id.* at 507.

failing to appear, the attorney may reveal that the client was advised of the appearance date. Similarly, the attorney may reveal when a deficiency notice from the IRS was received, enabling the court to establish the time at which a petition for review should have been filed.

Without explaining why informing a client of a time or place that the law (represented in an order by the presiding judge or a notice of deficiency from the IRS) requires him to *personally appear* or requires him to take action to protect his rights does not constitute legal assistance protected by the privilege, the court held that informing the client of a time or place that the law (represented in an act of Congress) requires a client's *assets "to appear"* is privileged legal advice.[339] This decision was a product of the recharacterization of the scope of the attorney-client privilege as protecting communications "between" the attorney and client—affording a *direct protection* to all responsive *attorney communications*.

Under the classical derivative theory for responsive attorney communications, this attorney's communication about the abstract requirements of the law would not have been privileged because the communication failed to apply or interpret those principles in light of the client's unique circumstances, and, thereby, did not reveal prior privileged communications of the client. Indeed, this conclusion would result regardless of whether the attorney's communications were characterized as "legal advice" or the "transmission of public information."[340] The fact that the response reveals that the bankruptcy advice was sought by the client does not make the lawyer's responsive communication privileged. Such information is not protected by the privilege because it must be disclosed in order to establish that "legal assistance" was the purpose of the consultation.[341] A conclusionary assertion

---

[339] *Id.* at 509.

[340] *See* Softview Computer Products Corp. v. Haworth, Inc., 2000 U.S. Dist. LEXIS 9457, *5-6 (S.D.N.Y. July 10, 2000) ("even if the content of the letter [from the attorney] can be considered legal advice, it is not legal advice that reflects a client confidence, and, therefore, is not privileged."); Transonic Systems, Inc. v. Non-Invasive Medical Tech. Corp., 192 F.R.D. 710, 2000 U.S. Dist. LEXIS 7366, *8-9 (D. Utah May 25, 2000) ("Biomet correctly argued before the district court, as it does here, that the opinion letter was not privileged because it did not reveal directly or indirectly, the substance of any confidential communication. The letter itself supports that assertion. The 'opinion letter' is not signed, is not addressed to Biomet or anyone else, and bears no letterhead or other indication of source. It discusses no prior action of Biomet and recommends no action to be taken by Biomet, but merely concludes that the '123 patent is invalid. Because the record is devoid of any indication that the validity opinion reveals the substance of a confidential communication by Biomet, we cannot view as clearly erroneous the district court's finding that the opinion was not privileged."); Midwestern Univ. v. HBO & Co., 1999 WL 329228, *2 (N.D. Ill. 1999) ("When a lawyer gives legal advice to the client it does not automatically trigger the attorney-client privilege. Rather, statements which would reveal the substance of the confidential communications [of the client] are protected. . . . Thus, this court will not protect documents based solely on the assertion that they reflect legal advice."). *See generally*, PAUL RICE, ATTORNEY-CLIENT PRIVILEGE IN THE UNITED STATES § 5:2 n.60 (Thomson West 2d ed. 1999).

[341] *See* **PRACTICE 136**, *infra. See generally,* PAUL R. RICE, ATTORNEY-CLIENT PRIVILEGE IN THE UNITED STATES, § 6:21 (Thomson West 2nd ed. 1999).

that "legal advice was sought" by the privilege proponent is insufficient because the judge is the finder of fact and must be given sufficient information from which that conclusion can independently be drawn. In addition, the opposing party must be provided sufficient facts from which an intelligent challenge can be made to the privilege claim.

128 PRACTICES

Confidential communications, not confidential information. Because the privilege focuses only on the communication, the *facts* incorporated into the communication do not have to be confidential. Neither the nature nor source of the facts is relevant to the confidential nature of the communication into which they have been placed.[342] Nevertheless, courts often mistakenly require that the protected communications contain confidential facts.

Example 1

If a client, through a letter, sought legal advice from his attorney about a possible cause of action in defamation for libel in a published comic strip, either the client's description of the comic strip or a copy of the strip would be part of the privileged "communication." The fact that the comic strip is public knowledge is irrelevant to the application of the attorney-client privilege protection in the context of what was "communicated," by way of being sent.[343]

Example 2

If a client sends non-confidential business information to the attorney with a request for an opinion on (1) the patentability of a product,[344]

---

[342] United States v. Woodall, 438 F.2d 1317, 1319 (5th Cir. 1970) ("If there is no fraud, or complicity in a proposed violation of the law, or breach of a duty to the Court, the content of the communication is immaterial. If there is a communication, it is privileged."); Minnesota Mining & Mfg. Co. v. North Amer. Science Assoc., Inc., 189 F.R.D. 406, 408 (D. Minn. 1999) ("Documents gathered from notebooks and monthly reports for the purpose of providing information to attorneys to obtain legal opinions or patentability are protected by the attorney-client privilege."). *See generally,* PAUL R. RICE, ATTORNEY-CLIENT PRIVILEGE IN THE UNITED STATES § 5:1 n.20 (Thomson West 2d ed. 1999).

[343] *See, e.g.,* Natta v. Zletz, 418 F.2d 633, 637 (7th Cir. 1969) ("It is also immaterial that some of the [letters] refer to technical or published information."); In re Ampicillin Antitrust Litigation, 81 F.R.D. 377, 389-90 (D.D.C. 1978) ("It is not necessary that the *information* be confidential. Under this standard, information the attorney learned from a client would be privileged if it was learned in a confidential client communication. Similarly, the attorney may be questioned about information obtained from public documents or other public sources because it was learned *outside* of the confidential attorney-client relationship (not because there is a requirement that the information be confidential). The *communication* of this publicly-obtained information, however, should be privileged to the extent that the communication was treated as confidential by the client and would tend to reveal a confidential communication of the client.").

[344] Knogo Corp. v. United States, 213 U.S.P.Q. 936, 940 (Ct. Cl. 1980).

(2) whether antitrust laws have /been violated, or (3) an opinion on whether a court order has been violated, if the facts communicated reasonably relate to the legal advice sought, the communication of those facts is privileged. The client cannot be asked, "What non-confidential facts did you send to your attorney?" The non-confidential facts have become part of a confidential communication. The non-confidential facts can be discovered, but not through the confidential communication.[345] Frequently, however, courts fail to appreciate

3c.

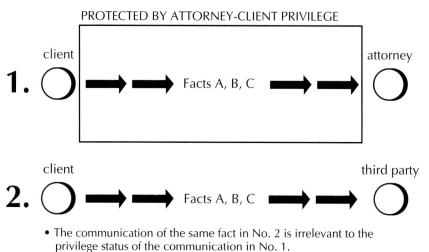

PROTECTED BY ATTORNEY-CLIENT PRIVILEGE

1. client → → Facts A, B, C → → attorney

2. client → → Facts A, B, C → → third party

- The communication of the same fact in No. 2 is irrelevant to the privilege status of the communication in No. 1.
- No. 2 will waive the privilege protection for No.1 only if the client tells the third party that the same facts were communicated to the attorney — if the content of the actual communication were acknowledged.

---

[345] *See generally*, PAUL R. RICE, ATTORNEY-CLIENT PRIVILEGE IN THE UNITED STATES § 5:1 pp. 16-20 (Thomson West 2d ed. 1999):

> [T]he privileged status that is given to the client's *communication* to the attorney is not affected by the client communicating those same *facts* to someone else. If, for example, a client communicated certain business information to his attorney to obtain advice on the legal implications of proposed business actions, the fact that the client subsequently communicated the same information to a business associate for other purposes would not affect the privileged status of his prior communication with his attorney.

> The confidential status of a communication is not dependent upon the source or nature of the information communicated. The fact that the client did not have personal knowledge of the facts confidentially communicated is irrelevant to whether the communication is protected by the privilege. Consequently, the public source or technical nature of the information communicated is irrelevant to the communication's privileged status. Therefore, if the client acquired information from the Patent Office or land records, for example, or collected technical information about a new invention and then communicated that information, confidentially, to an attorney for the purpose of obtaining legal advice or assistance, the communication relating that information to the attorney should be protected.

the distinction between confidential communications and the information contained within them.[346]

129 PRACTICES

Status of pre-existing documents. Pre-existing documents are simply older versions of copies of current documents. When either is sent to an attorney as part of an effort to obtain legal assistance (i.e., by regularly sending a copy for screening or by sending a pre-existing document with a cover letter), the attorney-client privilege should protect client-to-attorney communications, regardless of whether the incorporated material is itself otherwise privileged.[347] The fact the pre-existing documents can be obtained from the client, independent of the attorney-client communication, or the fact that the incorporated documents were initially used for business purposes (i.e., communi-

---

[346] *See, e.g.,* In re Case Corp., 1999 WL 1114209, *1 (8th Cir. Dec. 7, 1999) (concluding that a meeting was not held for the purpose of obtaining legal assistance, the court noted that the letters given to legal counsel reported unprivileged "factual matters and observations and opinions of Case's employees."); Larouche v. Dept. of Treasury, 2000 U.S. Dist. LEXIS 5078, *36 (D.D.C. Mar. 31, 2000) ("[T]he IRS has made no showing as to how the *information* that is specifically subject to this privilege is confidential.")(emphasis added); Softview Computer Products Corp. v. Haworth, Inc., 2000 U.S. Dist. LEXIS 4254, *31-32 (S.D.N.Y. Mar. 31, 2000) ("Accordingly, the extent that the challenged documents contain *confidential information* communicated by Haworth for the purpose of securing counsel's advice and assistance in obtaining the '798 patent, those documents are privileged. . . . Document 3 is an authorization from Haworth to counsel to file a patent application, and contains no *confidential information*.") (emphasis added); In re Gaming Lottery Securities Litig., 2000 U.S. Dist. LEXIS 3931, *12 (S.D.N.Y. Mar. 30, 2000) (concluding that the privilege was inapplicable because the client was using the attorney to perpetrate a fraud on regulatory agencies.); Eugene Burger Mgt. Corp. v. United States, 1999 U.S. Dist. LEXIS 22096, *9 (D.D.C. July 12, 1990) ("[T]he information communicated by the agency official must also be confidential"); DeSloover v. Daniels, 1999 WL 417322, *7 (N.D. Ill. June 6, 1999) ("It stands to reason that if the purpose for the attorney-client privilege is to protect the sharing of confidential information, then there is no need for the privilege if the *information* shared with the attorney was *not confidential* in the first place.") (emphasis added); Evans v. Atwood, 1777 F.R.D. 1, 5 (D.D.C. 1997) ("If, as is true of many of the documents, the client official sought the opinion without disclosing any confidential *information*, the existence of the opinion and its contents are not privileged.") (emphasis added). For an extensive discussion of the cases reflecting this mistake, *see* PAUL R. RICE, ATTORNEY-CLIENT PRIVILEGE IN THE UNITED STATES § 5:1 n.21 (Thomson West 2d ed. 1999).

[347] *See* Advanced Cardiovascular Systems, Inc. v. C.R. Bard, Inc., 144 F.R.D. 372, 374 (N.D. Cal. 1992) ("First, what the privilege presumptively protects from discovery is specific communications between client and counsel, not the relevant underlying facts, data or information. Thus, the kind of information that the *Jack Winter* and *Hercules* courts were concerned about making available to opposing parties and to the trier of fact ('technical information such as the results of research, tests, and experiments') will remain available, even if certain communications which include that information are presumptively privileged. In other words, opposing parties will remain free to discover, directly from the inventor, all the technical information the inventor had about the invention, all the results of tests the inventor performed, or had performed, all the documents related to experiments with the invention, everything the inventor knew about prior art, etc. The effect of the privilege only would be to block access to that kind of information indirectly, by blocking access to the private communications between inventor and patent lawyer.").

cation among vice presidents or with competitors), is irrelevant to the privileged status of the "communication" into which it was incorporated.[348]

130 PRACTICES

Discovery from attorney of pre-existing client documents. Failing fully to understand the distinction between "communications" and "information," the U.S. Supreme Court, in *United States v. Fisher*,[349] erroneously decided that pre-existing documents communicated by a client to an attorney for the purpose of obtaining legal assistance could be discovered *from the attorney*.[350] This decision is inappropriate because the method of discovery disclosed the content of prior "communications" between the attorney and client.[351]

---

[348] *See* Minnesota Mining & Mfg. Co. v. North Amer. Science Assoc., Inc., 189 F.R.D. 406, 408 (D. Minn. 1999) ("Documents gathered from notebooks and monthly reports for the purpose of providing information to attorneys to obtain legal opinions or patentability are protected by the attorney-client privilege."). *See generally,* PAUL R. RICE, ATTORNEY-CLIENT PRIVILEGE IN THE UNTIED STATES § 5:19 (Thomson West 2d ed. 1999):

Another justification for denying protection to the pre-existing documents used as part of the client's communications with his attorney is the fact that the documents were not *prepared* (created) primarily for the purpose of obtaining legal advice or assistance. This justification creates confusion, however, because the courts fail to differentiate between the *communication* (the transmission of information from the client to the attorney) and the *means of communication* (the document). If the primary purpose of a client *communication* with an attorney is to obtain legal advice, the privilege compels protection of the communication regardless of the nature of the instrument through which that communication was accomplished and regardless of whether the instrument was originally created for that purpose. The distinction between communications and the means of communication is as important to the proper application of the attorney-client privilege as the distinction between the communication and the information within it. The information within the client's communication need not be confidential for the privilege to attach. It is the act of communication that is encouraged and protected by the privilege rather than the content of the instrument. The means of transmitting information to the attorney is equally unimportant to the privilege's goal. It is important only that the communication itself is confidential.

[349] 425 U.S. 391 (1976).

[350] *Id.* at 399.

[351] *See* Advanced Cariovascular Systems, Inc. v. C.R. Bard, Inc., 144 F.R.D. 372, 374 (N.D. Cal. 1992). *See generally,* PAUL R. RICE, ATTORNEY-CLIENT PRIVILEGE IN THE UNITED STATES § 5:19 p.129 (Thomson West 2d ed. 1999):

If the client, when seeking legal advice based on the information contained in the pre-existing document, verbally communicated its contents to the attorney (via a telephone conversation, for example) or copied the information from that document into a letter he was writing to his attorney, (rather than attaching a copy of it to the letter), few courts would hold that the client's letter was not privileged. They would not even inquire about the source of the information communicated. Withholding the privilege's protection when the client incorporates the content of a pre-existing document through a more efficient means – attaching the original or a copy of the pre-existing document to his letter – is both illogical and unfair. It intolerably elevates form over substance without justification.

Contrary to the protestations of the Supreme Court, appropriately forbidding discovery from the attorney would not permit clients to avoid discovery by the simple expedient of having all documents screened by legal counsel. Discovery is always possible from the client, even if the client has sent the only copy to the attorney, because under the rules of discovery, documents possessed by a client's attorney are within the "possession, custody and control" of the client under Rule 34(a) of the Federal Rules of Civil Procedure.[352]

If a client, while seeking legal assistance, reads a pre-existing document to her attorney during a telephone conversation or copies the document into another letter, the conversation or the letter are protected by the privilege; and no court has held otherwise. To deny the privilege protection to the actual document copied and attached to the letter intolerably places form over substance.

PRE-EXISTING DOCUMENTS

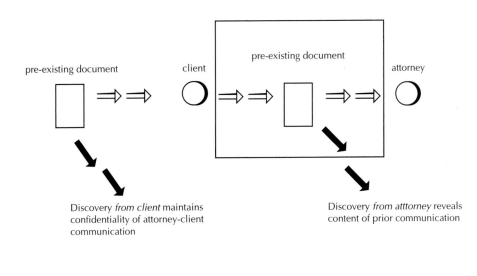

pre-existing document   client   pre-existing document   attorney

Discovery *from client* maintains confidentiality of attorney-client communication

Discovery *from atttorney* reveals content of prior communication

---

[352] Rule 34 of the Federal Rules of Civil Procedure provides, in part:

(a) Scope. Any party may serve on any other party a request (1) to produce and permit the party making the request, or someone acting on the requestor's behalf, to inspect and copy, any designated documents (including writings, drawings, graphics, charts, photographs, phone records, and other data compilations from which information can be obtained, translated, if necessary, by the respondent through detection devices into reasonably usable form), or to inspect and copy, test, or sample any tangible things which constitute or contain matters within the scope of Rule 26(b) and *which are in the possession, custody or control of the party upon whom the request is served*; (emphasis added).

131 PRACTICES

E-mail communications present special attorney-client privilege problems. With the advent of e-mail, communicating is quicker, easier, and less expensive. While all of this sounds positive, there are significant hidden consequences. When privilege claims are raised to withhold those communications from discovery, it radically increases the number, difficulty, and expense in asserting, establishing and resolving those claims.

First, because of the ease of this form of communication, lawyers (particularly in-house counsel) are being contacted *far more frequently*. This translates into many more claims being asserted that are unjustified. This over-assertion of the attorney-client privilege is exacerbated by the too-common practice of instructing associates and paralegals to claim privilege on anything that has a lawyer's name in the header. Many of these e-mail contacts are unnecessary and frequently are not even read by counsel. As a result, claims are multiplied and the cost of the privilege resolution process skyrockets with no corresponding benefit. Many of these documents are not seeking legal advice from the lawyer, and when they are, the primary purpose of the communications in which multiple employees are copied is business, rather than legal, in nature. And when there is a legal purpose in contacting the attorney, even though the primary purpose in communicating with everyone else is not legal, only the copy sent to the lawyer is protected by the attorney-client privilege. *See* **PRACTICES NO. 137**, *infra*. Second, the increased contact with lawyers has resulted in legal counsel being *brought into* discussions at a *much earlier time* when business strategy is developing. This has resulted in an increasing number of responsive communications from the lawyer that are purely business in nature.

Third, with the increased involvement of lawyers in business discussions, the difficulty in resolving privilege claims is compounded. Lawyers give legal advice on business matters, and give business advice on legal matters because the two are often inextricably intertwined. *See* **PRACTICES NO. 132**, *infra*. Identifying when the lawyer is giving business advice on business matters is often very difficult.

Fourth, because many corporate people place a lawyers name in the header to "take advantage of the attorney-client privilege," the headers have little or no circumstantial evidentiary value for the judge when resolving privilege claims. Because appearances are being manipulated, headers may reflect little about the true purpose for a communication. For example, many messages are addressed to an attorney, with copies being sent to corporate personnel, and the content of the document relates only to the individuals who were copied. Often, the individual paragraphs direct messages by name only to those who were copied, with little if anything directed to the attorney who was made to appear to be the primary recipient in the header.

Fifth, because e-mail users employ predefined address groups instead of selecting individual recipients from an address list, there are an increasing number of mistakes in dissemination. This has resulted in an increased number of *inadvertent disclosure* claims. When this occurs prior to litigation, rather than in a discovery process following the initiation of the action, disputes about the return, destruction, or non-use of the communication often lay dormant for much longer periods of time awaiting the commencement of litigation, thereby complicating the resolution of claims by the court.

132 PRACTICES

Concept of "inextricably intertwined" must only go one way. When a lawyer is consulted for the purpose of rendering a particular legal service, the responsive communications of the attorney often involve a mixture of both legal and business advice. Because legal problems arise from the business environment, complete and meaningful advice necessarily involves business direction that complements the legal service. The two are inextricably intertwined and courts have accepted this reality by extending the privilege protection to the *entire body of legal advice*.[353] However, when the lawyer is *not employed*

---

[353] In re OM Group Sec. Litig., 226 F.R.D. 579, 2005 U.S. Dist. LEXIS 3967, *28 (N.D. Ohio Feb. 28, 2005) (Advice given to Audit Committee by attorneys occasionally was business in nature. Court held privilege applicable because the legal and business concerns were inextricably intertwined.); Hercules Inc. v. Exxon Corp., 434 F. Supp. 136 (D. Del. 1977) ("The problem remains, however, of separating business from legal advice. An important responsibility of most patent attorneys, especially those employed by corporate patent departments, is to assess the business implications of the company's patent position. Many of the communications between the patent attorney and non-legal personnel of the corporation would therefore predominately reflect business concerns, such as the competitive position of the company, marketing strategy, licensing policy, etc. The Court recognizes that business and legal advice may often be inextricably interwoven. A single proposed course of conduct such as patenting and licensing of an invention will have both legal and business ramifications, and the lawyer may advise as to both in a single communication. As was pointed out in Jack Winter, Inc. v. KoratronInc. [54 F.R.D. 44 (N.D. Cal. 1971)], it is necessary to separate the two, in the interest of preserving the integrity of the privilege itself: 'As is not infrequently the case in patent matters, the problem of classification here was particularly troublesome as the attorneys for Koratron performed virtually every task incident to filing for and obtaining a patent or trademark registration. They were so closely associated with the activities of Koratron that picking out from the mass of documents presented to the court those which involved nonlegal transactions not soliciting or offering legal advice, and the separating of these from documents which did involve the exercise of the attorney's art, became at times an arduous and complex exercise. Yet we have sought to not lose sight of the importance of the distinction, for it is important that the attorney-client privilege not be downgraded in the interests of expedient results.' 54 F.R.D. at 47. . . . If the primary purpose of a communication is to solicit or render advice on nonlegal matters, the communication is not within the scope of the attorney-client privilege. Only if the attorney is "acting as a lawyer" – giving advice with respect to the legal implications of a proposed course of conduct – may the privilege be properly invoked. In addition, if a communication is made primarily for the purpose of soliciting legal advice, an incidental request for business advice does not vitiate the attorney-client privilege."); Coleman v. Am. Broadcasting Co., 106 F.R.D. 201, 206 (D.D.C. 1985); Chore-Time Equipment, Inc. v. Big Dutchman, Inc., 255 F. Supp. 1020, 1023 (W.D. Mich. 1966) ("Where a lawyer possesses multifarious talents, his clients should not be deprived of the attorney-client

primarily for legal assistance, and assumes a non-legal role (business consultant, for example), the extension of the privilege protection to the *client's communications* to the attorney under the inextricably intertwined concept is unjustified, inappropriate, and dangerous.

Extension of the privilege protection to legal and business advice that is inextricably intertwined was a practical necessity of effective legal service. The application of this concept, however, must be strictly limited to the context in which it originally was recognized. It should not be expanded to include (1) communications from the client *to legal counsel* in which business and legal matters are intertwined, or (2) communications from legal counsel that are a byproduct of nonlegal services. Unlike the needs arising when an attorney attempts to provide meaningful legal assistance, the mixture of legal and nonlegal communications in the two instances noted above is the product of client choice, rather than the inherent nature of the service being provided.

A similar type of problem arises when a corporation simultaneously sends an e-mail communication involving business matters to both business and legal personnel, the mixing of the two so that they cannot be separated is a voluntary decision by the client that is not compelled by the legal services being sought. For legal assistance purposes, the client could have sent a separate transmission of the e-mail message to the attorney, thereby separating the legal from the nonlegal. To give an expanded privilege protection to the business communications that were only protected under the common law to the extent that a *copy* was communicated to the attorney for examination and assistance, permits the client to engage in a form of funneling — sending everything through the attorney, even though business was the primary purpose, solely to get the protection of the attorney-client privilege. Having voluntarily chosen this means of transmission, the client should bear the loss of the privilege protection rather than the opposing party losing the discovery of otherwise non-privileged business information.

Similarly, when the client uses in-house counsel to perform nonlegal services (like public relations work or contract negotiations), and the lawyer subsequently finds it necessary to mix his factual reporting with his legal advice, this is a situation that the client created by assigning a lawyer to this nonlegal task, not one that is driven exclusively by the necessities of the advice being given. Consequently, the client should not be rewarded by broadening the privilege protection. Otherwise, corporations will be encouraged to employ lawyers to perform most critical functions that they would like to have the option of keeping secret when it serves their ends.[354]

---

privilege, where applicable, simply because their correspondence is also concerned with highly technical matters. Patent lawyers should not be banished to the status of quasi-lawyers by reason of the fact that besides being skilled in the law, they are also competent in scientific and technical areas.").

[354] *See* P.R. RICE, ATTORNEY-CLIENT PRIVILEGE IN THE UNITED STATES § 7:2.1 — E-Mail Technology Changes Everything (West Group 2nd ed. 1999)(2006 supplement)

133 PRACTICES

Are your outside consultants "virtual employees" or "functional employees" whose communications with your legal counsel are protected by your privilege? The ease of communication by e-mail has resulted in the increasing inclusion of individuals outside the corporation in e-mail threads. The newest wrinkle is outside public relations consultants helping put a public face on developments in pending litigation. In general, the reaction of courts has been mixed regarding outside consultants,[355] but courts are becoming increasingly receptive to treating some of them like "virtual employees" or "functional employees" of the client, particularly if they are performing work they previously performed as employees.[356]

Following the lead of *Bieter* the court in *In re Copper Market Antitrust Litig.*[357] concluded that an outside public relations consultant could be treated as an employee of the corporation and permissibly allowed within the circle of the corporation's confidential communications with legal counsel because the public relations firm "was, essentially, incorporated into [the corporation's] staff to perform a corporate function that was necessary in the context of various litigations; (2) the public relations firm "possessed authority to make decisions on behalf of [the corporation] concerning its public relations strategy;" (3) the public relations firm often consulted the corporation's attorneys in formulating this strategy; and (4) the communications at issue "were for the purpose of obtaining legal advice." The court *In re Currency Conversion Fee Antitrust Litigation*[358] characterized the positions held by the outside consultants in *Bieter* and *Copper Market Antitrust* as "functional employees." The court contrasted the services provided in those cases by noting that First Data, the consultant, "was merely a transaction processing and computer services corporation that provided standard trade services to First USA and a vast number of other credit card companies. . . . In this man-

---

[355] In re Beiter Co., 16 F.3d 929, 937 (8th Cir. 1994) (outside consultant); In re Currency Conversion Fee Antitrust Litigation, 2003 U.S. Dist. LEXIS 18636, *7 (S.D.N.Y. Oct. 21, 2003) (characterizing media consultants as "functional employees"); and In re Copper Market Antitrust Litig., 200 F.R.D. 213, 219-20 (S.D.N.Y. 2001) (public relations consultant within the scope of the privilege).

[356] *See* Twentieth Century Fox Film Corp. v. Marvel Enterprises, Inc., 2002 U.S. Dist. LEXIS 22215, *5-7 (S.D.N.Y. Nov. 15, 2002) ("In this case, I find that the non-employees to whom disclosure was made were the functional equivalent of employees. Fox's determination to conduct its business through the use of independent contractors is a result of the sporadic nature of employment in the motion picture industry; for a wide variety of reasons, producers, directors and actors generally do not 'turn out' movies with the same mechanical regularity with which most tangible products are produced. The fact that the nature of the industry dictates the use of independent contractors over employees should not, without more, create greater limitations on the scope of the attorney-client privilege.").

[357] 200 F.R.D. 213, 218 (S.D.N.Y. 2001).

[358] 2003 U.S. Dist. LEXIS 18636, *7 (S.D.N.Y. Oct. 21, 2003).

ner, First Data's role is akin to that of an accountant or other ordinary third party specialist, disclosure to whom destroys the attorney-client privilege."[359]

If outside consultants are *hired by the attorney* to help the attorney in the rendering legal assistance, they have long been recognized as agents of the attorney who are appropriately with the circle of confidentiality.[360]

IV. DRAFTS OF DOCUMENTS DISTRIBUTED TO THIRD PARTIES

A. PRINCIPLES

When a client consults with an attorney for the purpose of filing a law suit, the complaint ultimately served on the opposing party and filed with the court incorporates the contents of many client communications. However, no court has held that the public dissemination of that complaint waives the attorney-client privilege for all communications contributing to its content. The same result applies to drafts of all other types of documents being prepared for public dissemination.[361]

---

[359] Subsequently, *Bieter* has been construed narrowly. *See, e.g.*, Expert-Import Bank of the U.S. v. Asia Pulp & Paper Co., Ltd., 2005 U.S. Dist. LEXIS 28671, *24-25 (S.D.N.Y. Nov. 28, 2005) (The court recognized consultants as "de facto employees" when they assumed the functions and duties of full-time employees and met three conditions. First, whether the consultant had primary responsibility for a key corporate job. Second, whether there was a "continuous and close working relationship between the consultant and the company's principals on matter critical to the company's position in litigation. Third, whether the consultant is likely to possess information possessed by no one else at the company.); Freeport-McMorgan Sulphur v. Mike Mullen Energy Equip. Resource, Inc., 2004 U.S. Dist. LEXIS 10048, *12-13 (E.D. La. June 3, 2004) (The court focused on the facts that the consultant's "duties were varied and extensive," he appeared at public hearings on behalf of the company, he was viewed as and dealt with as the representative of Bieter, he had an equity interest in the development, and "he was an individual without which Bieter Company could not exist."[10.2] Although the independent contractor in *Freeport* had previously work for Freeport entities for twenty-five years, was working as full time consultant for Freeport, dealing most with a Vice President, the court refused to extend the privilege to cover communications with the consultant because Freeport had not established that the consultant held himself out as a representative of Freeport, was perceived by others as Freeport's representative, was an intimate link in the project being work on, or owned an equity interest in the project.

[360] *See* P.R. RICE, ATTORNEY-CLIENT PRIVILEGE IN THE UNITED STATES § 3:3 (West Group 2nd ed. 1999).

[361] *See* McCook Metals v. Alcoa Inc., 192 F.R.D. 233, 2000 U.S. Dist. LEXIS 2309, *19 (N.D. Ill. Mar. 2, 2000) ("A draft necessarily reflects the communications between a client and his attorney as the attorney attempts to put forth the invention in the best light possible to protect a client's legal right."); N.V. Organon v. Elan Pharm., *Inc.*, 2000 U.S. Dist. LEXIS 5629, *5-6 (S.D.N.Y. May 1, 2000) (holding draft settlement agreements confidential and protected by the attorney-client privilege); Softview Computer Prod. Corp. v. Haworth, Inc., 2000 U.S. Dist. LEXIS 4254, *53 (S.D.N.Y. Mar. 31, 2000) ("I believe that the better rule is one which extends the privilege to draft patent applications."); In re Brand Name Prescription Drugs Antitrust Litig., 1995 WL 557412, *2 (N.D. Ill. 1995) ("The mere fact that a final version of these documents may have been intended for public dissemination does not take them out from under the protection of the privilege, if the drafts of these

134 PRACTICES

What you see is what you get. Confidential drafts of communications between the attorney and client should not be affected by the ultimate use made of the final product. The validity of a legal complaint, patent application or prospectus is not judged on the basis of prior communications between the attorney and client but upon independent evidence that supports the factual representations made therein. Therefore, continuing to protect the drafts does not create a hardship for the party to whom the final document has been disclosed.[362]

Before dissemination, the privilege protects all communications relating to the developing document. After dissemination, the privilege protection is lost only for the disclosed document.

DRAFTS OF RELEASED DOCUMENT

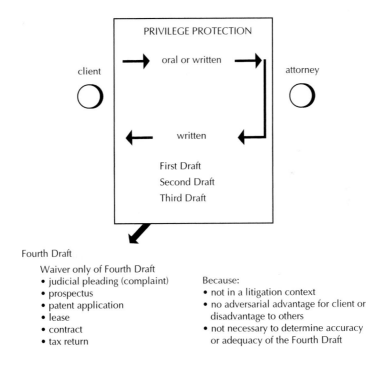

---

documents were intended to be confidential communications concerning legal advice. . . . Preliminary drafts of documents which were not distributed, and which reflect confidential communications regarding legal advice are privileged. . . . AHP's description of these documents reveals nothing from which we can infer that AHP did not intend these drafts documents and letters — which on their face reveal legal advice — to be confidential. These items are therefore privileged.").

362 *See* Grupo Sistemas Integrales de Telecomicacion S.A. de C.V. v. AT&T Communications, 1995 WL 102679, *1 (S.D. N.Y. Mar. 8, 1995) ("The discussion of the 'draft' was a confidential attorney-

- Drafts are only a form of communication — a preliminary iteration of something that will be made public when the client directs.

- Until the order to file, everything that precedes by way of communications that were privileged when made remain privileged.

- This is true of tax returns or prospectuses. Whether they adequately disclose what they purport to disclose must be determined from evidence other than what the client said and disclosed to the attorney and what the attorney said in response.

- If this were the rule, then the filing of a complaint would waive the privilege for all prior communications between the attorney and client leading up to the complaint. Drafts of communications — even communications intended to be disseminated to third parties — do not lose their privilege status when the communications are ultimately disseminated so long as the client intended the previous iterations to be confidential when they were created.

---

client communication; even if a complaint had eventually been filed (which did not occur), that act would not have waived the attorney-client privilege as to drafts."); Sequa Corp. v. Gelmin, 1994 WL 538124, *3 (S.D. N.Y. Sept. 30, 1994) ("Under the law of this circuit, a draft of a document that, in its final form, is intended for public dissemination may be privileged if the draft constitutes an attorney-client communication and was itself intended to be confidential. . . . Ms. Harmon avers that the draft contracts, which she prepared, have not been disclosed outside the attorney-client relationship, and the reasonable inference is that those drafts, when transmitted to Sequa's officers, constituted an attorney's rendering of legal advice. Under the circumstances, the draft is privileged."); Ball Corp. v. American National Can Co., 27 U.S.P.Q.2d 1958 (S.D. Ind. May 13, 1993) ("Information must flow freely between a client inventor and the attorney before the final patent application is signed and filed, just as it must in an ordinary civil case before the filing of a complaint. There is nothing inherent in patent practice that diminishes the value of respecting an intended confidential communication to an attorney. There is nothing sinister about the attorney-client privilege. One cannot assume that if a client inventor intends a confidential communication to his attorney, fraud on the PTO is afoot, and there is no need to equate 'privilege' with 'fraud,' or 'non-privileged' with 'candor.' This Court therefore joins with those which have recognized that the attorney-client privilege attaches to draft patent applications."); Allegheny Ludlum Corp. v. Nippon Steel Corp., 1991 WL 61144, *5 (E.D. Pa. 1991) ("Document no. 12 is a draft of the application which resulted in the '018 patent. After carefully reviewing document no. 12, I find that the document is privileged. It is apparent that the document, in draft form, was not intended to transmitted to the Patent and Trademark Office ("PTO") . . . . Moreover, document no.12 contains information which Allegheny Ludlum was considering but decided not to include in the application of the '018 patent. . . . The document contains a communication within the attorney-client relationship for the purpose of rendering a legal opinion in confidence."). *See generally*, P.R. RICE, ATTORNEY-CLIENT PRIVILEGE IN THE UNITED STATES § 5:13 (West Group 2nd ed. 1999).

V. CONFIDENTIALITY — A REQUIREMENT OF SECRECY

PRINCIPLES

For the attorney-client privilege to arise, the client must have communicated with the attorney in confidence.[363] Although confidentiality originally described the nature of the attorney-client relationship, over time it came to describe the context in which attorney-client communications usually took place—outside the presence of third-parties who were not agents of either the attorney or the client. Eventually, confidentiality became equated with secrecy — courts held that the privilege protection could not arise unless the communications between the attorney and the client were secret and could not survive unless that secrecy was subsequently maintained.[364]

135 PRACTICES

A condition precedent to the creation of the privilege, not a necessary condition to its survival. This concept of confidentiality evolved, in significant part, due to the influence of Professor Wigmore who proclaimed in 1905 that no privilege is justified unless the communications it protects are secret.[365] In adopting this view, neither the courts nor Professor Wigmore ever explained why secrecy is a logical imperative. Indeed, since it is the suppression of the communications as evidence that encourages clients to communicate openly with their attorneys (because it prevents them from being injured by their own words), the element of confidentiality serves little, if any, purpose.

Throughout the years, judges intuitively have understood this. As a consequence, when confidential communications are stolen by third parties, or released by agents after they have left the client's employ, courts no longer consider this either to have waived or destroyed the privilege protection.[366]

---

[363] *See* United States v. Tellier, 255 F.2d 441, 447 (2nd Cir. 1958) ("It is of the essence of the attorney-client privilege that it is limited to those communications which are intended to be confidential." *cert. denied*, 358 U.S. 821 (1958); Parkhurst v. Lowten, 2 Swanst. 194, 216, 36 E.R. 589, 611 (Ch. 1818) ("[T]he moment confidence ceases, privilege ceases.").

[364] *See* P.R. RICE, ATTORNEY-CLIENT PRIVILEGE IN THE UNITED STATES, § 6:3 (West Group 2nd ed. 1999); P.R. Rice, *Attorney-Client Privilege: The Eroding Concept of Confidentiality Should Be Abolished*, 47 DUKE L. REV. 101 (1998) (available at www.acprivilege.com).

[365] 4 J. WIGMORE, A TREATISE ON THE SYSTEM OF EVIDENCE IN TRIALS AT COMMON LAW § 2285 at 3185 (1905); 8 J. WIGMORE, EVIDENCE, § 2285, at 527 (McNauthton rev. 1961).

[366] *Contrast* In re Grand Jury Proceedings Involving Berkley & Co., 466 F. Supp. 863, 868 (D. Minn. 1979) ("The protection afforded by the privilege, however, does not apply to the documents obtained from Berkley's former employee, for the privilege does not apply to stolen or lost document.") *and* 8 Wigmore, EVIDENCE § 2325 (McNaughton rev. ed. 1961) ("All involuntary disclosures, in particular, through the loss or theft of documents from the attorney's possession, are not protected

Similarly, when documents have been inadvertently disclosed, confidentiality has been lost but courts (both state and federal) uniformly have refused to declare the privilege expired.[367]

Progressively, courts have treated confidentiality as a condition precedent to the creation of the privilege but not as a necessary condition to its continuation. Perhaps courts will eventually eliminate the requirement altogether.[368] This would eliminate most of the costs of the privilege resolution process arising from the need to document that "secrecy" has not been destroyed by the inappropriate circulation of the communications.

---

by the privilege, on the principle that, since the law has granted secrecy so far as its own process goes, it leaves to the client and attorney to take the measures of caution sufficient to prevent being overheard by third parties. The risk of insufficient precautions is upon the client. This principle applies equally to documents.") *with* Crabb v. KFC Nat'l Management Co., 952 F.2d 403 (6th Cir. 1992) (unpublished) (holding that ex-employee's possession of privileged document was excused, even though the breach of confidentiality was unexplained, because efforts to preserve confidentiality were perceived to have been adequate); Sackman v. Liggett Group, Inc., 173 F.R.D. 358, 365 (E.D.N.Y. 1997) ("[T]he assertion of privilege by "B&W" is not waived through public disclosure of a stolen privileged document."). Courts also have shown a willingness to ignore the voluntary, albeit inadvertent, loss of confidentiality through the client's disclosures to third parties. *See, e.g.,* Alldread v. Grenada, 988 F.2d 1425, 1434, (5th Cir. 1993) ("In our view, an analysis which permits the court to consider the circumstances surrounding a disclosure on a case-by-case basis is preferable to a per se rule of waiver. This analysis serves the purpose of the attorney-client privilege, the protection of communications which the client fully intended would remain confidential, yet at the same time will not relieve those claiming the privilege of the consequences of their carelessness if the circumstances surrounding the disclosure do not clearly demonstrate that continued protec-tion is warranted."); Lois Sportwear, U.S.A., Inc. v. Levi Strauss Co., 104 F.R.D. 103, 105 (S.D.N.Y. 1985).

At the same time the courts have vastly extended the permissible circle of confidentiality to include joint client of the same attorney, *see* Bernardo v. C.I.R., 104 T.C. 677, 696 n.11 (1995) ("Petitioners have joint representation in the instant proceeding. Consequently, we do not view the disclosure of information regarding petitioners' Federal income tax returns to Mr. Houlihan as a voluntary disclosure of privileged information to a third party."), clients of separate attorneys who share a community of interests, Hodges, Grant & Kaufmann v. I.R.S., 768 F.2d 719, 721 (5th Cir. 1985) ("The privilege is not . . . waived if a privileged communication is shared with a third person who has a common legal interest with respect to the subject matter of the communication."), or who are participating in a joint defense effort. *Matter of Bevill, Bresler & Schulman Asset Management Corp.*, 805 F.2d 120, 126 (3rd Cir. 1986) ("The joint defense privilege protects communications between an individual and an attorney for another when the communications are 'part of an ongoing and joint effort to set up a common defense strategy.'").

Agents of the attorney have been expanded from those who are necessary to the attorney's effective representation of the client, *see, e.g.,* Burlington Indus. v. Exxon Corp., 65 F.R.D. 26, 40 (D. Md. 1974) ("[A]gents of the attorney for purposes of the privilege . . . are those persons essential to the lawyer's performance of legal services"), to those who merely assist. *See generally,* P.R. Rice, Attorney-Client Privilege in the United States § 3:3 (West Group 2nd ed. 1999) (identifying an array of circumstances under which agents of the attorney have been recognized by courts).

[367] *See generally* P.R. Rice, Attorney-Client Privilege in the United States, §§ 9:70 - 9:76 (West Group 2nd ed. 1999)

[368] *See generally,* P.R. Rice, Attorney-Client Privilege: The Eroding Concept of Confidentiality Should Be Abolished, 47 Duke L. Rev. 101 (1998) (available at www.acprivilege.com).

136 PRACTICES

Information about the attorney-client relationship and privileged communications may be neither confidential nor protected by the privilege. Lawyer and judges often assume that far too much information about the attorney-client relationship and its communications are confidential, and therefore shielded by the privilege. The privilege only protects the communications of the attorney and client or their authorized agents. Generally, it does not protect information about the attorney-client relationship. A helpful rule of thumb is that information essential to the successful assertion of a privilege claim is not protected by the privilege because that information must be disclosed in the required privilege log. Consequently, information about the client, the communications, their confidential nature, the attorney, the purpose of each communication, is not protected and cannot be withheld. The client's identity must be disclosed so it can be determined whether third parties who were privy to the communications personified the corporate client or otherwise were the client's agents. The identity of the attorney must be disclosed so it can be determined whether the client could reasonably believed that legal advice was being sought from someone qualified to render it. Information about the communications (when, where, how, who was involved, and who was later allowed to be privy) must be disclosed so it can be determined that the communications were confidential. The general content of the communications must be characterized so that the opposing party has a fair opportunity to challenge whether legal, as opposed to business, advice was being sought, and who the appropriate recipients of that advice were. This is illustrated in the following graphic. All the information surrounding the privilege box is not protected by the privilege. As previously illustrated, only the communications placed in the box are protected.

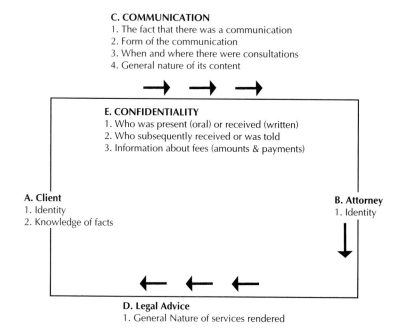

**INFORMATION ABOUT THE PRIVILEGE
THAT IS NOT PROTECTED**

C. COMMUNICATION
1. The fact that there was a communication
2. Form of the communication
3. When and where there were consultations
4. General nature of its content

E. CONFIDENTIALITY
1. Who was present (oral) or received (written)
2. Who subsequently received or was told
3. Information about fees (amounts & payments)

A. Client
1. Identity
2. Knowledge of facts

B. Attorney
1. Identity

D. Legal Advice
1. General Nature of services rendered

Another fact about the attorney-client relationship that is not protected is fees. What was charged by the attorney, what was paid by the client or third parties, how payment was made, and when payment was made have no relationship to the purpose of the privilege — encouraging the client to be open and candid in his communications with the attorney. Therefore, when relevant to a matter being litigated, all of this information can be discovered.

VI. LEGAL ADVICE OR ASSISTANCE

PRINCIPLES

The attorney-client privilege is applicable only when "legal" advice or assistance is sought from an attorney. The mere fact that a communication is to or from an attorney, or an attorney is copied on the communication does not mean that the privilege is applicable.[369] The resolution of whether legal advice was sought and given is a factual question that will turn on the nature of the assis-

---

[369] *See,* F.D.I.C. v. Hurwitz, 384 F. Supp.2d 1039, 2005 U.S. Dist. LEXIS 17907, *174-75 (S.D. Tex. Aug. 23, 2005) ("The log identified hundreds of documents that were not privileged. The FDIC said that work-product and attorney-client privileges protect documents sent by or to a government employee with a law license, even when that employee acts as an executive, investigator, or regulator. It is wrong. A person must give legal advice in a context of advice sought to render his communication privileged; that he has a law license is not enough."); Garcia v. City of El Centro, 214 F.R.D. 587, 590 (S.D. Cal. 2003) ("In the instant case, the communications that took place were

tance sought, the context in which the request is made, and the broader relationship of the attorney and client to one another.[370] Generally, when an independent lawyer is contacted by a prospective client, the operating assumption is that legal advice was sought. Wigmore referred to this as creating a *prima facie* case for legal advice or assistance.[371] With in-house counsel, however, such an assumption is inappropriate because in-house counsel too often assumes many different roles in the daily operations of a enterprise.[372]

137 PRACTICES

Legal advice or assistance must be the primary purpose of the consultation. When a lawyer is consulted for multiple purposes (this is usually situation that arises with in-house counsel), the privilege proponent must prove that the primary or predominant purpose of the communications was to obtain legal assistance. The older common law required that legal assistance be the sole purpose, but that standard has been abandoned. If the primary purpose of to obtain legal assistance, and the business assistance only complemented that legal purpose, the privilege protection would be given to the entire communication.

If a mixed purpose communication to or from an attorney is segregable. (*viz.*, the portions that relate to non-legal purposes can be identified and separated from the legal purposes), the non-legal portions must be produced with the alleged privileged portions excised and described in a privilege log.

---

between the claims adjuster and Officers Beltran and Hernandez. Even if the interviewing claims adjuster were an attorney (there has been no evidence offered that the interviewing claims adjuster is in fact an attorney), the attorney-client privilege would not attach because Officers Hernandez and Beltran were not seeking legal advice from the claims adjuster. The claims adjuster's capacity here was principally to determine whether to pay Plaintiff's claim, not to offer legal advice to Officers Beltran and/or Hernandez.").

[370] *See,* Giardina v. Ruth U. Fertel, Inc., 2001 WL 1658183, at *2 (E.D. La. Dec. 24, 2001) ("[C]ommunications must be made in the role of an attorney in order to qualify for the attorney-client privilege. Likewise, a full-time practicing attorney does not imbue all confidential communications with the privilege. Such an attorney may have multiple roles in his activities (*e.g.*, business advisor, corporate director, labor negotiator) that are not necessarily attorney-related roles for the purpose of the privilege. In the representation of corporate interests, counsel might find themselves performing multiple roles. Frequently the roles are closely related, which make it virtually impossible to isolate a purely legal role from the nonlegal. . . . [T]he Court is not satisfied that RUFI's attorney was acting in his capacity as an attorney during the relevant portions of the board meetings. The statements made by RUFI's attorney did not require the skill and expertise of an attorney. In addition, it appears clear from the redacted portions of the minutes of the board meetings that the purpose of the conversations was not to render legal advice. Finally, it does not appear that either RUFI nor its attorney understood that the purpose of the communications was to reveal and consider the legal issues pertaining to RUFI.").

[371] 8 Wigmore, EVIDENCE § 2296 (McNauthton rev. ed. 1961).

[372] *See generally,* P.R. RICE, ATTORNEY-CLIENT PRIVILEGE IN THE UNITED STATES, § 7:1-7:2 (West Group 2nd ed. 1999).

Mixed purpose communications should be distinguished from mixed purpose circulations of business communications. Many business letters, memos and e-mails are circulated among corporate employees with copies being sent to legal counsel for advice on proposed courses of actions. While the primary purpose of the communications is not business, the primary purpose of sending the copy to the attorney is to obtain legal assistance. Therefore, the copy to legal counsel is privileged, but the other copies are not.

Giving this protection to the copy going to the attorney is often meaningless, however, because the fact that it was communicated to legal counsel is often revealed on the face of the document (e.g., "cc: John Doe, Legal"). This is why the circulating of business communication to legal counsel should always be by blind copy. Most companies will not follow this advice, however, because they mistakenly believe that by sending a copy to legal counsel it makes the entire document privileged.

138 PRACTICES

Legal advice is more and less than what you might think. The law provides no definitive answer to what constitutes legal advice. Generalities that have guided courts include:

1. Services that involve the interpretation and application of legal principles;

2. Services that the lawyer's education and certification to practice qualifies him to render for compensation; and

3. Services that involve the judgment of a lawyer in his capacity as a lawyer.

The fact that a non-lawyer could perform the same services provided by the lawyer is not dispositive but it is a factor to be weighed. Lawyers often perform nonlegal types of tasks that complement legal services otherwise being performed.[373] For example, an attorney investigation internal corruption within a corporation may propose auditing standards that can help the client avoid similar problems in the future. Because auditing advice is so intimately tied to the fraud being uncovered and exposed, both will be considered legal assistance.

Things that have *not* been considered legal advice or assistance include: tax return preparation, accounting services; custodian; preparation of leases; writing advertisements and press releases; insurance claim investigation (claims adjustor); serving as a messenger or conduit of funds; monitoring

---

[373] In re Allen, 106 F.3d 582 (4th Cir. 1997) (investigative services are not legal assistance unless they are prefatory to giving advice based on the results of the investigation).

compliance with consent decrees; lobby efforts and preparing reports as source materials for congressional hearings; negotiating a business transaction; investment counseling; amending business records (scrivener); and supervising the publication of documents.

Things considered legal advice or assistance include: representing parties in litigation; advising individuals on the legality of proposed courses of action; investigations leading to further recommendations to avoid illegal conduct; drafting contracts and wills; giving tax advice; preparing and filing patent applications; and negotiating the settlement of a dispute.[374]

VII. GOOD CAUSE EXCEPTION

PRINCIPLES

The attorney-client is absolute. Once it attaches, its duration is forever, unless one of the exceptions discussed below are applicable or the protection is otherwise waived. The theory for a permanent rule is the belief that the client needs to be assured that his confidences will be perpetually protected in order to convince him to be completely open and candid with his legal counsel. Undoubtedly, the validity of this logic depends on the nature of the legal assistance sought and context it which it was rendered. For example, seeking advice about the disposition of your estate may require perpetual protection of communications, while confidences shared during the representation of someone at trial may not need such permanent protection when the cause of action has expired and there can be no collateral consequences from the disclosure of incriminating information. Whether either proposition is true has never been empirically tested, and may be unprovable. The same, of course, can be said for many of the applications of the privilege protection. Its extension to corporate entities may be the best example. *See* **PRACTICES NO. 126,** *supra*.

139 PRACTICES

A good reason won't do. It is said that hard cases make bad law. If a good cause exception to the privilege were recognized, it would be a perfect example. Fortunately, it's not. Courts have consistently resisted attempts to override the privilege when a compelling need is demonstrated to discover statements made to an attorney in confidence by a client. While factual patterns create compelling needs, the concern is that such an exception, once recognized, has no apparent limitation. Its application becomes totally discretionary, and as a consequence, the privilege protection becomes totally unpredictable.

---

[374] *See generally*, Paul R. Rice, Attorney-Client Privilege in the United States, § 7:10-7:26 (West Group 2nd ed. 1999).

VIII. CRIME/FRAUD EXCEPTION

PRINCIPLES

If you abuse it you lose it. The crime/fraud exception is that simple. If a client seek legal advice or assistance with the intention of using it to more successfully commit what he knows to be a crime or fraud, the law considers the privilege to never have attached to the client's communications with the attorney. For the exception to apply, the government need only demonstrate a *prima facie* case — putting aside issues of credibility, sufficient evidence upon which a reasonable person could find — that the client's purpose was bad. The judge making the decision need not be convinced that such a purpose existed.

140 PRACTICES

The prima facie confusion after Zolin. Even though *prima facie* is the standard for activating the crime/fraud exception, the Supreme Court in *United States v. Zolin*,[375] created confusion when it held that a judge need not conduct an *in camera* inspection of allegedly privilege communication unless a showing is made to support a reasonable belief that *in camera* inspection would "reveal evidence to establish the claim that the crime/fraud exception applies." This, simply stated, is a *prima facie* showing to make a *prima facie* showing. The first showing is that *in camera* examination reveal evidence of fraud. The second is the fraud that is revealed. The problem with the decision is its assumption that judges need not engage in the *in camera* inspection of all allegedly privileged communications before making a decision on those claims. *See* **PRACTICES NO. 147**, *infra*. If that is done, in the fulfillment of the judge's independent fact-finding role, the issue of *Zolin* becomes moot.

IX. FIDUCIARY DUTY EXCEPTION

PRINCIPLES

The extension of the privilege to entities, like corporations, created difficult situations where parties own an entity but are not considered the client. For example, shareholders own the corporation in which they hold stock, but the shareholders are not the client. The fictitious legal entity is the client. The entity, however, cannot speak. Therefore, the privilege protects the communications between the corporation's attorney and the entity's directors, officers and employees. Those folks, however, like the shareholders, are also not the clients, and therefore, have no control over the privilege's assertion or waiver. This cre-

---

[375] 491 U.S. 554. 109 S. Ct. 2619, 105 L. Ed. 2d 469 (1989).

ated uncomfortably difficult situations when the shareholders sued corporate directors for negligent mismanagement of corporate assets and needed to see their communications with corporate counsel in order to prove their allegations. Since there was no good cause exception, courts came up with another — the fiduciary duty exception.[376] By this exception, if a fiduciary duty were owed to a third party, that third party could gain access to confidential attorney-client communications to prove that the duty was breached.

141 PRACTICES

When duty demands, the privilege gives way. When first recognized, the fiduciary duty exception was limited to shareholder derivative actions where the shareholders had to demonstrate good cause. Good cause was determined by many factors like the nature of the shareholders' claim, the claim's apparent validity, the need for the information, the percentage of shares represented by the plaintiff, and the extent to which the communications were identified. Subsequently, the scope of the exception has expanded beyond corporate derivative actions to a variety of fiduciary contexts where the recognition of the privilege would favor the interests of one principal over another (*e.g.*, limited partners against general partners, union members against union officials, trust beneficiaries against the trust and its trustee, excess insurers against primary insurers and creditors against bankruptcy creditor's committees). Not only has the scope of the exception been expanded, with each expansion, courts appear to have progressively abandoned the good cause demonstration.[377]

X. WAIVER

PRINCIPLES

When a client takes actions inconsistent with the confidentiality of privileged communications, the privilege protection for those communications is waived. Courts often admonish that clients cannot use the privilege as both a sword and a shield. If the client strikes out with his privileged communications (including asserting claims premised upon those communications), the communications cannot be hidden behind the privilege shield. Therefore, the law has recognized many grounds of waiver: voluntary disclosures, evidentiary use of

---

[376] Garner v. Wolfinbarger, 430 F.2d 1093 (5th Cir. 1970). Subsequently, this decision has been followed throughout the country, in both state and federal courts. *See generally*, PAUL R. RICE, ATTORNEY-CLIENT PRIVILEGE IN THE UNITED STATES, §§ 8:17-8:25 (Thomson West 2d ed. 1999).

[377] This has particularly been true in state courts where the exception has been universally recognized and vastly expanded over its shareholder derivative origins. *See* PAUL R. RICE, ATTORNEY-CLIENT PRIVILEGE: STATE LAW, § 8.19 (Rice Publishing 2006).

privileged communications, producing them in a discovery process without properly raising privilege objections, and injecting privilege communications into litigation by raising issues to which privileged communications are central (*e.g.*, reliance on advice of counsel as a defense, raising claims like good faith, knowledge, and estoppel, or attacking counsel).[378]

142 PRACTICES

Waiver is a fairness, as much as a confidentiality, issue. Today, unlike the past, waiver of privilege is premised more on the standard of fairness, than on the existence or absence of confidentiality. Under the earlier common law when confidentiality disappeared, the privilege protection disappeared with it. Consequently, when documents were stolen (purloined communications), oral communications were seized by eavesdropping, or documents were produced pursuant to judicial order, the privilege vanished. Today, courts are more concerned about the culpability of the privilege holder in the loss of confidentiality. For example, if the voluntary disclosure was through inadvertence, or the documents were stolen by departing employees, courts have consistently refused to declare the privilege lost because the client did not voluntarily and intentionally engage in conduct justifying a finding of waived. Waiver is seen more as a sanction than a consequence. As a consequence the fundamental principle driving the waiver decisions today is fairness — fairness in finding a waiver and in deciding the scope of the waiver (the body of other communications that must be disclosed in order to give context and meaning to each).

143 PRACTICES

Limited waivers without the consequences. Courts have generally rejected the concept of limited waivers — voluntarily disclosing a privilege communication to one person and then resisting its disclosure to another under a claim of privilege. While sanctioned by one court in the context of disclosures to a government agency,[379] it has been rejected by all others.[380] This has given rise to great concern in the corporate world because U.S. Attorneys

---

[378] *See* PAUL R. RICE, ATTORNEY-CLIENT PRIVILEGE IN THE UNITED STATES, Chapter Nine, Waiver (Thomson West 2nd ed. 1999).

[379] United States v. Massachusetts Institute of Technology, 129 F.3d 681 (1st Cir. 1997); Salomon Bros. Treasury Litig. v. Steinhardt Partners, L.P. (In re Steinhardt Partners, L.P.), 9 F.3d 230, 236 (2d Cir. 1993); Permian Corp. v. United States, 665 F.2d 1214, 1221 n.13 (D.C. Cir. 1981); In re Weiss, 596 F.2d 1185 (4th Cir. 1979); Diversified Industries, Inc. v. Meredith, 572 F.2d 596 (8th Cir. 1977); In re Syncor Erisa Litig., 229 F.R.D. 636, 2005 U.S. Dist. LEXIS 22377, *31-39 (C.D. Cal. July 6, 2005); In re Columbia/HCA Healthcare Corp., 192 F.R.D. 575, 579 (M.D. Tenn. 2000) aff'd 293 F.3d 289 (6th Cir. June 10, 2002) Neal v. Honeywell, Inc., 942 F. Supp. 388 (N.D. Ill. 1995); Feinberg v. Hibernia Corp., 1993 WL 92516, *4 (E.D. La. Mar. 23, 1993).

[380] Genentech, Inc. v. U.S. Intern. Trade Com'n, 122 F.3d 1409 (Fed. Cir. 1997)

and government agencies are putting great pressure on them to voluntary relinquish their privilege claims to avoid regulatory and prosecutorial consequences that they find undesirable. They would like to cooperate, but they are concerned about the broader waiver implications when later involved in litigation with other parties.

The solution for these corporations is to have a judge issue a protective order preserving the privilege, even though the client is disclosing communications inconsistent with the requirement of confidentiality. Unlike confidentiality agreements, and reservations, which most courts will not honor in future litigation, because the client cannot say one thing and do another, when a judicial order is signed, the inconsistency is ignored.[381]

XI. BURDEN OF PERSUASION — IN CAMERA INSPECTION — PROCEDURES FOR RAISING AND RESOLVING CLAIMS

PRINCIPLES

The party raising the attorney-client privilege claim as an excuse for disclosing certain facts has the burden of persuading the court that the privilege is applicable. Relative to documents claimed to be privileged, the claiming party must properly assert the claim by notifying the demanding party, and, after informal attempts to resolve the dispute have failed, formally documenting the nature of the claim in a privilege log (giving details such as who wrote it, to whom it was addressed, who received copies, number of pages, purpose, and a general description of its content). When judicial intervention is sought by either the demanding or responding party, the privilege log must be accompanied by an affidavit from a knowledgeable person in which the expectation of confidentiality is documented with an assurance that the subjective expectation is objectively reasonable — that is, that confidentiality has, in fact, been maintained.[382]

To ensure the representations about the documents are accurate and all details of the documents are addressed, the court should examine the document *in camera* — outside the presence of the parties.[383]

---

[381] *See* PAUL R. RICE, ATTORNEY-CLIENT PRIVILEGE IN THE UNITED STATES, 311:23, Confidentiality Agreements (ThomsonWest 2d ed. 1999).

[382] *See generally*, PAUL R. RICE, ATTORNEY-CLIENT PRIVILEGE IN THE UNITED STATES, ch. 11, Procedures (Thomson West 2d ed. 1999).

[383] *See, e.g.*, United Coal Cos. v. Powell Const. Co., 839 F.2d 958, 966 (3rd Cir. 1988) ("proper procedure for [judicial] consideration [of any attorney-client privilege claim] is . . .in camera inspection by the court"); In re Grand Jury Witness, 695 F.2d 359, 362 (9th Cir. 1982) ("proper procedure for asserting the attorney-client privilege as to particular documents, or portions thereof, would have been for appellants to submit them in camera for the court's inspection, providing an explanation

144 PRACTICES

Privilege logs have been inadequate vis-a-vis e-mail communications. The manner in which privilege logs are constructed for e-mail communications has been both inadequate and misleading.

Each e-mail communication should be identified on the privilege log with a disclosure of who received copies and the general nature of its content. One description for an entire e-mail thread containing multiple messages is facially inadequate.[384] Both the content and recipients of each message are often different. In the past, when each message was exchanged through hard copy memoranda, separate claims had to be made for each memorandum. The modern convenience of electronic messaging doesn't eliminate the need for this.

When separate sentences and paragraphs of communications address different issues, each sentence or paragraph must be identified in the privilege log. This is a particular problem with e-mail communications that are more like conversations than letters. When individuals are in constant contact with one another on many different topics, numerous unrelated matters are often discussed in a single message. Therefore, one description is often inadequate.

---

of how the information fit within the privilege."); United States v. Tratner, 511 F.2d 248, 252 (7th Cir. 1975) ("The responsibility of determining whether the privilege exists rests upon the District Judge and not upon the lawyer whose client claims the privilege. . . . Where this evidence may be presented only by revealing the very information sought to be protected by the privilege, an in camera inspection of the evidence may be appropriate."); Schwimmer v. United States, 232 F.2d 855, 864 (8th Cir. 1956) ("[I]t is to be remembered that existence of the privilege is not a basis for keeping the documents from having to be brought before the court. The privilege is not self-operative against a judicially required production, since the court is entitled to an opportunity to make [in camera] inspection of any such documents in order to satisfy itself that they are in fact privileged . . . 'the individual citizen may not resolve himself into a court , and himself determine [a question of privilege as to] the contents of books and papers required to be produced.'").

[384] *See* In re Universal Service Fund Telephone Billing Practices Litig., 2005 U.S. Dist. LEXIS 39804, *6-15 (D. Kan. July 26, 2005) (The court explained why a separate listing of each e-mail message was critical to the privilege resolution process, but acknowledged the difficulties this creates. "[R]equiring each e-mail within a strand to be listed separately on a privilege log is a laborious, time-intensive task for counsel. And, of course, that task adds considerably expense for the clients involved; even for very well-financed corporate defendants such as those in the case at bar, this is a very significant drawback to modern commercial litigation. But the court finds that adherence to such a procedure is essential to ensuring that privilege is asserted only where necessary to achieve its purpose, e.g., in the case of the attorney-client privilege, protecting disclosures made to obtain legal advice which might not have been made absent the existence of the privilege. In any event, the court strongly encourages counsel, in the preparation of future privilege logs, to list each e-mail within a strand as a separate entry. Otherwise, the client may suffer a waiver of the attorney-client privilege or work product protection (and the lawyer may later draw a claim from the client).")

145 PRACTICES

Don't forget the metadata in your privilege log. Behind all electronic evidence (e.g., e-mails, spreadsheets, accounting records and even the most simple letter) is metadata — data about the information appearing on the face of the document. This is information about the history, tracking, or management of an electronic document. One report defined metadata as "information about a particular data set which describes how, when and by whom it was collected, created, accessed, or modified and how it is formatted (including data demographics such a size, location, storage requirements and media information)."[385]

This information is generally not visible when a document is printed or converted to an image file. This data can be altered, and can be extracted from a file and converted to its own document. It can be inaccurate because it can be altered. It can be misleading when a form document is used only as a template but another person drafted a document on that form. The metadata will show the original author of the template as the author of the document on the template. While the metadata is usually created automatically by a computer, it can also be supplied by a user. For example, Microsoft Excel spreadsheets and applications such as Word and PowerPoint will contain the following metadata: author name or initials, company or organization name, identification of computer or network server or hard disk where documents is saved, names of previous document authors, document revisions and versions, hidden text or cells, template information, other file properties and summary information, non-visible portion or embedded objects, personalized views, and comments.[386]

The metadata underlying word processor documents is seldom critical to understanding the substance of the document. Though not important to understanding the substance of the document, the underlying metadata of a word processor document will provide critical evidence of its distribution, and therefore, whether the document's confidentiality has been preserved. By contrast, the metadata underlying spreadsheets or undifferentiated masses or tables of data is often critical to understanding the relationships between the data presented. In the latter instances, it has been held that the producing party must produce the documents in the form in which they are maintained for business purposes.[387]

---

[385] The Sedona Guidelines: Best Practice Guidelines & Commentary for Managing Information & Records in the Electronic Age (The Sedona Conference Working Group Series, Sept. 2005 Version. http://www.thesedonaconference.org/content/miscFiles/TSG9_05.pdf.

[386] Microsoft Office Online: Find and Remove Metadata (Hidden Information) in Your Legal Documents, http://office.microsoft.com/en-us/assistance/HA010776461033.aspx.

[387] Williams v. Sprint/United Management Co., 230 F.R.D. 640, 2005 U.S. Dist. LEXIS 21966 (D. Kan. Sept. 29, 2005).

To avoid the inadvertent disclosures of irrelevant, proprietary, or privileged information not visible on the face of a document, software programs are available that remove the metadata. This "scrubbing" of documents, however, can constitute spoliation if it is done in a litigation context without the consent of the adverse party or permission of the court.[388] To avoid a spoliation sanction, the scrubbing must be done as a matter of course in the daily maintenance of the documents. In the absence of such a routine practice, the producing party must produce the documents as they are maintained in the ordinary course of business (with the metadata)[389] or assert privilege on those portions being withheld. This requires that each identifiable portion of metadata be listed on a privilege log, with a general description of its content documenting why it is privileged. Failure to do so can result in the waiver of all privilege claims.[390]

146 PRACTICES

Allocation of burdens. The privilege proponent does not have the initial burden of proving the inapplicability of all possible means of losing the privilege. Once the privilege proponent presents sufficient evidence to establish the basic elements of the privilege, the burden of going forward with evidence shifts to the opponent. Only after the party opposing the privilege presents credible evidence to support a claim that the privilege has been lost is the proponent required to negative the claim of waiver.[391]

---

[388] Spoliation is the intentional destruction of evidence that is relevant to pending or reasonably anticipated litigation. It is not spoliation to destroy documents and information on a regular basis, outside of any litigation context. Of course, when the prospect of litigation arises, the practice must cease. *See* Paul R. RICE, E-EVIDENCE: LAW AND PRACTICE, ch. 2 (ABA 2005)

[389] The producing party has the initial burden seek a protective order. "The initial burden with regard to the disclosure of the metadata would therefore be placed on the party to whom the request or order to produce is directed. The burden to object to the disclosure of metadata is appropriately placed on the party ordered to produce its electronic documents as they are ordinarily maintained because that party already has access to the metadata and is in the best position to determine whether producing it is objectionable. Placing the burden on the producing party is further supported by the fact that metadata is an inherent party of an electronic document, and its removal ordinarily requires an affirmative act by the producing party that alters the electronic document." Williams v. Sprint/United Management Co., 2005 U.S. Dist. LEXIS 21966, *39- 40 (D. Kan. Sept. 29, 2005).

[390] Williams v. Sprint/United Management Co., 230 F.R.D. 640, 2005 U.S. Dist. LEXIS 21966 , *44-45 (D. Kan. Sept. 29, 2005) ("Defendant has not provided the Court with even a general description of the purportedly privileged metadata that was scrubbed from the spreadsheets. As Defendant has failed to provide any privilege log for the electronic documents it claims contain metadata that will reveal privileged communications or attorney work product, the Court holds that Defendant has waived any attorney-client privilege or work product with regard to the spreadsheets' metadata except for the metadata directly corresponding to the adverse impact analyses and social security number information , which the Court has permitted Defendant to remove from the spreadsheets.")..

[391] Perkins v. Gregg County, 1995 U.S. Dist. LEXIS 6898, *3-4 (E.D. Tex. May 11, 1995) ("The burden of proof regarding a privilege's applicability rests on the party invoking it . . . Once the priv-

147 PRACTICES

In camera inspection a necessity. While judges may resist it because it is labor intensive, *in camera* inspection is *necessary* if the judge expects to serve as an independent fact finder vis-a-vis the elements of the privilege.[392] Without looking at the allegedly privileged communication, the judge cannot verify that the descriptions in the privilege log and supporting affidavits are either accurate or complete. Often portions of communications serve both legal and business purposes — and, if segregable, need to be excised and produced. It is common both for initials on documents to be neither mentioned nor identified and for interlineations to go unattributed (both of which could signal an inappropriate circulation of the communication and, therefore, a loss of confidentiality).

One judge concluded that the accuracy of adversarial descriptions was becoming an increasing problem because of the changing pressures of law practice. In *Bristol-Myers Squibb Company v. Rhone-Poulenc Rorer, Incor-*

---

ilege has been established, the burden shifts to the other party to prove any applicable exception."). *See generally*, P. R. RICE, ATTORNEY-CLIENT PRIVILEGE IN THE UNITED STATES, § 11:9 p. 84 (West Group 2nd ed. 1999) ("The opponent can succeed only if he is able to present evidence that is sufficient to establish a *prima facie* case of waiver, or an exception to the privilege is applicable and the proponent has failed to rebut the opponent's *prima facie* showing.").

[392] *See* PaineWebber Group, Inc. v. Zinsmeyer Trusts Partnership, 187 F.3d 988, 992 (8th Cir. 1999) ("Because privilege disputes can only be resolved by in camera review of a document, formal resolution of such disputes is tedious and difficult. When many documents are at issue, the tribunal will of course want the party seeking discovery to limit the number it challenges. The tribunal ultimately decides what information must be disclosed on a privileged document log. Because that log is the basis upon which the party seeking discovery decides whether to request in camera review of a particular document, when the disclosure is inadequate — for example, PaineWebber's use of blue sheets to replace allegedly privileged documents in the compliance officer's file — the party seeking discovery must either demand in camera review of all documents, or ask the tribunal to require greater disclosure on the log. While this awkward process may seem to present the opportunity for a party to 'hide' damaging documents by providing a deceptive or inaccurate privileged document log, inadequacies in the log will become apparent to the tribunal if the party seeking discovery demands in camera review of some documents, and stiff sanctions may be imposed on a party whose log is found to be inaccurate or dishonest."); In re Bevill, Bresler & Schulman Asset Management Corp., 805 F.2d 120, 125 n.2 (3rd Cir. 1986) (rejecting the contention that in camera review violates the attorney-client privilege "because in camera review is frequently the only way to resolve whether in fact the privilege asserted applies."); Avery Dennison Corp. v. Four Pillars, 1999 U.S. Dist. LEXIS 21019, *15 (D.D.C. Oct. 14, 1999) ("I cannot possibly fulfill my judicial responsibilities without seeing the documents."). *But see,* Nishika, Ltd. v. Fuji Photo Film Co., Ltd., 1998 U.S. Dist. LEXIS 21748, *6-7 (D. Nev. June 2, 1998) ("In camera review is not generally favored. . . . There must be a sufficient evidentiary showing which creates a legitimate issue as to the application of the privilege asserted. . . . In camera review is appropriate only after the party seeking it has submitted sufficient affidavits and other evidence to the extent it can."). This type of evidentiary showing is both unfair to the demanding party, with no access to the communication, and inconsistent with the judge's independent fact finding role.

porated[393] the judge concluded that the changing pressures of law firm work require courts to be particularly careful in reviewing privilege claims raised by outside counsel.

In civil litigation, the importance of strict construction, in the light of changes in the profession, is particularly noteworthy. Liberal construction of the attorney/client privilege leads to attorneys "pushing the envelope," as has been done in this case, which puts undue hardship on the court and can obfuscate the truth. Lawyers, particularly in larger firms, are no longer members of monolithic firms which will support them financially despite the loss of a client, as was often the case in the past. Accordingly, lawyers are increasingly dependent on the financial support of their clients to a degree similar to salaried in-house counsel. Under these circumstances, the substantial monetary rewards involved create financial pressure not to disclose relevant documents to opposing counsel to a considerably greater extent than was the case in a generation ago when law firms would support partners and associates willing to interpret the law correctly and not just in accordance with his/her clients' wishes. The attorney-client privilege in civil matters should be narrowly construed and, perhaps, reconsidered in light of these changes in the profession, by those appellate courts who have not yet adopted a strict construction rule.[394]

With the increased problems created by electronic communications, *in camera* inspection is even more critical to the fair resolution of claims. If judges don't have the time to attend to their responsibilities as an independent finder of facts, they should be encouraged to appoint special masters, who are paid by the hour, and require the costs of those substitute judicial officers to be borne by the parties whose claims are creating the expense.

XII. APPLICATIONS — ATTORNEY-CLIENT PRIVILEGE

ONE

Peter James believed that his wife was being unfaithful to him. Distraught, Peter went to the office of his attorney and close personal friend to discuss his marital problems. Upon arriving at the lawyer's office, Peter learned that his friend was out playing golf for the day. The attorney's investigator, however, was in the office and offered his services to Peter in the attorney's name.

On Peter's suggestion, the two of them went into a private office to discuss Peter's problem. Peter explained his suspicions to the investigator, stating, "I would leave my wife in a minute if I knew she was cheating on me." The inves-

---

[393] 1998 WL 474206, *2 (S.D.N.Y. Aug. 12, 1998).

[394] *See generally*, P.R. RICE, ATTORNEY-CLIENT PRIVILEGE IN THE UNITED STATES, ch. 11, Procedures §§ 11:14-15 (West Group 2nd ed. 1999).

tigator then told Peter that Peter could engage the law firm's services to ascertain whether Peter's wife was, in fact, being unfaithful to him. Peter agreed to the arrangement.

The investigator discovered that Peter's wife was having an affair with her aerobics instructor. Upon informing Peter of this fact during a private meeting arranged by Peter, Peter exclaimed, "What can I do? I really want to get back at her!" After his wife's death under suspicious circumstances, Peter is indicted for her murder.

At Peter's trial for murder, the prosecution calls the investigator as a witness. The prosecution then attempts to elicit from the investigator the substance of Peter's conversation with the investigator on the day that the investigator informed Peter of his wife's infidelity. Peter's counsel objects on the ground that the conversation is protected by the attorney-client privilege.

For communications to be protected by the attorney-client privilege, the party invoking the privilege must establish four elements to the trial court's satisfaction pursuant to Rule 104(a): (1) that the client consulted an attorney; (2) that the consultation was for the purpose of obtaining legal advice or assistance; (3) that the client intended that the communications be confidential at the time that he made them; and (4) that the requisite confidentiality has been maintained.

Although the investigator is not an attorney, courts have expanded the circle of confidentiality to include individuals who act as an attorney's agent in the attorney's representation of his client. Because the investigator offered his services in the attorney's name and Peter accepted them as such, the trial court should conclude that Peter did consult with an attorney when he engaged the law firm's investigative services, even though he never did actually confer with one. *See Baird v. Koerner*, 279 F.2d 623 (9th Cir. 1960); *Dabney v. Investment Corp. of Am.*, 82 F.R.D. 464 (E.D. Pa. 1979).

The trial court should also conclude that Peter intended his communications with the investigator to remain confidential, in that Peter expressly requested a private consultation, both in his first meeting with the investigator and in the meeting in question in this problem. In that there is no indication in the problem that the confidentiality of the communication has not been maintained, the court should also find that this element has been met.

It is not clear, however, that Peter consulted his attorney for the purpose of obtaining legal advice. The evidence indicates that Peter consulted his attorney to confirm or allay his suspicions concerning his wife's infidelity, not to obtain legal advice concerning a possible divorce proceeding. Courts have held that investigative services are not necessarily legal in nature. *See, e.g., In re Grand Jury Subpoena*, 599 F.2d 504 (2d Cir. 1979); *United States v. Demauro*, 581 F.2d 50 (2d Cir. 1978); *Diamond v. City of Mobile*, 86 F.R.D. 324 (S.D. Ala. 1978). Consequently, the trial court should reject Peter's contention that the conversation in question is protected from disclosure by the attorney-client privilege because Peter's primary purpose was investigative in nature.

Because the prosecution is attempting to introduce an out-of-court state-ment to prove the truth of the matter asserted, namely that Peter had the req-uisite intent to murder his wife, the statement's introduction has possible hearsay implications. The statement is still admissible, however, both under a common law exception to the hearsay rule and as nonhearsay under Rule 801(d)(2)(A) of the federal rules, as an admission.

TWO

John Doe has been the target of a grand jury investigation for more than a year. The grand jury has recently issued a subpoena duces tecum to Doe's attor-ney requesting certain documents that Doe sent to his attorney concerning Doe's personal and corporate legal affairs. The documents requested in the sub-poena include the following: Doe's personal tax return for that year which he signed but which is yet unfiled; notes relating to a contemplated lease; and a prospectus for a stock offering that Doe had instructed his attorney not to com-plete. Doe's attorney moves to quash the subpoena, objecting that all of the material requested is protected by the attorney-client privilege.

One of the requirements for the successful invocation of the attorney-client privilege is that the client intends that the communications in question remain confidential. If a client communicates information to his attorney with the understanding that the information will be revealed to others, the attorney-client privilege will not protect the communication from subsequent disclosure. *See In re Grand Jury Proceedings (John Doe)*, 727 F.2d 1392, 1356 (4th Cir. 1982) (quoting *United States v. Cote*, 456 F.2d 142, 145 (8th Cir. 1972)). In determining whether a client intended or assumed that his communications would remain confidential, courts look to the nature of the services for which the client had consulted his attorney to ascertain whether the client could reason-ably expect those services to entail publication of his communications. *See United States v. (Under Seal)*, 748 F.2d 871, 877 (4th Cir. 1984).

(1) Doe would not have expected his *personal tax return* to remain confiden-tial because although as yet unfiled, he clearly intended it to be filed, as wit-nessed by the fact that he signed it.

(2) The *notes relating to the contemplated lease* are problematic. It is not clear in the problem what the client intended when the communications reflected in the notes were made to the attorney for the purpose of having him prepare the lease. If the client simply related information that he wanted included in the lease, one could reasonably conclude that there was no expec-tation of confidentiality — the lawyer was simply serving as a conduit through whom the information was going to be conveyed to a third party. If, however, Doe can establish that the notes related to communications upon which he was seeking advice or assistance were part of the preliminary counseling stages preceding the finalization of a lease, then there could have been an expectation of confidentiality. This is a factual decision to be made by the presiding judge pursuant to Rule 104(a).

(3) The *prospectus* is like the lease notes but in a later stage of legal assistance. It was drafted by the attorney on the basis of information provided to him by the client that was probably summarized in notes of the attorney. Although the prospectus was drafted for eventual public distribution, this should not necessarily mean that the client would have had no expectation of confidentiality relative to any of his communications to the lawyer about what might go into it. Since the prospectus could not have been distributed without the approval of the client (as witnessed by the fact that work on it was discontinued at the direction of the client), there is no reason why confidentiality could not be expected.

THREE

Attorney A retained Attorney B for a confidential conference concerning the legal problems of a certain taxpayer. Attorney A specifically requested that Attorney B not divulge the name of either Attorney A or the taxpayer as such information could result in a civil or criminal tax suit against the taxpayer. Two weeks later, Attorney B delivered a check to the Internal Revenue Service (IRS) for $200,000 on behalf of the unnamed taxpayer. The IRS subsequently subpoenaed Attorney B to give testimony before a grand jury concerning the "tax liability of taxpayer John Doe, on whose behalf B delivered a check to the IRS in the amount of $200,000." Attorney B appeared before the grand jury but refused to answer any of the Government's questions regarding his profession or the identity of the client on whose behalf he delivered the check in question. Attorney B bases his refusal to answer on the ground that such information is protected from disclosure by the attorney-client privilege. The Government argues that the attorney-client privilege does not allow Attorney B to refuse to disclose his client's identity.

The attorney-client privilege extends to the substance of matters that a client communicates to his attorney in professional confidence. Thus, a client's identity, or the fact that a given individual is a client, are matters that the attorney-client privilege usually will not protect from disclosure. See *United States v. Tratner*, 511 F.2d 248 (7th Cir. 1975); *United States v. Pander*, 475 F.2d 37 (5th Cir. 1973). A narrow exception to this general rule of disclosure of a client's identity applies if, as a result of information already in the Government's possession, disclosure of the client's identity would supply the "last link" in an existing chain of incriminating evidence likely to lead to the client's identity. See *In re Grand Jury Subpoena Bierman*, 765 F.2d 1014, 1019 (11th Cir. 1985).

In this case, Attorney B's disclosure of his client's identity could ultimately result in the disclosure of the taxpayer's motive for seeking legal advice. Inasmuch as such disclosure could be tantamount to an acknowledgment of guilt by the taxpayer of the very offenses for which the taxpayer had sought legal advice, a court should consider the taxpayer's name to fall within the ambit of the attorney-client privilege. *In re Grand Jury Investigation No. 83-2-25*, 723 F.2d 447 (8th Cir. 1983); *see also In re Grand Jury Proceedings*, 517 F.2d 666 (5th Cir. 1975) (attorney-client privilege protects from disclosure client's motive for consulting attorney and also protects client's identity if such protection is necessary to protect privileged motive).

FOUR

An employee of the 1340 Corporation, during the course of his deliveries, struck a pedestrian with the company truck. The accident occurred on corporation property within viewing distance of the corporation's loading dock. Consequently, in addition to the truck driver, two other corporation employees witnessed the accident, the loading dock foreman on duty at the time of the accident, and an assembly line worker who was on his break. Pursuant to corporation policy, which required any witness to any accident on company property to report said accident to their immediate supervisor, each of the employees made written statements concerning the accident. When the pedestrian sued the corporation, the written statements were forwarded to in-house counsel. The plaintiff has served interrogatories on the corporation seeking any statements of witnesses to the accident that the corporation possesses. The corporation withheld the statements on the basis of the attorney-client privilege. This was inappropriate.

Communications by a corporation's employees are privileged if the employees made such communications to an attorney at the direction of corporate superiors on matters within the scope of the employees' corporate duties for the purpose of obtaining legal advice and assistance. *See Upjohn Co. v. United States*, 449 U.S. 383, 394 (1981). None of the statements meet these requirements.

Although the statements by the truck driver and the loading dock foreman relate to matters within the scope of their employment, that of the assembly line worker apparently does not. Consequently, the assembly line worker's statement would not fall within the protection of the attorney-client privilege for that reason alone. More importantly, none of the witnesses made their statements for the clear purpose of obtaining legal advice or assistance. The corporation's requirement for making accident reports should be viewed as a device for developing accurate statistics on accidents within the corporation, and not necessarily as a device for developing evidence for purposes of legal advice. Significantly, the corporation did not forward the statements to its attorney until after the suit was initiated, indicating that the corporation's purpose in maintaining the witness reports was primarily nonlegal in nature. *See D.I. Chadbourne, Inc. v. Superior Court of City and County of San Fran.*, 60 Cal. 2d 723, 36 Cal. Rptr. 468, 388 P.2d 700 (1964) (the question of whether a report that corporation requires its employee to make to attorney is privileged is determined by corporation's purpose in requiring report). Had the purpose for making the statements been to obtain legal advice, the fact that they were made to another employee (a supervisor) would not affect their privileged status so long as the element of confidentiality had been maintained. *See United States v. AT & T*, Special Masters' Guidelines for the Resolution of Privilege Claims, Guideline 10(a), 86 F.R.D. 603 (D.D.C. 1980). Because the statements would not have been privileged while in the corporation's possession, they cannot acquire a privileged status under the attorney-client privilege merely by their transfer to an attorney. Consequently, the corporation must retrieve these documents from its attorney and deliver them to the plaintiff pursuant to his interrogatory.

FIVE

Sam Jones was a widower with no children and only two living relatives. Jones determined that he should make a will and sent the following letter to his attorney:

Dear Mr. Smith:

Please prepare a will for me leaving all my property to my nephew Ralph Jones. I do not wish to leave anything to my nephew Joseph because he is possessed by demons and devils. I am determined that the devil will not get any of my property.

Sincerely,
Sam Jones.

Attorney Smith prepared the will as Jones had directed. At the execution of this will, Smith and his secretary witnessed Jones' signature.

After Jones' death, Joseph challenges the will on the ground that Jones was incompetent at the time of the will's execution. In support of his contention, Joseph seeks to introduce into the probate proceeding a copy of the letter that Jones had sent to Smith requesting him to draft the will in controversy. Joseph also seeks to elicit testimony from Smith regarding Jones' "insane delusion" that Joseph was possessed by devils and demons as evidenced, in part, by Jones' comportment at the will's execution. Smith, representing Jones' estate, objects to the letter's introduction and refuses to testify as to any communication between himself and Jones on the ground that both the letter and the testimony are protected from disclosure by the attorney-client privilege. Smith also refuses to testify as to Jones' behavior at the time the will was executed on the same ground.

The attorney-client privilege survives the death of the client. Consequently, if the letter met all the elements of the privilege, it would, in other circumstances, be entitled to the privilege's protection from disclosure. The privilege is not applicable in this instance, however, because the testator's heirs seek to introduce the communications in a contest of the will's validity. *See United States v. Osborn*, 561 F.2d 1334, 1340 (9th Cir. 1977); *Stegman v. Miller*, 515 S.W.2d 244 (Ky. 1974). *But see In re Estate of Karras*, 166 N.E.2d 781 (Ohio 1959). In this limited situation, courts have used the legal fiction that the testator would want his attorney to reveal the contents of his prior confidential communications to effectuate his intent through the will.

As to Smith's objection to Joseph's attempt to seek Smith's testimony concerning Jones' comportment at the time the will was executed, it is without merit. By making his attorney a subscribing witness to his will, courts deem the client to have waived all objections to the attorney's testifying with respect to the will signing.

SIX

Corporation Y has recently become the target of a takeover attempt by T. Good Pickins, an infamous and highly successful corporate raider. To oust Pickins from the corporation, the Board of Directors voted to pay Pickins a substantial sum to repurchase his stock in Corporation Y. A small number of shareholders in Corporation Y who had been in favor of Pickins' attempted takeover brought a derivative action on behalf of Corporation Y against the Board of Directors, alleging that the Board's "greenmail" payments were a waste of corporate assets. As part of discovery in the shareholders' derivative suit, the attorney for the shareholders requests copies of internal correspondence between the corporation's General Counsel and the members of the Board of Directors. The internal correspondence allegedly concerns the General Counsel's opinion as to the legality of the proposed payments to Pickins. The shareholders' knowledge of the correspondence stems from an unverified account of a junior member of the General Counsel's staff. The Board of Directors refuses to produce the document, stating both that the document does not exist, and that if it did, it would be protected from disclosure by the attorney-client privilege. The shareholders filed a motion to compel discovery.

In a shareholders' derivative suit against corporate officers, the corporation may assert the attorney-client privilege against shareholders seeking information relating to the suit. *See Garner v. Wolfinbarger*, 430 F.2d 1093 (5th Cir. 1970). The shareholders, however, may present evidence to show cause why the privilege should not be invoked in the particular instance. What constitutes good cause for holding that the attorney-client privilege will not apply in a particular case is determined on a case-by-case basis. Factors that a court should consider include: the small number of stockholders seeking the information in question; the nature of the alleged wrongful activity, i.e., the fact that the Board of Directors' alleged wrongdoings were potentially actionable, but not criminal; and the fact that the existence of internal correspondence was unverified and denied. All of these factors weigh against overriding the corporation's assertion of the privilege. The fact that the information sought by the shareholders might not be available from any other source, except perhaps through the testimony of the junior member of the General Counsel's staff, would not be sufficient to outweigh the considerations set forth above that weigh in favor of the corporation's ability to assert the privilege. Consequently, the corporation should be able to deny discovery of the internal correspondence on the ground that disclosure of the document would violate the corporate entity's attorney-client privilege.

SEVEN

Sawyer is being tried for bribing Crowe, a city official. Crowe had previously been convicted of accepting bribes on other occasions and is currently in state prison. Before Sawyer's trial, Crowe told his attorney that he had never accepted a bribe from Sawyer but that if the prosecutor would dismiss the remaining charges against Crowe, he would testify that he had. This was overheard by the lawyer's secretary. During Sawyer's trial, Sawyer's attorney seeks to introduce Crowe's statement to his attorney. Crow claims that is protected by the attorney-client privilege.

The trial court permitted Sawyer to introduce the statement. Although the attorney-client privilege protects confidential communications from a client to his attorney, the privilege does not prevent the disclosure of communications made in the furtherance of a crime. Crowe's statement to his attorney was an attempt to have his attorney assist him in the commission of perjury and obstruction of justice. Consequently, the attorney-client privilege should not bar the statement's introduction at Sawyer's trial. *See In re Sawyer's Petition*, 229 F.2d 805 (7th Cir. 1956).

EIGHT

Plaintiff is suing defendant for default on a loan. The terms of the loan are complicated, and the defendant denies that he defaulted. To establish default, the plaintiff seeks the testimony of the attorney who assisted in the preparation of the agreement in question. Specifically, the plaintiff seeks testimony concerning the particular requirements of the loan as contemplated by the parties at the time the attorney prepared the loan document in question. The defendant objects to this testimony, arguing that the attorney-client privilege prohibits its admission into evidence.

The court permitted the plaintiff to elicit the attorney's testimony. If an attorney represents two clients in a matter and the clients subsequently become adversaries over the matter about which they initially sought joint representation, the attorney-client privilege will not prohibit the disclosure of communications that either party had with their attorney. *See LeBlanc v. Broussard*, 198 So. 2d 193 (La. App. 1967).

NINE

Hexagon Corporation and Blairex Corporation signed a merger agreement under which each corporation gave the other access to its business records. The agreement further provided that if it was terminated, each corporation would return all documents it had obtained under the agreement and would hold in confidence all information obtained. Among the documents that Blairex obtained from Hexagon were those Hexagon had created or collected in preparation for litigation. When the merger agreement was terminated, Blairex returned all of Hexagon's documents, but retained microfilm copies with Hexagon's grudging consent.

A government agency began investigating Hexagon and subpoenaed from Blairex copies of all the documents Blairex had received from Hexagon. Hexagon intervened in a subsequent subpoena enforcement proceeding for the purpose of asserting the attorney-client privilege and the work product immunity. Hexagon had prepared the original documents in preparation for litigation.

The attorney-client privilege exists to protect the confidential attorney-client relationship. Any voluntary disclosure of communications made between an attorney and his client is inconsistent with the privilege's purpose and, therefore, results in a waiver of the privilege with regard to those communications voluntarily disclosed. Hexagon's transfer of its business records to Blairex and its subsequent assent to Blairex's retention of those documents constituted a voluntary disclosure of any documents that might have been protected by the attorney-client privilege. Thus, Hexagon has waived its attorney-client privilege with regard to those documents. Courts have rejected limited waiver — disclosing to one party while withholding from another.

The work-product privilege, like the attorney-client privilege, can be waived through disclosure. As the court explained in *United States v. Gulf Oil Corp.*, 760 F.2d 292 (Temp. Emer. Ct. App. 1985), however, there are different standards for determining the waiver of the attorney-client privilege and work product immunity. *United States v. American Tel. & Tel. Co.*, 642 F.2d 1285 (D.C. Cir. 1980). The court in *Gulf Oil* noted that unlike the attorney-client privilege, the work-product privilege protects information only from opposing parties. A disclosure that is not inconsistent with maintaining secrecy against opponents does not waive this privilege. To determine whether a disclosure is inconsistent with this secrecy, the court looks to the existence of common interests between the individual making the disclosure and the individual to whom the disclosure is made *at the time of disclosure*. Here, Hexagon and Blairex were not adversaries at the time of disclosure. Rather, they were in the process of becoming parent and subsidiary. This is a strong common interest. Disclosure from Hexagon to Blairex, therefore, was not inconsistent with secrecy and did not waive the work-product privilege.

TEN

AirCo, the inventor of an inhalant anesthetic, entered into a license agreement with Abbott Marketing, Inc., for the sale and marketing of the invention. Due to a subsequent dispute over the terms of the agreement, AirCo filed a diversity action against Abbott in federal district court in the Northern District of Illinois. Abbott counterclaimed against AirCo for an alleged breach of the license agreement.

During discovery, both sides sought numerous documents from the other relating to the license arrangement. Both sides also sought to prevent the disclosure of certain documents through an assertion of the attorney-client privilege. Abbott asserted the privilege for documents described in an index filed with the court as follows:

> Certain notes written by Ms. Mayer, secretary to Mr. Baker, the Executive Vice President of Abbott's International Division, transmitting summaries of legal advice from Mr. Barmak, division counsel at Abbott.

Abbott supplied the notes described above to the presiding judge for an *in camera* inspection. Abbott did not, however, supply any additional supporting materials.

AirCo asserted the attorney-client privilege for a series of documents involving Mr. Reich, the president and chief executive officer of AirCo from 1979 to 1983. From 1973 to 1978, Reich had held positions in AirCo as Senior Vice President and Executive Vice President. AirCo described the documents for which it claimed the privilege in an index of privilege claims as follows:

> AirCo Document #1: Multiple copies and excerpts of a draft of an internal memorandum on the FDA's position on testing isoflurans for carcinogenity. A portion of the internal memorandum discusses AirCo's legal and business options in response to a letter from the FDA. The internal memorandum was drafted by Mr. Mashek, an attorney at AirCo, and was signed by Mr. Reich. The memorandum was addressed to Mr. Rashek, a member of AirCo's board of directors. The identity of other recipients of the memorandum is unknown.

> AirCo Document #2: Memoranda drafted by an AirCo attorney reporting on conferences held between AirCo representatives and FDA officials. These memoranda advised members of the AirCo control group of possible actions that the FDA might take with regard to the continued sale of isoflurane.

In support of its claim of privilege for these documents, AirCo filed the personal affidavit of Mr. Reich, in which he recited his employment history at AirCo and the circumstances under which the documents in question were drafted and maintained.

The court's first step in resolving these privilege claims is to determine what law governs the question. Under Rule 501, a federal district court exercising diversity jurisdiction must apply the privilege law of the state whose substantive law governs the merits of the action. In the problem, the law of the forum, Illinois, presumably governs the action. Illinois follows the "control group" test enunciated in Philadelphia v. Westinghouse Elec. Corp., 210 F. Supp. 484 (E.D. Pa. 1962), to determine who personifies the corporation for purposes of the attorney-client privilege. Thus, to determine whether the corporations in question consulted an attorney for purposes of obtaining legal advice, one must consider whether the corporate individuals in question were "in a position to control or even to take a substantial part in a decision about any action the corporation may take upon the advice of the attorney [consulted]." *Westinghouse,* 210 F. Supp. at 485. With the "control group" test in mind, the court examined the applicability of the privilege to each of the documents.

Abbott Documents

Under the classical definition of the attorney-client privilege, for responsive communications from an attorney to his client to acquire a privileged status, the response must reveal *the client's* confidential communications. This necessarily requires that the individual claiming the privilege for his attorney's responsive communications must establish the privileged status of the initial communication to the attorney. Abbott clearly did not make such a showing. In Abbott's description of the documents in question, there was no reference to Abbott's initial communication to Mr. Barmak, Abbott's attorney. Thus, the court has no way of knowing whether legal advice was Abbott's primary purpose in its initial communication to Barmak, whether Abbott anticipated that its initial communication would remain confidential (as reflected, in part, by the persons to whom Abbott made the communication), and, if Abbott had anticipated confidentiality, whether it has subsequently been maintained (as reflected, in part, by the breadth of its distribution). Because the court cannot ascertain from the documents that Abbott has submitted whether Abbott's initial communication with its attorney Barmak was privileged, the court also cannot determine whether the attorney-client privilege should protect the documents that Abbott seeks to protect from disclosure. Inasmuch as the burden of establishing the existence of a privilege rests squarely with the privilege's proponent, and Abbott failed to carry its burden with regard to the classical requirement that a proponent establish the foundation for derivative protection of responsive attorney communications, the trial court should have denied the privilege with regard to the Abbott documents.

Courts, however, have been very lax in enforcing this requirement for the extension of derivative protection to responsive attorney communications to a client. Courts have tended to grant privilege claims for communications from an attorney to his client on the proponent's mere statement that the attorney rendered legal advice. *See Abbott Labs. v. AirCo, Inc.,* Docket No. 82-C-3292 (N.D. Ill. Nov. 5, 1985). Proposed Rule 503(b), which was never enacted, reflected the same laxity by the courts in the enforcement of the privilege's requirements. Rule 503(b) stated that the attorney-client privilege under the federal rules would protect communications "between" the client and his attorney, without distinguishing between who was communicating with whom. *See also Upjohn Co. v. United States,* 449 U.S. 384, 390 (1981). Under such a broad interpretation of the privilege's scope, the privilege might have protected the Abbott documents if Abbott had made a showing that the documents themselves, not the initial communications to the attorney that prompted the documents, met the requirements for the privilege's application. Mr. Baker, as Executive Vice President, would certainly qualify as a member of the "control group," and therefore would have personified the Abbott corporation for purposes of the communications from Barmak, Abbott's counsel. The fact that the notes themselves were drafted by Ms. Mayer does not alter this determination because Ms. Mayer was acting as Baker's secretary and agent. The notes, therefore, arguably were made in the context of an attorney-client relationship. There is no indication, however, of how broadly Ms. Mayer's notes were circulated. Thus, Abbott failed to establish that it anticipated that the notes would remain confidential or that such confidentiality, if anticipated, was maintained. Consequently, even under the more relaxed definition of the scope of the attorney-client privilege, the trial court should deny Abbott's claim of privilege and allow AirCo access to the documents in question. *But see Abbott Labs.* (granting claim of privilege in identical circumstances without considering whether proponent of privilege had adequately demonstrated that documents had enjoyed a limited circulation for purposes of demonstrating proponent's anticipation and maintenance of confidentiality).

AirCo Document #1

The trial court should deny AirCo's claim of privilege for these documents because by AirCo's own admission, the identity of those who might have received the memorandum is unknown. Consequently, regardless of whether the "control group" test or the "subject matter" test were used to define the scope of the privilege in the corporate context, AirCo has not met the requirement of confidentiality with regard to these documents. In addition, even if AirCo had established the requisite confidentiality for these documents, the privilege would not protect from disclosure those portions of the memorandum that address business as opposed to purely legal matters.

AirCo Document #2

As previously discussed, under the classical definition of the attorney-client privilege, an attorney's responsive communications are not protected unless they reveal a client's prior confidential communications. In this document, the lawyer is reporting on a conference between himself and FDA officials. Because the client was not involved in the underlying communication, the attorney's communications to his client could not possibly fall within the purview of the attorney-client privilege.

The court in *Abbott Labs* held that the attorney-client privilege did not protect these documents, both because they were a summary of non-confidential conversations and, significantly, because they *did not contain legal advice*. A comparison of this result with that reached on the above Abbott claim reveals what appears to be a rapidly developing attitude among judges. When an attorney communicates legal advice to his client, as opposed to communications about matters upon which legal advice may eventually be given (for example, communications relating what witnesses may have stated in depositions), courts tend to protect those communications regardless of what they were based upon or what they reveal directly or indirectly of the client's confidential communications. Courts have tended to treat the attorney's advice as a proprietary secret, not unlike a trade secret, that the client has the right to withhold from others.

ELEVEN

Ventura Corporation brought an action against Cygna Corporation, alleging that Cygna had violated the antitrust laws. During discovery, Ventura sought various documents the production of which Cygna opposed on the ground of attorney-client privilege. The documents fall into two categories:

I. Documents that were found in a file belonging to the attorney who, until his death, advised Cygna on antitrust matters. These documents consisted of letters to and from the attorney and client and dealt with a variety of antitrust matters.

II. Letters from Cygna's counsel to David Wolf, Cygna's president, expressing counsel's opinions as to the legality of the actions of Cygna's that are being litigated in this action. The letter is currently and unexplainedly in the possession of a company with which Cygna is presently litigating a similar antitrust question.

Pursuant to Rule 37(a) of the Federal Rules of Civil Procedure, Ventura moves to compel production of the documents in question.

In analyzing this problem, the trial court must first determine whether the attorney-client privilege is even applicable to the documents in question. If the privilege does apply, then the court must determine whether Cygna has waived the privilege's protection with regard to each category of documents sought. To establish that the privilege applies, Cygna must establish that both groups of documents satisfy each element of the privilege. As documents in an attorney's case file concerning a client's legal matters, absent some indication that Cygna has not maintained the requisite confidentiality, or perhaps that the documents do not reflect only Cygna's communications to its attorney, the documents described in Group I probably fall within the privilege's protection.

Although the attorney-client privilege could also apply to the documents in Group II, those documents will likely be subject to disclosure because Cygna has waived the privilege's protection. The disclosures to a third party of the letters between the attorney and client will constitute a waiver of the privilege, unless Cygna can adequately explain that the breach occurred as a result of an involuntary disclosure. Logically, even if the breach of confidentiality with regard to the letters was a result of involuntary disclosure, there is no reason for treating an involuntary disclosure differently from a voluntary disclosure inasmuch as the requisite confidentiality in either instance has been destroyed by the breach. Given that Cygna has failed to provide any explanation for the breach of confidentiality, it will be construed as destroying the privilege.

Finally, with regard to the documents in Group I, although Cygna has not disclosed the documents to anyone other than its attorney, thereby maintaining the requisite confidentiality with regard to them, it is possible that the waiver of the privilege with regard to the documents in Group II has destroyed the privilege with regard to the limited number of documents in Group I that relate to the same subject matter. Although decisions in this area have been inconsistent, the underlying premise for the "subject matter" waiver doctrine is that courts are not inclined to allow the client to unfairly use his communications with his attorney as a sword when they happen to be favorable to his case, while simultaneously using the attorney-client privilege to shield unfavorable communications. Because there is no indication that Cygna is invoking the privilege unfairly to shield unfavorable communications while using favorable ones to its advantage in this litigation, the court will construe the subject matter waiver narrowly — limiting the scope to opinions about the same conduct.

TWELVE

J.P. Manley Co. is an asbestos manufacturer that is currently involved in litigation throughout the country with individuals who claim to have been injured as a result of exposure to Manley's asbestos. In the most recent action against Manley, the plaintiff requests that Manley produce all documents that Manley had previously disclosed in prior litigation. These documents fall into four categories. Manley objects to the disclosure of all the documents in each category on the ground of attorney-client privilege. In an index filed with the court, Manley described each category of documents as follows:

Category #1: Documents that Manley produced in prior litigation after its claim of privilege was denied by the presiding judge and that decision was affirmed by an appellate court.

Category #2: Documents that Manley produced in prior litigation pursuant to a court order after the trial court considered and denied Manley's claim of attorney-client privilege.

Category #3: Documents that could be protected from disclosure under the attorney-client privilege but that Manley inadvertently disclosed in prior litigation during voluminous discovery under an expedited production schedule. In the prior litigation the presiding judge had issued an order that allowed the parties to retrieve from the opposition documents that had been inadvertently produced under the pressure of the expedited schedule, without prejudice to its claim of attorney-client privilege. All of these documents had been retrieved pursuant to this order, but no privilege claims were ever asserted because the demanding party withdrew its claim for them.

Category #4: Documents that could be protected from disclosure under the attorney-client privilege but that Manley voluntarily produced pursuant to a plaintiff's discovery request.

Each of these categories are evaluated seriatim.

Category #1

Theoretically, Manley destroyed its privilege with regard to the documents in this and every category by disclosing them to third parties because such disclosure eliminated the confidentiality necessary for the privilege's existence. Courts have held, however, that if a party discloses information solely at the direction of the court, such coercive disclosures are not considered waivers of the privilege. To consider such conduct a waiver would discourage parties' voluntary cooperation with court orders. This is particularly true in situations in which the party resisting disclosure has exhausted all legal recourse in his attempt to avoid disclosing his assertedly confidential papers. Thus, the trial court should consider the documents in Category #1 to have been involuntarily disclosed and hold that Manley had not waived its attorney-client privilege with regard to them. Consequently, the trial court would probably allow Manley to resurrect its claim of attorney-client privilege in this most recent litigation.

As an additional consideration, if a prior court has already considered the issue of attorney-client privilege and denied the claim, could that ruling be a bar in the nature of collateral estoppel to Manley's relitigation of that issue in this action? Although logically compelling, courts have not addressed this aspect of court-ordered disclosures of allegedly confidential documents.

Category #2

Theoretically Manley has destroyed its attorney-client privilege with regard to any documents it has disclosed in prior litigation, including the documents in this category, regardless of whether that disclosure was voluntary or involuntary. Nevertheless, courts have generally not considered the attorney-client privilege to be destroyed in these circumstances. Focusing instead on the involuntary nature of the disclosure, courts have held that court-ordered disclosure does not necessarily constitute a waiver of the privilege. *See, e.g., In re Grand Jury Proceedings (Vargas)*, 723 F.2d 1461, 1466 (10th Cir. 1983), *cert. denied*, 105 S. Ct. 90 (1984).

Thus, the issue centers on whether Manley's disclosure of the documents was involuntary despite Manley's failure to exercise all of its legal rights in contesting the documents' disclosure. Courts have not required a party to resist the production of documents that a district court orders disclosed until that order has been affirmed on appeal as a prerequisite to a determination that that party's disclosure of the documents in question was involuntary. Consequently, in this problem the trial court will probably find that Manley has not waived its privilege as to the documents in Category #2, despite Manley's failure to exhaust all of its avenues of legal recourse.

Category #3

The trial court in the previous action recognized the concept of limited waiver with regard to the documents in this category through its use of a protective order that alleviated the serious risk of privilege waiver through inadvertent disclosures of privileged documents during voluminous discovery. The trial court gave effect to that protective order by allowing Manley, upon discovering the documents' privileged nature, to withdraw the privileged document without prejudice to its privilege claim. Courts in subsequent actions have implicitly given effect to a prior trial court's decision to reinstate the attorney-client privilege with regard to documents inadvertently disclosed during voluminous discovery. *See Transamerica Computer Co. v. International Business Machines Corp.*, 573 F.2d 646, 650-51 (9th Cir. 1978). They have done so primarily to encourage parties to cooperate voluntarily with extensive, burdensome pretrial discovery orders. Following such reasoning, the trial court in the problem should respect the previous trial court's assurance of continued or revived protection of the attorney-client privilege, particularly inasmuch as there is no indication in the problem that Manley is attempting to use the attorney-client privilege unfairly in this most recent litigation.

Category #4

Unlike the previous categories of documents, the disclosure of each of which Manley contested in increasing degrees, Manley voluntarily disclosed the documents in Category #4. A client's voluntary disclosure of confidential material not only destroys the confidentiality essential to the privilege's theoretical underpinnings, it also constitutes a clear waiver of the privilege for all subsequent litigation.

Chapter 9

SHORTCUTS TO PROOF

I. PRESUMPTIONS — THE THEORY AND THE PRACTICE

A. PRINCIPLES

The presumption is a mechanism by which the law presumes certain facts to be true by proof of other facts. The facts that must be proven are the *primary facts*. The fact presumed to be true is the *presumed fact*. These presumptions are created on the basis of (1) probability, (2) convenience, (3) fairness and social policy.[395]

Example 1

Following proof that a letter was written, properly addressed to a specific person, stamped, and posted, the law presumes that the addressee received the letter in the due course of the mail. This presumption is based on probability because of the regularity of the public mail service.

Consistent with this presumption, the law makes the return letter received in the mail, without undue delay, referring to the original letter and professing to be a response to it, self-authenticating. Again, because of the regularity of the mails, the law presumes that the response is from the person who signed it, and that if that person is not the individual to whom the original letter was sent, the responding person was the authorized agent of the original addressee.

Example 2

If an individual gives an item to a trucking company to be delivered and can prove that the item was is good condition when delivered to the trucking company, the law presumes that damage to that item while in the company's custody was caused by the company's negligence. This presumption is based on both probability and convenience (the trucking company has the best access to proof).

If more than one carrier is involved in the transport, the law presumes that the last carrier to handle the item was at fault. This presumption

---

[395] *See generally* Paul R. Rice & Roy A. Katriel, Evidence: Common Law & Federal Rules of Evidence, § 10.01[A][1] (LEXIS 4th ed. 2000); McCormick On Evidence § 343, at 520-22 (West Group 5th ed. 1999).

is also based on convenience and access to proof. If the item had been damaged by a previous carrier, the next carrier should have declined to receive it without an acknowledgment of its condition upon transfer.

Example 3

If a child is born to a married woman, and it is proven the husband had sexual contact with the woman during the period when the child was conceived, the law presumes that the husband is the biological father of the child. This presumption is based on probability, fairness (access to proof) and social policy (protecting an innocent child).

Rule 301 FRE
Presumptions in General in Civil Actions and Proceedings

In all civil actions and proceedings not otherwise provided for by Act of Congress or by these rules, a presumption imposes on the party against whom it is directed the burden of going forward with evidence to rebut or meet the presumption, but does not shift to such party the burden of proof in the sense of the risk of nonpersuasion, which remains throughout the trial upon the party on whom it was originally cast.

148 PRACTICES

What they say is not what they do. A debate has persisted, both before and after the adoption of the federal rules of evidence, about the appropriate effect of a presumption. Two general theories have emerged:

(1) The first is the "bursting bubble" theory advocated by Professors James B. Thayer[396] and J. Wigmore.[397] Under this theory, the presumption is like a bubble — existing only until it is burst. The presumption shifts to the adversary only the burden of coming forward with evidence. Once *any evidence* of the nonexistence of the presumed fact has been presented, the presumption bubble is pricked and burst — disappearing because it has served its purpose. Nothing is ever said to the jury about the presumption, and the trial proceeds as if the presumption never existed.

(2) The second theory was advocated by Professors E. Morgan[398] and J. McCormick.[399] They wanted the presumption to have a greater

---

[396] PRELIMINARY TREATISE ON EVIDENCE AT THE COMMON LAW pp. 353-389 (1898).

[397] 9 WIGMORE ON EVIDENCE § 2491 (Chadbourn rev. 1961).

[398] BASIC PROBLEMS OF EVIDENCE, pp. 34-44 (1962).

[399] McCORMICK ON EVIDENCE, § 338 (West Group 5th ed. 1999).

legal impact than merely shifting to the opposing party the burden to produce *some* evidence. Since presumptions are based on many factors central to the original allocation of burdens of persuasion when the causes of actions were created — probability, access to proof, social policy, fairness — those factors should prompt a real-location of the same burden. Therefore, with the presumption that a child born to a married couple was the child of the husband, the husband would have the burden of proving he *was not* the biologi-cal father. Similarly, the addressee on a letter would have to prove to the jury's satisfaction he *did not* receive the letter mailed to him. Under this theory there would be no confusion about the instruction that should be given to juries — they would be told that the adver-sary had to disprove what had been presumed.

Though Rule 301 has adopted the "bursting bubble" theory, this has not resolved the debate.[400] Appreciating how little purpose this gives to pre-sumptions, because the alleged recipient of a letter could simply take the wit-ness stand and deny having received it (and that would be sufficient, no matter how little credibility he had), trial judges, through instructions given at the end of the trial, have manipulated presumptions to give them greater clout.

Contrary to the "bursting bubble" theory (which considers the bubble to have disappeared), many judges continue to mention the presumption to the jury in instructions. Further complicating the problem, these judges give widely varying instructions. Some judges simply mention the presumption without more, speaking of it as if it were evidence to be weighed by the jury. Others place a burden of persuasion on the adversary's obligation of coming forward with evidence, instructing that the adversary must come forward with *credible* evidence, or evidence *sufficient to disprove* the presumed fact (which, of course, is the equivalent of shifting the burden of persuasion to the adversary). Two factors compel these distortions of the presumption: (1) the logically compelling nature of the presumed facts from the primary facts (and the desire of judges to comment on the strength of those logical infer-ences — in the bubble metaphor, this would be the logical residue when the bubble bursts); and (2) a strong preference among members of the bench for the alternative theory of presumptions that shift the burden of persuasion.[401]

---

[400] *See* Texas Dept. Of Community Affairs v. Burdine, 450 U.S. 248, 257 (1981).

[401] *See, e.g.,* F.D.I.C. v. Schaffer, 731 F.2d 1134, 1137 (4th Cir. 1984) (stating that a presumption that a properly mailed letter was received can be rebutted only by clear and convincing evidence); N.L.R.B. v. Tahoe Nugget, Inc., 584 F.2d 293 (9th Cir. 1978) (concluding that the non-statutory pre-sumption in certain labor disputes shifted the burden of persuasion); United States v. Ahrens, 530 F.2d 781, 786 n.8 (8th Cir. 1976) (stating that a presumption requires the rebutting party to disprove the presumed fact); Child v. Beame, 412 F. Supp. 593, 599 & n.2 (S.D.N.Y. 1976) (shifting the bur-den of persuasion for a presumption that when an attorney appears on behalf of a client, the attorney is authorized to do so).

149 PRACTICES

Authenticating through the reply doctrine — a presumption that isn't a presumption. One of the circumstantial methods of authentication recognized by courts is the reply doctrine. If a letter is received in the due course of mail in reply to a previous letter, the authenticity of the reply, and the authority of the one who executed it, is sufficiently established to justify the admission of the document into evidence. This method of authentication was not explicitly codified in Rule 901, but it is generally encompassed in Rule 901(b)(4).

Rule 901 FRE
Requirement of Authentication or Identification

(a) General provision. The requirement of authentication or identification as a condition precedent to admissibility is satisfied by evidence sufficient to support a finding that the matter in question is what its proponent claims.

(b) Illustrations. By way of illustration only, and not by way of limitation, the following are examples of authentication or identification conforming with the requirements of this rule:

. . . .

(4) Distinctive characteristics and the like. Appearance, contents, substance, internal patterns, or other distinctive characteristics, taken in conjunction with circumstances.

Courts speak of the authenticity of such a reply letter as being *presumed* — a "presumption of genuineness."[402] Is this a presumption of authenticity in the true sense of the term? Because the question of authenticity is one of conditional relevance, the "presumption" arising from this reply doctrine could have significance at two levels in the trial — the first with the judge on the *question of the document's admissibility*, and the second with the jury on the *question* whether the document should be accepted as genuine and, therefore, given *weight* during deliberations on the substantive issues being litigated. On the first level, courts construe this "presumption" as establishing a *prima facie* case of authenticity that gets the evidence past the preliminary screening of the trial judge under Rule 104(b) and into evidence.

Is the reply doctrine a true presumption if it is employed to establish only a *prima facie* case of authenticity for purposes of admissibility? Would the opponent be entitled to present the judge with evidence to disprove the pre-

---

[402] *See* Reliance Life Ins. Co. v. Russell, 94 So. 748, 752 (Ala. 1922).

sumed fact, thereby rebutting the presumption? Or does this preliminary determination of authenticity, relating only to admissibility, conclusively established by the evidence of a reply, meaning that contradictory evidence is admissible only after the document's introduction, and only on the question of the weight that the jury should give to it?

Surprisingly, case law offers little guidance. Although courts speak of the presumption as rebuttable,[403] it is unclear whether this rebuttal evidence is to be offered to the court on the question of admissibility or to the jury on the question of weight. After surveying the cases, one may conclude that this "presumption" is really not a presumption at all at this first level of use at trial. Instead it is more of a conclusive assessment of the probative value of the reply relative to the admissibility determination, which is concerned only with whether the proponent has established a *prima facie* case of genuineness. So long as the trial judge is convinced that a reasonable jury could find the basic facts of the presumption (that the original letter that prompted the reply was properly addressed, stamped, and posted, and that the letter received was in reply to it) the evidence *is admissible*. The proponent need provide no additional evidence to get the document to the jury.

The second point in the trial when this reply presumption could have significance is after the document has been admitted into evidence and the jury must finally decide whether it is genuine and, therefore, whether it should be given any weight during jury deliberations. Does this presumption of authenticity continue to survive the admissibility determination and shift to the opposing side either the burden of going forward with evidence (the Thayer theory) or the burden of persuasion (the Morgan theory) on the authenticity issue? Or is the "presumption" nothing more than a device designed to ensure that certain documents and the authenticity questions connected to them get to the jury? Is it something designed solely for the purpose of determining admissibility?

Not surprisingly, confusion exists in the application of the "presumption" at this level as well. The courts that have discussed this presumption have done so only in reference to the admissibility question, but their discussions have been broader than the issue before them. Generally, courts indicate that the presumption continues to operate after admission and, contrary to the prevailing position on the presumption's effect in other contexts, those courts appear to have construed the presumption as shifting the burden of persuasion to the opposing party. The opposing party must prove that the letter is not genuine — that the named individual did not sign it and that the signature appearing on it was placed there without the individual's authorization or approval.[404]

---

[403] *Id.*

[404] *See, e.g.,* Capital City Supply Co. v. Beury, 72 S.E. 657, 658 (W. Va. 1911).

150 PRACTICES

Presumption of expertise in business and public records. Courts established the exceptions to the hearsay rule for business records, Rule 803(6), and public records, Rule 803(8)(C), because they considered the contents of those documents to have independent guarantees of trustworthiness. This belief is grounded in the regularity and routine nature of the notations; the independent needs of the author or the author's organization to have accurate records; the regular examinations, use, and accuracy checks to which the records are exposed; and the lack of any motive to falsify. When entries in these records are in the form of opinions requiring special expertise, the question has arisen whether those entries are admissible without a demonstration by the proponent, pursuant to Rule 702, of the expertise of the person making the entry. For example, should a court admit an insurance company's appraisal record if the proponent has not established the appraiser's qualifications? Similarly, in the public arena, should a court admit an FAA airline crash evaluation report if the proponent has not established the qualifications of the investigator and recorder? Courts have generally concluded that the proponent need not demonstrate the authors' special *expertise*. Because of the documents' nature, the courts will presume the expertise of those permitted to render expert opinions in them.[405]

Once this presumption of trustworthiness arises, it is subject to rebuttal through evidence that demonstrates the lack of qualifications of those responsible for the entries. Consistent with the confusion and disagreement that generally exists over a presumption's effect, and therefore, the quantity of evidence that must be presented to rebut them, courts have taken different positions on the effect of challenges to the expertise of entrants in business or public records. The Third Circuit, for example, apparently would assign the presumption a Thayer-Wigmore effect, shifting to the opponent only the burden of producing "some" evidence to challenge the presumed trustworthiness, whereupon the proponent would have to demonstrate appropriate expertise under Rule 702. Most courts have employed the presumption, but very few have not spoken to this issue.

---

[405] *See* United States v. Licavoli, 604 F.2d 613, 622 (9th Cir. 1979) (finding no need to establish special qualifications of persons responsible for business record entries); Melville v. American Home Assurance Co., 584 F.2d 1306, 1316 (3d Cir. 1978) (concluding that the opinion in an official report should be presumed reliable); Muncie Aviation Co. v. Party Doll Fleet, Inc., 519 F.2d 1178, 1183 (5th Cir. 1975) (considering government agency's recommendations inherently trustworthy).

B. Relationship of Presumption Rules to Other Rules[406]

Rule 104(b). Preliminary Questions of Conditional Relevance. Before an instruction on the existence of a presumption is appropriate, the trial judge must determine whether sufficient evidence has been presented upon which a reasonable juror could find the basic facts of the presumption have been established. The existence of the presumption is conditioned upon the establishment of the basic facts. This is a preliminary question of conditional relevance under Rule 104(b) which requires a preliminary screening by the judge to determine that the proponent has established a *prima facie* case.

Rule 201. Judicial Notice of Adjudicative Facts. On her own initiative, the presiding judge may take judicial notice of facts generally known or capable of accurate and ready determination from unimpeachable sources. In determining whether an opponent has successfully rebutted a presumption, the judge may rely upon such "noticed" facts, as illustrated in the case of *Sinatra v. Heckler*.[407] In *Sinatra*, Judge Weinstein took notice of delays in the delivery of the mail at the end of the calendar year in determining whether the opponent had rebutted presumption of receipt of a letter five days after it had been posted. The Social Security Administration mailed a notice of the denial of benefits to the plaintiff on December 21, 1979. Because the plaintiff did not file a request for a hearing on that notice of denial until March 3, 1980, the Administration claimed that the request was not timely because it had not been made within the required 60 days from his receipt of that notice. To establish the date of receipt, the Administration relied upon the presumption established in its regulations that a letter is received five days after it is posted. After concluding that this presumption only shifted to the plaintiff the burden of going forward with evidence of non-receipt, the judge found that burden to have been satisfied by the plaintiff's signed affidavit of non-receipt before January 3, 1980, coupled with the implications for delayed delivery because of the time of the year when notice was sent.[408]

The court takes judicial notice that a substantial number of federal employees take vacations at this time of year and that there is a general slowing down of office operations during this period. Fed.R.Evid. 201. The court also takes judicial notice that the mails are heavily burdened during and in the aftermath of the holiday season and that delivery is sometimes slowed.

Notices of denial of benefits upon reconsideration are mailed from the Bureau of Disability Determinations in Baltimore, Maryland. The Postal Service applies a two-day delivery standard from Baltimore to claimant's postal district 117 in Suffolk County. But the Post Office's Origin-Destination Information System

---

[406] PAUL R. RICE & ROY A. KATRIEL, EVIDENCE: COMMON LAW AND FEDERAL RULES OF EVIDENCE § 10.01 [C] (LEXIS 5th ed. 2005).

[407] 566 F. Supp. 1354 (E.D.N.Y. 1983).

[408] *Id.* at 1356-57.

reported that for the period December 29, 1979, through January 25, 1980, on-time delivery to district 117 from two-day delivery areas was down to 49%, the worst on Long Island. For the same origin-destination combination there was 76% on-time delivery from December 1, 1979, through December 28, 1979. The Post Office ordinarily aims for 91% on-time delivery from two-day delivery areas. FY '83 Goals (Internal Post Office Memorandum).

Even at ordinary times of the year the mailing of government notices is often delayed. For example, a letter from the Office of Hearings and Appeals sent to plaintiff's counsel in this case, plaintiff's exhibit no. 1, was dated October 14, 1982, postmarked October 19, and received October 22. . . .

The facts of this case are suggestive of untimely receipt. A glance at the calendar provides a credible explanation for delay. The notice was dated on the eve of the Christmas-New Year's holiday period. Many government employees take vacation at this time of the year, and office operations slow considerably. Not implausibly, January 2, 1981, was the first day a complete staff was available to clean desks of the remains of the previous year's work. In addition, the mails move more slowly during and after this period, because of the large holiday postal volume.

Given these factors, it is not unreasonable that a letter dated December 21, 1979, would be belatedly dispatched and then delayed in the mail so it would not have been received before January 3, 1980. Had it been received on that date, the March 3, 1980 filing of a request for a hearing would have been timely. Were this a jury trial plaintiff's case would be more than sufficient to defeat a directed verdict against him on the issue of timely receipt. It more than meets a claimant's burden of coming forward. . . .[409]

Rule 902. Self-authentication. A number of presumptions arise from proof of basic facts through documentary evidence. For example, in a deportation proceeding of alleged undocumented immigrants, the presentation of foreign birth certificates with names identical to those of the defendants gives rise to a presumption of identity. The certificates establish *prima facie* cases of nationality, places of birth, and dates of birth.[410]

C. Applications — Presumptions

ONE

After the plaintiff presented a *prima facie* case of employment discrimination it gives rise to a presumption of discrimination that must be rebutted by the employer. The presumption arises because if the employer is silent in the face of such evidence it is more likely than not that the disparate treatment was

---

[409] Id. at 1356-57, 1360.

[410] *See* Corona-Palomera v. I. N. S., 661 F.2d 814, 815-16 (9th Cir. 1981).

based on the consideration of impermissible factors. At the trial the employer came forward with testimony indicating that there was a nondiscriminatory reason for the plaintiff not being given a position that was given to a man. A lower court held that after the *prima facie* case, the defendant had to prove, by a preponderance of the evidence, that the nondiscriminatory reason given for the disparate treatment was, in fact, true. The Supreme Court disagreed. Because the effect of a presumption under Rule 301 is only to shift the burden of going forward with evidence, "the defendant bears only the burden of explaining clearly the nondiscriminatory reasons for its action." The plaintiff retains the burden of persuasion. "She now must have the opportunity to demonstrate that the proffered reason was not the true reason for the employment decision. This plaintiff now merges with the ultimate burden of persuading the court that she has been the victim of intentional discrimination. She may succeed in this either directly by persuading the court that a discriminatory reason more likely motivated the employer or indirectly by showing that the employer's proffered explanation is unworthy of credence." *Texas Dept. Of Community Affairs v. Burdine*, 450 U.S. 257 (1981).

TWO

An application for a patent filed within twelve months after filing an application for a foreign patent on the same invention is statutorily accorded the filing date of the foreign application and effect thereof. If a U.S. application is not filed within that time-frame, patent protection in the United States is not available. An attorney placed four patent applications in a package, properly addressed it to the Patent Office in Washington, D.C., place the proper amount of air mail postage on it and placed in a mail receptacle. The Patent Office claims it did not receive the package until after the twelve month period had elapsed. The plaintiff relies on a presumption that a properly addressed, stamped and posted package was received by the addressee in the due course of mail. The Patent Office relied upon another presumption of procedural regularity based upon the normal manner, custom, practice and habit established for the handling of incoming mail at the Patent Office. Received mail is processed immediately and the time-stamp on the applications revealed it was received too late. The presumption of receipt of mail operates unless the contrary is proven. The presumption of procedural regularity operates until evidence proves it was not handled routinely. The trial court ruled that the procedural regularity presumption was not strong enough to overcome the strong presumption about the receipt of mail. The appellate court disagreed. It held that the two presumptions are the equivalent of evidence that rebut each other. The court characterizing all presumptions as "bats of the law, flitting in the twilight, but disappearing in the sunshine of actual facts." This is a more poetic characterization of the "bursting bubble" theory of presumption. The lower courts error was treating presumptions as though they could wage war among themselves. They cannot. As a consequence, all that is left are the logical inferences flowing from the facts that form the foundation of each presumption. This is a factual question that must be resolved at trial, thereby makes the disposition of a claim of this nature inappropriate for summary judgment. *Legille v. Dann*, 544 F.2d 1 (D.C. Cir. 1976).

INDEX

[References are to pages.]

[References are to pages.]

[References are to pages.]

[References are to pages.]

[References are to pages.]

[References are to pages.]

[References are to pages.]

V

VICARIOUS ADMISSIONS
Party-opponent's admissions . . . 88-90

VICTIMS OF CRIMES
Character evidence
    Generally . . . 32; 34
    Sex offense victims . . . 37-38
"Perry Mason" defense . . . 36

VITAL STATISTICS
Public records hearsay exception and . . . 177

W

WITNESSES AND TESTIMONY
Character evidence to prove witness's propensity (See CHARACTER EVIDENCE)
Confrontation right and hearsay
    Generally . . . 180-183
    Co-conspirator admissions . . . 94
    Declarations against interest 123-124
    Former testimony exception 116-117
Credibility of witnesses
    Cross-examination . . . 4
    Expert opinion testimony . . . 220-221
    Hearsay declarants (See HEARSAY)
    Impeachment evidence (See IMPEACHMENT OF WITNESSES)
Cross-examination (See CROSS-EXAMINATION)
Direct examination (See DIRECT EXAMINATION)
Exclusion of expert witnesses . . . 221-222
Expert opinion (See EXPERT OPINION)
Former testimony
    Generally . . . 115-121
    Forfeiture by wrongdoing exception and . . . 128
Impeachment of witnesses (See IMPEACHMENT OF WITNESSES)
Interrogation of witnesses
    Control by court . . . 2; 192
    Cross-examination (See CROSS-EXAMINATION)
    Direct examination (See DIRECT EXAMINATION)
Lay witness opinion (See LAY WITNESS OPINION)

WITNESSES AND TESTIMONY—Cont.
Opinion testimony
    Expert witnesses (See EXPERT OPINION)
    Lay witnesses (See LAY WITNESS OPINION)
Personal knowledge, lack of
    Business records . . . 167
    Declarations against interest and . . . 124
    Excited utterances and . . . 136
    Expert opinion . . . 212
    Expert witnesses . . . 220
    Present physical condition and 147-148
Presentation of testimony . . . 2-5
Prior statements of witnesses
    Generally . . . 76-77
    Admissions and . . . 96-97
    Applications . . . 83-85
    Completeness doctrine . . . 82-83
    Consistent statements . . . 81-82
    Declarations against interest . . . 124
    Forfeiture by wrongdoing . . . 125-130
    Former testimony exception and . . . 119-120
    Impeachment evidence . . . 228-229
    Inconsistent statements . . . 77-81
    Original documents rule and . . . 196
    Party-opponent admissions . . . 87-88
    Preliminary questions . . . 82
Religious beliefs or opinions . . . 230

WRITINGS AND RECORDED STATEMENTS
Business records (See BUSINESS RECORDS)
Hearsay, as . . . 62-63
    (See also HEARSAY; HEARSAY EXCEPTIONS)
Judgments from felony prosecutions 178-180
Original writing rule (See BEST EVIDENCE RULE)
Past recollection recorded (See PAST RECOLLECTION RECORDED)
Public records and reports (See PUBLIC RECORDS AND REPORTS)
Refreshing memory from writing 153-154; 243-247
Remainder of related writings, admission of (See COMPLETENESS DOCTRINE)